D0899053

A Story

*Masterworks
of the Classical Haida Mythtellers*

BOOKS BY ROBERT BRINGHURST

Poetry

The Shipwright's Log · 1972
Cadastre · 1973
Eight Objects · 1975
Bergschrund · 1975
Tzuhalem's Mountain · 1982
The Beauty of the Weapons: Selected Poems 1972–82 · 1982
The Blue Roofs of Japan · 1986
Pieces of Map, Pieces of Music · 1986
Conversations with a Toad · 1987
The Calling: Selected Poems 1970–1995 · 1995
Elements (with Ulf Nilsen) · 1995

Prose

Visions: Contemporary Art in Canada
    (with Geoffrey James, Russell Keziere & Doris Shadbolt) · 1983
Ocean/Paper/Stone · 1984
The Raven Steals the Light (with Bill Reid) · 1984; 2nd ed., 1996
Part of the Land, Part of the Water: A History of the Yukon Indians
    (with Catharine McClellan *et al.*) · 1987
The Black Canoe (with Ulli Steltzer) · 1991; 2nd ed., 1992
The Elements of Typographic Style · 1992; 2nd ed., 1996
*A Story as Sharp as a Knife: The Classical Haida Mythtellers
    and Their World* · 1999

A Story

as Sharp as a Knife

The Classical Haida Mythtellers and Their World

as Sharp

Robert Bringhurst

as a Knife

DOUGLAS & MCINTYRE · *Vancouver/Toronto*
UNIVERSITY OF NEBRASKA PRESS · *Lincoln*

▸ DOUGLAS & MCINTYRE LTD.
Suite 201
2323 Quebec Street
Vancouver, BC V5T 4S7

Published simultaneously in the United States of America by the
▸ UNIVERSITY OF NEBRASKA PRESS,
Lincoln, NE 68588-0484

Draft portions of some of the text and translations in this book have appeared in *Canadian Literature* (Vancouver), the *Journal of Canadian Studies* (Peterborough, Ontario), Sean Kane's *Wisdom of the Mythtellers* (Broadview, 1994, 1998), Brian Swann's anthology *Coming to Light: Contemporary Translations of the Native Literatures of North America* (Random House, 1994), and – courtesy of Jim Cheney – in *An Invitation to Environmental Philosophy*, edited by Anthony Weston (Oxford University Press, 1999).

00 01 02 03 · 5 4 3 2

Canadian Cataloguing in Publication Data:

Bringhurst, Robert, 1946–
   A story as sharp as a knife

Includes bibliographical references and index.
ISBN 1-55054-696-1 (cloth)
ISBN 1-55054-795-X (pbk)

1. Haida Indians – Folklore.
2. Indian mythology – British Columbia – Pacific Coast.
3. Legends – British Columbia – Pacific Coast.
4. Indians of North America – British Columbia – Pacific Coast – Folklore.
I. Title.
E99.H2B74 1999   398.2'089'972
   C95-911229-4

The publisher gratefully acknowledges the support of the Canada Council for the Arts and of the British Columbia Ministry of Tourism, Small Business and Culture. The publisher also acknowledges the financial support of the Government of Canada through the Book Publishing Industry Development Program.

Library of Congress Catalog Card Number: 00-100327,
ISBN 0-8032-1314-X (cloth, USA)
ISBN 0-8032-6179-9 (pbk, USA)

Printed and bound in Canada by Friesens

In memoriam
BILL REID
of the Qqaadasghu Qiighawaay
of the village of Ttanuu,
whose names were
Iihljiwaas, Kihlguulins, Yaahl Sghwaansing,
1920–1998

Contents

Illustrations

PHOTOGRAPHS

Acknowledgements

THIS BOOK is fundamentally an exercise in listening. Much of it, nonetheless, took shape through talking, when I found myself, a nonacademic, visiting in academic settings.

The title and some of the published text come from a short series of lectures delivered under the terms of the Ashley Fellowship at Trent University in 1994. I'm grateful to Sean Kane & Kelly Liberty, Stephen Brown, Theresa Topic, Morton Berkowitz, John Wadland and my other hosts at Trent, and to the late Prof. Charles Allan Ashley, whose bequest sustains the fellowship I held.

I'm similarly grateful to my hosts at the Asociación de Escritores en Lenguas Indígenas de México; Universitat Central de Barcelona; Clare Hall, Cambridge; Universidade de Coimbra; Universidad de la Laguna, Tenerife; Università degli studi di Lecce; Universidad Complutense de Madrid; Università di Pisa; University of British Columbia; Yukon College, Whitehorse; and the Western Literature Association's 30th annual meeting in Vancouver in 1995, who heard and questioned early drafts of many portions of the book, in the form of isolated lectures.

Because this is a voyage of discovery into classical, not contemporary, Haida oral literature, it relies almost entirely on documentary sources. These sources exist because of the extraordinary patience, perseverance and good will of several individuals, both Haidas and outsiders, whose names are mentioned often in the text. This book is an homage to them and to the long tradition they served. It is also now an homage to my master and my friend Bill Reid, who understood when no one else did why a poet should apprentice with a sculptor.

Reassembling the story would have been impossible without the aid of archivists at many institutions. I'm grateful to people at the National Anthropology Archives, Washington, DC; American Museum of Natural History, New York; American Philosophical Society Library,

Philadelphia; British Columbia Archives and Records Service and the Royal British Columbia Museum, Victoria; National Archives of Canada, Ottawa; United Church of Canada (British Columbia Conference) Archives, Vancouver; and the University of Washington Library, Seattle. I owe particular thanks to Belinda Kaye at the Department of Anthropology, American Museum of Natural History, for help of many kinds over many years. I'm grateful too to Celia Duthie, who knew what I was up to before I knew myself.

The John Simon Guggenheim Memorial Foundation helped me find my way by awarding me a fellowship in poetry in 1987. I was forty years old at that time, yet my studies of the languages and literatures of the land where I was born, and in which I was living, were still at a preliminary stage. Neither I nor the Foundation could tell where this would lead. A decade later, vital help came from the George Woodcock Fund, Toronto, and from two cherished friends, Sean Kane and Dennis Lee.

For help with Blackfoot, Cree, Hupa, Karuk, Pawnee and Sahaptin spelling, I owe thanks to William Bright, Donald Frantz, Victor Golla, Thomas Morning Owl, Douglas Parks, Bruce Rigsby, Noel Rude and Christoph Wolfart. But I have now and then pigheadedly rejected their advice. They are not, of course, to blame for my decisions. For sharing facts and ideas, my deep thanks to Judith Berman and Dell Hymes.

Roo Borson, Gudrun Dreher, Sean Kane, Dennis Lee, Don McKay, Louise Mercer and Jan Zwicky offered many helpful comments on the manuscript. I am grateful to them, and I am grateful to Scott McIntyre for his superhuman patience and his deeply human trust, lavished on this book and on the volume of translations now intended as its sequel.

Vancouver · Winter Solstice 1998

HÍghagilda, Xhaaydla Gwaayaay, 1881. Photograph by Edward Dossetter.

(American Museum of Natural History, Library Services, 42268)

Prologue:

Reading What Cannot Be Written

A HUNDRED MILES INTO THE PACIFIC, drenched in rain and wind and mist and sunlight, lie the islands known as Haida Gwaii. In September 1900, a young, soft-spoken linguist with a new degree from Harvard and a bundle of instructions from his mentor stepped ashore there, planning to stay half a year, learning what he could of the Haida language, and of Haida life and thought and social structure.

The linguist found himself confronted by great art, great devastation and great literature. His teacher had forewarned him to expect the devastation and the visual art as well. It was the literature that took him by surprise. And so for three and a half years he did nothing whatsoever but transcribe, translate and study Haida mythtexts, stories, histories and songs.

Back in Washington and Boston and New York, the linguist's learned colleagues did not hear what he had heard nor see what he had seen in the texts that he transcribed, and he was not a man to force his views on others. He published what he could, blamed himself for others' failings, and went on to other work, with other persecuted languages, elsewhere in the world.

The fact remains that he had heard, and had recorded as well as he was able, one of the world's richer classical literatures, embodying one of the world's great mythologies.

Everything we have in the way of classical Haida literature comes through the transcriptions of one man – and so the subject is a small one. It is one specific phase of one specific oral literature, shrunk now to only about 40,000 lines of written text. But the world as a whole is what that literature, like every healthy literature, is really all about – and so the subject is beyond the ability of any human being, or of all human beings, to exhaust.

⸕ ⸕ ⸕

All classical Haida literature is oral. By definition, therefore, it is something printed books cannot contain, in precisely the same sense that jazz, or the classical music of India, is music that a score cannot contain. Every healthy, living culture holds its stories to its heart, and so *the book,* in the fundamental yet intangible sense, is a cultural universal. This however is a book composed in homage to what script and print omit – and to the intellectual richness of a world where no written books exist.

Reading, like speech, is an ancient, preliterate craft. We read the tracks and scat of animals, the depth and lustre of their coats, the set of their ears and the gait of their limbs. We read the horns of sheep, the teeth of horses. We read the weights and measures of the wind, the flight of birds, the surface of the sea, snow, fossils, broken rocks, the growth of shrubs and trees and lichens. We also read, of course, the voices that we hear. We read the speech of jays, ravens, hawks, frogs, wolves, and, in infinite detail, the voices, faces, gestures, coughs and postures of other human beings. This is a serious kind of reading, and it antedates all but the earliest, most involuntary form of writing, which is the leaving of prints and traces, the making of tracks.

The works of literature translated and discussed here were made in such a world – where the *performance* could be read but the *work* could not. Now they are frozen, verbatim transcriptions of single performances. Voices hide in these transcriptions. If they are to speak, we must find a way to listen. That is difficult to do so long as we keep thinking of the fixed and silent texts that have come to overshadow every other kind of literature in the European tradition.

All literature is oral at its root, so the dilemma is unreal. Dante, Shakespeare, Melville, Flaubert, Joyce are read because they speak, although the pedants' books are mum. Yet the oral poet's strategies and tactics differ from the writer's, and the tactics of the listener are different from the reader's. Once it is transcribed, oral literature *looks like* writing – but as every reader senses, that is not quite what it is.

Native American oral literature in general, and Haida oral literature in particular, seem to me far closer in spirit and in form to European painting and to European music than to European literature. This is one way out of the dilemma. Reading works of oral literature is more like reading notes and reading paintings than it is like reading books. In my attempts to set the best Haida poets in a global context, I have found Bach and Titian and Velázquez more immediately helpful than Racine.

To those concerned about such things, I think it will be clear how much I owe to the work of several scholars. Dell Hymes and Claude Lévi-Strauss are among the first who come to mind.

My differences from Hymes, I like to think, are superficial. He uses the words *measured verse* to describe the structural patterns of thought and language he has patiently unearthed in Kathlamet, Kiksht and many other oral literatures. Hymes and I are completely in agreement about the reality, vitality and importance of these patterns – and I wish I had his great gift for discerning them. I also wish that he had given them a different name. Perversely, then, I have expressed my admiration for his work, and for his skills as a polylingual critic, by redefining or avoiding his key terms.

I would be happy to have Lévi-Strauss's gift for seeing narrative patterns too – since I suppose, as he does, that stories very often tell us more than their tellers ever know, and that structural analysis is one important means of finding out what stories have to say, to us and to each other. Unlike him, I think it quintessential to root this kind of listening in real and original texts, and to identify the speakers and occasions as precisely as I can. I want to know, as he does, *how myths think themselves in people,*[1] but I also want to know how people think themselves in myths. These are two quite different modes of thinking. Only one of them is, strictly speaking, human, though both are in the broad sense humanistic, and both take place in human hearts and heads. When we listen to a real human being telling a real myth, we can hear, feel and see the way these two modes of thinking interact.

The endnotes begin on page 439.

Walter Ong and others have written at great length on the nature of oral culture, but rarely in such works do we encounter an actual oral text. Still less often do we meet an actual speaker. The result is that the real human beings who inhabit oral cultures disappear, and stereotypes replace them. Native American oral poets have so often been mistreated in this way that their namelessness has come to seem routine. It is true that a few myth-tellers, working in unusual conditions, have preferred to remain anonymous. But myths are always told by individuals, not by language groups or tribes. Even when the speakers are unnamed, to hear what they are saying, we have to learn to hear them one by one, in the time and in the place where each is speaking.

Not many of the immigrants arriving in North America, from the sixteenth century through the twentieth, have grasped the fact that they were coming to take refuge with indigenous societies of genuine antiquity and cultural complexity. Not many immigrants have taught this simple truth to their children either. Even the philosopher George Grant – a man not often tolerant of unexamined assumptions – could call North America "the only society on earth that has no indigenous traditions from before the age of progress."[2] Grant made it his vocation to fight against defining human life in terms of human will, but he was captured, in that sentence, by the will that he decried.

The Old World and the New are not two regions marked reliably on maps. The Old World is wherever indigenous traditions are permitted to exist and acknowledged to have meaning. The

16

New World is wherever such traditions are denied and a vision of human triumph is allowed to take their place. The Old World is the self-sustaining world – worldwide – to which we all owe our existence. The New World is the synthetic, self-absorbed and unsustainable one – now also worldwide – that we create.

Every language and its literature – written or oral – is also a world, linked to other worlds, of which the speakers of that language are often unaware. Every language and its literature form an intellectual bioregion, an ecosystem of ideas and perceptions, a watershed of thought. The several hundred oral literatures indigenous to North America – though constantly remade in the mouths of oral poets and new to every listener who comes from somewhere else – are parts of the old-growth forest of the human mind.

,   ,   ,

Because this is a book about a Native American literature, I have used native names for places and for people as often as I could. I use, for instance, the old village names Hlghagilda, Ghadaghaaxhiwaas and Qquuna in place of the more current English names, which are Skidegate, Masset and Skedans. And except in a few cases where I know the individuals or their communities would disapprove, I use people's indigenous personal names: Skaay instead of John Sky; Daxhiigang rather than Edenshaw; Kilxhawgins, not Abraham Jones. I know most readers of this book will find the Haida and other native names harder to spell, remember and pronounce. Acknowledging these names seems to me nonetheless an essential gesture of respect and recognition – one I hope most readers of this book will also want to make.

Appendix 1 (page 415) gives detailed information on the pronunciation of Haida, and appendix 2 recounts the short but checkered history of Haida as a written language. For other Native American tongues, pronunciation and spelling are treated briefly in appendix 3. These appendices are, I am sorry to say, written in technical language and could not serve their function

17

if they weren't. There is no accurate way to portray, in any language, sounds that language disallows. That is why linguistics, like all the other sciences, relies upon a language of its own, and why this language – though that is not its aim – shuts other people out. Mouth-to-mouth training in phonetics is the only real solution, but anyone prepared to spend an hour reading the article on phonetics in a decent encyclopedia will be able to make headway. All that is really involved is learning the anatomy of the human mouth.

Readers impatient with the jargon will find some consolation in appendix 6 (page 436). This is a short, nontechnical pronouncing glossary of essential Haida names that recur throughout the book. Using that as a basis, most readers can begin to sound out other Haida words that crop up in the text.

A few Haida names also appear – simply because they seemed to invite it – in English translation. Xhuut Tsiixwas ("Harbor-Seal Ebb-Tide"), for example, has turned into Seal Beach, and Jaat Sttagha Gaxhiigans into Thunder Walking Woman. I could not translate every Haida name, because the meanings of some are obscure, and to do so would in any case anglicize the Haida texts too much.

The problems that arise in translating from Haida to English are many and quite interesting, of course, and some are discussed in the course of the book. One may be worth mentioning up front. From time to time I use the English words *god* and *gods* to translate the Haida noun *sghaana* and the verb phrase *sghaana qiidas*. I know that to those who think of God in Biblical terms (which many native speakers of Native American languages now do) this usage can seem startlingly wrong. The texts translated here speak from an older world in which gods are as innumerable, numinous, mortal and local as killer whales, rocks and trees. *Spirit-being* is an alternate translation of the same Haida terms, and one I also often use. Anyone troubled by one translation is at liberty, of course, to substitute the other.

Very literal, inch-by-inch translation – what scholars call a strict morphemic gloss – is fashionable now in Native American linguistics, and such translations can be wonderfully revealing. They also give a false sense of security and of scientific precision. (To anyone who doubts this, I suggest taking a short passage of poetry, or a snippet of conversation, and translating it morpheme by morpheme from English into English.) I have resorted now and then to such forensic translation myself, but on the whole I think that this procedure tends to cast its light entirely on language and leave literature in the dark.

I confess that all translation seems to me at best approximation – but translation also seems to me a necessary part of what Ngũgĩ wa Thiong'o calls decolonizing the mind, and what Plato calls νοεῖν: that is, approximately, thinking.

⸼   ⸼   ⸼

Together with its rucksack of appendices, the book now carries a substantial load of endnotes. Most readers, I imagine, will need some of these; few will need them all. They include a lot of leads to important literary texts in other Native American languages. These are leads I hope some readers will decide, in their own time, to follow up. To make that easier to do, the ninety or so Native American mythtellers and the sixty-odd Native American literatures mentioned in the text or in the notes are tracked through a systematic index.

The notes include a lot of background information too: on history and language, and especially on natural history. They include, in other words, a part of the large reservoir of facts on which any fruitful hearing of Haida oral literature depends. Once upon a time, a Haida mythteller's older listeners would have had this information in their heads. Others could get at it, when and if they wished, through conversation, observation and example. That was the back of the oral book.

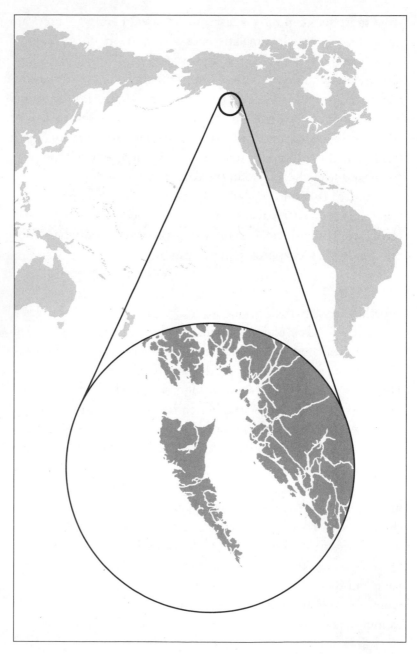

Haida Gwaii – or in classical Haida, *Xhaaydla Gwaayaay*: the Islands on the Boundary between Worlds

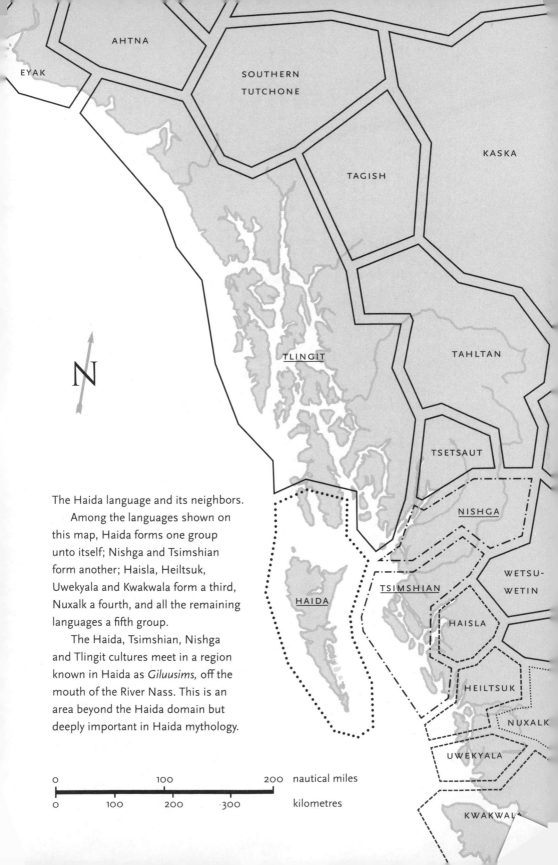

AHTNA

EYAK

SOUTHERN
TUTCHONE

KASKA

TAGISH

N

TLINGIT

TAHLTAN

TSETSAUT

The Haida language and its neighbors.
    Among the languages shown on
this map, Haida forms one group
unto itself; Nishga and Tsimshian
form another; Haisla, Heiltsuk,
Uwekyala and Kwakwala form a third,
Nuxalk a fourth, and all the remaining
languages a fifth group.
    The Haida, Tsimshian, Nishga
and Tlingit cultures meet in a region
known in Haida as *Giluusims,* off the
mouth of the River Nass. This is an
area beyond the Haida domain but
deeply important in Haida mythology.

NISHGA

WETSU-
WETIN

TSIMSHIAN

HAIDA

HAISLA

HEILTSUK

NUXALK

UWEKYALA

0   100   200 nautical miles

0   100   200   300   kilometres

KWAKWALA

▲ **Eyak villages**

1 Iiyaaq (*Eyak*)
2 Anax̌anaq (*Alaganik*)
3 Itl'aandaya
 (*Mountain Slough*)

● **Tlingit villages**

4 Yaakwdáat (*Yakutat*)
5 Klukwan
6 Jilk̲ut (*Chilkoot*)
7 Xunaa (*Hoonah*)
8 T'aak̲ú (*Taku*)
9 K̲ák'w (*Basket Bay*)
10 S'awdáan (*Sumdum*)
11 Xutsnoowú (*Angoon*)
12 Sheet'ká (*Sitka*)
13 K̲éix̲' (*Kake*)
14 Kuyú
15 Shtax'héen (*Stikine,
 Old Wrangell*)
16 Tuxekan
17 Lawáak (*Klawock*)
18 T'angaas (*Tongass*)

■ **Haida villages**

19 Kasaan
20 Xhaada
21 Saqqwaan
22 Ghawkkyan
23 Kkaykkaanii (*Kaigani*)
24 Qqwii Ghandlas
25 Hlinqwan
26 Yaakkw
27 Kkyuusta
28 Yan
29 Ghadaghaaxhiwaas
 (Ghaw, *Masset*)
30 Ttii
31 Tiiyan
32 Hlghagilda
 (*Skidegate*)
33 Ttsaa'ahl
34 Qaysun
35 Hlqiinul

36 Qquuna
37 Ttanuu
38 Hlkkyaa
39 Sqiina
40 Skwaay
41 Yaku
42 Qayju
43 Sghan Gwaay
44 Sqay

❖ **Nishga villages**

45 Gitwinksiiłkw
 (*Canyon City*)
46 Gitlax̲'aws (*Gitlakaus*)
47 Lax Nkit'wah (*Angida*)
48 Ay'ans (*Aiyansh*)
49 Kwinwo'a
 (*Kwunwoq, Gunwa*)
50 Gitlaxt'aamiks

◆ **Tsimshian villages**

51 Maxłaqxaała
 (*Old Metlakatla*)
52 Q'aaduu (*Qqaaduu*)
53 Kitsiis (*Gitsees*)
54 Kinax'ankiik
 (*Ginakangeek*)
55 Kit'antoo (*Gitandau*)
56 Kitsmqeelm
 (*Kitsumkalum*)
57 Kitsalaasẅ (*Kitselas*)
58 Kitsaxłaał
 (*Gitzaklalth*)
59 Kitqxaała (*Kitkatla*)
60 Kitqa'ata (*Kitkiata*)

✦ **Haisla villages**

61 Kitamaat
62 Kitloop (*Kitlope*)

◆ **Haihais villages**

63 Lhṁdu
 (*Klemtu, Kitasu*)
64 Láiq (*Mussel River*)
65 Qínát

◆ **Heiltsuk villages**

66 K'émx̌k'vitx̌v
 (*Kimsquit*)
67 Sxváxviylkv
 (*Scowquiltz*)
68 Q'Íc ₵ Wáglísla
 (*Bella Bella*)
69 N'xvám'u (*Namu*)
70 Yálátli

✳ **Uwikeeno villages**

71 Núxvants (*Neechanz*)
72 K'ítit
73 GÍdala (*Kiltala*)
74 Ǧádlmbalis

➤ **Centers of religious &
 mercantile intrusion**

75 *Novorossiisk*
 (1796–1805)
76 *Novo Arkangel'sk*
 (1804–)
77 *Fort Wrangell* (1834–)
78 *New Metlakatla*
 (1887–)
79 *Kincolith* (1864–)
80 *Fort Nass* (*Old Fort
 Simpson*, 1831–1834)
81 *Port Simpson* (1834–)
82 *Metlakatla Mission*
 (1862–1887)
83 *Masset* (1869–)
84 *Skidegate Mission*
 (1883–)
85 *Gold Harbour*
 (1851–1854)
86 *Port Essington*
 (1871–1964)
87 *Fort McLoughlin*
 (1833–1843)
88 *Bella Coola* (1869–)
89 *Fort Rupert* (1836–)
90 [300 sea miles south-
 east of Fort Rupert]
 Fort Victoria (1843–)

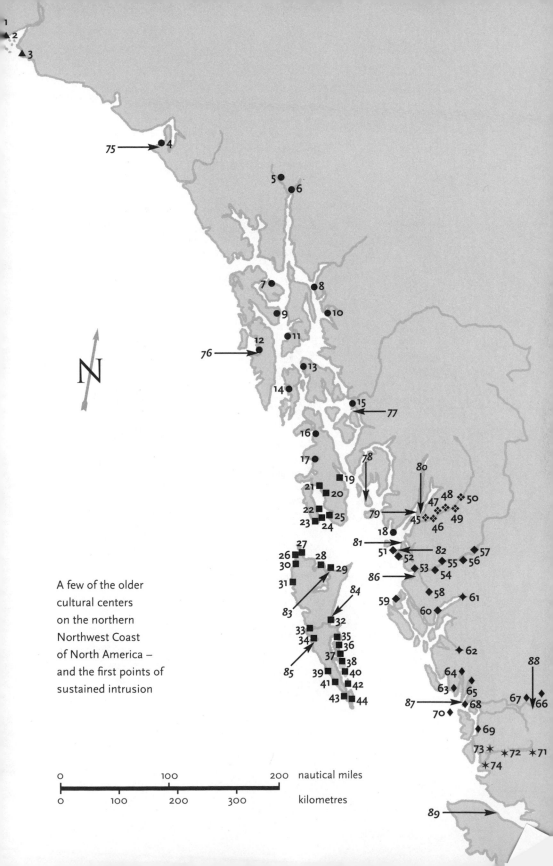

A few of the older
cultural centers
on the northern
Northwest Coast
of North America –
and the first points of
sustained intrusion

N

0   100   200   nautical miles

0   100   200   300   kilometres

1 **Ghadaghaaxhiwaas**
  (Ghaw, later called
  Masset)
2 Ghiijaw
3 Qqayaang
4 Hliiyalang
5 Naay Kun
  (*House Point*)
6 Xhuuya Ghandl
  (*Raven's Creek*)
7 Ghahlins Kun
8 Daxwa
9 Hlghaayxha
10 **Hlghagilda** (later
   called *Skidegate*)

11 Guuhlgha
12 Gawjaaws
13 Gaasins
14 Kixhlagas
15 **Xayna** (*Sunshine,*
   later called *New
   Gold Harbour*)
16 Sqiina [1]
17 Jiighugiiga
18 Qqaasta
19 Suuxhans
20 Laanaaya

21 Kunji
22 Kunxhalas
23 Quughahl
24 **Hlqiinul** (later
   called *Cumshewa*)
25 Jiigwa
26 Ghaw Quns
27 Qqaadasghu
28 **Qquuna**
   (later called *Skedans*)
29 Yawgas
30 Ttlxingas

31 Xiltsi
32 Singgi
33 **Ttanuu**
34 Skkuudas
35 Ttaahldi
36 Xhuut Ttsiixwas
37 Hlkkyaa (*Merganser,*
   later known as
   Windy Bay)
38 Gaysigas Qqiit
39 Ataana
40 **Qinggi**

41 Xhiina
42 Ghaduu
43 Skwaay
44 Hlanaaygwas
45 Llaana Daaganga
46 Qqiit
47 Xhaagi
48 Ghaaydi
49 Sqaws Giidawaay
50 Qayju

51 Styuujin
52 Sindas Kun
53 Xhyuudaw
54 Sqay
55 Ghangxhiit Kun
56 Swaanaay
57 Saw
58 Taada Sttling
59 Sinit
60 Sghan Gwaay (later
   called *Ninstints* and
   Anthony Island)

61 Taajil
62 Hlghadan
63 Qayjudal
64 Sttlindighaay
65 Naagas
66 Gwaayakanjus

67 Kawdas
68 Juuqqyuu
69 Yaku
70 Jiihlinjaaws

71 Ghuuski
72 Sghilgi
73 Sqiina [2]
74 Gwiitku
75 Ghaw Ghawdagaas
76 Singga
77 Gasindas
78 Stanhlaay
79 Saqaaydi Gilgaana
80 Sqaytaaw
81 Juu

82 **Qaysun** (later known
   as *Scots Guy's Cove*
   and *Gold Harbour*)
83 Niisi
84 Skuusindl
85 Ttsaa'ahl
86 Guudal
87 Ghattanas
88 Sqiilu
89 Tiiyan
90 Ttii

91 Qqanan Ghandlaay
92 Yaakkw
93 Kkyuusta
94 Daadans
95 Yaa'ats
96 Qang
97 Naydan Qaahli
98 Yan
99 Llaanas
100 Ghawaay Qaahli
   (later known as
   Masset Inlet)

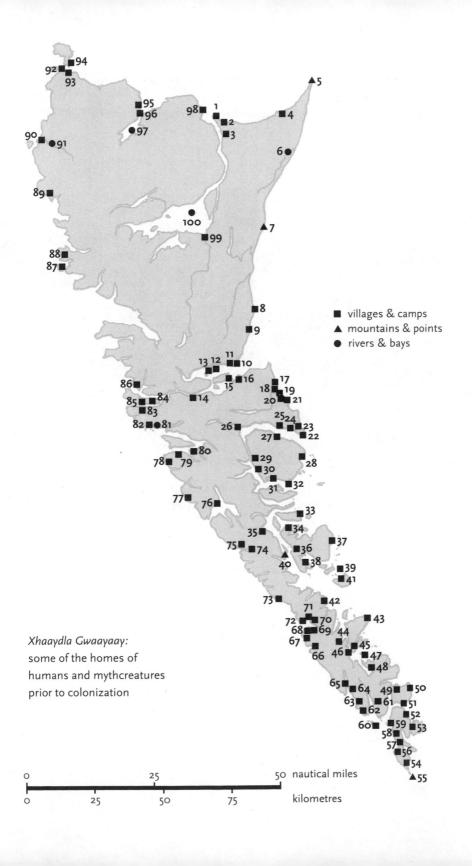

Xhaaydla Gwaayaay:
some of the homes of
humans and mythcreatures
prior to colonization

villages & camps
mountains & points
rivers & bays

nautical miles

kilometres

Hlghagilda, 1881. Photograph by Edward Dossetter.

(American Museum of Natural History, Library Services, 42267)

SGHWAANSING

[•]   square brackets mark editorial restorations

⟨•⟩   angle brackets mark insertions

{•}   curly braces mark deletions

†•†   daggers flag passages that seem corrupt

1   Goose Food

T HE LARGEST AND MOST COMPLEX works of classical Haida literature belong to a genre known as *qqaygaang*. *Qqay*, the root, means *full* or *old* or *round*; the suffix *-gaang* means *enduring* or *continuing to be*. The word is often rendered in English as *story, myth* or *tale*, and these are sensible translations, but they give no overt clue to the artistry involved. Like all works of literature, the *qqaygaang* are constructed from inherited materials and filled with shared ideas, but they are made, in every case, by individuals. How they are built is a matter of personal skill and sensitivity and style. The best transcriptions that we have of classical Haida myth, and the best performances occuring in the present day, are works of art, like the finest pieces of Haida weaving, painting and sculpture. The *qqaygaang* are what people fond of literature call oral narrative poems.

Since the *qqaygaang* are the subject of this book, we should begin with an example. But a book is a dehydrated voice, set adrift in many copies, like a seed, and a work of oral literature is rooted like a tree, in time and place and in the person who is speaking. The poems we want to hear are colored and shaped by a language other than this one, and informed by an oral tradition that books know nothing about. It accomplishes nothing to ask the poem to come to us. We must try to make the pilgrimage to the poem.

The author of this poem, the teller of this myth, was born and raised on the brink of the North Pacific, on the exposed west side of an island off the Northwest Coast of North America. He spoke the Haida language from childhood, and in time he learned some words of the Chinook trade jargon, perhaps a little Tlingit and some Tsimshian but virtually no English. Nevertheless he acquired, in the course of his extraordinary life, both a Haida and an English name. In Haida we should call him Ghandl or Ghandls, which means Fresh Water or River or Creek. But the few Europeans he knew referred to him as Walter. He was born in Qaysun Llanagaay,[1] or Sealion Town, in Xhaaydla Gwaayaay, the Islands on the *xhaaydla*, which is to say, the Islands on the Boundary between Worlds. English-speaking Haida now call these islands Haida Gwaii,[2] the Islands of the People, and that is the name I will use, but to find them in the atlas, you must look for them under the British colonial name imposed on them in 1787: the Queen Charlotte Islands. They lie at the same latitude as Amsterdam and Warsaw, Dublin and Berlin, but in the grip of different weather, in a different fold of time.

Appendix 6, page 436, gives non-technical advice on pronouncing Haida names; technical details are in appendix 1, page 415.

The Gregorian calendar meant nothing in these islands at the time of Ghandl's birth. It was at most a mysterious rumor – like the Christian faith, the roman alphabet, the Greenwich prime meridian, and the reigns of the English kings. But if later missionary records are accurate, the year of Ghandl's birth, by European reckoning, was 1851.

He belonged to a family called the Qayahl Llaanas, the Sealion People, of the Eagle side or moiety. Because inheritance is matrilineal in the Haida world, all children, male and female, take the family name of their mother. Ghandl's father (whose name I do not know) belonged to a family or lineage called Hlghaaxhitgu Llaanas, the Pebble Beach People, of the Raven side. But Ghandl was a Sealion Person, because that was his mother's lineage, and he was an Eagle, because that was his mother's family's moiety or side.

The people of Qaysun abandoned their village about 1875, after a series of smallpox epidemics had swept through Haida Gwaii. With other refugees, they built a new town at an old site known as Xayna, which means Sunshine, on the sheltered east side of the archipelago, where traders came more often. In the 1890s, after more bouts of smallpox, measles and other disease, the survivors moved to Skidegate, the new mission town displacing the old Haida village of Hlghagilda.

Hlghagilda is west of Attawapiskat and Wetaskiwin, east of Petropavlovsk and Unalaska, south of Tuktoyaktuk and Chutine, and north of 5000 miles of open ocean and a rock called Pitcairn Island. If you triangulate from Paris and New York, Jerusalem and Rome, the Haida village of Hlghagilda may seem, in consequence, remote. It is true the outside world has taken from it less than what it offered and a great deal more than it could give – and that is one definition of remote. But it needed, and still needs, little or nothing of what the colonial world can offer. In that sense, it is not remote at all. In fact, like every place where birds sing and people pause to listen and a storyteller speaks, it is the center of the world.

⁊   ⁊   ⁊

The verb *to be brave* in Haida is *sqaatsi*. A number of names, titles and nicknames have grown from this root. There are elaborate forms like Sqaatsidaahlging (Belly Full of Bravery) and simple ones like Sqaatsigins (Always Brave), Nang Sqaatsis (One Who Is Brave), and Sqaatsigaay (Bravery Itself). The latter name, used by a headman of the Qayahl Llaanas family of Qaysun, caught the ears of the early British traders who anchored near the town and was transmuted into *Scots Guy*. The few Europeans who had seen Qaysun began to call it Scots Guy's Cove, and the people of Qaysun learned that Scots Guy was a handy name to use in all transactions involving Europeans.[3] A short-lived gold rush around 1852 gave Qaysun another English name, Gold Harbour, but the anchorage is charted even now as Skotsgai Bay.

In 1884, Methodist missionaries started a steady campaign of conversion among the smallpox survivors in southern Haida Gwaii. Hundreds of southern Haida were baptized over the next

Stormblown poles in the empty village of Qaysun, on the west coast of Haida Gwaii, summer 1901. The pole at right is the housepole of Wiixhaws of the Qaayahl Llaanas, still erect in front of the disintegrating houseframe. Photograph by C. F. Newcombe.

(Royal British Columbia Museum, PN 46)

few years, and in the village of Xayna on Sunday, 25 December 1887, Ghandl of the Qayahl Llaanas joined their number.[4] The officiating clergyman recorded Ghandl's age as 36 and interpreted his name in the colloquial terms of the time: not as Fresh-Water-Person of the Sealion People but as Water of Scots Guy's Family. The missionary gave this name what he regarded as a proper Christian form, and Ghandl was henceforth known to speakers of English as Walter McGregor.

The worst single outbreak of smallpox to hit Haida Gwaii came in 1862, when Ghandl was about eleven. During that year alone, the Haida population fell by more than half.[5] Six years later came a severe epidemic of measles, lethal to many more native people up and down the Northwest Coast. Ghandl survived these disasters and others, but sometime before his move to Hlghagilda in the 1890s, a bout of smallpox or measles cost him his sight.[6] From that point on, the time he might have spent on the traditional professions of an adult Haida male – fishing, seahunting, woodworking, trading – went largely into listening instead. Even in his forties, he possessed extraordinary skill as an oral poet and extraordinary insight as a scholar of the seen and the unseen. In the midst of continuous death, evacuation and destruction, followed by aggressive transformation of his culture, Ghandl collected the remnants of an old and fundamentally celebratory tradition. We owe him much of what we have in the way of classical Haida literature, and much of what we know of Haida thought before the Christian missionization.

>   >   >

Ghandl of the Qayahl Llaanas of Qaysun, or Walter McGregor, the blind poet of Sunshine and Sealion Town, spent the month of November 1900 telling stories – that is to say, dictating his condensed, tightly woven narrative poetry – to a 27-year-old linguist from the state of Maine. The linguist was John Reed Swanton (1873–1958), a self-effacing man who spent a year in

Haida Gwaii and years more making sense of what he learned while he was there. He became, by what we might call accident, a figure of considerable importance in Haida cultural history.

A third important person joined Ghandl and Swanton at each session: a young bilingual Haida whose Christian name was Henry Moody (c. 1871–1945). He was Swanton's tutor, assistant and guide, and during these long sessions of dictation – typically six hours a day – he was the storyteller's primary audience and the linguist's second tongue and set of ears. His task was to listen to the poem and repeat it sentence by sentence in a loud, clear, slow voice, proving to the poet he had heard each word and giving Swanton time to write it down.[7] Ghandl spoke, a sentence or two at a time, Moody repeated, and Swanton wrote, hour after hour, day after day. On one of those wet November days, Ghandl began a poem with the following words:

Ll gidaagang wansuuga.
Kkuxu gyaa'at gutgu lla giistingdas.
Ll xhitiit ttsinhlghwaanggwang qawdi
llanagaay diitsi qahlagaagang wansuuga.

Ttsalaay waghii gwatxhaawasi   5
suu ghii lla qaagyaganggandixhan
ll gyuugha hlgitghun kyingaangas.
Gyaanhaw gha la qaagasi.

Ga jaada sting suugha ghaadangdyas.
Tlaagi giina sqqagidaasi gu   10
hlgitghun qqaal ttlsting xhasiiwas.
Kkit qqul ghaada qqaghatiisgasi

Lla qindi qawdihaw
lla dawghattlxhasi....[8]   14

There was a child of good family, they say.
He wore two marten-skin blankets.
After he took up the shooting of birds,
he went inland, uphill from the village, they say.

Going through the pines,
just to where the ponds lay,
he heard geese calling.
Then he went in that direction.

There were two women bathing in a lake.
Something lay there on the shore. 10
Two goose skins were thrown over it.
Under their tails were patches of white.

After watching for a while,
he swooped in.
He sat on the two skins.
The women asked to have them back.

He asked the better-looking one to marry him.
The other one replied.
«Don't marry my younger sister.
I am smarter. Marry me.» 20

«No. I will marry your younger sister.»

And she said that she accepted him, they say.

«Well then! Marry my younger sister.
You caught us bathing in a lake
that belongs to our father.
Now give me my skin.»

He gave it back.
She slipped it on
while she was swimming in the lake.

A goose swam in the lake then,   30
and then she started calling,
and then she flew, they say,
though leaving her younger sister
sickened her heart.

She circled above them.
Then she flew off, they say.
She passed through the sky.

He gave the younger woman one of his marten-skin blankets,
and he brought her home, they say.

A two-headed redcedar stood at the edge of the village,   40
and he put his wife's skin between the trunks.
Then he brought her into his father's house.

The headman's son had taken a wife.
So his father invited the people, they say.
They offered her food.
She did nothing but smell it.
She would eat no human food.

Later, her husband's mother
    began to steam pine noodles,⁹ they say.
Then she paid closer attention.
When her husband's mother was still busy cooking,   50
she asked her husband
to ask her to hurry, they say.

They placed it before her.
It vanished.
And then they began to feed her this only, they say.

A*fter a time, as he was sleeping,*
   his wife lay down beside him,
      and her skin was cold.
When it happened again,
he decided to watch her, they say.

He lay still in the bed,   60
and he felt her moving away from him slowly, they say.
Then she went out.
He followed behind her.

She walked along the beach in front of the village.
She went where the skin was kept.
From there, she flew.
She landed beyond the point at the edge of town.

He started toward her.
She was eating the eelgrass[10] *that grew there,*
and the breaking waves were lifting her back toward shore.   70
He saw her, they say.
And then she flew back where they kept her skin.

He got back to the house
before she did, they say.
There he lay down,
and soon his wife lay down beside him, cold.

A *famine began in the village, they say.*
   One day, without leaving her seat, she said,
«*My father is sending things down through the clouds to me.*»

35

Back of the village, geese began landing and honking.   80
She went there.
They followed her.
Food of many kinds was lying there:
pine noodles and clover roots.[11]
They carried it home.
And her father-in-law invited the people, they say.

When that was entirely gone,
 she said it again:
«My father is sending things down through the clouds to me.»
Geese began landing and honking again in back of the village.   90

They went there.
There were piles, again, of many kinds of food.
Again they brought it home.
And her father-in-law again invited the people.

Then, they say, someone in the village said,
«She thinks very highly of goose food.»

The woman heard it.
She got up to leave at that moment, they say.
Her husband tried to dissuade her.
No use.   100
She had settled on leaving.

It was the same
     when he tried to dissuade her in front of the town.
She went where her skin was.
Then she flew.
She flew in circles over the town,
and leaving her husband sickened her heart, they say.

And then she passed through the sky.
After that, her husband was constantly weeping, they say.

A*n old man had a house at the edge of the village.*
He went there and asked, 110
«*Don't you know the trail that leads to my wife?*»

«*Headman's son, you married a woman*
whose mother and father are not of this world.»

And the old man began to fit him out.
He gave him a bone marlinspike
for working with cedar-limb line.
Then he said,
«*Now, sir, get some oil.*
Get two sharp wedges too.
And a comb and a cord and salmon roe
and a coho skin and a spearhead.
Get all these.»

After he gathered what he needed, 120
he came back to him, they say.
«*Old one, here are all the things you spoke of.*»

«*Now, sir, you may go.*
Take the narrowest of the trails that lead from my house.»
Then he set off.

A*fter walking awhile,*
he came upon someone infested with lice.
He was trying to catch the lice by turning around.

After he had stared at him awhile,
the other said, 130

37

«Sir, don't just tickle me with your eyes.
I have long been expecting you.»

Then he went up close,
and he combed out his hair.
He rubbed him with oil
and picked off the lice.
And he gave him the comb and the rest of the oil.

The other one said,
«This is the trail that leads to your wife.»

Again he set off.   140
After walking awhile,
he saw a small mouse in front of him.
There was a cranberry in her mouth.

Then she came to a fallen tree,
and she looked for a way to go over it.
He let her step onto his open hand
and put her across.

She laid her tail up between her ears
and ran ahead.
Not far away, she went under some ferns.   150

He rested there,
and something said,
«A headwoman asks if you wish to come in.»
Then he parted the fronds of the ferns.

He was standing in front of a large house.
He walked through the door.
There was the headwoman dishing up cranberries.

She spoke with grace.
Her voice had big round eyes.

Once she had offered him something to eat,   160
Mouse Woman said to him,
«When I was bringing a bit of a cranberry
*   back from my berry patch,*
you helped me.
I intend to lend you something that I wore
for stalking prey when I was younger.»

She brought out a box.
She pulled out four more boxes within boxes.
In the innermost box was the skin of a mouse
*   with small bent claws.*
She said to him,
«Put this on.»   170

Small though it was, he got into it.
It was easy.
He went up the wall and into the roof of the house.
And Mouse Woman said to him,
«You know what to do when you wear it.
Be on your way.»

He set out again on the trail.
After walking awhile,
he heard someone grunting and straining.
He went there.   180

A woman was hoisting a pile of stones.
The cedar-limb line she was using kept slipping.
He watched her awhile
and then he went up to her.

«*Excuse me,*» *he said,*
«*But what are you doing?*»

The woman replied,
«*They told me to hold up the mountains*
        of the Islands on the Boundary between Worlds.
That is what I am doing.»

Then he remembered his spruce-root cord   190
and he said, «*Let me help you.*»

He made splices with the cord.
«*Now take the load on your back,*» *he said,*
and she hoisted it up on her back.
It did not slip off.

And she said to him,
«*Sir, you have helped me.*
Here is the trail that leads to your wife.»

Then he went on.
After a time, he came to a hump in the muskeg.   200
Something slender and red grew from the top of it.
He went up close to it.
All around the bottom of the tall, thin thing lay human bones.

He saw no way of going up.
Then he entered the mouse skin.
Pushing the salmon roe ahead of him, he climbed.
He went up after it.
When he came to the top,
he pulled himself onto the sky.

The trail stretched ahead of him there too.   210
He walked along.

40

After travelling awhile,
he began to hear a noise.

After travelling further,
he came to a river.
It was running high.

Near it perched an eagle.
A heron perched on the opposite bank.
A kingfisher perched upstream.
A black bear sat on the opposite bank,   220
and he had no claws, they say.

Then, they say, the black bear said to the eagle,
«Lend me something, grandfather.»
Then, they say, the eagle did as he asked.
Then and there the black bear got his claws.

When the young man had been sitting there awhile,
half of a person lurched by,
leaning himself on a fishing spear.

He had one leg and one arm,
and his head was half a head.   230
He speared the coho that were swimming there
and put them into his basket.

The man unrolled his coho skin and put it on
and swam in that direction.
When the half man speared him,
he was unable to pull him in.

The young man cut the spearhead from the spear, they say.
And the half man said,
«Human beings sometimes do this sort of thing.»

The younger man went up to him then, they say.   240
«Sir, did something take your spearhead?»

«Yes,» he said.

And the young man gave him the one he had.
That was Falling-Forward-in-the-Forest-God, they say.

When he went up further,
two men, old and fat, came out collecting firewood.
They chopped at the roots of windfall trees,
and they scattered the chips on the water.
The coho were coming from there.

He went back of the fallen tree,   250
pushing stones in from behind,
and their wedges shattered, they say.
And one of them said,
«Ahhh! We'll get a beating!»

Then he went up to them.
He gave them the two wedges that he had.
And they stared at him and said,
«This is your wife's house.»

Then he went up to it, they say.
He stood waiting in front of the house.   260
His wife came out to meet him.
Then he went in with her.
She was happy to see him.
She was the village headman's daughter, they say.

In that village too, they were man and wife.
And everything they gathered,
he gathered as well.

A fter living there for a time,
   he began to dislike the entire country.
Then his wife spoke to her father.   270
And his father-in-law called the villagers in.
There in the house, he asked them, they say,
« Who will carry my son-in-law back? »

And a loon said,
« I will carry your son-in-law back. »
« How will you do it? » he asked.

The loon said,
« I will put him under my tail
  and dive right in front here.
Then I'll come up again at the edge of his father's town   280
and release him. »

They thought he was too weak to do it, they say.

His father-in-law asked the question again.
A grebe gave the same reply.
They thought she was also too weak.

And a raven said he would carry him back.
And they asked him, « How will you do it? »

« I will put him under my wing
  and fly with him from the edge of the village.
When I am tired,   290
I will let myself tumble and fall with him. »[12]

They were pleased with his answer, they say,
and they all came down to the edge of the village to watch.

He did as he said.

When he grew tired,
he let himself fall
     down through the clouds with him
and dropped him onto a shoal exposed by the tide.

« Hwuuu! What a load I have carried.»

Becoming a gull, he squawked and went on squawking.

This is where it ends.   300

⟩   ⟩   ⟩

If you are a storyteller yourself, or a student of European oral literature, you may say, "I know that story. That's the Swan Maiden tale!" It is, more broadly, the universal story of the hunter who sees, as in a vision, the beauty of his prey and falls in love with what he came to kill. The two basic plots – man marries a bird who is a woman, or a woman who is a bird, then loses her again; and man climbs a pole to visit the sky but cannot remain where he doesn't belong – are part of the ancient stock of human stories. They could well be 100,000 years old. All around the world, people who can neither read nor write still tell stories on these themes.[13] And people who *can* read and write still find them in fairytale books and venues like the *National Enquirer*. But unless you know the work of this particular Haida poet, you cannot have heard the story told in quite this form before.

Lumping all the world's Swan Maiden tales together and saying they're the same is like walking into the Uffizi or the Prado or the Louvre, looking around at all those paintings of the Adoration or the Crucifixion, and saying, "These are all the same!" So they are – and when you see their similarity, you've taken one large step into the rich and densely layered world of the European imagination. They're the same, and that's an essential part of the truth. At the same time, every one is different.

44

Each is an individual human vision of a widely shared idea. That too is an essential part of the truth.

The narrative tradition in European painting is very strong, yet we understand that a painter, commissioned to produce an altarpiece, panel painting or fresco, is not usually asked *to invent a new story*. The story will come, as a rule, from the shared feast of Roman or Greek or Jewish or Christian mythology, and the painter's task is *to see the story afresh*: to make it live in his viewers' minds. This is one of the reasons why it is often more informative to compare Native American oral poetry to European painting than to European literature.

We can plot a possible route by which the Swan Maiden tale might have reached Haida Gwaii from Europe or Asia – or, since its place of origin is unknown, we could plot a route by which it might have reached Europe and Asia from Haida Gwaii. But even if we trace the route correctly, that will not explain how Ghandl reenvisioned the story as he did. We could also – with a greater chance of success – plot the route by which stories of the crucifixion and resurrection of Christ made their way from Palestine to Spain, but that will not explain how generations of Spanish painters reenvisioned them as they did.

The gospel of Saint Luke, the patron saint of painters, depicts the risen Christ wandering like a lost ghost on the road out of Jerusalem, where he meets two friends, walks with them to Emmaus and joins them for dinner at an inn. But nothing in the gospel of Luke explains how, in Seville, around 1618, Diego Velázquez saw the story afresh through the eyes of a kitchen maid, and painted it as no one had ever painted it before – and as no one except a few copyists have ever painted it since. The originality and power of that painting depend in part on the *unoriginality* of the story. We have to know the story beforehand in order to grasp what Velázquez has done with it – how he has pulled it back, tautly, into a corner, over the woman's shoulder, and suddenly let it go, so we can see it ricocheting through her eyes.

45

Diego de Silva y Velázquez, *Kitchen Maid with the Supper at Emmaus, c.* 1618. Oil on canvas, 55 × 118 cm. National Gallery of Ireland, Dublin.

What dawns on us as we stand in front of the painting is what is dawning on the woman in the kitchen: one of the three men sitting in her restaurant died three days ago, yet there he is, elbows on the table, talking with his friends. In that instant of recognition, the real world and the mythworld collide, much as they do in Ghandl's story when the woman goes out of the house at midnight to eat eelgrass, dressed in the skin of a goose, and comes back in to lie beside her husband in the form of a human being.

Both the meal and the story, strictly speaking, are invisible in Velázquez's painting. There are plates, but they are washed, stacked and drying. The place of honor in the central foreground is occupied by nothing but a wadded rag. The only food in sight is a single bulb of garlic in the bottom righthand corner, as far away from the table as it can get. But for those who know the story, the hints that Velázquez provides are enough. For those who don't, there is no single image or tableau, however literal or detailed, that could make the action clear.

46

A myth is a story, and it is a story that insistently recurs: a piece of timelessness caught like an eddy in narrative time. Once the story is known, a single image or even a single word can evoke it. But only a linked sequence of images, words or gestures can *tell* it. A story is not a solid object or a solitary entity but a transformative relationship. In musical terms, it is not a note or a set of notes but an episode: a large phrase made from other phrases, which are made in turn of intervals – relationships *between* notes – more than from notes themselves. In linguistic terms, it is a plot: a large sentence made of other sentences. Once you know the verbs, bare names or nouns will call them back to mind,[14] though nouns alone can never tell the story. And stories, whether mythical or historical, timeless or temporal, never exist in isolation. They are linked to other stories, forming a timeless or temporal web.

Velázquez's *Kitchen Maid with the Supper at Emmaus* has not been dated exactly, but it comes from early in his career. He was probably between 18 and 20 when he painted it. In 1623, the King of Spain, Philip IV, appointed him court painter. Velázquez was then 24 years old, and his infatuated patron was 18. From that moment on, while he painted many portraits of the royal household, Velázquez's skills as a mythteller in oils got very little exercise. Perhaps they got little appreciation as well. Some time after it left his workshop, the *Supper at Emmaus* was altered to suit the taste of someone other than its maker. The tiny background scene which contains the real subject of the painting was covered over entirely; the shape of the maid's headdress was changed, and several centimeters of canvas were cut from the left edge of the painting – evidently to make it fit an existing frame or a handy spot on the owner's wall. By this simple procedure, Velázquez's work was demoted from the realm of myth to the realm of anecdote; it was reduced from a vision to a picture.

In the original painting, mythtime and historical time intersect. The result gives depth, humanity and something more than that – transhumanity, we could call it – both to the woman in the painting and to those who stand in front of it, sharing her surprise. Even for non-Christians (I am one) the young Velázquez's painting opens a door; it confirms what every mythteller, physicist, biologist and hunter-gatherer knows: that man is not the manager and measure of all things. The altered version of the painting differed only at the margins. That was enough to reduce the whole to a skillful character sketch or snapshot of a servant in the kitchen, and to confine the scale of value to an implied social hierarchy flattering the European viewer.

If we cut the human element away, keeping only the upper lefthand corner, the painting would become little more than a pious allusion. It would also lose its power as a piece of material craftsmanship, because that corner, where the myth is told, is only a sketch. If we reverse this procedure and mask out the myth, as a former owner did, the painting keeps its surface energy – but all of it is trapped within the human-centered realm. When we see the work in full, something comes from juxtaposing these two views. The painting's power, like the power of Ghandl's story, comes in part from its skillful execution, but also it comes from the juxtaposition and interpenetration of timelessness and time.

Velázquez's painting gives less direct attention to the mythworld than Ghandl's story does. It doesn't take us on a grand tour of the universe. But it does, like Ghandl's story, bring the mythworld right into the house. Whoever decided to paint out the background was responding to its power in the same ungrateful way as the peevish neighbor in Ghandl's story. A harsh word or a few strokes of the brush is enough, in the myth or in the ordinary world, to drive the myth away and cancel out the vision.

In its edited form, Velázquez's painting nevertheless had its admirers. It was copied at least once,[15] and the masked original passed from hand to hand among private collectors, mostly in England, bearing titles such as "The Kitchen Maid" and "The Mulatta." The real subject of the painting was finally rediscovered in 1933, when it was given a thorough cleaning and the overpainting came away. Not until 1987 did it pass into the care of a public museum, the National Gallery of Ireland, to which it now belongs.

Ghandl's spoken poem, like an apple or a loaf of homemade bread – or a coho skin or a cedar tree or Diego Velázquez's painting – is both familiar and one-of-a-kind. It is something new and locally flavored, fulfilling age-old, independently recurrent and widely travelled themes. And it is part of a whole forest of themes and variations, echoes and allusions, spreading out through space and time. It is one piece of work; it is also part of a fabric that is torn and patched, woven and unwoven day after day, night after night, and sentence after sentence, like the cloth on Penelope's loom.

2   Spoken Music

THE POETS PORTRAYED in the *Odyssey* – Demodokos and Phemios – are singers. Ghandl's poems were spoken, not chanted or sung, but they are musical in other important ways – so much so that I think his work deserves to be compared to European music as much as to European sculpture and painting.

Musicologists like to distinguish between intrinsically musical abstract structures – fugues, sonatas, and so on – and program music, in which the composer has an extramusical plot to represent or an image to convey. The two kinds of structure very often coexist in the same piece – and the abstract structures of music have their counterparts, of course, in painting and in literature too. A painting or a poem can tell a story or represent an image and be rigorously abstract, or in some sense absolutely musical, both at the same time. Ghandl's poem about the man who married a goose is an example.

Consider, for instance, some of the symmetries in the poem. It begins at a lake – a patch of water surrounded by land – where a young man falls in love with a soft-spoken, beautiful goose. It ends with the same man marooned on a reef – a patch of land surrounded by water – where the man himself is squawking like a loudmouthed gull. At the center of the story is a pole that links the earth and sky. Either side of the pole is a series of tests and exchanges, and framing these sequences are the two domestic scenes. The first is in the groom's father's house, where a vegetarian bride, who cannot speak directly to her mother-in-law, is offered food she cannot eat. The second is in the bride's father's house. There the omnivorous groom, who cannot speak directly to his father-in-law, tries to eat the same restricted diet as the birds. In the groom's village, the people insult the bride, whose connections with the skyworld have saved them from starvation, and the bride flies off. In the bride's village, the groom insults the people, who nevertheless respond with perfect courtesy, offering to fly him back to earth since he cannot fly himself.

There are more of these symmetrical inversions in the story, but they are linked, like all good symmetries, to structures of other, more dynamic kinds.

The old man gives the younger man a gift: a tool called *skiiskil tlxhahlgaaw*, which is a marlinspike or bradawl used for working with cedar-limb line. Then he instructs him to get eight things for himself. The total is nine. At this point, every listener familiar with Haida narrative will know that there is one more gift to come. In Haida, five and ten – *tliihl* and *tlaahl* – are perfect, or consonant, numbers. Two, four and eight – *sting, stansing* and *stansingxha* – are perfect numbers too, though in a different mode or key. But nine is not. Nine in Haida is *tlaahl sghwaansing guu,* "ten one minus," or *tlaahlinggiisghwaansingghu,* "ten-less-one-many." Nine is a dissonance. It is waiting to be completed. In this poem, what completes the series is the mouse skin.

page 37: lines 113–119

These ten items are like musical themes or motifs. They are undissipated energies. All ten must be resolved in the unfolding of the story. But Ghandl of the Qayahl Llaanas is an artist, who likes to make a plot stand up and dance, so there is something like a fugal structure to this aspect of the poem. The second subject – putting the ten medicine objects to use – begins before the first, their acquisition, has come to an end.

The ten things are put to use in pairs, so five occasions are required. One of these occasions is the sky pillar itself. The other four – symmetrically arranged around the pillar – involve extraordinary beings. Between their acquisition and their use, the

ten charged objects, from marlinspike to mouse skin, are melod-
ically and rhythmically recombined.[1] The rhythm and the
melody involved have less to do with sound than with the order
and the tempo at which images are called before the mind – but
they are called up in the context of a set of expectations and conventions, much like a system of musical modes or keys, which can
work by a mixture of statement and suggestion. Ghandl has to
tell us that the salmon roe is used in combination with the mouse
skin, but the other gift, the marlinspike, is never directly mentioned a second time. A reference to cedar-limb line and spruce-
root cord is enough. That allusion brings the spike to mind.

*page 40:
lines
205–206;
pages
39–40:
lines
181–192*

The first pair of objects – oil and comb – goes to the holy fool:
a talented clairvoyant who cannot find his own lice. (Elsewhere
in the world, the same joke has been told of many wise men, including Herakleitos.) When a louse bites the back of his head, he
turns around and looks for it behind him. This seer who is busy
accomplishing nothing is followed by a woman who tries to do
everything exactly as she is told. She is holding up the country:
Xhaaydla Gwaayaay tldaghawaay, the mountains of the Islands
on the Boundary between Worlds. Beyond the pillar to the sky
are two more figures – or two and a half. The first is half a man;
the second is a pair of fat old guys who act as one. The pair create the coho out of salmon-colored woodchips, while the half-
man downstream spears them and puts them in his creel.

*pages
37–38:
lines
126–139*

*page 40:
line 188*

The structure created by these characters alone is a kind of
complex narrative crystal, or a piece of conceptual music. But
other structures are linked to it. On the terrestrial side there are
the benefactors: the old man who lives at the edge of the village,
and the Mouse Woman, whose large house is hidden in a clump
of ferns. On the celestial side there is a conclave of three carniv-
orous birds and a bear. Later comes another foursome consisting
of three omnivorous birds – loon, grebe and raven – linked to a
man who is evidently also a bird, since his daughters are geese as
well as women. In each of these two groups, one bird acts while
the other two stand by. And there is one more bird in the last

scene: the gull, who counterbalances the brace of geese with which the plot began.

Very early in the story, the man takes one of the two goose skins – his wife's – and gives her one of his two marten skins in exchange. After losing his wife, he gets two other skins: a coho skin and a mouse skin, which is the only skin in the story that comes with claws. This skin-swapping is linked to that innocent, even irrelevant-looking transaction between the eagle and the bear. The story of the bear getting claws from the eagle is a stock piece of North American folklore, slipped into the poem like an innocent bit of folksong inserted into a string quartet or sonata.[2] But it fulfills here an essential musical function.

page 41:
lines
217–225

The human husband is in heaven, where he cannot stay. He got there by means of a salmon egg and a mouse skin. Before he can return to earth, the energy residing in these images has to be resolved, the way an errant theme in music must be modulated back to its home key. But this is *narrative* music; it is not performed on a keyboard; it is played by calling images into the mind with spoken words. For the story to seem complete, tensions that are built up by that means must be discharged in the same way. The energy of the mouse skin is resolved, or answered, by the transfer of claws from eagle to bear, and the energy of the salmon egg is answered by the woodchips that transform themselves to salmon.

Between these events comes another resolution or response. The story began with two geese who came out of the sky and undressed, becoming recognizable as women. Both were caught, and one was released, by a single man. In the sky, that scene is answered by another in which the roles are reversed and the numbers cut in half. The man comes up from earth, dresses as a salmon, and evades being caught by half a man. These scenes balance one another much as episodes balance one another in sonata form, and as figures balance one another in pictorial composition. The "unnatural" figure of the clawless bear also mirrors the "unnaturally" meatless diet of the famine-stricken humans, and the bear's unmistakeable politeness in dealing with the eagle balances the rudeness of the unnamed human whose words drove the Goose Woman back to the sky.

The transfer of the claws is nicely symmetrical with another *page 42: lines 240–244* event: the transfer of the spearhead from the hunter to the being with one leg. It is, as we shall see, an old requirement that talons, claws or fingers should *change hands* in this story. It seems that they must also fall to earth – which they do when they are passed from eagle to bear. The webbed feet and wings that belong to the geese must also go back to the sky, and a man who masquerades as a mouse and a coho must return to earth and water.

This structure was built by an artist enraptured by a story that unfolds behind his eyes. And the story is more than just a dance of the animal transvestites, a display of imagistic acrobatics, structural pattern or surreal cartoon ballet. It is grounded, let us remember, in a poignant story of love and loss. It is grounded in a world where perfection is perceived but imperfection rules, and where humans and nonhumans sometimes both want more than they can have.

Superficially, the story turns on the distinction between *xhaayda gataagha,* human food, and *hlgitghun gataagha,* goose food. The Goose Woman's arrival in her human husband's village, and the terms of her remaining there, are stated in a simple *page 34: line 47* sentence: *Xhaayda gataagha waadluxhan gam lla taaghangas*: "She ate no human food at all." Her departure is provoked by the in- *page 36: line 96* version of this sentence: *Hlgitghun gataagha lla quyaada-ttlxhawgwa aa*: "She thinks very highly of goose food." Both a famine and a feast intervene between these sentences. The Goose Woman's father sends the feast – but does he also send the famine? Is the famine *caused* by the Goose Woman remaining among the humans and in human form? If so, is the famine a test for the human community to pass, or is it simply an inevitable symptom of disorder in the world?

When her father sends food to the hungry humans, the Goose

Woman tells them what is happening. *Hakw dii xhaatgha diighi* *pages*
dangghattlxhattahlga, she says: "Now my father is sending *35–36:*
[something] down to me." She speaks this sentence twice, to her- *lines*
79 & 89
ald the arrival of two shipments of food. The complex verb she
uses, *ghattlxhattahl,* means "to move quickly downward." This
verb will reappear, once only, later in the story – when the raven
delivers the Goose Woman's husband back to the surface of the
earth. There the verb is differently inflected to form the second
half of a double subordinate clause (a convenient construction in
Haida which I cannot gracefully replicate in English). The prefix
changes too, from *dang-* (which points to the object of the verb)
to *giit-* (which points to the subject). The root form, nonetheless,
is unmistakeable:

> Ll ghaaxhaghihljihliigaay dluu *page 44:*
> Ila dangat giitghattlxhattahldalaay dluu *lines*
> *295–297*
> nang qwaagadaaganga qqaayghudyas gha Ila Ila qqaa'adas.

> *When he grew very tired*
> *and let himself fall with him,*
> *he dropped him onto a shoal exposed by the tide.*

The verbal echoes or thematic repetitions that are clear in the
Haida have been submerged in these line-by-line translations. In
the full translation with which we began, I added a phrase,
"down through the clouds," to each of the three sentences in
which the verb *ghattlxhattahl* appears. "Down" and "through"
have counterparts within that verb itself, but clouds are nowhere
mentioned in the Haida. I put them in, to achieve in English a
noun-centered echo equivalent in weight to the *verb-centered echo*
in the original. This is far from a perfect solution, yet I think
something like it is required. The poem's thematic echoes are not
mere accidents of language or ornamental rhymes.

It is a tale of transformation, or transposition, as musicians say: bird transposed to woman; man to bird. In the interim, a mouse becomes a woman and her burrow a big house; a man becomes a mouse and then a salmon; joy becomes despair. Dead redcedar springs to life as fish with cedar-colored flesh, and passion and devotion die. Even as the headman's loveliest and youngest daughter's husband in a fine house overhead, a hunter's life becomes routine.

But there are other transformations here, and other continuities, that summaries know nothing whatever about. In the beginning of the poem, when the hunter sees the women in the water and the goose skins on the shore, Ghandl says, in two superbly simple lines,

*pages
32 & 33:
lines 13–14*

> *Lla qindi qawdihaw
> lla dawghattlxhasi.*
>
> *After watching for a while,
> he swooped in.*

The verb in the first line is *qing,* to watch or to see. It can apply to anything with eyes (and that includes, in Haida biology, the earth, the sea, the forest and the sky, and nearly everything that lives in all these realms.) The verb in the next line is *dawghattlxha.* It means to swoop in order to catch prey. It calls to mind one class of creatures only: the small hawks and falcons that in English are called kestrels, merlins and sharp-shins. In Haida, these three species have one name: *dawghattlxhaayang.* The hunter of the birds, transformed into a gull at the end of the poem, was himself a bird of prey in the beginning.

After Swanton put this poem in writing, he asked Ghandl if it had a name. Ghandl called it *Ghungghang llanaagha gha nang xhitiit ttsinhlgwaangxidaghan.* This means "In his own father's village, someone was just about to go out hunting birds." The verb used here includes a component, *-xidi-*, that makes it a verb of anticipation or inception. The young man is getting ready to go, or thinking of going, out to hunt birds, but he hasn't yet gone.

In the opening lines of the story itself, Ghandl uses a different form of the verb: not *ttsinhlghwaangxidaghan* but *ttsinhlghwaanggwang,* which implies that the hunting has begun. I wonder if this subtle shift in the verb has something to tell us. Should we take this story at face value as a tale of what happened, maybe, once upon a time? Or does Ghandl's title set it into a different context, as something that hasn't happened yet but that could occur tomorrow and tomorrow and tomorrow: something like a dream, or a young hunter's preparatory vision?

᠈   ᠈   ᠈

It is easy to imagine – and not very difficult, at present, to go to a few galleries and see – how the elements in Velázquez's *Supper at Emmaus* could be differently combined by other painters. Rembrandt, for example, painted the same subject ten or twelve years later, while he was still in his early twenties and living in Leiden. There is very little chance that he had seen Velázquez's painting – a work by another young artist like himself, with as yet only a local reputation, living 1600 sea miles to the south – but Rembrandt also knew the story. He assembled the same figures on his canvas, while turning the arrangement inside out. The result (never trimmed or overpainted) now hangs in the Musée Jacquemart-André in Paris.

Rembrandt's serving maid occupies the spot Velázquez gave to the disciples. She is far off in the background to the left, perhaps suspecting nothing. Both she and Christ, who looms up large and ghostlike on the right, are potent silhouettes. In the foreground, also faceless, is a nearly invisible figure: a pilgrim crouching down in sudden recognition. But at the center of it all, as in a mirror, there is a face. It is drawing back, twisted with astonishment. It belongs to the other pilgrim – and to us.

Ghandl's poem, like Rembrandt's painting, or Velázquez's, takes the form it does because that is the form its author gave it. It has the human poignancy it does because that poignancy is something its author had learned to perceive and communicate. The images and themes of which it is made are largely materials he inherited – and along with these components, he inherited a narrative and visionary grammar for putting them together. He could however have built them into a vastly different structure – a more sentimental structure, for example, or a colder one, with a lower emotional charge – just as any fluent speaker of a language can assemble a cluster of words into sentences with very different values.

Pokhodsk is farther from Hlghagilda than Leiden from Seville. It is an overgrown mission station, trading post and neolithic village near the mouth of the Kolyma, which empties into the East Siberian Sea, 3000 rough and windy miles north and west of Haida Gwaii. There in the summer of 1896 a Yukaghir woman told several stories to a listener willing, like Swanton, to take dictation. I do not know her Yukaghir name, but a royalist Russian missionary had given her another: Ekaterina Rumyantsev. Her listener was a Russian political activist, anthropologist and novelist named Vladimir Germanovich Bogoraz.[3]

Ekaterina Rumyantsev had not only a Russian name; she had considerable exposure to Russian colonial culture. She therefore told her stories to Bogoraz in the Russian language. And some of Bogoraz's research in Siberia was funded, like Swanton's work in Haida Gwaii, through the American Museum of Natural History in New York, at the instance of Franz Boas. The stories Rumyantsev had learned in Yukaghir and told to Bogoraz in Russian were, for this reason, ultimately published not in Leningrad or Moscow but in New York, in Bogoraz's English translation.

In the absence of an actual transcription, there is no hope of appraising Rumyantsev's skill or stature as a mythteller, and no hope of studying her work and Ghandl's together on equitable terms. But one of her stories has something important to tell us, even when reduced to English prose. Side by side with Ghandl's poem, it shows how the same events and characters can be assembled very differently by different human beings, just as the same figures can be grouped very differently in different painters' paintings and in different people's dreams. This is Rumyantsev's story as rendered by Bogoraz:[4]

There was a family of Tungus. They lived in a tent. They had three daughters. The girls, when going to pick berries, would turn into female geese. In this form they visited the sea islands. One time they flew farther than usual. On a lonely island they saw a one-sided man. When he breathed, his heart and lungs would jump out of his side. The Geese were afraid and flew home.

After some time, they had nothing to eat, so they went again to the sea islands for berries. Wherever they chose a spot on which to alight, One-Side appeared and frightened them away. At last they found a place full of berries. They descended and laid aside their wings. They picked so many berries that they could hardly carry them all. They went back to the place where they had left their wings. The wings of the youngest daughter were gone. They looked for them a long time. At last, evening came and the sun went down. It grew very dark. The two elder sisters reproached the youngest one: "Probably you have taken a liking to One-Side, and you have asked him to hide your wings. Now remain here alone and let him take you!"

She almost cried while assuring them that their suspicions were unjust. "I have never seen him and never thought of him." They left her and flew away. She remained alone.

As soon as they were out of sight, One-Side appeared carrying her wings. "Well, now," he said. "Fair maiden, will you not consent to marry me?" She refused for a long time. Then she gave in and said, "I will!"

"If you are willing," said One-Side, "I will lead the way." He took her to his house. It was the usual house, made of wood, with a wooden fireplace. He proved to be a good hunter, able to catch any kind of game. Still he had only one side, and with every breath his heart would jump out. They lived together for a while, and the woman brought forth a son. The young woman nursed the infant. But One-Side did not want to stay at home. He would wander about all the time and bring back reindeer and elk. They had so much meat that the storehouses would no longer hold it. He was a great hunter. He hunted on foot on snowshoes, for he had neither reindeer nor horses for traveling.

One time he set off to hunt as usual. Then his wife's sisters suddenly came and carried the youngest sister and her little son off to their own country. The small boy, while carried on high, shouted, "O father! O my father! We are being carried by aunties to their home, to their home."

One-Side ran home as fast as he could, but he came too late. They were out of sight. Only the boy's voice was heard far away. Then he shot an arrow with a forked head in the direction whence the voices seemed to come, and the arrow cut off one of the boy's little fingers. One-Side found the arrow and the finger and put them into his pouch.

Then he started in search of his boy. He walked and walked. A whole year passed. Then he arrived at a village. A number of children were playing sticks. He looked from one to another, thinking of his boy. There was one poor boy who was dressed in the poorest of clothing. His body was mangy, and his head was bruised and covered with scars. First, One-Side paid no attention to him, but when he finally looked at this boy, he saw that the little finger on his left hand was missing. He snatched the finger out of his pouch and placed it beside the hand, and indeed it fit! The poor boy was his son! "Whose boy are you?" asked One-Side.

"I am mamma's boy."

"And where is your father?"

"I have no father. I used to have one, but now I have none."

"I am your father."

The boy refused to believe it and only cried bitterly. "If my father were alive, we should not be so wretched, mother and I."

The elder sisters had married and made their youngest sister a drudge in the house.

"Why is your head so bruised and scarred?" asked One-Side.

"It is because my aunts order me to enter the house only by the back entrance, and every time I try to go in by the front entrance, they strike my head with their heavy staffs."

"Let us go to your house."

They arrived at the house. The boy went ahead and One-Side followed him. They came to the front entrance. As soon as the boy tried to go in, his eldest aunt jumped up and struck him with her iron staff. Then the woman saw the boy's father and felt so much ashamed that she fell down before him.

He entered the house. They hustled about, brought food of every kind, and prepared tea. They ate so long that it grew very late and it was time to go to bed. On the following morning after breakfast, he said to his brothers-in-law, "Let us go and try which of us can shoot the best with the bow! You are two and I am only one."

They made ready their bows and arrows and began to shoot at each other. The elder brother-in-law shot first, but One-Side jumped upward, and the arrow missed him. The second brother-in-law also shot. One-Side jumped aside and dodged the arrow.

"Now I shall shoot," said One-Side, "and you try to dodge my arrows." He shot once and hit his elder brother-in-law straight through the heart. With the second shot he killed his other brother-in-law. Then he went back to the house, killed his wife's sisters and took home his wife and son.

One time he set off as usual to look for game. When he was out of sight of his wife, he took off the skin that disguised his true form and hung it up in the top of a high larch tree. He became a young man, quite fair and handsome, just like the sunrise. He went home and sat down on his wife's bed. While he was sitting there, he was about to take off his boots. The woman began to argue. "Go away from here! My husband will be here soon, and he will be angry with me. He will say, 'Why have you let a strange man sit on your bed?'"

"I am your husband," said he. "Why do you try to drive me away?"

"No," said the woman. "My husband is one-sided, and you are like other men."

They argued for a long time. At last he said, "Go and look at that tree yonder. I hung up my one-sided skin on it." She found the tree and the one-sided skin, and now she believed him. Then she caught him in her arms and covered him with kisses. After that they lived happier than ever.

➤ ➤ ➤

Ghandl's poem about the hunter who married his prey has been spared the indignities visited on many works of indigenous oral literature. It was transcribed in the language in which it was spoken, and it has quietly been travelling the world since 1905 in Swanton's admirably faithful prose translation. In that form it is also the subject of a sensitive, close study by the poet Gary Snyder.[5] It is nonetheless a literary work that we have only just begun to understand.

I have been calling it a poem and a piece of spoken music. That is because I hear in it resonant textures and densities, and vividness and shapeliness and clarity that, for me, define the terms I want to use. I cannot tell what terms to use for Rumyantsev's story, because Bogoraz's translated paraphrase is all that now remains.

Some things, nonetheless, can be known about the story on the basis of the paraphrase alone, just as some things can be known about a painting on the basis of a poorer painter's copy or a second-hand account.

The paraphrase can tell us, first of all, that the list of narrative ingredients is very much the same – almost uncannily the same – in Rumyantsev's story and in Ghandl's. The ingredients are very much the same, but they are differently assembled by two very different cooks, one of whom has learned the European fairytale custom of serving happy endings for dessert. "The same story" has become two wholly different meals for the mind. That much is clear, though in the one case we can still attend the feast – because we have the actual text – and in the other we can only read the menu and collect the empty plates. There is no supper at Pokhodsk because no one took dictation – just as, in the legacy of Velázquez, there was once no supper at Emmaus because vandals, in whose hands the treasure rested, chose to have the painter's vision blotted out.

Digesting the sense of the world – of which we are made, and to which we return – is just as essential to life as digesting its physical substance. The mythteller's art is as old, universal and vital as that of the cook. The congruences between these tales told by Ghandl and Rumyantsev are reminders of that fact. Drawing on this old, shared recipe – as dormant in its way as Luke's abbreviated version of the supper at Emmaus – and adding some significant resources of his own, Ghandl could construct a work of art that can stand beside the paintings of Rembrandt and Velázquez or, I think, beside the sonatas of Haydn and Mozart. It is a work of music built from silent images, sounding down the years. It is a vision painted indelibly in the air with words that disappear the moment they are spoken.

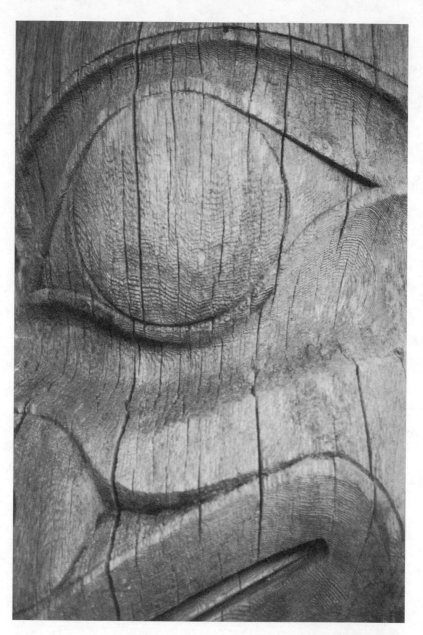

Bear's eye from the housepole of Naagha Hliman Xhunandas (House of the Cascading Elk Hides), Ttanuu. The pole is now in four sections at the Museum of Anthropology, University of British Columbia, Vancouver.

(MOA A50,000a)

3   The One They Hand Along

Pᴇᴏᴩʟᴇ ᴅᴇᴩᴇɴᴅᴀɴᴛ ᴏɴ ʜᴜɴᴛɪɴɢ and foraging are
almost always mobile, while gardeners and farmers stay put and
build towns. In Haida Gwaii, as elsewhere on the Northwest
Coast of North America after the last glaciation, this rule ceased
to hold. Shellfish are there for the taking twice each day when
the tide recedes – and salmon, halibut, cod, herring, eulachon,
sealion, seal and other species pass like an edible calendar along
the open coast and through the maze of inshore waters. In precolonial times the Haida planted no crops,[1] and yet they lived,
like wealthy farmers, in substantial towns. The rich tradition of
Haida art and oral literature is simultaneously rooted in the
powerful social forces of the village and in the hunter's acutely
personal relations with the wild. It is also rooted in the constant
presence of the sea. Manna falls only rarely from the heavens; it
emerges daily from the waves. And the primary realm of the
gods, in Haida cosmology, is not celestial; it is submarine.

This vision is a part of the complex intellectual ecology of the
North American continent – not by virtue of any political union
engineered by Europeans, but through physical proximity and
centuries of cultural exchange between the Haida and their
neighbors, both human and nonhuman. Ideas are widely shared
and thought is sometimes deeply rooted. This does not, however,
mean that Haida literature, philosophy and art are entirely joint
and anonymous tribal creations. The dwelling place of culture, as
the linguist Edward Sapir tried often to explain to his anthropologist colleagues,

is not in a theoretical community of human beings known as society.... The true locus of culture is in the interactions of specific individuals and, on the subjective side, in the world of meanings which each one of these individuals may unconsciously abstract....[2]

Franz Boas (1858–1942), who was John Swanton's mentor and the father of American anthropology, taught by contrast that "Ethnology ... does not deal with the exceptional man; it deals with the masses."[3]

The writings of many ethnographers, both popular and scholarly, are well supplied with sentences in the form "The Haida believe that..." or "The Navajo believe that...." Perhaps not all such sentences are altogether false, but it is certain that no such sentence is ever entirely true. What people think, and what they believe, from moment to moment and day to day, is for each of them to say or not to say, as each of them may choose. Many people choose to speak instead of what they remember or what they imagine. Some choose not to speak at all, or not to speak to those who ask too many questions. If we come to the study of culture by way of literature and art, we have an advantage: we can generally be sure that what we are studying is something someone has actually chosen to say. What one poet says is not necessarily what another poet would say, nor what the poet's neighbors would say if asked what they believe. We know, however, that Ghandl had listened to earlier Haida poets, as well as to the world, and we know that those who knew him chose to listen to him too, even in very difficult times. His knowledge and skill as a mythteller are remembered in the Islands even now – and not entirely by people who have read his words in books.

Why Ghandl of the Qayahl Llaanas of Qaysun has not also been adopted with full honors into the polylingual canon of North American literary history I do not know. He seems to me a great deal more accomplished – and therefore far more worthy of celebration as a literary ancestor – than any Canadian poet or novelist who was writing in English or French during his time. In fact I know of no one writing in any language, anywhere in North America toward the end of the nineteenth century, who uses words with greater sensitivity and skill. He seems to me not just an exceptional man, as Boas would say, but a figure of durable importance in the history of literature.

Like Homer and the author of the *Beowulf,* Ghandl was a poet who never learned to write – and who therefore did not need to. We have some of his poetry nevertheless – about 5000 lines of it, in fact – and we have it in written form, because he spent a month painstakingly dictating it while John Swanton patiently wrote it down. Swanton's wages were paid by the Bureau of American Ethnology in Washington, DC, but his work was guided primarily by Boas, at the American Museum of Natural History. Swanton had just completed his PhD under Boas's direction, and Boas had picked him to make the first serious study of Haida culture from a European perspective.

Ghandl explained to Swanton in some detail how the gods as well as human beings are divided into Raven and Eagle sides. This web of reciprocal interrelations, as Ghandl describes it, is not a social contract; it is part of the intrinsic structure of the world. The Raven is a raven and a Raven – a member of the raven species and the Raven side – and the Eagle is an eagle and an Eagle; but no one – neither a human nor a mythcreature – is the leader of a species or a nation or a side. Each side consists of a varying number of independent matrilineal families or clans, and each of these families is an ordered aristocracy. Rank within the family is heritable rather than hereditary. Family rights to fishing grounds and other resources are recognized. Status nevertheless depends in the long term on the character, skill and luck of individual hunters and traders. Each house has a head; each lineage or family has a head; each village has a head, who is a family head as well; and that is as far as the apparent political infrastructure extends. Yet there are unwritten contracts between families, villages, nations, and also between species, including humans and gods. The culture as Ghandl describes it depends – like every hunting culture – not on control of the land as such but on control of the human demands that are placed upon it.

Europeans had been coming to the Haida country for more than a century when Swanton finally arrived, but most of them, it seems, had been interested in taking things or changing things far more than in learning things. They had brought the gospel and the smallpox, gunpowder and money, and on the whole, had acted in reality much as the Raven does in myth: making unrestrained and unsustainable demands. The first European fur-buying mission to the Haida came in 1787. Less than a century later the sea otter had vanished, the migratory populations of sealion, seal and whale were greatly reduced, and other species – the spring-running sockeye; the coho, chinook, chum and pink salmon that run in the fall; the red cod and black cod and halibut; the big Sitka spruce and the western hemlock, the redcedar and yellowcedar – were waiting their turn as objects of uncontrolled harvest. But of all the indigenous species of Haida Gwaii, the two that suffered the heaviest losses during the nineteenth and early twentieth centuries were *Enhydra lutris*, the sea otter, and *Homo sapiens*, the human being. Overhunting, overfishing and clear-cut logging notwithstanding, the single most persistently abused and heavily damaged ecosystem in Haida Gwaii to date has been the fragile, half-tangible ecosystem of language, thought, memory and behavior: the ecosystem of culture.

>

Swanton headed west by rail from Washington, DC, in September 1900. He was on Vancouver Island by the middle of the month, and he caught the coastal steamer *Princess Louise* north from Victoria on the night of Monday, September 17th. He got his first Haida lessons on shipboard, from the master carver Daxhiigang, known in English as Charlie Edenshaw (1839–1920),

who was his fellow passenger.[4] Swanton disembarked with
Daxhiigang at the mouth of the Skeena River, in the Tsimshian
country, on the British Columbia mainland, on Sunday, September 23rd, and on Tuesday, September 25th, he made the hundred-mile crossing out to Haida Gwaii, landing at Skidegate. On
Sunday the 30th, he reported his first impressions to Boas:

*The island population is now shrunk to not over seven hundred, of
whom three hundred are here. There is not an old house standing [at
Skidegate] – all have modern frame structures with the regulation
windows.... The missionary has suppressed all the dances and has
been instrumental in having all the old houses destroyed – everything
in short that makes life worth living.... I have taken down one text
and begun a study of the grammar using that as a basis. The verb
promises to be difficult....[5]*

Swanton's population estimate – 700 Haida in the entirety of
Haida Gwaii – looks fairly accurate in retrospect, and almost all
700 of them were living in the two mission villages, Skidegate
and Masset. Later, after visiting all the surviving Haida communities in Canada and Alaska, Swanton put the total at 850.[6] If we
add the absentees – Haida who had gone to the cannery towns
and south to Vancouver Island in search of jobs – the total still
cannot be much above 1000. A century earlier, there were several dozen villages, and perhaps 12,000 Haida altogether. That
change in population, from 12,000 to 1000, is one important
measure of the price the Haida paid for European contact. Some
of this reduction can be credited to typhoid, measles, syphilis and
gunshot, but the principal killer – the one that took more than
ninety per cent of the Haida population over the course of the
nineteenth century – was smallpox.

The Haida poets whose works Swanton transcribed over the
following year were not living in the idyllic Canadian wilderness, nor were they living in raw, new frontier towns. They were

living in something more like the Warsaw ghetto. Europe and Asia, at this date, remembered nothing worse than the Black Death, which killed perhaps thirty per cent of their population during the fourteenth century. The Haida who were alive to meet John Swanton in the fall of 1900 had lived through a series of epidemics three times more virulent than that. And instead of being left then to rebuild their culture in peace, they were targeted by missionaries, government agents and traders who were certain, by and large, of the innate superiority of English customs, the Christian religion and the Anglo-Saxon race.

Cultural warfare is a practice of great antiquity, possibly as old as culture itself. But death and forced reeducation came to the Haida with stunning force. Europeans, so far as we know, tasted cultural warfare in a similarly concentrated form only when Stalin and Hitler opened their camps.

Swanton declined an invitation to board with the missionary and his family, but he did not join a Haida household either. Haida culture has never had a more devoted foreign student, but it was not Swanton's plan to leave his own identity behind or to submerge himself entirely in Haida life – especially not in Haida life as it was in a mission village in 1900. This does not mean the world he hoped to enter was a world of his own romantic imagining. The world he was seeking was the real world of Haida memory and imagination. Swanton was not wrong in thinking he would find this world more vividly alive in Haida art and oral literature than in mission-village routine. He chose, therefore, to rent peaceful quarters of his own near the dogfish oilery, half an hour's walk from the village where he worked each day. Three months later, he discovered to his delight that he was living on the site of the old Haida village of Guuhlgha, a place as important in classical Haida literature as Ithaka or Argos in the literature of Greece.

Within days of his arrival in the Islands, Swanton took another crucial step. He hired as his teacher, guide and assistant a bilingual Haida by the name of Henry Moody of the Qaagyals Qiighawaay, who was only a year or two older than Swanton himself. Swanton explained to Moody what he wanted, and Moody arranged their first experiment with taking dictation in Haida. The result – the text Swanton mentioned in his first report to Boas – was a story about Jilaquns ("Big Bait"), a creature of the mythworld who destroys a whole village in reprisal for human arrogance. It was the first written piece of Haida literature, dictated to Moody and Swanton on 29 September 1900.[7] The author was Henry Moody's father, Job Moody, whose Haida title – as hereditary headman of the Xhiida Xhaaydaghaay and the abandoned village of Hlqiinul[8] – was Gumsiiwa.

Swanton spent several days studying this text with Henry Moody, getting a feel for the work to come. Then on Friday, 5 October 1900 – ten days after he had first set foot in Haida Gwaii – he began the serious taking of texts. Swanton and Moody spent four hours of that day taking dictation from a man known in English as Philip Jackson and in Haida as Na Yuuwans Xhaayda Sghiidagits, or Big-House Person Little-Red-Chiton.[9]

Sghiidagits was the hereditary headman of Hlghagilda – the old Haida village displaced by the mission town of Skidegate. The English name of the town is taken from that of the man, and Sghiidagits has been the hereditary name of the headmen of Hlghagilda for more than two centuries. This particular Sghiidagits – who held the office from his predecessor's death in October 1892 until his own death a decade later – dictated to Swanton a linked set of three stories, beginning with the widely told tale of a woman who married a grizzly and continuing with the stories of the Tsimshian heroes Dzagmdaawła and Ganaxnox Sm'oogyit.[10] The latter name has been absorbed into Haida in two forms: Nanasimgit or Gunanasimgit.

Nanasimgit is a figure often compared to Orpheus. His story involves a voyage to the bottom of the sea to retrieve his wife after she is kidnapped by a killer whale. But why, we may ask, is

Hlghagilda (Skidegate), summer 1881, photographed by Edward Dossetter. At this date the village consisted of 25 or 30 houses with more than 60 exterior poles – including housepoles, memorials and mortuary poles. Immigration from outlying villages had increased the population, but not as fast as small-pox had reduced it. Only about 20 of the houses were still inhabited.

(American Museum of Natural History, Library Services, 42268)

Sghiidagits, a Haida, telling John Swanton a Tsimshian story? Is this what is known nowadays as cultural appropriation – or is it a sign of healthy intercultural trade? Haida artists imported beaver teeth (for chisels), porcupine hair (for paintbrushes), mountain sheep and mountain goat horn (chiefly for bowls, ladles and spoons), mountain goat wool and many other things from the Tsimshian. They imported raw copper from Alaska and the Yukon, and abalone shell from Oregon and California, insisting that California red abalone shell had better iridescence than the species available at home. There is plenty of evidence that poets imported storylines and metaphors as well. By telling a tale that takes place across the water, Sghiidagits was acting very much like Sophocles and Shakespeare. He was also acting in accord with Haida literary tradition.

Skidegate (Hlghagilda), *c.*1912. All the traditional houses are gone, but four memorial poles and one detached housepole are still standing. (Three of the five remaining poles are visible near the center of the photograph. The leftmost of these is a memorial pole for Daxhiigang's mother, Kkaawquuna, who died about 1879.)

(Royal British Columbia Museum, PN 5336; photographer unidentified)

Swanton, by buying his first story from Sghiidagits, was at the same time proving his respect for Haida protocol. It was diplomatically correct of him to begin his search for Haida narratives with the headman of the village where he was working. On the following Monday, when Sghiidagits announced he had other commitments, Swanton was free to go in search of the best mythtellers in town, whatever their rank or family. Henry Moody, in the meantime, had arranged to introduce him to the person he was looking for.

⸙　　　⸙　　　⸙

It was on that day, Monday, 8 October 1900, that Swanton met the finest poet he would ever meet, in any language or tradition. His name was Skaay, which is the Haida name of a small, inedi-

73

ble mollusk with a spiral shell, called a periwinkle in English and *Littorina sitkana* in Latin. Skaay's family or lineage was the Qquuna Qiighawaay, of the Eagle side. *Qii*, as a verb, means to give birth, and as a noun it means descendant. *Qquuna Qiighawaay* means "the Descendants of [the village known as] Qquuna." Not all members of this lineage were themselves born at Qquuna, but Skaay almost certainly was, in or about the year 1827. For most of his adult life his home was a village south of Qquuna, called Ttanuu.

There are few written records from those days in Haida Gwaii, and none more oblivious to indigenous Haida culture than the missionaries' ledgers, the account books of souls. Yet even these reveal many facts of interest. They reveal, among other things, that Skaay – and evidently Skaay alone, of all the surviving southern Haida – had several Christian names over the years. In 1884 he was entered in the missionary's roll as Robert McKay. This name evidently slipped his mind or did not suit him. On Sunday, 13 March 1892, at the village of Qqaa-dasghu, he was baptized and registered again simply as "Sky." On 31 January 1894, he was baptized a third time, together with his wife, and their marriage was confirmed by a Christian wedding. It was on this date that Skaay took the English name John Sky, by which he has been known to outsiders ever since. On the same January day, his wife, whose Haida name I do not know, was christened Esther. This was Skaay's last recorded transaction with the church.[11]

Daxhiigang, who was Swanton's first tutor in the Haida language and the greatest Haida sculptor of his time, used to carry around in his pocket a Haida translation of the gospel of Saint Luke.[12] It is not very likely that he read this book, but it is likely that Daxhiigang, like Velázquez, knew and relished the tradition that Saint Luke had been a painter. Skaay of the Qquuna Qiighawaay – the greatest Haida poet whose work survives – could neither read nor write, but when he settled on the Chris-

Qquuna in September 1902: the deserted birthplace of Skaay of the Qquuna Qiighawaay. Photograph by C.F. Newcombe.
(Royal British Columbia Museum, PN 10)

tian name John Sky, he had probably been told that John was the poet among the evangelists and that Saint John's totem animal, the eagle, corresponded with his own.

On Sunday, 14 October 1900, when he had known Skaay for a week, Swanton wrote again to Boas. He has now started working, he says,

with an old man in the village who has a crippled back but is admitted on all hands to tell the old legends very correctly. His first story covers one hundred and twenty six pages.... The second is not yet complete but will probably cover about seventy. It seems that a certain set of tales were told ... in a definite order.... Of this series the Raven story comes last, and this old man is almost the last in Skidegate who remembers the whole of it.... I consider him quite a find....[13]

The pages Swanton is counting here are field notebook pages, double-spaced to leave room for interlinear translation. In printed form, that first narrative poem takes a mere 50 pages. Told at a normal pace – which is a better way to measure oral literature – it lasts about two hours, and it is composed in three distinct movements. The translation which follows will carry us only through the end of the first movement – about an hour's worth of telling. In Haida, the poem opens as follows:

Ll gidaagang wansuuga.
Ll jaadagang wansuuga.
Skyaamskun ghinwaay llaghan ttl gitghan
     jihlgwagaangang wansuuga.
Ll xhaatgha llagha kkuugagang wansuuga.

Ll daaghalang stins: 5
nang dlquunas
gyaan ising nang hittaghaniina.

Waaygyaanhaw ll xhaatghaga llanagaay gu ga
     xyaahldaal ttl xhaayang wansuuga,
tluugha tlaahlgugha.
Waaygyaan xyaahldaalang wansuuga.   10
Waaygyaan gaytlgistlaayang wansuuga...[14]

There was a child of good family, they say.
She was a woman, they say.
They wove the down of blue falcons[15]
     into her dancing blanket, they say.
Her father loved her, they say.

She had two brothers:
one who was older
and one who was younger than she.

And then they came to dance at her father's town, they say,
in ten canoes.
And then they danced, they say.   10
And then they waited, they say.

And someone – one of her father's servants, they say –
stepped forward and said to them,
« Why are these canoes here? »

« These canoes are here for the headman's daughter. »
    Someone responded, they say:
« The woman refuses. »
    They went away weeping, they say.

They came to dance again on the following day,
        in ten canoes, they say.   20
    And again they were questioned, they say.
« Why are these canoes here? »

« These canoes are here for the headman's daughter. »
    And then they refused them again.
    And they went away weeping.

Now, on the following day someone was there,
in a harbor-seal canoe, in a broad hat,
        at early morning, they say.
Surfbirds lived in his hat, they say.

After they had looked at him in his harbor-seal canoe,
they asked him, they say,   30
« Why is this canoe here? »

He said nothing, they say.
They refused him.

They said to him, so they say,
« The woman refuses. »

Something encircled his hat.
It was white, they say.
It moved like breaking surf, they say.
It was foaming and churning, they say.

And when they refused him,   40
the earth became different, they say.
Seawater surged over the ground.
When they found themselves half underwater,
the villagers feared
that they might have to give him the woman.

And she had ten servants, they say.
And they dressed one to resemble her, they say.
And they painted her, they say.

They painted red cirrus clouds on her face, they say,
and gave her two skyblankets to wear   50
and sent her out to their eminent visitor.
He turned her down, they say.
He wanted the headman's daughter, they say.

And yet again they painted one, they say.
They painted her with seaward dark clouds
and gave her two marten-skin capes to wear
and sent her out, they say.
He refused her too, they say.
He refused all ten the same way.

Then the villagers took their children
into her father's house, they say.   60

And they wept,
and they let her go down
without painting her, they say.   .
And her ten servants went with her, they say.
When she stood by the sea,
the canoe came of itself, they say.
⟨*And the visitor placed his hat on the shore*
    as a gift for her father, they say.⟩[16]   66a
She and her ten servants stepped aboard, they say.

No one could see what moved the canoe.
After the girl had come aboard,
they saw the canoe standing offshore again.   70

Then they poked holes in the housefront, they say.
Peering through these,
they watched the canoe departing, they say.
And then, wherever they looked,
they saw nothing, they say.

They did not see that the canoe had gone back down.
And so they did not know
where the girl of good family had been taken.

Day after day, her father turned to the wall,
and he cried and cried and cried.   80
And her mother turned to the wall
and cried and cried and cried.
Her father's head servant stood with them, day after day.
Then her father stopped weeping and said to him,
«*Find where my child was taken.*»

«*Be patient. I'll be gone in a little while.*
I will find where your child was taken.»

Later, one day, at first light, he stirred up the fire
and bathed, they say,
while those in the house were still sleeping.
The day looked right to him,   90
so he took care that no one should see him.

Now, as his skin dried, he turned to the wall,
and he spread out his fishing tackle, they say.
He opened a bundle
and took out a hellebore stalk[17]
and touched it to the fire.

After it had smoldered for a while,
he quenched it,
smearing the ash on a flat stone.
He marked himself with it.   100

Now he set out, they say.
He went after the girl, they say.
And the girl's mother was with him, they say.

From then on, he moved like a hunter.
He carried a sea-otter spear, they say.
He pushed off,
and he threw the sea-otter spear.
It wiggled its tail.
It towed them, they say.

After a time, the canoe ceased moving, they say.   110
So, they say, did the sea-otter spear.
And then, they say, he beached the canoe.

The lady stepped out of the boat
and he turned it keel-upward.

Green seaweed grew from the hull.
This is what slowed the canoe.
They had travelled for one year, they say.

And he took off his redcedar cape,
and he rubbed the canoe with it.
He rubbed the lady as well,   120
and he rubbed his own body
until he was clean.

Again he launched the canoe,
and again he threw the sea-otter spear,
and again it swam forward.

Again the sea otter towed them along.
They went on and on and on and on,
and then, once again, the canoe ceased moving, they say.

He beached the canoe again,
and he turned it keel-upward.   130
Green seaweed had covered it,
and seaweed had covered the lady.
It covered him also.

Again he took off his cape,
and he rubbed the canoe and the lady.
He rubbed himself also.

When he was clean,
he launched the canoe.
And again he threw the sea-otter spear,
and it towed them along.   140

After a time, he came to where charcoal was floating, they say.

The canoe made no headway, they say.
He brought out his tackle box and looked in.

He had old scraps[18] from repairing his halibut hooks.
After he scattered them on the water,
the channel was opened,
and then he passed through it, they say.

Not far away, the channel closed over.
Again, when he put what he had in the water,
the passage was opened, they say.   150
Then he went through it, they say.

And he came to the edge of the sky.
After it opened and shut four times,
he thrust in his spear, propping it open.

In that way, they went under, they say,
and he pulled out the spear.
From then on, he kept it inside the canoe.
Then he took out his paddle and used it, they say.

Now, they say, he could see smoke from a large town.
He beached the canoe to one side of the village, they say.   160
He turned it keel-upward
and seated the lady beneath it, they say.
After that, he walked to the village, they say.

It was low tide when he came to the edge of the village.
A woman with a child on her back had come down on the foreshore.
She carried a basket and digging stick, probing for something.
As she placed something into her basket,
she looked at him sitting there.
Then she went back to what she was doing.

She looked up again.   170
She was prying up the beach rocks,
picking up sea-cukes[19] and putting them into her basket.
It was Wealth Woman.

The next time she looked at him sitting there,
she spoke to him, they say.
She said, «I know who you are.»

Then she beckoned, they say,
and then he went down on the beach
and stood near her.
She spoke to him, they say.   180

«You are here in search of the girl.»
«Yes,» he said.

«You see this town.
  The one who took the girl gave away his father's hat.
  That's why his father poured grease[20]
    into his son's wife's mind.
  She's been resting since then in that cave.

«After you enter the headman's house,
  go around to the right
  and walk behind the screen.
  There you will hear what people are saying.»

Then he set out, leaving Wealth Woman there,   190
  and he entered the cave where the girl was lying.
  She lay still,
  but her eyelids were fluttering.
  He took off his redcedar cape and used it to rub her,
  trying to wake her.

Nothing.
He tried it again,
and he failed again, and grew angry.
Then, having failed, he went on his way.

He dressed in two figured blankets 200
and wandered among them.
They failed to see him.
Then he went into the headman's house, they say,
going round to the right.

They say that the floor descended in ten tiers to the fire.
On the upper tier, on one side,
    a figured blanket hung on the weaver's frame,
and a voice came from the blanket.
«Tomorrow one of my faces will still be unfinished, unfinished.»

Then, they say, he went back of the screen,
and there, they say, he saw something surprising. 210
He saw a large bay, with sandspits and beaches,
and cranberries ripening on the outcrops.
Women were singing.
Close to the stream flowing into the bay,
a fire was built for heating saltwater,[21] *they say.*

Women emerged from the berry patch then
and walked past him.
    The last one was sniffing, they say.
«I smell a human being.»
«Excuse me,» he said. «Are you speaking of me?» 220

«My dancing blanket came from one
    of the young woman's ten servants,
  the ones who were eaten,» she said.
«It must be myself that I smell.»

Mink Woman, that was.

He went up to the fire
built for heating saltwater.
When he came near,
one of those who were sitting there said,
«What will he do
when they come here to look for the girl?»   230

«What are you saying?
The family of the girl must return his father's hat.
When that is returned,
he will make her sit up.»

After hearing what was said,
he turned around.
Remembering the mother of the girl,
he ran to the canoe
and lifted up the hull.

All he saw there were her bones.   240
Then he took off his redcedar cape
and moved it across her.
She stirred and sat up.
She was sweating.

He righted the canoe
and pulled it to the water.
When the lady had boarded,
he paddled in front of the town.
There, they say, he roped her to her seat.
He roped himself to his own seat too.   250
Wealth Woman had told him to tie himself down
    – and also the lady.

Roped to their seats,
they floated offshore from the headman's house.
Someone came out of the house, saying,
«Cousins, they ask the lady to wait where she is
while they make preparations.»

When they had floated there awhile,
lightning struck the house, they say.
After that, the point of a feather rose from the smokehole.
It came up and broke off.   260
It came toward them,
striking the two of them, knocking them cold.

Then he awoke on the upper tier of the house floor.
There he untied himself, they say.
There he untied the lady as well.
He came to assist her
as soon as he found he was able to move.

Her son-in-law sat toward the rear of the house,
and they spread out a mat for her
    down near the fire, they say.
Then she came forward.   270
She sat in the center of one of the tiers.

Food was brought out in a basket, they say.
There were butter clams, horseclams
    and two kinds of mussels, they say.
And they offered it to the lady.
They offered her food.

Once she had eaten,
another basket was brought near the fire.
Fresh water was poured in the basket.

Stones were put into the fire.
When the stones had been roasted,   280
they lifted them into the basket with tongs.

Soon it was boiling.
Her host spoke to a youngster
who stood near the basket.
The boy went to the back of the house.
He returned with humpback whale on the end of a stick.
This he put into the basket.

Soon he tested it with the stick.
When it was soft,
he lifted the whaleflesh onto a tray
    made in the shape of a red chiton[22]   290
and set it in front of the lady.

Her host spoke again,
and the boy brought her the rotten shell of a horseclam
to spoon up the soup.
She was unwilling to eat in this way.

Reaching into her purse,
she took out a fresh pair of clam shells,
and with them a fresh pair of mussel shells.
Silence fell in the house.
Even her host looked at nothing except the shells.   300
She paused when she noticed his eyes fastened upon them.

Then she handed the shells to the servant,
who passed them in turn to her son-in-law.
He cradled them in his cape.
When he had admired them for a while, he spoke again,
and they put them away behind the screen.

Then it was evening.
The house went to sleep.
The servant slept also, they say.

*A*t daybreak, a seal pup cried in the corner, they say.   310
  And at daybreak, they say,
   the servant prepared for departure.
The canoe sat on the upper tier of the house floor.
There he tied the lady into her seat.
He tied himself down too.

Behind the screens set end to end in the rear of the house,
a lightning bolt exploded, they say,
and the point of a feather came forward
and struck them, they say,
knocking them cold.

They awoke floating on open water, they say.   320
And the servant untied himself from his seat
and went to the lady.
He untied the lady as well.

They had left in midsummer, they say,
when the seal pups cry.[23]
Now he took up his paddle and used it, they say.
After taking the second stroke, they say,
he found himself in front of his master's town.

The lady entered the house and sat down.
She revealed to her husband   330
what she had learned of her child's location, they say.

Then the head servant went to his master.
He revealed what he had heard

from those near the fire for heating saltwater.
He spoke precisely as they had spoken.

His master spoke to the firekeepers, they say.
Two of them went through the village calling, they say,
and the people came.

The house overflowed with them, they say.
Then he brought food from the storeroom, they say.   340
He fed them and fed them.
When they had eaten, they say,
he told the people his thinking.

He told the villagers
he was going to take back his daughter.
He proposed that the headmen travel in ten canoes.
They agreed to do it, they say.

On the following day his elder son vanished, they say.
And the day after that,
when they started their work,   350
the younger vanished too, they say.

For the father and mother, cumulus clouds
    were painted on ten sets of clamshells, they say.
Ten mussel shells were within them.
Ten were painted for the elder son.
Ten were painted for the younger son as well.

Each man of the village preparing to go
gathered ten shells,
and each of the women five.
And when they had gathered them,
they sat waiting.   360

The two who were missing had gone to get married, they say.
The others were ready to search for the girl
and eager to leave, they say.
The villagers were fully prepared
and were waiting.

The elder brother returned at midday
with cedar twigs tied in his hair.
«Mother, I bring you my wife,
who is standing outside.
Will you welcome her?»   370
That's what he said to his mother, they say.

«Aiii! My child has come!»
She went out.
A woman with whiskers and round eyes was standing there.
It was Mouse Woman, they say.

The younger was gone somewhat longer.
He too, they say, returned at midday.
He entered with fern fronds tied in his hair.
Haiiii, hai hai hai haiiii!

«Mother, I bring you my wife,   380
who is standing outside.
Will you welcome her?»

Something astonishing stood there, they say.
No one could look at her.
A creature with short hair, wearing armor.[24]

«Lady, come in.»
She declined to come in.

«*She declines to come in.*
She refuses.
My child, your wife refuses.»   390

«*She is given to doing things backwards.*»
Then he went out to his wife
and escorted her in.

O*n the following day, they set off at first light.*
The villagers launched their canoes
and went seaward.
The elder son's wife sat on a thwart toward the bow.
The wife of the younger concealed herself in the crowd.
The first sat up high to see well, they say.

A small box was with her wherever she was.   400
As they headed seaward, she opened it.
Reaching inside,
she brought out her sewing needle, they say.
She tossed it into the sea, they say,
and it sliced through the water, they say.

They lined up behind it, they say,
and the needle towed them, they say.

When the needle had towed them awhile, they say,
they saw smoke from a town, drifting seaward.
Some distance away, the elder son's wife told them to land.   410
She gave them directions.
They say she had married the elder son
so that she could advise them.
Mouse Woman had.

Going ashore, they cut long poles, they say.

They cut them in pairs.
The younger son's wife concealed herself,
while the elder son's wife gave them directions.

The ten canoes stood offshore.
At the bow and amidships they linked them with poles.   420
They lashed the poles to the thwarts.
They managed it easily, they say.
Then they paddled in front of the town.

They took the most favored position, they say,
and someone came out of the headman's house, they say.
«Wait. They ask you to stay where you are
while they make preparations.»

After waiting awhile,
they lost track of themselves, they say.
They awoke in the house, they say,   430
on the uppermost tier of the floor.
There they unfastened the lashings.
There they untied the poles that linked the canoes.

Mats were spread on the upper tiers,
and on either side of the housepit, the people assembled.
The headman's daughter was not to be seen –
the one they had come to reclaim.
Only her husband was seated there.

They unrolled a pair of mats directly in front of him,
and he continued to sit there, they say.   440
The voyagers piled their clamshells in front of him.
They heaped them up as high as the house.
Ho ho ho hoooo! Up to the top!
And they placed the hat at the top of the pile.

«*Call in my father.*
  Ask him not to delay.»

 A youngster set off on the run, they say.

«*Is he not here?*»
«*He is close by.*»

 Hwuuuuuuuuuu!   450
 The house quivered, they say,
 and the earth shook.
 Together they all shied away.
 No one looked upward.

 But the youngest son's wife raised her head
 as the rest of them cowered, they say.
 She looked to the rear of the house,
 and she looked to the door.

«*Raise yourselves up!*
  Have you no power?»   460
 Those were her words.

 The house quivered again,
 and the earth shook.
 Hwuuuuuuuuu!
 And again those in the house lowered their heads.

«*Raise yourselves up!*
  Have you no powers?
  Have you no powers?»

 At that moment he entered, they say.
 What they saw made their hearts go crazy, they say.   470

His eyes bulged so that no one could look at him.
When he planted his foot, they say,
he stood there awhile.

And he took one more step,
and the earth and the house shuddered, they say.
And he took one more step,
and the house and the earth quivered,
and all together they cowered.

She said once again,
«Raise yourselves up!» 480

As she lifted her chin,
something powerful came to her,
and their heads rose like the tide.
«A powerful woman you are.»

After that he sat down,
and the tremors subsided.
He sat near his son.
But he reached for his hat
before he sat down.

With his father's staff, the son divided the shells. 490
He took less for himself.
He gave more to his father.

«Have you not yet sent for your wife, my son?»
«No. I have waited for you.»
«Send someone now for your wife, my young headman.»

A youngster went to call her then, they say.
«Is she not here?»
«Yes. She is close by.»

Soon the one they were looking for entered, they say.
She came from the cave where she had been sleeping.   500
She went to her mother directly, they say.
She did not go down to sit next to her husband.

And his father began to dance for power, they say.
After a time he fell over, they say,
breaking in two.

Feathers came out of his body and out of his neck.
One of the servants emerged from his body.
Another came out of his neck.
And another came from his body, and one from his neck.
He restored the ten that he had eaten.   510
That was his reason for dancing, they say.

Because of the hat, he had eaten the ten servants, they say.
It was he who put grease into the girl's mind, they say.
Because of the hat, they had put her into the cave, they say.

After a time, his body grew whole.
He ended his dance.
He sat down.

They built up the fire then, calling them forward.
They started to offer them food, they say.
They continued to midnight.   520
And then it was finished, then it was finished.
They gathered the dishes, they say.

At daybreak a seal pup cried from the corner, they say,
        just as before,
and then they prepared for departure, they say.
The canoes were still there,
    on the highest tier of the house floor.

95

Her father-in-law summoned her then, they say.
«Lady, come here. I have something to tell you.»

He took her aside, they say,
and she sat down beside him.
Then he advised her, they say.   530

«Lady, you will give birth to me from your body.
Do not be afraid of me.»

He gave her a skull made of copper, they say.
Something stuck out from it at each side.
Its name, they say, is Between the Neck and the Body.

«Let Master Carver[25] make my cradle, lady.
Let cumulus clouds be placed on the top of it, lady,
and also below.
Let the clouds be flat on the bottom.
When the sky is like this,   540
even ordinary humans may come out to me for food.
When they see me like this,
common surface birds may come to me for food.»

Her family was waiting on the upper tier, they say,
while her father-in-law was advising her below,
and she was listening, they say.

After he spoke, she went up to her father.
They had already lashed the canoes together
and already roped themselves into their seats.
When the headman's daughter stepped aboard, they say,   550
they lost track of themselves.

They woke on the open water, they say.

At once they set off.
And at once they came to the village, they say.

A*fter a time, the woman was pregnant, they say.*
When she started her labor,
they built her a shelter, they say.
They drove in a birthing stake,[26]
told her to hold it, and left her, they say.

Then he emerged.   560
As soon as she saw him,
her heart went crazy, they say.
Something stuck out of his eyes.
She raised herself up
and drew back from him, frightened, they say.

«*Awaaayaaaaa!*»
Her cry shook the houses, they say.

Then she turned back to him, they say, picking him up.
«*Aiii! I am here, grandfather.*»
This is the term by which she addressed him, they say,   570
and the town was as quiet
        as something that someone has dropped.

She brought him into the house, they say,
and her father brought out his own urinal[27] *for him.*
In that, they bathed him, they say.

⟨*Then, they say, she asked for Master Carver.*⟩[28]   574a
They sent for him,
and he came directly, they say.
He had already started his work in the forest
and brought it half-finished, they say.

As soon as he entered,
he made the design, they say,   580
as the woman described it.
He drew cumulus clouds together in pairs.
He drilled holes for the laces
to straighten the baby's legs.

And they fastened him in it, they say.
Two skyblankets were brought,
and they wrapped them around him
and laced him into the cradle.

Then, they say, they launched the canoe.
   Five of them climbed aboard,   590
and the woman was with them,
   and so was her child.
And they started seaward, they say.
They travelled and travelled and travelled.

To the landward towns and the seaward towns
   it was equally far,
they could see that it was,
when they put him over the side, they say.

When they put him over the side,
he turned
   around and around and around and around
      to the right four times
and lay quiet, they say,
like something that someone has dropped.   600
And they left him
and went to the place they had come from, they say.

➤   ➤   ➤

Sometime after Skaay dictated this story, Henry Moody added a postscript, which Swanton also dutifully took down:

Llahaw siis yakw tsyadyang wansuuga.
Sttii isghasas gyaanhaw gyaghitga
lla ttl qinggangang wansuuga.
Ll qadlaagang wansuuga,
    Nang Ttl Dlstlas aa.[29]

He lives there in the midst of the ocean, they say.
Sometimes when sickness is coming
they see him, they say.
He is a reef, they say –
    the One They Hand Along is.

This remark is the only authority for the title, *Nang Ttl Dlstlas,* "The One They Hand Along" or "The One They Put in Place," by which the poem has come to be known. Skaay himself, so far as we know, said nothing about a title.

Nang is the Haida impersonal singular pronoun, corresponding to English "someone" or "something." *Ttl* is the third-person plural animate pronoun, parallel to English "they" or "them" – but also often used in Haida where in English we say "we." Its position in the phrase suggests we hear it as the subject of a verb. That verb opens with the animate diminutive prefix *dl-*, which tells us that its object (*nang*) is a being, not a thing, and a being that is probably small or young. The root of the verb is *-stl-*, which means to put, to place, to handle or to hand. (Its cognate noun *stlaay* means "hand" or "paw" in Haida.) The suffix *-as* recasts this tenseless verb as a definitive verbal noun: the living one they timelessly have, or once and always have had, in their hands.

4   Wealth Has Big Eyes

THOUGH HIS STORY IS COMPLEX, Skaay's language is simple and direct. Still, some very basic terms, such as *canoe* and *house* and *cape*, had substantially different meanings for him than they may have now for his readers. Since his sense of myth is grounded in the real and immediate world, not in a misty fairytale existence, it is worth understanding quite precisely the things he has in mind.

A Haida canoe (*tluu*) is an ocean-going redcedar dugout, up to around 20 m (60 ft) in length and sometimes over 2 m (6 ft) in the beam. The crew and passengers might number anywhere up to thirty. Smaller dugouts were used for solo travel. Some Haida had surely also seen the sealskin boats of the Eyak, Aleut and Yupiit, but the self-propelled harbor-seal canoe (*xhuut tluu*) is a craft that is only seen on the ocean of literature. Skaay may have imagined that canoe to be made from the bones and skin of a seal, or he may have imagined it to be made, like other canoes, of good redcedar, painted or carved in the Haida way with the form of a seal. The sea-otter spear may likewise have been, in his imagination, alder carved to embody the sea otter's form. Form as much as substance, in the mythworld, can and does embody knowledge.

page 77: lines 26–29; page 79: lines 65–70

A proper house (*na*), in Skaay's experience, was a solid, square structure with a low-pitched gable roof and a central smokehole. The frame was built of large redcedar posts and beams, and the walls were of redcedar planks, vertically set. Light and air could

leak through the chinks, but there were no windows and there
was only one door. The house of Skaay's family head at Ttanuu,
for example, was 15 m × 16 m on the ground and 7 m high at the
central beam. An area roughly 10 m square – the entire center of
the house – was excavated to a depth of 1.5 m. Halfway up the
sides of this housepit was a terrace or middle tier some 1.5 m
wide. At the center of the housepit was the fire. Before the smallpox epidemics, twenty or thirty people would normally have
lived in such a house, but the head of the house had private quarters at the rear, often separated from the rest by a painted
wooden screen.[1]

The largest house in Haida Gwaii (built about 1840 by Wiiha,
the headman of Ghadaghaaxhiwaas, the largest Haida town) was
roughly 21 m square. Its central gallery or housepit was nearly
3 m deep and 16 m square, but still, the sidewalls of the gallery
had only two tiers, which Wiiha had equipped with sets of
European stairs.[2] The house in Skaay's story, where the housepit
is ten tiers deep and a fleet of canoes can pass through the
smokehole, is bigger than any house the poet or his neighbors
could have seen outside their dreams.[3]

A Haida town or village (llaana) consisted of one, two or three
(in the myths, more often five) rows of houses, built just above
the beach, facing the sea. Canoes were brought up on the beach
stern-first, directly in front of the houses. After standing offshore to await an invitation, visitors were expected to land in
front of the houses as well. Many such details are visible in a
photo of Skaay's town, Ttanuu, taken by George Dawson in 1878.
But we should read side by side with this photograph the remarks of another visitor, James Swan, who was there in 1883.
Swan performed a little census, counting 29 houses, 23 housepoles, 31 memorial poles, 11 mortuary poles and 15 mortuary
houses. "The monuments of the dead," he wrote, "outnumber
the monuments of the living."[4]

The cedarbark cape (Haida qqaayx) has remarkable and vital

The photo is reproduced on pages 104–105.

regenerative powers in this narrative, but in precolonial times it was an everyday garment. The woven bark of the redcedar is breathable, waterproof, comfortable and warm. The poem, in taking all this utterly for granted, may have something else to tell us. Death did become a vastly greater burden to the Haida, and the worlds within the world grew more separate from each other, as the people took to wearing European clothes.

The figured blanket (*naaxiin*) is what is now commonly called a Chilkat blanket: a cape that is also a stylized portrayal of an animal, woven of mountain goat wool and yellowcedar bark. Skaay is the only poet on the Northwest Coast, so far as I recall, who *page 84:*
lines
200–208 ever suggested that these animated garments could speak to one another, but that suggestion has the air of absolute discovery, not invention. Such blankets are like stories: they are alive. And all those figured blankets from the Northwest Coast, now hanging in museums around the world, must certainly be waiting – like the uncompleted blanket in the poem – for a visit from another of their kind. By donning such a blanket – such an animated skin – a skinless human being is empowered to cross the *xhaaydla*, to pass from realm to realm, like a sea mammal or bird.

The skyblanket or cloudblanket (*qwiighaalgyaat*) – rarer and possibly older than the figured blanket – is a cape of white mountain goat wool, plainwoven or with stylized rainclouds added in black.[5] In ordinary life, figured blankets and skyblankets alike are normally worn one at a time, but in Haida poetry, where two is a number of great importance (just as it is in the Haida social order), blankets are often worn in pairs. One of the few surviving early *qwiighaalgyaat* is actually designed in such a way that, when worn, it looks like two blankets rather than one. This blanket, known as the Swift Robe, has been for many years in the collection of the Peabody Museum at Harvard University.[6] Swanton must have seen it there, in fact, when he worked at the museum as a graduate student, three or four years before he came to Haida Gwaii.

Like the blankets who can speak to one another, the long eyes of the old god on the seafloor startle a few visitors in museums around the world. Haida sculptors, by convention, make the heads impossibly large for the bodies of their figures, and the eyes impossibly large for the heads, but these exaggerated eyes are of many different kinds. The eyes of amphibians and fish, for instance, are usually represented as circular, the eyes of sharks as vertically elliptical, and the eyes of mammals and birds as ovoid. But throughout the Northwest Coast, elongated eyes are a distinguishing mark of the god of wealth, who lives in a house on the floor of the sea, surrounded by seals.[7] The usual Haida name for this spirit-being is *Tangghwan Llaana,* or Sea Dweller. His Tlingit name is *Gunaakadeit* (a word whose etymology still stumps me). In Tsimshian he is *Nagunaks,* which simply means "located in the water." A two-dimensional, frontal view of his face appears on the sides of countless Haida, Tlingit and Tsimshian storage chests. In these representations, the eyes are generally stretched sideways and equipped with doubled pupils. Each eye becomes a face within a face. In three-dimensional representations, the eyes more often protrude.

The Nuuchahnulth trader and hunter Saayaacchapis put it this way to Edward Sapir in 1913: *A'iihh'atma qasii hhawwihlmis'i. … Cchushaama yaaqwihl'itq cchusha*: "Wealth has big eyes…. He is wary of those he suspects."[8]

Common though he is on Haida storage boxes, this god of wealth is rare on Haida poles. Nevertheless, he appeared in a prominent form on three of the two dozen housepoles standing in Skaay's village, Ttanuu, in the latter half of the nineteenth century. Here his eyes are elongated vertically, in keeping with the form of the pole itself. They reach across his cheeks and well beyond his chin. In the end of each such elongated eye, where the pupil ought to be, there is not just a face but a complete small creature, like a not-quite-human child.[9]

The system used here for writing Nootka is explained in appendix 3, page 427.

Ttanuu, 9 July 1878. This photo, made by the geologist George Dawson, is the first ever taken of the village. The view is from the south, showing six of the roughly thirty houses in the town.

In the middle of the left half of the photo, behind and to the left of the

tallest pole, is the house of Xhyuu, who was headman of the village and also of
the lineage called Qquuna Qiighawaay. Skaay lived in this house, from perhaps
as early as 1840 until 1886.

(National Archives of Canada, National Photography Collection, PA 37753)

Xhyuu's house at Ttanuu, 9 July 1878 (detail from the photo overleaf). Some Tsimshian visitors are clustered near the base of Gitkuna's memorial pole in front of the house. At lower left (marked by the arrowheads), a sculptor is at work on Xhyuu's new housepole, raised shortly after the photo was taken.

The remains of Xhyuu's house at Ttanuu, September 1902. Photograph by C.F. Newcombe. The new housepole (the middle one of the five poles in the photo) has been raised, but the inhabitants are missing.

(Royal British Columbia Museum, PN 342)

Houses at Ttanuu, 1 May 1901. The village had no full-time residents at this date, but the house at left, with the frontal boards still on, remained in seasonal use. This was the house of Gwiisukuunas of the Qqaadasghu Qiighawaay. The topmost major figure on the housepole is the *skyaamskun* or blue falcon. Below this is the long-eyed spirit-being of the sea, Tangghwan Llaana. Photograph by C. F. Newcombe.

(Royal British Columbia Museum, PN 97)

The long-eyed spirit
of the sea on the
housepole of
Gwiisukuunas
of the Qqaadasghu
Qiighawaay, Ttanuu,
photographed by
Marius Barbeau in
1947, when the village
had been empty for
sixty years.

(National Museums of
Canada, 102731)

Daxhiigang, *The Face of Tangghwan Llaana*, c. 1890. Carved black argillite panel, 15 × 36.5 cm, forming one side of a fully enclosed chest. Royal British Columbia Museum, Victoria.

(RBCM, CPN 10622 V2)

5   Oral Tradition and the Individual Talent

S KAAY WAS AN ORAL POET in a mesolithic culture. He spoke his stories in a supple, stylized language, as precise and economical as that of his contemporary Flaubert, though Skaay's style is of an oral, not a writerly, kind. I call these stories poetry because they are dense, crisp and full of lucid images whose power is not confined by cultural fences – and because they are richly patterned. But the patterns are syntactic and thematic more than rhythmical or phonemic. For all the acoustic beauty of these poems, that is not where their obvious formal order resides. They are distinguished by a thinkable *prosody of meaning* more than by an audible prosody of sound. In the familiar Indo-European sense of the words, then, this language is not verse any more than it is prose.

Poetry of the sort that Skaay and Ghandl composed still lacks an established typographic form because it hasn't been absorbed, like the language of Greek and Hebrew oral poets, into a literate tradition. The question of how their work should look on the page is also, understandably, not a question Swanton asked these poets, since none of the Haida poets he met had ever worked with words in written form. The most obvious meaningful unit in this poetry seems to me the sentence or the clause, and I have treated these units as separate lines. But a Haida clause or sentence is generally different in shape from its English counterpart, because in Haida much more of the information is usually loaded into the verb, and the verb usually comes at the end of the sentence. For

this reason among others, many of Skaay's sentences have an intrinsically dramatic or suspenseful shape – almost always different from the shape they acquire in English translation.

We know that Skaay was also an animated performer, because
Swanton wrote down some of his cries, chuckles, hoots, stretched
syllables and other vocal gestures; and we know it from his handling of dialogue. He rarely uses markers such as "he said" and
"she said." Most other Haida mythtellers use them often. Skaay
dramatized his dialogue more than he narrated it.

page 32:
line 1
&
page 76:
line 1
It is not accidental that Ghandl's poem about the fate of a
young man and Skaay's about the fate of a young woman both
begin with the same phrase, *Ll gidaagang wansuuga*: a phrase I
have usually translated "There was a child of good family, they
say." The first word, *ll* (a glottalized vocalic *l*), is the passive form
of the third-person animate singular pronoun. It means *he* or *she*
or an animate *it*. The second word, *gidaagang,* is a form (the "past
putative" form) of the verb *gidaa,* which means to be an heir, a
scion, a descendant. It means to be a favored child of favored parents: a creature with a family to depend on, a tradition to inherit,
and a heritage and duties to fulfill. Henry Moody taught John
Swanton to translate *gidaa* as "to be the child of a chief," but in
classical Haida, the word is freely used in referring to whales,
bears and other creatures, as well as human beings.[1]

The last word in the phrase, *wansuuga,* is the classical Haida
quotative. It corresponds to the English phrase *they say* or *it is
said.* The root is *suu,* which is the verb *to say* in Haida. The prefix *wan-* means *far away,* and the suffix *-ga* puts the verb in the
present tense. (It is because of this quotative, incidentally, that
the other verb, *gidaa,* carries the putative ending, *-gang.* In Haida,
putative verbs are used when the language points to itself. They
are used when an action is *talked about* but not directly *told.*)

Most, if not all, Native American languages have quite convenient and precise ways of labelling information as oral tradition or as hearsay. These syntactical devices take many different
forms and can be used by skilled narrators to put many rhetori-

cal spins on a scene or a sentence. As Native American languages go, Haida has a very simple quotative system, but Skaay and others show how much can be done with it.[2]

The quotative casts a statement into narrative relief. It can suggest that what is said has been tested by tradition and found true, or warn that it bears no guarantee because it lies outside the speaker's own experience. It lifts a statement out of the realm of history or experience and drops it into one of the two realms (the timeless and true, the persistent and false) we now call myth.[3] Skaay uses this device more frequently and shrewdly than any other Haida poet Swanton heard. He uses it to dance back and forth between his own fallibility and the perdurable truth of the myth, and to give weight to certain passages by slowing the pace of events. He also uses it – the twinkle in his eye is clearly audible – to feint, to dodge, and actually to leap back and forth across the line between the credible and the outlandish.

Speech itself is neither verse nor prose, and myth itself is neither fact nor fiction. Myth is a species of truth that precedes that distinction. Yet even in Skaay's world it must wear the appearance of one or the other, and Skaay can skip at will between them. So it seems to me essential, in transcription and also in translation, not to obscure or omit or relocate these marks of oral style. What we have to do instead is learn to read them.

Ll gidaagang wansuuga tells us that "distantly it is said that there was a creature, species and gender unspecified, with a favored place in the order of things." It implies, but does not guarantee, that the creature in question is also young in years.

Skaay goes on to clarify the gender of his subject in the simplest imaginable way. He says *Ll jaadagang wansuuga*: "He/she was-being-a-woman, is-said-there." We know then, without needing to be told, that she will be eagerly sought in marriage, and that only a suitor of adequate rank will be acceptable to her parents. From this simple narrative seed, Skaay's geography of the universe and his poem about the rebirth of a god unfolds.

In the Birdhunter poem, Ghandl resolves the ambiguity of

the same opening line in a different way. *Ll gidaagang wansuuga,*
he says – and then, *Kkuxu gyaa'at gutgu lla giistingdas.* This means
"Marten cape(s) together he/she flattish-double-wore." In other
words, this still unidentified creature is wearing a pair of
marten-skin blankets. That confirms his or her high rank, and it
suggests that he or she belongs to the human species or to another species seen in human form. It still leaves the issue of gender in doubt. The next thing Ghandl says is:

*pages
32–33:
lines 3–4*   *Ll xhitiit ttsinhlghwaanggwang qawdi
llanagaay diitsi qahlagaagang wansuuga.*

This means, if we continue with bone-literal translation:

*He/she bird(s) shooting-here-and-there awhile
the-village behind-it was-going-uphill, is-said-there.*

In the Haida mythworld, women may snare birds, but only
males shoot them. Young males do so in particular. Hunting
birds is the male rite of passage into adulthood in the world of
Haida myth, just as puberty seclusion is for women. So the verb
ttsinhlghwaanggwang tells us by implication that the potentially
valuable person in Ghandl's poem is a newly marriageable male.

Ll gidaagang wansuuga is a formulaic opening, used repeatedly
by these two professional poets, Ghandl and Skaay, and by none
of the fifteen other Haida mythtellers Swanton recorded. The
two poets who used this formulaic opening belonged to different
families and came from opposite sides of the archipelago. They
also had very different creative minds, but they shared a literary
tradition.

The formula is not used to open just any narrative poem. The
extant poems that begin with these words all go on to involve either abandonment or kidnapping *and* marriage or childbirth. But
ll gidaagang wansuuga is not a formula in the sense of formula
fiction. It is not a metrical formula either: not the kind of for-

CHAPTER FIVE: *Oral Tradition and the Individual Talent*

mula we meet in Homer's epics or in other poems orally composed in metered verse. It is a gesture as meaningful and simple as picking up the instrument or lifting the baton. It tells us that a story is beginning – and something about the kind of story it is and the kind of artist who is telling it.

Formulaic phrases are used in oral literature worldwide, especially for starting and ending stories. Perhaps they are used in every realm of human and nonhuman communication. *Once upon a time* and *happily ever after* are two examples born in the oral world. *To whom it may concern* and *Yours sincerely* are examples born in the world of writing. Handshakes and waves are gestural examples. Some traditions are richer than others in such formulae, and some oral poets take obvious delight in them while others shy away.

Kootye, a mythteller who dictated hundreds of pages of stories to Franz Boas at Laguna Pueblo, New Mexico, between 1919 and 1921, began most of his stories with the formal invocation *Hamaha! ehe! Hama...*: "Long ago! Indeed! Long ago...." He ended certain kinds of stories (but not all kinds of stories) with the formulaic phrase *Tomee ts'itsa s'ak'ooya tsiyuts'išpityits*, "My aunt's backbone is this long." Kootye shortened the closing phrase from time to time, to *Tomee ts'itsa*, "It is this long." His colleague Gyiimi liked to lengthen the formula instead, to *Tomee ts'itsa s'ak'ooya Kšyeena k'ayoots'išpityits*, "My aunt Kshyeena's backbone is this long."[4]

The Blackfoot poet Káínaikoan, a contemporary of Ghandl, took more obvious delight in his repertoire of formulae. He opens certain kinds of stories with the formulaic phrase *Omá nínaawa ni'tsitápaokonnaayiwa*, "A man was camping there alone," and others with the phrase *Ninóóhkanistohtsimaahpi*, "As I have heard the news." In place of simple formulaic endings such as *Ki ánniayi*, "That's how it is," or *Ki sápanistsowa*, "It is completed," he liked to say *Ki áániitooyi imitáíksi*, "The dogs have gone off in different directions," or *Ki ánniayi niitakótsiwa*, "It has boiled long enough."[5]

The Karuk mythteller known as Imkyánvaan liked to end her narratives with elaborate strings of formulae. This is an example, recorded on the Klamath River in northwestern California in the late 1920s by the most eccentric of all American linguists, John Peabody Harrington:

> *Kupánnakanakana!*
> *Chéemyaach ík vúr ishyâat imshîinnaavish.*
> *Nanivási vúra veekyiniyâach!*
> *Chéemyaach ík vúra ataychúkinach i'uunúpraveesh.*[6]

> *Kupánnakanakana!*
> *Gleam soon in the shallows, spring salmon.*
> *My spine is quite straight!*
> *Gleam soon in the earth, little lily shoot.*[7]

The first of these four lines – whatever it may once have meant – is evidently spoken for its own sake now, much like *hickory dickory dock* or *eenie meenie minie mo* or *hosanna* or *amen*. The second line and the fourth are invocations, appropriate for tales told in winter, to the coming foods of spring. The third constitutes Imkyánvaan's claim that she has told the tale fully and correctly. Among many native nations of the Oregon and California coast, it is proverbial that anyone who tells the stories poorly or listens inattentively will soon have a stooped and crooked back. Skaay and other crippled myttellers remind us that this metaphor has limits. Conceptual links between stories and backbones are widespread nonetheless. The Hupa myttellter Tahseench'e', who dictated a number of stories to Edward Sapir during 1927, asserted her correctness with a formula much briefer than Imkyánvaan's but based on the same principle. *Shaan! Wheene' tseelitsow-nehwunt-te!* was her usual conclusion to a story: "Done! My back is like bluestone!"[8]

The differences here are not simply functions of language nor patterns of culture; they are individual differences. No other Blackfoot mythteller on record uses formulae like Káínaikoan, and no other Karuk poet ever recorded uses them precisely like Imkyánvaan. No classical Haida poet flourishes the stock of verbal formulae as ebulliently as Káínaikoan or braids them like Imkyánvaan either, but there are interesting things to be learned from the Haida mythtellers' formulae even so.

The closing phrase that Skaay and Ghandl use most often is *haw tlan ll ghiida*. The word *haw* means "here"; *tlan* means "end" or "stop" or "closed" or "finished"; *ghiida* is the plain present tense of the verb *ghit*, which overlaps the English verbs "to be" and "to become." That leaves only the pronoun, *ll*. This is a word we have already met. It is third-person singular and animate – and it is why simple translations like "the end" or "it is finished" don't do full justice to the phrase. When they use the pronoun *ll*, the storytellers tell us that their stories are alive.[9]

The distinction the mythtellers make here is not, in fact, linguistic. It resembles the cultural decision made by English-speaking sailors to speak of boats as feminine and animate, not the grammatical obligation, incumbent on every speaker of French, to treat *le bateau* as a masculine noun. Most things treated as inanimate in English are inanimate in Haida usage also. Even the canoe – a living thing in some sense, and a quintessential element of life in Haida Gwaii – is normally inanimate in Haida. Songs, words, and pieces of information are treated by convention as inanimate. Many of the Haida who told stories to John Swanton treated the myths as inanimate too. But those who told them best spoke of the myths the way they spoke of plants and animals: as living things.[10] Most recorded speakers of classical Haida also paid this courtesy to *places*.

❧   ❧   ❧

"One They Hand Along" is one movement of one poem, spoken by old John Sky to young Henry Moody, who echoed it in turn to Swanton. There are many other stories in the world that speak of kidnapped women who are retrieved, and many other stories of journeys to the bottom of the sea, but to the best of my knowledge, no stories we could really call "the same" as this one have ever been recorded, in any language or at any time. The story is one artist's individual work. At the same time, it is part of the great web of tradition. Its setting and central characters link it to the North Pacific Coast and to the large and living body of Haida mythology. In Skaay's mind, moreover, it was only a third of an evening's work. Skaay liked to tell stories in sets or suites, the way many chamber musicians like to play, and he told this story as the opening movement in a suite of three. The two stories he joined to it are set in the Tsimshian country, and both are well known in Tsimshian versions. Swanton, in fact, protested that these tales had nothing to do with one another. Skaay, however, insisted the link was real.

Swanton was looking for continuity of character or setting, which is scant. But structural and thematic echoes abound. A close analysis of the relations among the three stories would fill many pages, but the rudimentary outlines are as follows.

In the FIRST MOVEMENT, *the daughter of a headman living in the Islands comes of age and is ready to marry. When all suitors are refused, the son of a headman living on the bottom of the sea abducts her. In the second episode, a servant locates the girl, lying mindlessly in a cave in the other world. This exploratory voyage or dream, which occupies much of the story, involves the death and resurrection of the girl's mother. In the third major episode, the girl's two brothers (one of whom is very young) take superhuman wives. One marries Mouse Woman; the other marries a powerful shaman who is unnamed. These women take charge of a second expedition (fourth episode) which succeeds in reclaiming the girl. Back at home, in a final episode, the girl bears a child who is her father-in-law reincarnate. In accordance with his instructions, she returns this child to the sea, midway between the Islands and the mainland.*

The SECOND MOVEMENT *opens in a mainland town, on the bank of the Nass River. The headman's wife is a woman distinguished by her modest appetite. A creature emerges from the forest, kills the woman, enters her skin and returns in her stead to the village, eating like a fiend. The woman's two sons (one of whom is very young) run away from home and marry superhuman wives (Mouse Woman and another, unnamed, who is a powerful shaman's daughter). These women take charge of a voyage to find and revive the boys' mother, and to kill the imposter.*

(Skaay called this second movement of the poem *Simnaasum nang awgha daghiyalaghan,* "One Who Acquired Simnaasum for a Mother." The name Simnaasum conceals a Tsimshian pun, and only by unravelling the pun do we discover the identity of the ravenous forest creature at the center of the story. In Tsimshian, the prefix *sm-* means real, important or genuine, and *noo* [becoming *naa* in Haida] means mother, but *noosü* means wolverine. This is the story of "One Who Obtained What-was-actually-a-Wolverine for a Mother.")

In the THIRD MOVEMENT, *the shaman's daughter from the second story has borne her husband seven boys and a girl. The boys are married; the girl is not; and the whole extended family has settled at a place called Qqaaduu, on an island off the Tsimshian coast. Just across the strait is a larger town called Qaahlaqaahli. When the eldest brother dies in an accident, the cause is divined as his wife's infidelity. This suspicion is tested and confirmed. The youngest brother then kills the adulterer, whose father is the Qaahlaqaahli headman. When the murder is discovered, there is a war between the towns. The six remaining brothers are killed, and their mother and sister escape alone into the trees. There the mother offers her daughter in marriage. Animal suitors emerge from the forest and are rejected one by one. The son of a headman living in the sky then presents himself. He is accepted and marries the girl. In the world above the clouds, the girl bears her husband eight sons and two daughters. These children return to earth, resettling at Qqaaduu. War breaks out again with the town across the channel. The eight brothers are fine warriors, and both sisters have miraculous powers as healers; even so, they are beaten back. The youngest brother seeks their celestial grandfather's aid, and the grandfather drops a deadly cloud on his grandchildren's opponents. Here the final movement of the suite comes to an end.*

Human beings, in classical Haida, are called *xhaaydla xhaaydaghaay,* "surface people." Skaay also calls them *xhaaydla xhitiit ghidaay,* "ordinary surface birds." Such ideas are widespread in Native American philosophy. The corresponding Navajo term, for example, is *nihokáá dine'é,* "earth-surface people." But the Haida term evokes in particular the surface of the sea. "One They Hand Along" is a narrative map locating the world of surface people in relation to the world beneath the waves, which is of special concern to the Haida. The trilogy of which it is a part extends this map to the forest and the sky. We can pass from one world to another, according to these stories, by paddling a canoe across the horizon, or by making a moral choice.

This is the first story Skaay chose to tell John Swanton, and only the third Haida text Swanton transcribed. Not surprisingly, there are glitches in the transcription. Understanding precisely what Skaay said or meant to say is sometimes a difficult task. But I think he chose this story for a reason. Skaay had spent much of his lifetime watching a long and immensely destructive cultural war. The old matrilineal order was centered on reciprocal relations between Raven people and Eagle people, and between human beings and the sea, whose power is incarnate in the killer whale. Skaay had seen this system crushed under the force of insatiable greed and then displaced by a new order, patrilineal and fixated on the powers of a father in the sky. Even the pun that the new language makes of Skaay's name records this transition. The war he had witnessed was a catastrophe on a scale the older mythtellers, who taught him his art, had never known. Yet I think they had left him a means with which to address it.

➤   ➤   ➤

Swanton was deeply interested in literature, and he was prepared, as we shall see, to believe that a poet like Skaay, in an oral
culture like that of the Haida, could create an epic structure – a
large, sequential structure, built of concentric or linear episodes,
like the *Iliad* or the *Beowulf*. Swanton knew much less about the
architectural principles of Renaissance, Baroque and Neoclassical
painting and music. These are subjects not routinely taught to
American students of anthropology, in his time or our own. So
the structures he encountered in Skaay's first trilogy threw
Swanton for a loop. He encountered such an architecture first in
simplified form, in the tale told to him by Sghiidagits, just a few
days before his encounter with Skaay. That poem too unfolds the
story of a woman who is kidnapped by a more-than-human being, and it too is structured in three parts. The three-part form
was a puzzle to Swanton, precisely because he knew the separate
plots already. Boas had recorded them, linked in the same way,
on earlier trips to the Northwest Coast, but Boas liked to think
of them as separate, self-sufficient elements, not as parts of a
larger whole. He had tried to teach his students – Swanton and
others – to think in the same terms.[11]

Surprised though he was to hear these stories linked, Swanton had no trouble following Sghiidagits's path from scene to
scene. In the opening movement, a woman, finding grizzly dung
in the berry patch, says unkind words about the bear. A grizzly
then appears to her in the guise of a human being, brings her to
his village and takes her as his wife. She lives long enough
among the grizzlies for all of us to learn that bears are people
too. And then, *tlga ll gutdaghanggadaaghan*, says Sghiidagits in a
familiar sounding phrase: "she came to dislike the country." The
woman plots her escape from the village of grizzlies, makes her
break and is pursued. At the end of an interesting chase scene,
she reaches the beach with the bears not far behind. Here the
second movement begins.[12]

Wiidhaw qaada tluguugha nang gaayaangaghan.
Wiidhaw nang jaadas lla gi agang kingguusghaayaaghan.   100
Nang ittlxhaagidas dajing yuuwan gu dajaaghan.
Dajingaay ungut llagha xhitiit ngataaystlgaangaghan.
Saghadila'u hanhaw ll kighaayaghan....

N*ow someone sat offshore in a canoe.*
   Now the woman hollered to him.   100
He was wearing the big dancing hat of a headman.
Perched on the hat was a flock of waterbirds.
His name was Going Ashore.[13]

«*If you take me aboard,*
   my father will give you ten copper shields,»
   said the woman to the headman.

Now the headman tapped his club against the side of his canoe.
Now it came ashore in front of the woman.
Now she stepped aboard.
Again he tapped the side of the canoe,   110
and it moved back out to sea.

Now the grizzlies erupted from the trees.
A pack of wolves ran out beside them.
Again he tapped the side of his canoe.

Now the canoe sank its fangs in the throats of the grizzlies.
Now it bit open the throats of the wolves.
It killed them all.

Now he told the woman to look through his hair.[14]
Frogs were what she found there.
She was too afraid to bite them.   120
She squeezed them with her fingernails instead.
Going Ashore, as I said, was his name.

And now he headed home.
On the way he filled his boat with harbor seal.
And now he started walking toward his wife,
who was standing in front of the house.
And now his wife came down to meet him.

She was pleased that he had taken a second wife.
Dark Woman was his first wife's name.
He went with the two of them into the house. 130

On the following day he went hunting again.
He gave his second wife instructions.
«Never peek at her while she is eating.
She strangles those who see her.»
But the woman stole a look.

She saw the other woman swallow a whole seal.
She saw her spit the bones out toward the door.
And as she looked at her, she choked.
The woman died.
Dark Woman made it happen. 140

Now she lay dead in the house
when their husband returned.
He saw the body of his wife,
Going Ashore did.
Now he killed the other wife.

He cut his first wife's body clean in half.
He set a whetstone in between the pieces.
That was it for her.[15]
And now he brought the other back to life
and married her again. 150

Now she bore a child.

Now she was the mother of a boy.
His father held his feet down with his own feet
and stretched him with his hands,
and so he grew.

He made his son a small canoe just like his own.
He made him a club –
that too the same as his own –
and when the boy took his canoe out in the cove,
it chomped on little bullheads. 160

Now the woman came to dislike the country.
She returned to her own homeland,
and she took along the child.

Now they arrived in her own country.
He took his mother's brother's daughter as his wife –
the son, that is –
and now he started hunting.
Where they were is known as Qqaaduu.

This concludes the second movement. Without a pause, so far as we know, Sghiidagits continued with the third.

N*ow, when he had hunted for a while,*
a silver otter[16] *swam in front of the town.* 170
Now he headed out in his canoe.

He shot it just at the base of its tail.[17]
Now he skinned it –
or rather, his wife did.
He asked her not to let the blood get on the skin.
She let no blood get on the skin.

Now she asked if she could have it.
He gave it to his wife.
She took it out to wash it in the sea.

She touched it to saltwater.   180
Now it swam away to seaward.
She swam out to bring it back.
It swam still further out to sea.
She swam after it again.

Now a killer whale caught her with its double dorsal fins[18]
and swam along the surface with her, spouting.
Now her husband headed out in his canoe.
He chased the killer whale.
He chased it hard.

He followed it all the way up to the Nass.   190
In front of Spouting Killer Whale Mountain,[19]
his wife went down below the waves.
Now he returned.
He paddled back to Qqaaduu.

He started picking hellebore.
He also gathered urine.
He collected things from menstruating women.
He saved things from their puberty seclusion.
He stored them in a box.

Now he went to sea.   200
He went back where he had seen his wife go down.
He had cedar-limb rope, a marlinspike, a whetstone.

Where his wife had disappeared below the waves
grew a two-headed kelp.

Now he went into the water,
descending the kelp,
and Plain Old Marten stayed behind in the canoe.

Now he came upon a broad main trail.
He followed it.
He came to Lamas Channel.[20]   210

Now near Gyadiigha he met a group of women.
And some of the women spoke.
«I smell Nanasimgit.»[21]

One of the women said that.
And another woman said,
«I smell him too.»

Now he went up to one of the women
and opened her eyes.
«My eyes are open! My eyes are open!»

She shouted with happiness.   220
Now he opened the eyes of another.
So at last he learned his name.

Now the women asked what he had come for.
«They took my wife away.
I want her back.»

«Not long ago they passed here with your wife.
Isniigahl's son married your wife.
Your wife's new husband's name is Northwest Wind.[22]

«When you get to the town,
look out for yourself.   230

A Heron spirit lives at the edge of the village.
He keeps watch.
And he is constantly repairing a canoe.»

Now he continued on his way.
Now he came to the edge of town.
And now the Heron saw him.

Now he gave a cry –
the Heron did –
and Nanasimgit put the cedar limbs
and marlinspike and whetstone in his hands.
And now the Heron picked up Nanasimgit.   240
He stuck him under his arm.

The people of the town came rushing out.
«Old man,» they shouted,
«Why did you cry out?»

«I spoke because I saw my own reflection.»
Now they all went home.
Now he let Nanasimgit out from underneath his arm.

«Two servants will be going out tomorrow,
felling the dry hemlock[23]
that stands behind the house   250
owned by the one who took your wife,
here in the middle of the town.

«One of the servants is known as Raven.
The other is known as Crow.
The wood is for steaming a dorsal fin for your wife.»

Now when it was evening,

he visited the town.
Now he peeked inside
where his wife was,
in the housepit of the house. 260

He saw his wife, seated close beside her husband.
He went back to the old man.
He stayed at his place for the night.

Next day, he went behind the town.
He came to where the leafless hemlock stood.
He sat there, waiting.
Now a pair of servants came along.
And now he slipped inside the hemlock.

Now they started chopping down the tree.
He nicked and cracked the blade of their stone axe. 270
And now they started wailing.
«My master will give me the usual talking to,»
one of the servants said.

Now he came back out of the dry tree,
Gunanasimgit did.
And now he sucked the blade of the stone axe.
Now it came to be as good as new.
Now he felled the hemlock for them.
Now he split it for them too.

«When evening comes, 280
they are going to steam the fin for your wife,»
one of them said.

«We will go to get the water.
As soon as evening comes,

stand in front of the house.
When we have carried in a load,
we will carry you in too.

«When we bring another load,
we will trip ourselves and fall,
waterbuckets and all, into the housepit.   290
After we spill water on the fire,
you can grab your wife.»

As soon as it was evening,
he stood outside the door.
Right away they brought him in.

Now they continued bringing water.
Now the cooking stones grew hot.
Now they had her dorsal fin prepared.
They put a cooking box of stone beside the door.
Now the servants went to get another load.   300

Now as they were packing in the load,
the last one toppled over with the water.
Now it gushed into the fire.

Now there were billows of steam.
Now he ran to get his wife.
Now he took her in his arms.
Now he ran away with her,
back the way he came.[24]

Now seeing she was gone
they ran out after her –   310
the whole town.

The One that Outruns Trout looked around for them above.
Plain Old Marten[25] looked around for them below.
The pair of servants ran ahead.
When they were very close behind him,
one of the servants tripped himself again.

Now his belly swelled up huge.
Mainland Mouse bit his belly open.
Now they chased him once again.

When they closed in on him again,   320
the other servant tripped himself.
Mainland Weasel[26] bit his belly open.

Now Nanasimgit reached the place
where he had gone beneath the waves.
Now he climbed aboard his own canoe.
The watchman, who was still aboard the boat,
had grown old.

Now Nanasimgit paddled hard.
Now the killer whales surfaced off the stern.
They chased him down.   330

As they were starting to capsize him,
he scattered them with hellebore.
Now his pursuers fell away.
Now when they closed in on him again,
he scattered more.

Now he paddled into Qqaaduu.
And now he brought his wife inside the house.
And now he kept his wife inside a box.
There were boxes within boxes,
five in all.   340

Now when it was morning,
he looked in the corner for his wife.
And now, one day, when he went looking for his wife,
his wife had vanished from the box.
In the bottom of the box there was a hole.

It is finished.   346

       ➤   ➤   ➤

In Haida, the closing lines are these:

Wiidhaw Qqaaduu gu lla dangahl lla tluqattlxaayaaghan.
Wiidhaw na gi jaaghang dangahl lla isgaawaghan.
Wiidhaw ghuda sttling gha jaaghang lla daghayaghan.
Ghudaay gutghii daguuhlagaay
tliihlayaaghani.   340

Wiidhaw singgadlana,
wiidhaw kun gu jaaganggha lla qiyattsaayaghan.
Wiidhaw gyaghitaaxhan jaaghang lla qins dluu
wiidhaw ll jaagha ghudaay gha gaawaghani.
Ghudaay sttlinga xhiilaayaghani.

Tlan ghiidang.[27]   346

This or any ten-line sample makes it clear that the author of
this poem is not Ghandl and not Skaay. The dialect or idiolect is
different, to begin with. Sghiidagits uses more northern Haida
forms than Skaay or Ghandl. More importantly, Sghiidagits's
rhythms are not theirs. He also has his own way of deploying in-
troductory particles and handling the tenses of the supple Haida
verb. His closing formula differs slightly as well. It is *inanimate,*
though its meaning is otherwise the same. And the word *wan-*
suuga is nowhere to be found; it does not appear in these ten
lines nor anywhere else in the headman's poem.

Sghiidagits spins a good yarn and weaves a serviceable myth. There is something to be said for the plainness of his style (*wiidhaw … wiidhaw … wiidhaw*, or *now then … now then … now then*), and there is something to be said for the strictness of the five- and three-part patterns into which he fits his images.[28] Still, he does not build his sentences or episodes as fluently as Skaay nor as subtly as Ghandl. His repetitions, parallels, inversions and thematic variations are crude compared to theirs. The rhythm of his thought, like the rhythm of his tongue, is sturdy but comparatively wooden.

Swanton transcribed Sghiidagits's story on a Friday, worked through it with Moody all day Saturday, thought about it on Sunday, and on Monday he had just begun to grasp its architectural complexity. On that day, he met Skaay – and Skaay began to tell him the most intricate and complicated narratives he had ever heard in his life. Swanton understood at once, as his letters tell us, that Skaay was the better mythteller, yet Skaay was telling him suites and cycles of stories in which the connections eluded Swanton completely.

Skaay's first three-part suite links the sea, the land and the sky, and its movements do indeed hang together, though they seem to be as different in their way as the individual movements in one of Haydn's or Mozart's or Beethoven's string quartets or piano sonatas. They are different in structure, different in tone, different in setting. Yet innumerable echoes, contrasts and structural parallels link them.

We can't learn much about the structure or the nature of a string quartet so long as we are exposed to only one example. The form becomes perceptible as such only after we have listened closely to several, heard how they differ and heard what they share. The same is true of these poems – and even the shortest of them takes about an hour and a quarter to perform. It takes a lot of listening to grasp Skaay's artistry, but artistry it is. It is art on a scale John Swanton, sympathetic though he was, did not expect to find in a "remote" and "primitive" village on the raped frontier. In that respect again, the old Haida village of Hlghagilda was something like the Warsaw ghetto.

⟩ ⟩ ⟩

Ghandl's poem about a man who married a woman who came from the sky, and Skaay's poem about a woman who married a man from under the sea, are both typical of the best classical Haida narrative poetry. They are typical in that they are subtly constructed and intricately balanced. And they are typical in that they link stories of poignant human emotion to the structure of the cosmos. But structure is a word with many shades of meaning, some of which, in this case, threaten to lead us astray. The cosmos as Skaay and Ghandl portray it is made in part of numbers, but it is not a Pythagorean numerical crystal.[29] It can be navigated by travelling through space, but not through a space that obeys Euclidean rules. The mythworld is structured like a forest or an animal. It wakes and feeds and sleeps and dreams and changes. And it is made of separate parts that live and die. These poems, when they were oral, did the same. The poems themselves were ecological components of the world they describe.

Properly speaking, what we have here are the fossils of poems, the transcripts, and not the poems themselves – not the living bodies that exist in a flourishing oral tradition. Fossils often provoke discussions of structure, because structure is what they retain and reveal. But the function of the structure is not to call attention to itself; it is to serve the living body. No structural analysis is ever an end in itself – not in literature, not in music, not in biology. The structure disappears from view in the living poem, in the sonata, in the body. The structural analysis should slip from view as well, as soon as it serves its purpose – which is simply to rekindle some of the amazement and respect that the poem itself deserves.

It interests me, however, that Ghandl's poem, which begins

with a young hunter – a marriageable male – later turns on the significance of plant food, which in a culture of hunter-gatherers is food that is usually furnished by women rather than men. No meat is eaten in that story, and though there is a marriage, no child is ever born. The birdhunter gains only momentary joy by marrying his prey, who is a goose who is a woman. Ghandl makes it clear that the hunter and his young wife love each other dearly, but she is not at ease or happy in his world, nor is he content in hers.

Things go differently in Skaay's poem, which begins with a marriageable woman rather than a man. The woman bears a child, though her marriage does not last. She bears the child and hands it on, and her momentary marriage is transformed into a long-term pact bringing fish to surface people from a god beneath the sea.

In both poems, real spiritual power belongs to the underprivileged, not to the tycoons. In Ghandl's poem, the spiritual guides are an old man who lives at the edge of the village and an old woman who is a mouse. In Skaay's poem, the great spiritual journey is made by a servant, and the balance of power is tilted by a spirit-being who is a social misfit, married to a prepubescent boy. It may not be altogether incidental that the makers of these literary masterworks were blind and crippled men. But that is not the explanation either. In many other Haida poems, told by straight-backed, sighted Haida headmen, knowledge and power are vested in a heron with a broken beak, or in an orphaned child. Like all societies whose members are concerned with attaining social dominance and amassing material wealth, the Haida needed countervailing values: nonmaterial and nonauthoritarian. Those are the values manifest in classical Haida literature.

2

STING

6   The Anthropologist and the Dogfish

FRANZ BOAS made his first trip to the Northwest Coast of North America in the fall of 1886, when he was 28 years old, and his last during the winter of 1930–31, at the age of 72. In 1895, after six intensive seasons in the field, he produced the first anthology of the region's literature: *Indianische Sagen von der Nord-Pacifischen Küste Amerikas.* Behind this book lie stories told in almost every language of the Coast – but the originals of all these texts are missing. Every story in the book is reduced to German paraphrase. Few of the mythtellers are named, and none is presented in a way that might preserve any personal style.[1] Boas did, over the years, transcribe and publish many texts in Kathlamet, Shoalwater Chinook, Kwakwala, Nishga, Tsimshian, Pentlatch and other coastal languages, but the individual voices, visions and styles of Native American mythtellers were never his primary interest.

Like his eminent successor Claude Lévi-Strauss, Boas was fascinated by far-reaching thematic comparisons, and for this purpose, plot summaries seemed to him sufficient. The work that appears, in retrospect, closest to his heart is a detailed comparative analysis of the indigenous mythologies of western North America, published when he was 58. It is typical of Boas that this immense undertaking was published as the appendix to something else: it occupies the last half of his thousand-page monograph *Tsimshian Mythology,* which is itself, in theory, nothing more than the accompanying paper to one of the Bureau of

American Ethnology's annual reports. This vast comparative enterprise pays no attention to individual authorship and makes no allowances for individual artistry, intelligence or style. Many of Boas's students – which is to say, many of the next two generations of American anthropologists – continued with this method. It lent to their work an air of scientific impartiality, but it involved the habitual omission or suppression of many sorts of data. Sometimes there were reasons for this omission of information. Sometimes, for example, people demanded a promise of anonymity before agreeing to answer the kinds of questions anthropologists wanted to ask. But Boas persistently preferred the study of shared ideas to the study of individual insights. This made the anonymity of sources desirable in itself.

It is interesting to compare the view of Boas's student and colleague Ruth Benedict. Like Boas, Benedict habitually ironed the style of all the mythtellers she worked with into a seamless uniformity. Ruth Bunzel, Benedict's own student and colleague, was far more attentive to the individuality of the superb Zuni mythtellers both of them knew and admired. Nonetheless, working at Zuni in the early 1930s, Benedict formulated a theory that was far in advance of her own practice:

There is no more communal authorship in folklore than there is a communal designer in ironwork or a communal priest in religious rites. The whole problem is unreal. There is no conceivable source for any cultural trait other than the behavior of some man, woman or child. What is communal about the process is the social acceptance by which the trait becomes a part of the teaching handed down to the next generation. The role of the narrator in such a body of folklore as that of Zuni remains as real as that of any story teller in any civilization though its scope is somewhat changed by the role of the audience.[2]

John Swanton, like Ruth Bunzel, loathed and feared the battles over theory, at which Benedict and Boas both excelled. But his work as an ethnographer in 1900 silently embodies the same theory Benedict was arguing in 1935. Swanton's interest in oral literature was just as intense as Boas's and very different in character – yet the two men really clashed on this issue only once. That clash – as we shall see – came amid the editing of Swanton's massive collection of Haida texts.

Early in his career on the Northwest Coast, Boas acquired some fluency in conversational Haida, but he recorded only a few short texts and word lists in the language.[3] If we had, in transcript, all the Haida oral literature he heard – or all he might have heard, if he had been a patient listener – the record of classical Haida literature would be much richer than it is. Yet we owe Boas one set of secondary texts that is of fundamental importance for understanding Haida art and culture.

>

The Coast Mountains dance into the sea in the rain-wet, grey-green light at the mouth of the Skeena River. It is one of the painfully beautiful places in what is still, after a century of industrial savagery, an exceedingly beautiful land, and the rich submarine archaeological sites north of the river mouth suggest that this is one of the cradles of classical culture on the Northwest Coast.[4] The lower reaches of the Skeena are Tsimshian country, but the Haida sculptor Daxhiigang spent much of his time here. Kkwaayang of the Yaakw Llaanas,[5] his wife, often worked for part of the year at canneries near Port Essington, while Daxhiigang carved, and this is where Swanton left Daxhiigang when the two men sailed north together from Victoria in September 1900.[6] Swanton then caught another boat to Haida Gwaii – where a few old men, speaking a language he did not yet understand, were about to change his life. Daxhiigang was their colleague and their peer, but he was also by then a seasonal emigrant. When he and Swanton parted, Daxhiigang was returning to his family and his work while Swanton reembarked alone to visit his new friend's ancestral home.

Three years earlier, Boas himself was marooned for two weeks

Port Essington, at the mouth of the Skeena River, *c.* 1900. Bleak as it may look, this was the seasonal home of one of the finest artists working in North America at the end of the nineteenth century: the Haida sculptor Daxhiigang (Charlie Edenshaw).

An independent trading post was built here in 1871. An Anglican mission was added in 1876, a cannery in 1877. The latter provided the seasonal work that gave the town its Tsimshian name, *Spaksuut* (Autumn Place).

At its peak, Port Essington included about half a dozen stores, four canneries, three restaurants (two Japanese, one Chinese), two hotels with gaming rooms and bars, a pool hall, at least one brothel, a sawmill, a makeshift jail, two churches and a school. There were two residential areas – one for indigenous people, the other for Europeans. A special dormitory was built for oriental laborers. The fortunes of the town began to fade when a rail line was laid along the Skeena in 1914. The line brought traffic to the new port of Prince Rupert rather than Port Essington – and incidentally destroyed every Gitksan and Tsimshian village in its path.

(Royal British Columbia Museum, PN 15102; photographer unidentified)

138

at Port Essington, waiting for a boat that didn't come. Daxhiigang was there, and Boas hired him, first to make drawings and carvings, then to interpret other Haida artworks – including a few of his own – that Boas had bought for the American Museum of Natural History, and finally to tell stories. From Wednesday, 11 August, to Wednesday, 25 August 1897, Daxhiigang answered Boas's questions, talked about the principles of Haida painting and sculpture, and told Boas a dozen myths or more.[7] These conversations – conducted in Chinook Jargon salted with Haida – inform an important book that Boas published in English thirty years later under the title *Primitive Art*.[8]

If Boas had asked Daxhiigang to tell the myths in full, and had made it plain that he would listen as long as required, and if he had then transcribed Daxhiigang's Haida word for word, we would now have the luxury of comparing the master carver's sculpture with his poetry. Since the links between classical Haida poetry and classical Haida sculpture are unusually close, this could prove much more than just an interesting exercise. In the absence of full Haida versions, transcriptions of exactly what Daxhiigang said in Chinook Jargon would be extremely welcome.[9] But Boas had other work on his mind. He recorded the myths only in English paraphrase. Back in New York, he had them typed, in a slightly bowdlerized form, and in 1900 he passed the typescripts on to Swanton, restoring the bowdlerized passages by hand. Swanton (to Boas's surprise) published most of these paraphrases as supplements to his own Haida transcriptions and translations.[10] One of them is the only version we have, from a classical source, of the story of Qqaaxhadajaat, the Dogfish Woman. The group of drawings[11] Boas bought from Daxhiigang in 1897 includes a detailed image of this creature, and Boas asked the artist to explain it. What Daxhiigang said is lost, but this is what Franz Boas thought he meant:

A woman went travelling with her husband. She used to make fun of the dogfish. They went to visit a small rock in the sea. When they were

Daxhiigang, *Qqaaxhadajaat* [*The Dogfish Woman*], 1897. Pencil with red ochre and blue pigments (probably colored pencil) on paper, 28 × 23.5 cm. (The image itself is 24 cm tall.) Boas Collection, 1943. Dept. of Anthropology Archives, American Museum of Natural History, New York.

(AMNH, 132560: Jackie Beckett, 1996.)

out there, the dogfish, whose home the rock was, came and took the woman down into the sea. There she discovered that the dogfish were really people. They had taken off their dogfish blankets. After she had stayed in the house for some time, fins began to grow upon her arms, her legs, and her back. Her husband was searching for her everywhere, but he was not able to find her. After a number of years he found her. Her face had remained unchanged; but fins had grown on her arms, on her legs, on her back, and on her head. She never returned. Ever since that time her family have used the dogfish crest, and their house is called Dogfish House.[12]

Dogfish do not have fins on their heads, and it is highly un-likely that Daxhiigang said the Dogfish Woman had fins on her head either. I suspect that he said something much more careful and precise than the paraphrase suggests, and quite possibly just as precise as the image he drew. That image was made quickly but with absolute assurance. It incorporates with surgical clarity the gill slits, the crescent-shaped mouth full of sharp, triangular teeth, the vertical pupils, elongated forehead, asymmetrical cau-dal fin and spined double dorsal fins of the dogfish. The woman within the dogfish is just as clearly shown. She is hairless like a slave but wears the face paint and labret of a Haida woman aris-tocrat. She also has – or she and the dogfish jointly have – what seem to be the talons of an eagle or a raven. There are multiple transformations and interrelationships here of which Boas's par-aphrase gives only the scarcest hint. There is also a considerable range of tone, from the severity and grace of the emaciated woman within the dogfish to the muscular poise of the body and head of the dogfish itself to the impish humor of the twins in-habiting her dorsal fins. Silent though it is, the drawing has some of the properties familiar in well-told Haida narrative. There are no stray lines, no anecdotal shading or coloration. The logic of the form is as sleek as a fish and as spare as a skeleton. There are enigmas, but there are no irrelevant details or loose ends.

Daxhiigang made his drawing of the Dogfish Woman in black pencil enlivened with dark red and bluegreen pigments – canonical Haida colors, though not quite traditional Haida media – on the back of one of the large preprinted forms that Boas had prepared for a study of Northwest Coastal face painting.[13] There is a note in Boas's hand on the front of the drawing and a longer one in Swanton's hand on the back. It appears, in fact, that Swanton may have taken the drawing with him when he left for Haida Gwaii in 1900 and made his annotations in the Islands. Which of his Haida teachers he consulted when he did so is harder to say. He too sometimes omitted crucial information. But his notes tell us some interesting things.

Boas's notes tell us, first of all, and Swanton's notes confirm, that heraldic rights to the use of the image of the Dogfish Woman were claimed by three families of the Eagle side: the Yaakw Llaanas, the Gitins of Hlghagilda, and the Qquuna Qiighawaay, Skaay's family. Swanton's notes tell us further that the Hlghagilda branch of the Gitins – which includes Sghiidagits's family, the Na Yuuwans Xhaaydaghaay – caused dissension by starting to use the image without permission from the Qquuna Qiighawaay. Finally and most importantly, Swanton's notes tell us that Qqaaxhadajaat, the Dogfish Woman, "is the sister of Nang Ttl Dlstlas": the sister of the One They Hand Along.[14]

If we take this statement narrowly and literally, it means that Qqaaxhadajaat is the daughter of the woman who was kidnapped by a creature from the sea. She is the sister of the reincarnated sea god who is born to a human mother, laced into his cradle, and returned to his rightful place on the floor of the sea. Skaay, in that case, knew the story of the Dogfish Woman well – but the story of the Dogfish Woman's human mother, her uncles and the god who was her brother is the one that he decided Henry Moody and John Swanton ought to hear.

Qqaaxhadajaat, not her brother, is the figure who fascinated Daxhiigang, and he carved and drew her image often over the years. Boas did not grasp the depth of this relationship – even after Daxhiigang had explained to him, and Boas had recorded, that the image belonged to the Yaakw Llaanas family. Yet this was the clue, if Boas had thought about it, revealing how the story and the drawing had become not just heraldic furniture but vehicles of an intensely personal meditation on the permanence of love in a world filled with death and sudden disappearances.

To those who *think* the myths, the creatures who inhabit them are real and not fictitious. One of the members of the Yaakw Llaanas family – thus one of the spiritual daughters and potential reincarnations of the woman captured by the dogfish – was Kkwaayang, Daxhiigang's wife. One potential reincarnation of the abandoned and bereaved human husband of the Dogfish Woman was, therefore, of course, Daxhiigang himself.

Stylized and hieratic though it appears, Haida art can be and frequently is that personal and intense. This does not mean that the art requires a personal explanation by the artist, nor does it mean that the art is obscure. Daxhiigang took the story of the Dogfish Woman very personally indeed – and so did his successor, the Haida sculptor Bill Reid. But they are not the only people on the Northwest Coast who have understood a link between dogfish and lost love. A Haida man known as Giikw of the Daayuuwahl Llaanas (*c.* 1820–1907) wove such a link into a family history that he dictated to Swanton at Hlghagilda sometime during the winter of 1900–1901.[15] More than a decade later and nearly a thousand kilometers south – on Tuesday, 7 October 1913, to be precise, in the village of Ttsuum'as on the west coast of Vancouver Island – the Nuuchahnulth mythteller Qiixxa (known in English as Big Fred) told Edward Sapir a handsomely crafted and detailed story, in the Nootka language, about a man who tried to retrieve his wife after she was kidnapped by creatures from the sea. Sapir, with his European education, heard in it many resemblances to the Greek story of Orpheus. A listener from the northern Northwest Coast would have recognized it at once as the story of Nanasimgit – part three of the trilogy that Sghiidagits dictated to Swanton on 5 October 1900. But there is one intriguing difference. As Qiixxa tells the story, it is not a killer whale but a dogfish who abducts the hunter's wife.[16]

Is there a reason for these connections that is independent of the logic of the myths? I do not know. But perhaps it is not irrelevant that, of all the sharks and rays, dogfish are the nearest to human form and scale. On the Northwest Coast, they are also the most frequent in the vicinity of human villages. Sharks and rays also differ from most fishes in having what mammals like ourselves can recognize as a sex life. Their eggs are fertilized internally, like the ova of warm-blooded animals, not externally, like the roe of herring, halibut and salmon. The male dogfish penetrates the female. Dogfish, like other sharks and rays, also appear to be doubly potent, since the males have two penises (actually claspers) and the females two vaginas. In Haida – but not so far as I know in any other language of the Northwest Coast – the link between adultery and dogfish is reinforced by a pun. The dogfish is called *qqaaxhada* in Haida; *qqaaxhii* is one of the Haida words for penis.

And then there is the matter of the fins. Killer whales, in ordinary life, have large and impressive dorsal fins, but only one dorsal fin each. In Haida myth and Haida art – as in the Nanasimgit story told by Sghiidagits – they frequently have double dorsal fins. Dogfish – evidently doubly potent in this respect as well – have two dorsal fins even in daily life.

Humans and dogfish, then, like men and women, are close in some respects, and in others blatantly different. Some of their differences, however, are subtle and complex. Where physical love is concerned, one difference of importance is the skin. Dogfish skin is rough – so rough that Haida carpenters and carvers use it for sandpaper. Sometime in the 1930s, a Tsimshian mythteller known as Arthur Lewis told the Nishga ethnographer Gwüsk'aayn (William Beynon) a story in which the Raven visits a village of beautiful women. They allow him to make love to them one by one – but he wears his penis to shreds as he does so, because they are sharks.[17] A man whose wife is potentially a dogfish is a man potentially too fragile to make love to the very woman he loves most.

›   ›   ›

Now that Daxhiigang has taught us a little about the relationship of mythtellers and myths, we might think back to Ghandl and his story of the young man who meets and falls in love with a woman from another world. Love is tested in the story, and it seems to meet the test, yet the marriage quickly fails. I do not know the date of Ghandl's blindness, nor whether he himself was ever married, nor how his disability affected his relationships with women. But from his poetry alone we know that Ghandl was an expert on the potency of vision, the impermanence of joy, the durability of love, and the unsustainability of all love's practical conditions. His understanding of these matters is palpable in many of his poems, and especially in the way he tells the tale of the man "who was just about to go out hunting birds." In Ghandl's poem, as in Daxhiigang's drawing, the human is contained within the hieratic, and that containment proves to be a source of power. Human features and emotions are rendered potently as human, and as more than human, both at the same time.

We might think back, too, to the story of Nanasimgit, which Sghiidagits told to Swanton on his first official call. Did Sghiidagits choose to tell a Tsimshian story just to keep the anthropologist at bay? Was the headman of the village artfully avoiding a stranger's curiosity, protecting himself and his culture by dishing up a story full of foreign names, set in foreign places, when he might have told a story closer to the bone? Or could this myth, known in one form or another, in 1900, to every native person up and down the Northwest Coast, be a means of real self-revelation?

The Sghiidagits whom Swanton met in 1900 was in his early sixties. He had served as headman of the village since his elder

brother's death in 1892.[18] In the 1870s and 1880s, when the old poles and houses of Hlghagilda still stood, the senior male members of his lineage (Na Yuuwans Xhaaydaghaay, the Big House People) lived in three adjacent houses at the center of the town.[19] The memorial and mortuary poles for all three houses stood together in front of the middle house. In 1882, when more than sixty poles were standing in the village, there were six poles here in the Big House Family yard. Three of them were mortuary posts, and all three held the bones of women. Though each was independently designed, these three poles portrayed a single theme: a woman being carried between worlds by a two-finned killer whale.[20]

The names of these three women are now lost, but all three were apparently deceased wives of headmen of the town. The last of these three mortuary posts was raised in 1881. In 1883, Hlghagilda acquired a new name – Skidegate Mission – and with it, an industrious new resident, whose first priorities included the construction of a church and European-style graveyard.

Swanton did not see any of the houses or the poles in the Big House Family complex. Between 1889 and 1894, the poles were emptied and cut down, the bones were buried, and the houses were demolished and replaced with smaller structures in the European style. When Charles Newcombe photographed the village in 1895, only sixteen poles were standing, where more than sixty had stood twelve years before. Daxhiigang, who knew far more than we about the three dead women, carved Swanton a small model of one of those three mortuary poles. The one he chose was the last one to be raised – but he did not explain its significance to Swanton.[21]

FACING PAGE: Two of the three mortuary poles in front of the house of Sghiidagits, headman of Hlghagilda, probably 1888. Both contain allusions to the Nanasimgit story. Photograph by Richard Maynard.

(American Museum of Natural History, Library Services, 39992)

The Nanasimgit story, as Sghiidagits chose to tell it, is a tale of adventure and a wonder tale, mapping the connections between the visible and not-so-visible realms. It is also – like Ghandl's story of the man who married the goose and Daxhii-gang's story of the woman taken by the dogfish – a story of lost love. It does not have to be so. At least thirteen versions of the Nanasimgit story were recorded on the Northwest Coast before 1910.[22] Only one of them – the version that Sghiidagits told to John Swanton in October 1900 – ends with the final loss of the hunter's wife.

The story Swanton heard is the story of three mortuary poles he was a bit too late to see, and of a fourth pole that Sghiidagits would have raised in the same place if the world had not, within his lifetime, changed beyond belief. If, that is, the world he was born in had not vanished from his grasp, like a certain rescued woman from the bottom of a box.

Swanton heard Sghiidagits's Nanasimgit story on a Friday and returned the following Monday prepared to transcribe another tale. Sghiidagits sent him away instead – all to the good, because Henry Moody led him straight to Skaay. But Swanton was slightly peeved by the rejection. He thought Sghiidagits "too lazy or grasping" to dictate another tale at the going rate.[23] Swanton may have got it right – but another possibility deserves consideration. It may be that the headman of Hlghagilda was occupied that Monday, gazing at the changed face of his village and nursing a broken heart.

⸙   ⸙   ⸙

Of all the Haidas' early European visitors, only Swanton had the training, the time and the patience for taking dictation, and evidently only Swanton sensed something of the way in which oral literatures actually function. As a consequence, no Haida texts of any substance were transcribed before Swanton set to work in October 1900, and nothing more of substance was recorded or transcribed for seventy years after Swanton left the Islands in August 1901. When those seventy years had passed, the Haida world, and even the Haida language, had irrevocably changed. That is why the preserved body of classical Haida literature comes to us focussed and constricted through the passion of one man. It consists of the roughly 250 narratives and songs that Swanton recorded during a single year.

A number of the songs and stories Swanton heard in 1900 and 1901 are still in circulation, and new ones are still made. Haida oral literature has by no means disappeared. But a century of churchgoing, hymn-singing, Bible study and English-language schooling, abetted in recent years by radio and television, magazines and films, has also left its mark on the narrative tradition.[24]

The Haida poets themselves and the mythcreatures they speak of, not the anthropologists and linguists who have put them into writing, are the significant figures in Haida literary history. But Swanton's role is singular enough, and his work substantial enough, that he too merits some of our attention. By following the course of Swanton's thoughts about his work in 1900 and 1901, we also stand to learn something more about the mind of his teacher Skaay.

John Swanton was born 19 February 1873 in Gardiner, Maine, a little town on the tidal reach of the Kennebec River. He was the youngest of three boys, and he was fatherless all his life. The father of the three Swanton boys was killed while his youngest son was still in the womb. The three were therefore raised by a triumvirate of women: mother, grandmother and great aunt. Their neighbors included a budding poet by the name of Edwin Arlington Robinson, four years older than John Swanton.

The older Swanton brothers studied science and engineering at MIT. The youngest, John, was happier, like Robinson, at Harvard. There as an undergraduate he took courses in philosophy with George Santayana and in psychology with William James. Global perspectives appealed to him early. Even before he entered college, he had written what he called "a history of the world [in] a series of composition books."[25]

Swanton's mother also introduced him to the works of Emanuel Swedenborg (1688–1772) – a trained and evidently able scientist who nonetheless, in later life, recorded countless visits to worlds that only he could see and conversations with beings that he alone could hear. Swedenborg inspired Blake and Yeats with the power and exactness of his visions, at the same time that he scandalized them both with his evident unwillingness as well as inability to sing what he had seen. "It was indeed Swedenborg," says Yeats,

who affirmed for the modern world, as against the abstract reasoning of the learned, the doctrine and practice of the desolate places, of shepherds and of midwives....

In his fifty-eighth year he was sitting in an Inn in London, where he had gone about the publication of a book, when a spirit appeared before him and told him that henceforth he could commune with spirits and angels. From that moment on he was a mysterious man describing distant events as if they were before his eyes, and knowing dead men's secrets.... And all this happened to a man without egotism, without drama, without a sense of the picturesque, and who wrote a dry language, lacking fire and emotion.... He considered heaven and hell and God, the angels, the whole destiny of man, as if he were sitting before a large table in a Government office putting little pieces of mineral ore into small square boxes for an assistant to pack away in drawers.[26]

Swanton experienced no such gargantuan visions and trances himself, but he did become, like Swedenborg, a scientist who trusted there were things he could not see. He was certain of the value of empirical observation and rigorous logic, yet equally convinced that mind inheres in everything, and quite prepared to credit the existence of innumerable immaterial beings and parallel worlds. He remained a lifelong member of the Sweden-borgian Church, and he preferred, throughout his life, a gentle science of experience to a science of relentless analytical dissection and experiment. In his own brief book on Swedenborg, which he published in 1928, at the age of 54, Swanton praises the science of Swedenborg's time, when

students of nature were oftener content to observe her in the open than to carry her captive into a laboratory and put her through her paces under "controlled" conditions.[27]

In 1896, Swanton started graduate studies at Harvard in archaeology and ethnology. Or as his friend Alfred Kroeber preferred to put it, "he was sent to one of the interminable diggings in Ohio, with half a following winter to wash skeletons in the [Peabody] Museum basement."[28] Swanton endured this regime just long enough to obtain his master's degree. He then enrolled as a Harvard doctoral candidate but arranged to do the rest of his course work at Columbia, where Livingston Farrand[29] was teaching anthropology and Franz Boas was teaching ethnology and linguistics. Under their direction, he spent the summer of 1899 at Rosebud, South Dakota, learning the rudiments of Lakhota. (This is a language with many names. Boas and Swanton called it Dakota; outsiders often call it Sioux).

At this point, Swanton planned to do his doctoral work on Lakhota. His expectations were subverted, by Boas and also by a mythteller Swanton never met and whose voice he never heard. In 1890, 1891 and 1894, Boas had spent several weeks with a quadrilingual oral poet by the name of Qqiltí,[30] on Willapa Bay, near the mouth of the Columbia River. Though he was not yet ready to admit that individual artistry was an issue in oral literature, Boas was deeply impressed with Qqiltí's knowledge and intelligence. Writing to his parents only a few days after he and Qqiltí met, Boas says that "he is worth his weight in gold, he knows so much."[31] The sessions with Qqiltí produced the most extended and successful transcriptions Boas had yet made. The two books that resulted – *Chinook Texts* (1894) and *Kathlamet Texts* (1901) – were published unceremoniously as numbers 20 and 26 in the Bureau of American Ethnology's long-running series of bulletins, but they represent something new for Boas, for the Bureau, and for Native American studies as a whole.

It was a predecessor of Boas's, the French priest Émile Petitot, who in 1888 issued the first substantial volume of Native North American oral literature in full bilingual form. But Boas's editions of Qqiltí's *Chinook Texts* and *Kathlamet Texts* are the first book-length publications by a single Native American author. They are also the first such works in which the aboriginal author is prominently named. As a concession to monolingual readers and librarians, however, he is called by his anglicized baptismal name: not Qqiltí but Charles Cultee.

Boas knew very well that his work with Qqiltí was the best linguistic work he had done, and that Qqiltí had set him on a new direction. He also knew that the languages of these two books of texts – Shoalwater Chinook and Kathlamet – were very close to extinction.[32] (Shoalwater Chinook, or Lower Chinook, is a Penutian language spoken until the end of the nineteenth century around the mouth of the Columbia River. It is different in every way from Chinook Jargon, a pidgin language once widely used by travellers and traders all along the Northwest Coast.) Boas asked Swanton and others of his students to join in a detailed study of Qqiltí's texts. Swanton complied and dutifully wrote his doctoral dissertation on "The Morphology of the Chinook Verb."[33]

After defending his dissertation at Harvard in June 1900, Swanton still planned to resume his work on Lakhota. But Boas once again had other plans: Swanton should take up the study of Haida, and he should become the first trained anthropologist on the staff of the Bureau of American Ethnology.[34] Once again, Swanton did as he was asked. He applied for a job at the Bureau and remained in the east to take a specially tailored civil service exam and await its results. The degree to which ethnology and continued colonization were confused in the minds of civil service examiners can be judged by Swanton's letter to Boas dated 5 August 1900:

I did not find very much difficulty with the examinations – although I made one or two little blunders – until I came to the last question, a translation of the Ten Commandments into Dakota. I doubt whether any such Ten Commandments were ever before heard of as the ones I gave them. Still, I did fill the sheet.[35]

On 1 September 1900, Swanton was appointed to the BAE at a salary of $50 per month, and he left within days for the Northwest Coast. Boas, from his position at the American Museum of Natural History, had arranged for the Museum to pay Swanton's expenses while the Bureau paid his salary. Swanton was therefore obligated to both, but there is no doubt that Boas commanded the greater share of his allegiance and respect. Boas commanded a lot of other things as well. W J McGee, then acting head of the BAE, had intended to set his new employee to work on Mayan languages, but Boas would not hear of it. His letter of instruction, laying out the program of work Swanton was to follow in Haida Gwaii on behalf of both the Museum and the BAE, is dated 5 June 1900: three months before Swanton was hired by the Bureau, and two months before he had even taken the exam.[36]

Boas asked Swanton to investigate in detail several things: the Haida system of heraldic crests and its role in the social order; the significance of the figures in Haida sculpture; Haida ceremonial life; the use and significance of masks; personal and family guardian spirits; and rules governing intermarriage with the neighboring native nations. Then he listed a number of artifacts, ranging from housepoles to spoons, that he wanted Swanton to buy for the American Museum. His letter of instruction makes no mention of oral literature, except insofar as "myths" might explain Haida social organization and elucidate the artifacts that Swanton was to buy. Swanton did not quite forget these other assignments, but he did very little to fulfill them. From the moment he arrived in the Haida country, he was consumed with the task of transcribing and translating stories, songs and narrative poems. He kept Boas fully informed of this radical shift in priorities – and Boas, to his everlasting credit, accepted this shift and continued to support him.

So it was that in October 1900, wholly unprepared yet perfectly equipped, John Swanton stepped into a world in which dogfish, geese and killer whales are bearers of the heart's truth as well as potent agents of creation, guides and escorts through the maze of space and time.

7   Who's Related to Whom?

I‌‌T IS A PECULIARITY – or a pathology, perhaps – of centrally administered and urbanized societies to want to see the world, including the gods, in strictly human terms, or to see it still more narrowly, in terms of a single language, faith and culture. Industrial societies habitually go further, dropping the gods overboard and classifying all nonhuman beings – and often other human beings too – as "natural resources" waiting to be used. In classical Haida literature and art, humans never exercise such dominance. The ritual combat of man against man, man against nature, and man against himself – reputedly the elemental themes of modern European literature – are never more than secondary subject matter here. Classical Haida poets spend much more time exploring the connections between humans and non-humans – sea mammals, land mammals, fish, birds, and the *sghaana qiidas*, "those who are born as spirit powers," the gods. Skaay and Ghandl speak of three distinct realms – forest, sea and sky – each with its native populations. None of these, however, is the human realm. Humans are only at home on the *xhaaydla*, the boundary or intertidal zone, at the conjunction of all three. A few strokes of the paddle or a few steps into the bush are enough to leave the human world behind.

Who are these creatures called the gods? They are dismissed as idle fictions by atheists and monotheists, capitalists and clergymen alike. But gods, in the plural, are found wherever human beings are found – unless the human beings claim exclusive rights, power and privilege, dispossessing the gods of their homes. Those who have to ask what a god is, like those who have to ask what a mountain or an eagle or a forest is, will not learn the answer from a book. Still, those who think the gods are fictions may be interested in José Ortega y Gasset's attempt to acknowledge their existence in human and secular terms. Ortega is discussing what is missing from Velázquez's later painting. He does this in part by comparing the work of Velázquez with that of his predecessor Titian, who seemed to see the gods in a much more frank and literal way. "The gods," Ortega says,

are the higher intelligence that things possess when they are perceived in interrelation with one other.... To say there are no gods is to say things do not have, in addition to their material constitution, the odor or glow of intellectual significance, of meaning. It is to say that life is senseless, that things are bereft of interconnections.[1]

The precolonial world was not, like the modern world, saturated with human interconnections – the telephone, the radio, the interstate, the internet, and so on. It was not starved for them either. Neither the Haida nor any other Native American nation lived in timeless isolation, waiting for the gifts of history and progress to be brought by Europeans. Haida Gwaii stood at the junction of three great provinces of stone-age and iron-age culture, and Haida intellectual and artistic life was altered and enriched by contact with them all. These cultural provinces are the Oceanic, the Circumpolar and the Continental North American. The Oceanic province includes Melanesian peoples such as the Asmat of New Guinea, Polynesians such as the Maori, and others such as the Ainu of Japan, whose visual art and oral literature resemble those of the Haida in many intriguing ways.[2] The Circumpolar province includes both arctic and subarctic hunters and herders such as the Inuit, Aleut, Yupiit, Chukchi, Koryak and Yukaghir.[3] The Continental province consists of Athapaskans,

Algonkians, Salishans, Penutians, Siouans, Iroquoians, and the other linguistic and cultural groups who peopled North America in precolonial times, and who, after half a millennium of attempted extermination, people it still.

It is, of course, deeply instructive to compare works of Haida oral literature with works in other Native American languages and traditions.[4] We should remember nonetheless that aboriginal North America is only one of several human domains with which the Haida have long-standing cultural associations. Native American literature is an immense field in itself, but not a field we can fully understand by treating it in isolation.

The Haida Swanton met in 1900 were well aware and proud of the cultural links between themselves and their nearest neighbors, the Tsimshian and Nishga to the east and northeast and the Tlingit to the north. Many Haida ceremonial and honorific names – for people, for houses, for objects – are Nishga, Tsimshian or Tlingit in origin. Several creatures important in Haida art and literature (grizzly, beaver, mountain goat, wolf) are found in the Tsimshian, Nishga and Tlingit country, but not in Haida Gwaii. Many of the songs that Swanton heard in the southern Haida country were Tsimshian, and in northern Haida Gwaii, many of the shamans and shamanic spirits mentioned by his teachers were Tlingit or at least had Tlingit names. Myth and history mix easily in classical Haida narrative, just as they do in Elizabethan drama, and the stories told by classical Haida poets are often set in Tsimshian or Nishga or Tlingit territory – just as the mythohistorical plays of Shakespeare are often set in mainland Europe. Swanton's thumbnail analysis, dashed off in an early letter to Boas, still bears consideration: "There is a wash of Tsimshian varnish over everything Haida, but the underlying influence I should say was Tlingit."[5]

Cultural ties between the classical Haida and their neighbors to the southeast and the south appear less intimate, though they too are substantial. This is the country of the Wakashans and

Salishans, who are jointly known in classical Haida as *Tljing
Xhaaydaghaay,* "the Distant People." It was here, Skaay says, that
the Raven first caught salmon, and here that the Raven found his
wife: an amphibious woman he brought back to Haida Gwaii,
where he installed her in a house he had stolen on the mainland
from its builders, who were beavers.[6]

Art historians now routinely group the Haida, Tlingit,
Nishga, Gitksan and Tsimshian together as cultures of the northern Northwest Coast. The northern Wakashans and the Nuxalk
(the northernmost of the Coast Salish peoples)[7] form a second
convenient division, the central Northwest Coast. On the southern Northwest Coast are the rest of the Coast Salish nations and
the southern Wakashans (speaking Nootka, Nitinaht and
Makah). The visual art of the Coast reaches its maximum tension, poise and sensuous restraint in classical Haida painting and
sculpture. It is possible, however, that the styles prevailing in the
southern art are older. There is not much doubt in any case that
the *visual* languages elaborated by early sculptors and painters all
along the Northwest Coast, from the Bering Sea to the Strait of
Juan de Fuca, are historically related. They are different visual
languages, but there is very little doubt that all belong to the
same family. It is otherwise with the languages that are *spoken*
over the same stretch of ground.[8]

*These
languages
are mapped
on page 21.*

The Nuxalk speak a Salishan language. The rest of the *Tljing
Xhaaydaghaay,* or peoples of the central Northwest Coast, speak
northern Wakashan tongues – Haisla, Heiltsuk, Uwekyala and
Kwakwala – which are clearly related to the Nootka, Nitinaht
and Makah languages spoken farther south.[9] These two families
of languages, Salishan and Wakashan, differ a great deal but are
probably connected – perhaps in the same degree that the
Romance languages are connected to Urdu and Hindi.

The Tsimshian, Nishga and Gitksan are three separate nations speaking two (formerly three) distinct languages, closely
related to each other but thoroughly distinct from the languages

around them. The Nishga (people of the Nass River) and the Gitksan (people of the Skeena River) share a single language, known as Nishga or Gyaanmx. Another, known as Tsimshian or Smalgyax, is spoken by their coastal relatives. The study of classical Nishga and Tsimshian literature is a natural counterpart to the study of classical Haida literature, and it could be of crucial importance – but the task is not so easy as it sounds, because early Nishga texts are scarce, and most early Tsimshian texts are in dubious condition.[10]

Tlingit and its more northerly neighbor Eyak are distant relatives of the Athapaskan languages,[11] which are spoken in much of Alaska and western Canada, in the Coast Mountains of Oregon and northern California, and in much of the American Southwest. (On the map on page 21, Ahtna, Southern Tutchone, Tagish, Kaska, Tahltan, Tsetsaut and Wetsuwetin are Athapaskan languages. Navajo, Hupa and the five Apache languages – spoken far beyond the boundaries of the map – are Athapaskan too.)

Insofar as we can reconstruct it, the map of thematic interrelationships among the classical oral literatures of the Northwest Coast seems to a large extent congruent with the map of interrelationships in the visual arts. The literatures of the northern coast – Eyak, Tlingit, Nishga, Tsimshian and Haida – form a recognizable and relatively close-knit group, which is more loosely related in turn to the literatures of the central and southern Northwest Coast. But the pattern formed by the language map is different. Eyak, Tlingit and their farflung Athapaskan relatives form one linguistic entity. Nishga and Tsimshian form another. Nuxalk, the southern Coast Salish and the Interior Salish languages together form a third group. The seven Wakashan languages form a fourth group – and Haida forms a fifth unto itself. Speakers of these five different families of languages have lived in close proximity for centuries, sharing their experiences, art forms, ideas, and a modest number of words. They have also come to share, as neighboring languages usually do, a palette of phonemes – that is, linguistically meaningful speech sounds. How the sounds are used is something else. In vocabulary and structure, these language groups are as different from one another as Arabic, English, Japanese, Persian and Finnish.

This is prima facie evidence – if any further evidence were needed – that literature is not made simply out of language. Language to the linguist is a wonderfully complex object of study in itself, like rock to the geophysicist or blood to the biochemist. To the classically minded storyteller or poet, language is a substance, a material – like wood, stone, ivory or bone – that is available, pleasant and practical to work. Complex though it is, it is still homogeneous enough in density and texture so that forms seen in the mind can be answered with forms that are spoken by the voice – and vice versa.

Accidents of language and material can substitute for ideas among artists who have none of their own, or who have come to be distrustful of ideas altogether. Such art has been in fashion now and then in European history – but so far as we now know, there were no artists of that kind at work on the Northwest Coast in the classical period.

In classical Haida art, the material substance gives the piece some of its character and sets certain limits on the form. That substance could be alder or redcedar, for example, or it could be the Haida or Tlingit language. Whatever the substance is, it encourages certain developments, certain techniques, and discourages certain others. There is always something to be learned by examining the physical material of a classical Haida sculpture – or the language of a classical Haida poem – and something further to be learned by studying the use to which the artefact was put. (Not much art on the Northwest Coast was made to sit on the shelf and do nothing.) But there is also always a form – a statement-making form, like a metaphor or a sentence – incarnate in the substance yet distinguishable from it. There is always an idea, envisioned in the substance by the artist, and clinging to the substance, yet perfectly able to leave the substance behind. In classical Haida art, forms can enter and leave physical substances much as spirits can enter and leave physical beings in classical Haida myth.

A molded plastic copy of a piece of Haida art is nevertheless always a disappointment, because the form has lost its bite. Paraphrases of classical Haida literature fail on precisely the same ground. The form must be reborn when it moves to a new substance; this occurs not when it is copied but when it is reenvisioned and recarved. Classical Haida literature and art, like the culture from which they come, live at the intersection between the material and the immaterial realms, where the substance, the idea, the artist and the tool all unite.[12] The poetry in a classical Haida story is, in the same way, easy to lose in translation – yet it is not so inextricably bound to the language that it is certain to be lost. That is one of the reasons it makes sense to call this literature classical.

> > >

Many attempts have been made to show that Haida is linked to Tlingit, Eyak and the Athapaskan languages, as part of a large linguistic family or phylum called Nadene.[13] Most linguists who have studied the languages closely have found this linkage unconvincing. For them, Haida constitutes, by default, a family all its own.[14]

Conservative taxonomists count dozens, even hundreds, of such isolated languages around the world. Some others besides Haida that continue to resist convincing classification are the Basque language, spoken in northern Spain; the Burushaski language of northern Kashmir; the Kutenai language, spoken around the borderland of Montana, British Columbia and Alberta; Gilyak, which is spoken near the mouth of the Amur River and on Sakhalin Island in eastern Siberia; and Ket, which is spoken in central Siberia, in the Yenisey basin. In the eighteenth century, Ket was a language that had several obvious relatives, but all their speakers perished in the smallpox epidemics that swept through Siberia with the Russian colonization. How many languages have vanished in the same way from North and South America without leaving any trace remains a potent but unanswerable question.

It is curious but true that if the Haida language had some obvious living relatives (which it did, no doubt, once have), the taxonomic urge to assign it to Nadene, while it would not disappear, would be miraculously lessened.

In 1929, Edward Sapir proposed a draft classification in which all the indigenous languages of North America were sorted into six large families. Sapir never claimed that this system was foolproof or complete, and decades of study by specialists have steadily teased it apart, though its skeleton remains. No one has yet proven the truth or falsity of Sapir's classification, and since his death in 1939, most professional students of Native American languages have focussed on the lower levels of classification: the subspecies, species and genera, rather than families, orders and phyla to which languages belong.

In 1987, however, Joseph Greenberg undertook to classify all the surviving languages of North and South America together into three large families. He counted over 600 languages still living (and as such left many out), and he put 94% into one of his three groups. This taxonomy is part of a systematic effort by Greenberg and his colleagues to classify all the world's recorded languages – there are more than 5000 – into a small number of phyla, and to trace those phyla to a single common root.

Greenberg's classification, like Sapir's, remains unproven. The methods Greenberg used to build the system were plainly insufficient to the task, and his data – sometimes limited to missionary wordlists – were frequently corrupt. This however does not tell us whether his thesis is false or true. Greenberg's critics, who are many, have proven that the case is far from closed, but none of them has proven that his theory must be wrong.[15]

Elephants and apple trees are noticeably different from each other, and they do not interbreed. Yet the molecular biologist, and even an observant physiologist, can see beyond a doubt that they have many things in common. Not only can they nourish one another as parts of the same biochemical system; they share an evolutionary root. Comparative linguistics has failed to advance in recent decades at the same pace as biology, and that is why the phylogenetic relations among languages remain so much in doubt. But the comparative isolation of Haida, Burushaski and a number of other languages is not in doubt at all. What is uncertain is the nature of their early, distant links.

Haida, it is safe to say, is a linguistic counterpart of *Struthio camelus*, the ostrich; of *Ginkgo biloba*, the ginkgo tree, and of *Homo sapiens*, the human being. Each of these species constitutes a monotypic family or order. Each has lost its closest relatives and is now out all alone on a long and slender taxonomic limb. This does not mean that these or any plants or animals are "completely unrelated" to the rest of what exists.

Like the boundaries between minds, the boundaries between languages can scatter or refract and rearrange the elements of stories. They do not prevent their passage. On the contrary, the boundaries and distinctions between languages clearly *encourage* the growth and regeneration of stories. That is one of the things – and possibly the chief thing – languages are for. The forest of language in its entirety forms an ecology in which ideas feed and hide. The mother tongue of Ekaterina Rumyantsev, whom we met in chapter 2, was Yukaghir, and her second tongue was Russian. No one has convincingly traced a genetic connection between either of these and Haida.[16] Rumyantsev and Ghandl are joined nevertheless, unknown to one another, in narrative communion. So are Skaay and a number of Tsimshian and Nishga mythtellers – though the hereditary links between their languages, for all their geographical proximity, have never yet been mapped. Haida and Tsimshian (or Haida and Yukaghir) appear to be as different as Haida and English, or English and Yoruba, or Yoruba and Mandarin Chinese.[17]

"Chinese," like "Greek," is for many English speakers just a way of saying "absolutely foreign." But in language as in life, no foreignness is ever absolute. Edward Sapir, though he never had a chance to work extensively with Haida, was deeply intrigued by the language, precisely because of its stalwart resistance to comfortable classification. And Sapir sensed resemblances that have eluded almost everybody else. He wrote a four-volume manuscript dictionary of comparative Nadene, one volume of which is devoted to cross-comparisons between Haida, Tlingit and the Athapaskan languages on the one hand and Chinese and its cousins on the other. Sapir was enthusiastic enough about Haida-Tibetan comparisons to write to his colleague Alfred Kroeber about them in 1921. "Reading Tibetan text," he says, "gives you precisely the same feeling as reading Haida text."[18]

Modern students of linguistics, trained on more conservative taxonomies, often smile and squirm at these suggestions. But Sapir was neither an amateur nor a crank; he was arguably the most gifted, literate and humane scholar yet to make a serious study of Native American languages, and we should leave him to discuss these questions with his peers.

In a deeper sense, no matter what classification system we use, and no matter how fragmentary or poor our historical records, it remains the case that all human languages are related – and all human literatures too – because all human beings are related. All human beings, let us remember, are *closely* related; and all human languages are born, bear their fruit and die in the minds and mouths of human beings.

Skaay, the poet and scholar, also insisted, like Edward Sapir, the scholar and poet, that divergent, widely separated things can still form very large and meaningful wholes – as we shall see.

        ➤   ➤   ➤

The histories of languages can frequently be sketched, in the barest outlines, by comparing one language with another. We can guess at the history of stories by comparing oral literatures too, but this is not enough. To write the history of art, we need real artworks. To write the history of literature, we need real works of literature as well. The first texts transcribed in Haida are those transcribed by Swanton in September 1900. This appears, at first, to be the limit of our knowledge. As it turns out, we can reach perhaps half a century farther back.

Sghaagya of the Yaakkw Gitinaay was a lively, widely travelled old warrior and trader, born about 1825 in the village of Ttsaa'ahl on the outer coast of Haida Gwaii. In December 1900, he dictated ten autobiographical stories to Swanton. In so doing, he became the first and most prolific Haida autobiographer. He dictated two brief *qqaygaang* too, but that is not a form he seemed to love. He excels at another kind of story, known in Haida as *gyaahlghalang*. To speak in borrowed genres, and therefore tongue-in-cheek, though not dishonestly, Sghaagya is one of the two principal authors of Haida nonfiction.[19] (The other is Kilxhawgins of Ttanuu, whom we will meet in due course.)

Sghaagya is no poet, but one of the most compelling tales that he told Henry Moody and John Swanton centers on a poem. The poem differs radically in language and in style from the story in which it appears, and that is one of the reasons to think it is a genuine quotation. When the poem was composed and first performed, Sghaagya was a young man, but he was there to hear it.

Families on the north and west coasts of Haida Gwaii, Sghaagya says, became embroiled in a feud which was largely fought across moiety lines. Since every Haida has a mother of one moiety and a father of the other, such a feud tears families apart, pitting sons against their fathers, men against the brothers of their lovers, husbands against the brothers of their wives. Sghaagya summarized one of several outbreaks of this feud with words that will do for them all: *Ga aahljaaw yuujaaw at gyaahlghalangaay ttla laagang*: "It was a terrible disaster, but the story is a good one even so."[20]

As the tale nears its climax, a man of Sghaagya's family, the Yaakw Gitinaay, Eagle side, has shot a member of the Kyaanusili family, Raven side. In turn, the younger brothers of the Kyaanusili man have stabbed a headman of the Eagle side named Gaala, a resident of Ghaw (Ghadaghaaxhiwaas, now Masset), the largest Haida village. At home in his bed, Gaala dies of his wounds. The uncle of the three Kyaanusili men – one of whom is dead, while the other two are wanted for the murder of a headman – now embarks on an effort to make peace. He approaches the town from behind, dancing alone, and singing a dirge.[21] After that, Sghaagya says, *ll kwiisuugang,* "he measured out his words." Those words turn out to be a poem, a political address and a concise allegorical monodrama, all in one. Down feathers – *hltang-ghu* – are the traditional emblem of peace on the Northwest Coast (there are no feathered war bonnets here, nor any peace

---

THE KYAANUSILI PEACE POEM

littlxhagit hl qiyadagan,
Naay Injawa llaana yaguhlsi gha
  gagaalang kkyuwaay at hltangghu kkyuwaay
    kitgitxhan ttlxhagan.
Gagaalang kkyuwaay gut hl qaylgan.
Hltangghu kkyuwaay gut hl qaattlxhaga.

«Gasing llaana ghiida haw aa iijin?»   5

«Kilstlaay hlqin, Gaala dang ghunggha llanaagha iiji.
  Dang ghunggha llanaagha yaguhlsi gha
    gagaalang kkyuwaay kit·ttlxhagan gut
      daa qaydan.
Dang ghungghalang danggi ngaygulgan.
Hltangghu kkyuwaay guthaw daa qaattlxhaga.»

Aa dii ghunggha llaana gwa iija – aa hayingii?[22]   10 pipes). Feathers therefore are central to the theme, contrasting throughout with *gagaalang* or vengeance.

After he had spoken, Sghaagya says, the old man once again began his solitary dance and disappeared. It was quiet for two days, with people hiding in the woods. Then there was one more round of fighting, followed by a difficult but finally successful peace negotiation. Evidently, then, the author of the poem was not just a master of literary structure and political theater but of practical diplomacy as well. Lucky for us that Sghaagya, who was there to hear the poem, repeated the words to John Swanton, and lucky for us that he set them in context. We are missing, it seems, only one vital piece of information. That is the poet's name.

[Ghadaghaaxhiwaas, *c.* 1850]

Princes, I am one of those who are married to your sisters.
At Trophy House in the middle of the town,
    the path of vengeance and the path of feathers
      start and end together.
On the path of vengeance I departed.
By the path of feathers I arrive.

«*What town have I come to?*»   5

«*Prince, my son, this is your father Gaala's town.*
From the middle of your father's town,
    where the path of vengeance starts,
      you departed.
Your fathers were concerned about you.[23]
Now by the path of feathers you arrive.»

Is this my father's town – or someone else's?   10

The Kyaanusili peace poem is as tightly patterned as a sonnet, as symmetrical and strophic as a Greek choral ode, and in its way as richly rhymed as a troubadour song – and yet these patterns, strophes, rhymes, are made primarily of ideas and of images, and only secondarily of sounds. This is *noetic prosody*. Words and phrases are repeated; so therefore are their syntax and their sounds – and the sounds exhibit order, as sounds always do in meaningful speech. But the pattern in the foreground, and the pattern in control, is a pattern made of thought. There is no autonomous arrangement of syllables or stresses, consonants or vowel sounds. In other words, the poem is not composed in verse, in the narrowest sense of the term. Laid out logically on the page, it *looks* like verse, and it is every bit as orderly as verse, but this is music of the mind more than music of the ear. This priority of imagery and syntax over sound is typical of classical Haida literature. It is typical in fact, of the literature of hunting and gathering peoples all throughout the world.

I have not been able to date the Kyaanusili poem precisely, but if Sghaagya was on hand to hear it, it could not have been composed much earlier than 1840. Nor could it be later than 1876, when the first of a series of missionaries took up residence at Ghaw. I estimate the date at 1850. It appears, as such, to be the oldest extant piece of oral literature from the Northwest Coast of North America.[24] It could, by a thin margin, be the oldest surviving piece of native literature from anywhere in Canada.[25]

       ➤   ➤   ➤

The kinds of order we will find in larger works of Haida literature – in Skaay's and Ghandl's poems in particular – are reminiscent of the kind of order present in the Kyaanusili poem. This is true even though the Kyaanusili poem belongs to another genre, and here where the scale is smaller, the patterns are tighter. In all these works, whatever their size, patterns of vision, patterns of thought, are more potent than patterns of sound.

In chapter 3 we heard the long first movement of the first narrative suite that Skaay performed for Henry Moody and John Swanton. It is the story of Nang Ttl Dlstlas, the One They Hand Along – who according to a rumor, written in Swanton's hand on the back of Daxhiigang's drawing, is in some sense the Dogfish Woman's brother. Skaay's second suite, like the first, is in three parts. It begins with what is now a familiar phrase, *Ll gidaagang wansuuga.* The opening movement, lasting something over an hour, tells the tale of a boy who is abandoned by his family, then acquires material wealth and spiritual power, marries two non-human wives and is finally reunited with his people. The second movement tells the story of a man who marries a sow grizzly, is killed by her for infidelity and avenged by their two sons: grizzly cubs who kill their mother after she has killed their father. The tiny closing movement (much to Swanton's surprise in October 1900, and much to the surprise of later readers) says nothing about marriage. It tells with innocent simplicity how *Sttluujagadang*, the Redheaded Sapsucker,[26] came by his fine feathers.

Here again, the most apparent structural patterns are intangible: made from images, events and grammatical gestures more than from the sounds of Haida speech. These images or gestures or events form regular patterns of five and three. Such conceptual patterns function like time signatures in music. And if we arrange the poem on the page so this numerical order is manifest, a verse-like structure of five- and three-line stanzas is what we will see. Perhaps it is the first thing we will notice about the poem, but it is not at all the first thing a listener will hear.

The structure is quite real, but if we listen to the poem, what we will hear first is not a numerical pattern. We will hear a tiny myth. We will hear, in other words, a story that unfolds in a musical shape that mimics eternity, not the unmusical march of time. It is a story of a world in which humans, however long their history, however rich their culture, have at best a minor place. The full text follows, in Haida and English translation.

STTLUUJAGADANG [*The Qquuna Cycle,* § 2.3]
Skaay of the Qquuna Qiighawaay

Anang qqaayghudyis haw,
qqan aa qqaayghudaayang wansuuga.
Lla guut lla qaaganggwaangas
Sttluujagadang aa.
Ll ttaaghun dlsguxhan llagha gawus.

Gyaanhaw unsiiya gu qayt yuuwan qqalgawgyagangas.
Gyagaang lla kkutdlskidas.
Gyaan lla kkuudadighandixhan,
giina ll suudas,
«*Dang tsin·gha quunigaay gwahlang dang qaattsixhalga.*»   10

Gyaan gii lla qiixhagasi.
Gam giina gut qqaahlghaghangas.
Gyaan ising gangaang giina ll suuwudaghaay dluu
qaydaay naxhul xhiilaayasi gii lla qiixattsiyaay dluu
tajxwaa nang ghaadaghaghaagha sqqin gangaang ghiida qqaawas.

Gyaan ll qattsaayas.
Nang qqayas anggha ghuuda skajiwaay ghii daayaangisi.
Gut ghiista lla lla dangttsisatliihliyaay dluu
ghin ll xiyaay ttaaghun lla ttawustaasi.
Waaaaa.   20

Gyaan ll kkiida ising waaghii lla giijas.
Gyaan lla lla tlghuuhlghadlstlas.
Sagwii lla lla sghiit hltabxiyaangdas.

Gyaan han lla lla suudas,

170

[Hlghagilda, October 1900]

There was something just awash –
　a grassy place, remaining just awash, they say.
He was always going back and forth along it –
Sapsucker was, that is.
He didn't have a feather to his name.

Then up above there was a big spruce sloughing off its skin.
He whacked it with his beak.
And as he drummed his beak against it,
something said,
«Your father's father asks you in.»　　　　　　　　10

Then he looked for what had spoken.
No one was there.
Then, after something said the same thing again,
when he peeked inside the hollow of the tree,
someone shrunken and sunken, white as a gull, sat at the back.

Then he stepped inside.
The elder took the lid off a little round basket.
After he had opened up five nested one inside the another,
he presented him with feathers for his wings.
Oooooooooooh my!　　　　　　　　20

Then he gave him tailfeathers too.
Then he shaped him with his hands.
He colored the upper part of him red.

Then he said to him,

«Hay ttakkin·gha hittaghan 〈hl〉 na qayt.
Hawhaw giina gagi diiga daa iijiniittsi.»

Gyaan ll qaasuwalasi.
Gyaan ll xidas.
Gyaan tlagu ll waagansas gangaang
qaydaay gii agang lla ttahlghaasgitsi,   30
gyaan lla kkuudadigangasi.

Haw tlan ll ghiida.[27]

«Now, my little grandson, you should go.
This is why you have been with me.»

Then he went back out,
and then he flew,
and then he did the same thing as before.
He clutched the tree,   30
and then he struck it with his beak.

And so it ends.

8   The Epic Dream

LET US RETURN now to Sunday, 14 October 1900: a quiet day in the mission village of Skidegate. After three weeks in the Islands, Swanton is writing a nine-page letter to Boas – a letter we have peeked at once already. It is the one in which Swanton first mentions his work with Skaay:

I can already report considerable progress. My interpreter is an excellent young fellow who has helped me to a very fair start in the language.... Monday, as Jackson [Sghiidagits] was too lazy or too grasping to tell us any more, I made arrangements with an old man in the village who has a crippled back but is admitted on all hands to tell the old legends very correctly.... It seems that a certain set of tales were told by the Haida and always in a definite order, though I do not know whether they have anything to do with each other beyond this.... I imagine that this series is a kind of Haida saga common to all of the race and independent of the clan legends. All of these the old man has promised to tell, and I consider him quite a find.... My old man says he has still longer stories of wars between the different towns, which I shall move heaven and earth to secure "in the original." My method of taking down texts is not perhaps what you would altogether recommend, but under the circumstances I think it is best. The story teller first repeats a short section of his story which my interpreter then dictates to me very slowly and I take down.... I find that the old man easily gets reconciled to frequent pauses while I think it would be very difficult to get him to tell me directly, slow enough to get it all in. So far the plan has worked admirably.[1]

It worked so admirably, in fact, that by the beginning of November, Swanton had recorded Skaay's complete extant works, a total of some 7000 lines of oral poetry.

In the meantime, Swanton had made one other important connection. He had befriended Charles Frederic Newcombe (1851–1924), a Scottish-born physician turned natural historian, who was then buying Haida artifacts on contract for a number of museums.[2] Newcombe and Swanton are two of the most devoted foreign students Haida culture has ever had. But Swanton turned his concentrated year in Haida Gwaii into three thick books and a couple of thin ones. Newcombe on the other hand spent twelve or fifteen seasons in the Islands, accumulating massive notes on Haida history, geography, zoology, botany and art, and published next to nothing. Swanton turned to him at first for help in satisfying Boas's requests for artifacts. In time, he would turn to Newcombe for ethnobotanical specimens, for identifications of plants, shellfish and birds, for maps of empty village sites, and much else. He was already making excuses to Boas – in the same long letter of 14 October – explaining his decision to put off several tasks, especially buying older artifacts.

The texts keep me too busy, besides, and I care more about them.... I have not investigated many of the problems, architectural and other, which you set before me in your letter because I am too busy with the stories and the language.... If the stories keep me as busy as I have been the past week, other matters will be crowded out.

Sundays – because the missionary discouraged Swanton's teachers from working on that day – became the anthropologist's best day for writing letters. His next report to Boas therefore comes exactly a week later, on Sunday, October 21st:

I am especially delighted over the discovery of this "Haida Epic," a sequence of five stories. I have three of these complete in Haida and sixty-nine pages of another. The Raven story comes last. If nothing interferes I shall have them all by the end of this week.

Skaay did indeed tell Swanton five long stories in addition to *Xhuuya Qaagaangas* or *Raven Travelling*. Three of the five stories are three-part suites or trilogies; the others can be heard as two long, single movements. And *Raven Travelling*, as Skaay chose to tell it, is itself a five-part suite. But Swanton's letters make it crystal clear that Skaay was not dredging half-forgotten tales one by one from a cluttered memory, nor was he assembling episodes at random. Skaay, not Swanton, was in control, and Skaay mapped the whole dictation project out for Swanton in advance. He told Swanton what was on the program before his concert series began.

Later on, when he was making his translations, Swanton had trouble understanding how even the individual trilogies hung together – but if Skaay said what Swanton thought he was saying, then to Skaay *the entire series,* including the three trilogies, is one large work. If that is what it is, it is a Haida epic poem -- or a mythological partita for solo speaking voice – about ten hours long. That would make it close to half the length of the *Odyssey.* And if that is what is it, we should learn how to read it.

On Monday, October 29th, Swanton wrote to his new friend Newcombe, speaking with a freedom he was rarely willing to risk when writing to Boas:

I have nine or ten stories covering in the neighborhood of four hundred pages. I have a poetic feeling about my work, as if I were constructing a nation's literature or rather like Homer collecting and arranging a literature already constructed. I have the whole of the saga or epic and am now adding short figurative tales, many of which are however of great interest. Wednesday I shall begin to work out the English.... I hope to have the spirit to infuse into the body you are so patiently putting together.[3]

Three weeks later – on Sunday, November 18th – he reported to Boas again:

I have now become so familiar with the Haida phonetics that I can take down forty-five pages a day, an increase of about fifty per cent. I finished taking stories from the Skedans man [Skaay] ... and have been working with one from the west coast [Ghandl]. I must have at least six or seven hundred pages of manuscript by this time and shall probably increase it above a thousand here in Skidegate....

I have the words of thirteen cradle songs from the west coast with the promise of more. Of course, and much to my regret, I can do nothing with the music, which is very sweet....

I am somewhat appalled by the amount of manuscript which I have to translate. I do not see that I can get away to Masset before February....

The Bureau of Ethnology, on Swanton's instructions, sent part of his salary to him and part of it to his mother, and the American Museum opened an account with a Victoria bank on which Swanton could draw for research expenses. He paid his tutor, interpreter and coworker Henry Moody $1.50 per day and kept him busy six full days a week. He paid poets, singers and storytellers 20¢ per hour and budgeted $35 per month for this purpose. If we compare these rates to Swanton's own workload and salary, we will find that he was paying his Haida colleagues pretty much the same hourly rate he was making himself.[4] But the size of the task he had undertaken, and the amount he stood to learn from a few old men and women inhabiting the wreckage of a preliterate civilization, continually amazed him. On Tuesday, December 4th, he wrote Boas a 12-page letter, saying among other things:

The chief anxiety I now have is about time. Since the first of October, I have put in nearly six solid hours a day taking down texts and must have in the neighborhood of one thousand pages. I know of only two [mythological] stories which I have not in my collection, though undoubtedly a very careful canvass would reveal more. I am now upon the war stories, and the man who is telling them [Sghaagya of the Yaakw Gitinaay] will probably fill in the entire week that way. I am continually impressed with the importance of taking these texts. Only today a historical point was discovered in one of the war stories which my informant had forgotten in every other connection. Besides a great many new words turn up in them which have dropped from the modern language…. But meantime I have only had opportunity to get a small amount of my material translated, and at the rate we usually do it, it will be far into February before I can complete it…. That would not leave time to repeat my work at Masset or begin to…. Now, shall I hurry through, take my time at Skidegate, or may I dare to hope for an extension?… If I could stay here next summer while the Indians are away and put in my time studying what material I have gathered, very likely a couple of months of work and questioning in the fall would clear things up and I could be home not later than January 1902. Privately, I do not want to remain isolated for so long. I simply write what it seems may be necessary to complete my work…. You told me to be thorough, and I am trying to be so. In one point I cannot be thorough, and that is when it comes to the songs, for I am no musician. I am satisfying myself with taking the words….

In mid December, Swanton stopped taking texts and began working over his transcriptions word by word with Henry Moody. Early the next year – another Sunday, 13 January 1901 – he brought Boas up to date:

During the last four or five weeks I have been doing nothing but translate, and there are still about eight days of this kind of work before me…. My interpreter and I have now got matters running very smoothly when it comes to taking down texts, and I cannot bear to leave until my resources run dry….

On the following Wednesday, Swanton was ill as well as exhausted. The letter he wrote to Boas that night is scrawled, partly in pencil, and the prose is running wild, but in the midst of his delirium he was taking an even longer perspective:

I have got to that point in my career on this coast when my career seems to call me to a seriatim conquest of legends, beginning at Skidegate, extending to Masset and Kaigani and thence continuing its papery way from the Tungas [Tongass] to Copper River.[5] At the same [time], I should shrink from the undertaking and I expect I shall be back within a year. But supposing *I cannot make a complete sweep of Masset and Kaigani before it is time to return, it would break my heart to feel there was a story left that I had failed to gather.... Haida mythology, I want to state here, can* not *be defined as animal worship. The Haida pantheon was decorated just as lavishly as the Roman, and they seem even to have risen to the level of an Olympian Jove.*

On the heels of this fevered celebration of a culture he had just begun to know, Swanton suddenly lost heart. On Sunday, February 10th, just before his 28th birthday, and perhaps under pressure from Boas,[6] he had in essence reversed his position:

I think it is entirely possible to put in too much time taking texts. I can take new ones now with very little trouble, but it would only be adding the known to the known. After having taken a good number of texts, unless one has unlimited time, it seems to me just as well to take the rest in English.

That is a plan which Swanton did, alas, put into practice among the Alaskan Haida six months later, and again in 1904 during his brief stay with the Tlingit. But so long as he remained in Haida Gwaii – this February letter notwithstanding – his idealism held, and he continued to transcribe in the original virtually every story he heard.

The gloomy coastal winter and long hours of labor had nevertheless taken their toll, and when he wrote to Boas on Friday, March 1st, he said, "I get along very well now but I am afraid I should find trouble in getting through another winter in isolation, especially on the Alaskan coast."

Four days after that, his sense of mission had returned:

I have worked about three times as hard as I expected and twice as hard as I ought, but it did not seem as if I could let anything I heard of go. The result is contained in about seventeen hundred mss. pages, about fifteen hundred of which I forward by the next steamer.... Day after tomorrow I have arranged to leave for Masset where I shall stay until the first of June. Then I propose to return to Skidegate, where I hope to find and communicate with Dr Newcombe.... Up to the very end my time was practically absorbed in text taking and translation of the same....

My judgement in regard to this work is as follows. To do the best work and secure the best all around results, some one person ought to take the north west work, or perhaps the Tsimshian, Haida and Tlingit work, together. By taking it in charge I mean being on the spot for most of each year, if not [continuously] for several years, taking texts and investigating all branches of Indian life. I have spent about five months now and have just got to where I can do comparatively rapid and effective work. My ear is now fairly well broken in to the sounds, and if I work at Masset or among the Tlingit I can work five times as fast as a person of my calibre sent there afresh. One thing leads to and bears upon another in such a way that to make the most intelligent study he should go back and forth from one tribe to another. At my single sitting, I have to work much in the dark....

I hope the boxes will arrive safely, especially the manuscripts, which indeed must arrive safely. I would not want to repeat my work contained in them for any money.

⸱   ⸱   ⸱

Swanton left Hlghagilda as planned, going north by dugout canoe as far as Naay Kun and walking west along the beaches,
30 km or so, to the old Haida metropolis of Ghadaghaaxhiwaas –
Masset to the Europeans.[7] There he spent three months wholly
absorbed once again in the task he had set himself, doing nothing but taking dictation. He transcribed stories from five men
during this period, and two of them – the two most prolific
mythtellers he met in Haida Gwaii – are of particular interest.
One was Kingagwaaw of the Ghaw Sttlan Llanagaay, of the
Raven side, from the village of Yan. The other was Haayas, head
of the Eagle family called Hliiyalang Qiighawaay and titular
head of the long-abandoned village of Hliiyalang.[8]

In the nineteenth century, even southern Haida found the
name Ghadaghaaxhiwaas (which means White Hillside) an un-
necessary mouthful. They routinely used the nickname Ghaw
(meaning Inlet or Bay). Before the missionaries came, Ghaw was
one of the largest aboriginal settlements on the Northwest Coast
and one of the largest stable settlements of hunter-gatherers
anywhere in the world. John Work, a nineteenth-century trader
with a keen interest in Haida demographics, estimated that there
were 160 houses and some 2400 people there in the 1830s, but
these figures are plausible only for "greater Ghadaghaaxhiwaas,"
including perhaps half a dozen villages ranged around the mouth
of Masset Sound. In 1883, after smallpox had emptied the outlying towns and brought all the survivors to Ghaw, there were 65
houses standing in the village proper, and most of these were
new, but only forty or fifty were occupied. The population then
was perhaps 400.[9]

Swanton found lodging at Ghaw with Daxhiigang's cousin
Kihlguulins (1868–1935). Kihlguulins's father, Gwaayang Gwanhlin (c. 1812–1894), was hereditary head of the Stastas family of
the Eagle side. When he was baptized at Ghaw in 1885, Gwaayang Gwanhlin elected to be called by the same name as Queen
Victoria's son and heir, Albert Edward, Prince of Wales. As a sur-

name, he chose Edenshaw: an anglicized form of the Tlingit name Idansaa, his hereditary title in the matrilineal line.

By the old way of reckoning, Kihlguulins's primary parent was his mother, Sinhlagutgaang of the Yaakw Llaanas,[10] who was Gwaayang Gwanhlin's second wife. Gwaayang Gwanhlin's rightful heir was not his own son Kihlguulins but his sister's son Daxhiigang – and Kihlguulins was rightfully the heir not to his father's name and position but to those of his mother's brother instead. Kihlguulins was baptized nonetheless as Henry Edenshaw. Accepting that surname meant rejecting the old system, in which the name was immutably the property of people *on the other side*. It appears that no Christian missionary posted to the Haida country ever doubted for a moment that a right and proper life required patrilineal inheritance and the nominal preeminence of the male line.

On Sunday, March 31st, after three weeks at Ghaw, Swanton reported his progress to Boas and outlined his plans:

I began text taking the fifteenth and have amassed about five hundred and fifty pages since then.... I do not know how much I could collect before the first of June, but according to present indications it might amount to two thousand more.

Now that I am here on the spot, have the text taking business reduced to the easiest terms and yet have plenty of money to continue the work, it seems to me it would be a shame to break off as early as I must to be in Washington by July....

The following programme is the one I should like to fill out before returning.

a) Collect Masset texts until the end of May.

b) Go to Skidegate the first of June, meet Dr Newcombe if he comes up, complete a little of my work which is left over and ship what articles I am having made.

c) Return to Masset, complete the translation of my Masset texts, complete my investigations of the customs, tabus and so forth, and

work a while with the assistance of Henry Edenshaw [Kihlguulins]
upon the language, in which the tenses are very puzzling....

d) I should like to follow that up with a trip to the Kaigani coun-
try....

e) It will be an easy matter when I am among the Kaigani to se-
cure one or two Stickeen [Stikine] or other Tlingit texts.... I am rather
anxious to have one or two texts to compare with my Haida.... Unless
I make a very prolonged stay in the Kaigani country I shall be through
with all my work by the end of summer....

To fulfill this plan, Swanton needed a further extension of his
leave from the Bureau of Ethnology. Boas secured it on Swanton's behalf and replenished his Victoria expense account with
funds from the Museum. He was not now expected back in
Washington before the end of September.

On Sunday, May 12th, Swanton had been nearly eight
months in Haida Gwaii. He had not, so far as we know, come
there consciously intent on doing nothing except documenting
Haida oral literature, but that is where the whole of his energy
had gone. As he put it to Boas:

I have written nearly three thousand pages in Haida and have trans-
lated most of the same.... I have found it impossible to resist the temp-
tation to get any new-old story I hear about, and text taking has con-
sequently monopolized ninety-nine one-hundredths of my time....

Another thought that my studies this year have awakened is that
in commonly supposing scriptures to be things of comparatively re-
cent historical development we are exactly wrong. It seems to me that,
although unwritten, the entire life of an ancient Haida was referred to
nothing but scriptures or what may fairly be called such.[11]

At the end of February 1901, Swanton imagined he had captured these scriptures in written form. By the end of May, he
wondered whether all his work had been in vain. He had still

heard nothing about the 1500 pages of transcript and translation mailed to New York three months before. Only his steady involvement in new work tempered his anxiety over the possible loss of the old.

Sunday, June 2nd:

I am worried that you say nothing of my manuscripts.... I had almost as soon drop out two years of my life as to lose them.... By the first of July I hope to be about through translating the stories still left and ready for my Alaskan trip.... By the first of August I hope to reach Inverness[12] on the Skeena where Charlie Edenshaw [Daxhiigang], who is doing carving for me, will be camping during the summer. After shipping my purchases from there I shall go to Port Simpson and thence to Victoria and home.

Mail normally travelled between Haida Gwaii and New York in 1901 at the same speed it did in 1991: two weeks each direction. But the bundle of pencilled phonetics encoding the voices of Ghandl and Skaay took twelve weeks to make the same trip. Boas reported its arrival on May 27th. After a few days basking in relief, Swanton was faced with worry of another kind. Thursday, June 20th, he was back at Hlghagilda, checking details with Henry Moody and deep in discussion with Ghandl about the structure of the universe. Then:

I have just learned that small-pox has broken out in Alaska, and has been brought to the Skeena. Charlie Edenshaw has been quarantined....

The century of grief was not yet over. The scare, in this case, was short-lived, but Swanton registered the message: living voices are just as easy to lose, and just as impossible to replace, as voices transcribed onto paper. At the end of June, despite the smallpox warning, Swanton sailed north with Newcombe to visit the Alaskan Haida villages. When he finally headed east, at the beginning of September, he carried 2000 pages of fresh text and the knowledge that Daxhiigang – who had just turned 62 – was still alive and well and carving.

Back in what is called the civilized world, the principal item of news on Swanton's return was the assassination in Buffalo, New York, of President William McKinley.

, , ,

Swanton saw his southern Haida notebooks again on Friday, 18 October 1901, seven months after he had mailed them from Haida Gwaii. He was freshly installed in his office at the BAE in Washington, and Boas shipped the parcel, still smelling of wood smoke, fish and beach weed, down from New York. Swanton was eager to get to work, but now the Bureau had him in its hands as well as on its payroll, it found things for him to do. He complained of these delays, Boas lobbied on his behalf, and he was freed at last to work on the Haida materials at the beginning of December. The first task he set himself was typing out, in Haida, a fair copy of the poems Skaay had spoken to him fourteen months before. On Saturday, December 7th, he wrote to Boas:

I am working away copying the Raven story and shall have it done in a little more than a week. I believe, however, it will take a whole year to copy off all of my texts – probably more....

The Raven was reconstituting himself in a sixth-floor cubicle on F Street in Washington, DC, a few hundred yards from Theodore Roosevelt's White House.[13] But Swanton was the juniormost employee of the Bureau of American Ethnology and, by his own account, "the only member of it who had even what purported to be an anthropological education."[14] Swanton's superiors at the Bureau grumbled from time to time that he was still working for Boas, not for them. And bit by bit, Boas proved that even he had no idea what Swanton really saw in all those Haida texts. The gulf between the elfin, unassertive Dr Swanton and his hale and hearty colleagues deepened, but Swanton persevered. Saturday, 2 August 1902:

Since the first or middle of May I have copied and translated on the typewriter about one thousand pages of my texts. I expect to have all the Skidegate texts copied and translated before the end of November.... Six months from that time, if I work steadily, the Masset texts might be completed.

Two other tasks filled Swanton's time while he was typing these texts and revising his translations. He was writing his own first book, *Contributions to the Ethnology of the Haida,* and from the summer of 1902 to the fall of 1903, he also served as editor of the Swedenborg Scientific Association's quarterly journal, *The New Philosophy.*

Late in 1903, he had finished drafts of all the Haida texts and what he thought was a final draft of the ethnology as well – but he was not through having to defend what he had edited and written. As early as the end of 1902, Boas had asked him to remove all Haida place names and words from the ethnology. Swanton diplomatically refused. Then there were disputes over who should publish the works and how. In May 1903, Boas agreed to allow the Bureau to publish the Skidegate texts – in the mistaken belief that they were the least important. He held out for both the ethnology and the Masset texts, which he wanted to include in the American Museum's series entitled *The Jesup North Pacific Expedition.*

Nothing in this arrangement suggested to Boas that he should relinquish editorial control over any of Swanton's Haida publications, and he continued to offer instruction and advice on the Skidegate texts. But Boas was baffled, far more than Swanton was, by the size and shape of many of the stories. He asked

Swanton to abridge and rearrange these texts, and to sever Skaay's trilogies into individual tales. Swanton admitted his own inability to explain why or how the stories were linked, but he stood by the mythtellers, insisting that the texts be printed bilingually and in full, and that most of Skaay's work be organized in print in the same way Skaay presented it aloud.

Once the texts were published, Swanton gave up quarreling with Boas's harsh view that Skaay's trilogies, and even the components of the trilogies, were linked by nothing but the storyteller's whim.[15] But so long as Skaay's legacy was actively under his care, he refused to give in. Swanton was a quiet and deeply courteous man, and the letter he wrote to Boas on Monday, 12 October 1903, is the only one I have ever seen in which he flatly rejects his imperious teacher's authority.

Dear Prof. Boas:

I will answer your questions categorically.

1) The woodpecker [Sapsucker] episode at the end of the story of The One They Abandoned for Eating the Flipper of a Hair Seal belongs to this story according to my informant. I think it should be left where it is, inserting a line before it or indicating in some other way that it stands somewhat by itself.

2) ... I do not wish to remove the story of Ḡodañxē'wat [Ghudangxhiiwat] from the Skedans series of tales where it belongs....[16]

The story of Ghudangxhiiwat, or Quartz Ribs, which Swanton mentions in this letter, is the second movement of Skaay's third trilogy.[17]

For all his trust in Skaay, Swanton did permit – in fact, he created – one important departure from Skaay's plan as he had earlier understood it. He collated two large versions of *Raven Travelling* – one composed of all the episodes he had heard from Skaay, Ghandl and other mythtellers at Hlghagilda, and the other composed of all the episodes he had heard from

Kingagwaaw, Haayas and others at Ghaw. Much as he admired Skaay and wanted to believe that he had narrated "a kind of Haida saga," he still accepted Boas's teaching that each aboriginal nation of the Northwest Coast possessed its own ideal, communal version of the tale of the trickster. Swanton thought of this accumulated narrative more as oral scripture than as a kind of communal mindprint, but he accepted that it existed. And he accepted that one of the challenges of anthropology was to reconstruct it, much as Elias Lönnrot claimed to have reconstructed the ideal *Kalevala* out of fragments he had heard from many different Finnish singers – and much, perhaps, as the editors of the Pentateuch had conflated into one standard version the inconsistent texts that later scholars have tried to sort back out again.

Sometime after writing his enthusiastic letters of October 1900, Swanton also became convinced that *Raven Travelling* was after all something separate from Skaay's monumental sequence, and not its final act. He placed it first, not last, in his edition of the Skidegate texts, and he confirmed at least three times that this decision was deliberate.[18] It would be nice to know exactly when and why he came to this conclusion, but the evidence is scant. I suspect he had made up his mind on the issue well before the end of 1901, when he started copying texts in Washington, because he made a point, then, of beginning with *Raven Travelling*. My hunch is that Swanton changed his thinking on this issue very early, perhaps during the last days of October 1900, when Skaay was actually telling the story. There is no doubt that Skaay did put it last when he unfolded what he chose of his life's work to Moody and Swanton – but his performance of the poem took a couple of strange turns, as we shall see.

We know, then, that in order to hear or read Skaay's version of *Raven Travelling*, we have to disentangle it from the episodes told by Ghandl and others, which Swanton strung together into one long tale. This is not hard to do, because Swanton scrupulously labelled his additions to Skaay's text. But several questions still remain. Is Skaay's large cycle of stories really an artistic whole? If so, is *Raven Travelling* really part of it? If so, does it come first in the series or last? Before we tackle these questions, let us see what else John Swanton's professional career reveals about the study of Native American oral literature.

In October 1903, Swanton was still making corrections to his typescript of the Masset texts. He was also still hoping to return to the Northwest Coast to do comprehensive research on all the oral literatures of the region. These plans got scant encouragement from the new director of the Bureau, William Henry Holmes.[19] Boas was no longer the perfect ally either. Boas had bitterly and publicly opposed the appointment of Holmes, and relations between the two were accordingly chilly. Worse, Boas himself still had no grasp of the importance of Swanton's encounters with the Haida poets nor even the real focus of Swanton's interests. No one, it seems, understood either the work he had already done or his reasons for wanting to do so much more of it. Under these conditions, he allowed himself at last to think of something other than that work, and in December 1903, in his thirtieth year, John Swanton was married. Days later, he left on his second and last trip to the Northwest Coast, to study Tlingit. But the Bureau of Ethnology had given him a mere four months to do a job that needed years, and Swanton could not work night and day transcribing and translating texts in southeastern Alaska as he had in Haida Gwaii, because he and his bride, Alice Barnard, were not only on an anthropological field trip; they were also on their honeymoon.

The Swantons paid a brief visit to Newcombe in Victoria just before Christmas 1903, then crossed to Vancouver where they stayed through New Year's Eve. By luck, Henry Moody was in town, and he and Swanton spent several evenings deep in conversation. Moody explained to Swanton some of the complexities of stick-gambling – crucial to understanding some of the stories – and tried once again to clarify the basics of potlatch etiquette. Then the discussion turned to metaphysics. Swanton asked about the difference between *ghahlanda*, the life-essence or parallel form; *xhants*, the reincarnatable soul; and *qqatxhana*, the ghost or spirit that hovers near a body after death, and he asked about the relationship between two of the most important and elusive beings in Haida mythology: the Raven and Ttsam'aws, the Snag. Moody's answers to these questions – scribbled hastily by Swanton onto a couple of scraps of paper and then recounted in an eight-page letter to Boas, written on New Year's Eve – have remained important keys to the interpretation of classical Haida literature and visual art.[20] There was much more to ask, and there was no end of other things to learn, but this was Swanton's last chance to talk with Henry Moody. It was, in fact, his last conversation with any member of the Haida nation.

Swanton was in Sitka from early January to the middle of March 1904, then at Wrangell through the end of April. He met some very capable mythtellers in the Tlingit country, just as he had in Haida Gwaii three years before. One of these was Deikinaak'w of the Kookhíttaan. Another was an old woman known as Léek of the Kaasx'agweidí, the first female mythteller Swanton ever recorded at length. But whether either of these was really on a par with Skaay and Ghandl is impossible to say. Swanton made no effort to record the full repertoire of Deikinaak'w. Sadder yet, though Léek told him thirty-five stories, he recorded them only in abridged English paraphrase. Never again would Swanton live the way he did during his year in Haida Gwaii – as if nothing in the world were more important than to record what a Native American oral poet wanted to say in precisely the way that poet wanted to say it.[21]

Another compromise awaited him back in Washington in the summer of 1904. The Bureau's new chief could see no reason to use his congressional appropriation typesetting hundreds of pages of Haida, which only a few Indians, linguists and missionaries could read. The Skidegate texts were therefore published in 1905 with fewer than fifty pages of Haida, where there should have been 400.[22] Despite Swanton's work on their behalf, Skaay

of the Qquuna Qiighawaay and Ghandl of the Qayahl Llaanas –
who are, on the evidence, two of the finest poets ever to live in
North America – have languished in manuscript to this day.

Swanton remained at the Bureau of Ethnology all his working life, and the Bureau assigned him many other tasks which
drew his attention away from oral literature and away from the
Northwest Coast. He studied some twenty Native American languages in depth,[23] wrote half a dozen works on indigenous cultures of the southeastern United States, and at the end of his career, he compiled the Smithsonian's large but bloodless work of
reference, *Indian Tribes of North America* (1952). A younger, more
idealistic Swanton had railed against such books half a century
before, lamenting that the Bureau and its parent the Smithsonian had lapsed into institutions "where editors and private sec-
retaries flourish while scientific workers are back-listed, where
compilation is made to count for more than original research,
and where talk runs to saving a hundred dollars instead of solv-
ing ethnological problems."[24]

Between 1908 and 1930, Swanton recorded substantial bodies
of text in the Natchez and Koasati languages. Like the best of his
Haida texts, these have remained unpublished except in translation. Swanton's work in the Southeast never put him into contact with a storyteller or poet of the stature of Ghandl or Skaay,
but he found there a field in which to practice his overtly unin-
trusive, even courteous, brand of ethnology. His colleague Alfred
Kroeber assessed this work in 1940:

*Field work by direct inquiry and observation, such as was and still is
largely possible in the Plains and Plateau, Southwest and California,
Northwest and Arctic, was enormously diluted in its possibilities for
the Southeastern tribes. It was like working over tailings instead of following a fresh vein. The cultural material ... is imbedded in a matrix
of long acculturation;... the most authentic data are often to be found
in the written records of preanthropological centuries.*

Such a field discourages and repels the average American ethnologist. It uncovered a streak of historical genius in Swanton. What informants could not give, good documents did yield, in many cases; and the information was one, two, three, and even four centuries nearer the purely aboriginal. He mastered the documentary sources..., synthesized and interpreted them, fused them with the products of field work. The result is something unique in American anthropology....[25]

▸   ▸   ▸

In 1905, when the Bureau had failed to publish the Skidegate texts as Swanton intended, he sent his unpublished Haida typescript up to Boas, hoping that his mentor would somehow steer it into print. It remained in Boas's office, on the seventh floor of the Journalism Building at Columbia University, for nearly forty years – and Boas, to the end, remained oblivious to its merits. Over the years, Boas seemed to grow increasingly sympathetic to the kind of work Swanton had done in Haida Gwaii. Yet all that while, working in the same room with the evidence, he remained unaware that Swanton had done it.[26]

"The importance of the record in the original language has become more and more apparent," Boas wrote in 1914. "Even the best translation cannot give us material for the study of literary form – a subject that has received hardly any attention, and the importance of which ... cannot be overestimated."[27] Boas repeated this sentiment now and again, sometimes with considerable eloquence,[28] yet the difference between oral and written literature continued to elude him. Time and again he urged his colleagues to do what Swanton had already tried to do: study the artistic side of Native American narrative. But he regularly coupled this injunction with advice that rendered it void.

"Since 1901 I have done next to nothing but copy, correct and translate texts," wrote Swanton in 1905. "I can never do my best work unless I am all alone by myself."[29]

"Dr Swanton is an indefatigable worker," Boas wrote in 1910, but "Swanton has not the qualities of a leader.... In his field investigations he is always somewhat one-sided, taking up one line and pursuing it to extremes."[30]

Boas led with great effect, not only in scholarship but in the fight for racial equality and intellectual freedom in the United States – causes that occupied an immense amount of his time from 1900 until his death.[31] But Boas himself had not the qualities of a listener. He lacked Swanton's patience and his self-effacing skill at transcribing oral poetry. He failed to grasp both the point of Swanton's method and the object of his study. And from 1900 to 1923, Boas paid no visits to the Northwest Coast.[32] He continued his encyclopedic studies of Northwest Coast mythology all this while, but he depended on written texts supplied to him in Kwakwala and English by Q'ix̲itasu' (George Hunt) and in English and Tsimshian by Henry Tate.[33] Enthralled by this new way of working, he now devalued the old, insisting that all anthropologists' transcriptions of oral literature were likely to give corrupt results because the process was so slow, and that narratives written directly in aboriginal languages by literate Native Americans were much to be preferred.[34]

Boas was right, of course, that the slow and fussy business of dictation and transcription can smother a good story and stifle a mythteller's skill. But Swanton is not the only anthropologist who overcame this problem. Others also managed to transcribe long and complex works of oral literature with nothing more than pencil and paper and a far from perfect knowledge of the language in which they were working. Edward Sapir performed this feat time and again – with the precocious Ute mythteller and singer Tony Tillohash in 1910, with the Nuuchahnulth elders Saayaacchapis and Qiixxa in 1913–14, with the Hupa shaman Tahseench'e' in 1927, and with two Navajo mythtellers and chanters, Charlie Mitchell and Chiishch'ilíts'ósí (Slim Curly), in 1929. Ruth Bunzel had equally spectacular success in 1926 when she worked with the Zuni mythtellers Nick Tumaka and Leo Zuni. Sapir and Bunzel rarely relied, as Swanton had in Haida

Gwaii, on intermediary listeners. But both of them had the gift of listening, like Swanton, with unflagging attention and genuine delight. The mythtellers they met responded in kind.[35] This symbiosis between mythteller and listener underlies the written record of oral literature.

And Boas was right to insist on the importance of Native American writers and writing. This tradition reaches back at least to the middle of the sixteenth century – to early monuments such as the Quiché Mayan book called *Popol Vuh* – and forward to the work of Boas's own Native American teachers, students and coworkers: John Napoleon Hewitt writing in Tuscarora, Ahyö'iini in Cherokee, Ápétu Wašté (Ella Deloria) in Lakhota, Archie Phinney in Nimipu (Nez Perce), William Jones in Sauk, Hochángkxátega (Sam Blowsnake) in Winnebago, Gwüsk̲'aayn (William Beynon) in Nishga, Q'ix̲itasu' and Pal'nakwala Wakas (Dan Cranmer) in Kwakwala, and Hiixuqqin'is (Alex Thomas) in Nootka. But transcribing oral literature and writing written literature are two quite different tasks. It is probably not an accident that all the polylingual writers on this list did their best transcription work in languages related to but different from their own: Hewitt in Mohawk, Onondaga and Seneca instead of Tuscarora, Jones in Ojibwa rather than Sauk, Gwüsk̲'aayn in Tsimshian rather than Nishga. It was then that they listened most carefully. It was then that, being at least a little unsure of themselves, they resisted the temptation to "improve" the oral text.

In a self-sustaining oral culture, faith, hope, and even charity are invested very differently than in cultures that are learning or have learned the use of writing. A shift from oral to written culture affects the functioning of memory, the understanding of truth, and the place of voice and language in the working of the world. It affects not just the meaning of words but the meaning of language itself. It affects the meaning of meaning. On the Northwest Coast, the shift from oral to written culture was linked to other changes just as rapid and profound. It was linked first of all to a shift from a culture of hunting and gathering to a culture of seasonal wage work and industrial predation – from harvesting for use to harvesting for export. In the world that came with writing, fish and timber go to market, and food and clothing come from stores. It was also linked, in this case, to a catastrophic drop in population, a shift from matrilineal to patrilineal inheritance, and a conceptual inversion of the world. Whole villages of relatives and benefactors – aerial, sylvan and submarine – were displaced by God the father up above, a crucified redeemer on the surface, and a Satan tempting sinners in the shadows and punishing their errors underground. The Americas were invaded on many fronts at once. But there is no such thing as introducing writing into a world of oral poets and hunter-gatherers while holding the other factors of culture the same.

Skaay's voice lay for four decades in Franz Boas's office in inaudible paper form. It could continue to sit in the library forever with precisely the same results – because it is painted over with silence, like the dining room at Emmaus. And so long as the myth, and the truth of the myth, is hidden, everything else that was once in the picture with it will be changed. The cure in Velázquez's case was to remove the editorial accretions and learn to see the painting. I think we can get similar results if we apply the same techniques to one of Skaay's works: if we undo the editorial "improvements" and listen to the poem. The poem, like the painting, has suffered some irreparable damage. Yet the moment we have learned to *see* the painting or to *listen* to the poem, the world breathes again. Imkyánvaan's wish stands a chance of coming true. The spine, if not quite straight, is not so crooked as before. One can begin to think of lily shoots and salmon.

⸙   ⸙   ⸙

There is one more pair of letters important to the story. On 5 February 1942 Boas was 83, retired but still active; Swanton was nearly 69 and still employed at the BAE.

Dear Swanton:

As you remember, I still have your old Haida texts in my care. It has been proposed that material of this kind should be microfilmed. I am not quite certain that it can be done with your manuscript because you used a light blue ribbon, but if it can be done would that be agreeable to you?

I am sorry I never see you any more, but I have not been in Washington for a long time and I do not get about very much nowadays.

With kindest regards,
　　　　Yours very sincerely,
　　　　　　Franz Boas[36]

Swanton answered this letter on February 10th:

Dear Professor Boas:

Please feel free to make any disposition of my Haida text material you desire. I fear much of it is pretty crude but had hoped that it might be good enough for a better linguist to correct....

I thank you for your kind remembrance and reciprocate the wish to meet, although I feel that your time is employed on such important matters that I would hesitate to intrude upon it.... I always think of my association with you as one of the most stimulating chapters in my life, and I know how widely shared that stimulation has been.

With kindest regards, I remain,
　　　　Sincerely yours,
　　　　　　John R. Swanton[37]

Less than a year after this, Boas was dead, and the Haida manuscript was shipped, with a vast number of other papers, to the American Philosophical Society Library, Philadelphia. There it remains – a document potentially as vital – or so I like to think – to the future life of North American culture as any classical manuscript in the Marcian Library at Venice or the Laurentian

Library at Florence is to the continuing self-renewal of the heritage of Europe. As vital and, of course, just as easy to forget.

❧   ❧   ❧

Three questions are still with us. Is Skaay's large cycle of stories really an artistic whole – or was Swanton merely leaping to wild, romantic conclusions in thinking Skaay had promised him a work of epic size? If the cycle is a whole, is *Raven Travelling* really part of it or not? And if it is, does it come first in the series or last?

There are, I suppose, two ways to approach these questions. One is to enumerate and measure all the themes and variations, all the images and characters, and write or draw up the results. Depending on the kind of notation we choose, this will yield a large and impressively tangled chart, a sheaf of interlocking lists or several dozen pages of dense and tedious prose. The other approach is to read the works aloud, over and over, in various combinations, asking the ear and the heart, as well as the mind, what seems to fit. That is closer to the way in which musicians and oral poets normally work, and it seems to me a necessary exercise for everyone who studies oral literature reduced to written form. The first approach may prove things, but I think that only the second can actually convince.

After several years of listening as well as several attempts to draw the chart, I have no doubt the cycle is just as whole as Swanton thought Skaay said it was. It is not a continuous linear thread, like the *Aeneid,* but I think that it is much less episodic than the *Georgics* or the later poems of Ovid. It is a whole made of a few large parts, each made of a small number of smaller parts which are constructed from still smaller parts in their turn. As such, the big poem's architecture is different from what we expect in a sonnet sequence or a cycle of personal lyrics, just as it is different from the structure of a European epic or drama with a single central character. We are better off to compare it with architectural wholes such as Haydn's Opus 33 and Beethoven's

Opus 18 – both of which are integrated series of six four-movement string quartets. Perhaps in its way it is also as integral as J. S. Bach's nearly complete *Art of the Fugue*. But these assertions are not like theorems in geometry or hypotheses in mechanics; they can be "proven" only in the sense that professional competence, personal honor or criminal responsibility are proven. This kind of proof can only occur when there is a jury able and willing to sift the evidence, and a community willing to let the jury decide. Only one such juror was really to be found among all Boas's colleagues. That juror was Edward Sapir.

Like *The Art of the Fugue*, Skaay's Large Poem seems to me convincing on the question of integrity even if its sequence and scope remain a subject of debate. *Die Kunst der Fuge*, after all, was published in 1751. Its order and extent remained unknown until 1983, when the puzzle was solved by the musicologist Gregory Butler.[38] Skaay's work – which has so far been ignored about as thoroughly as Bach's was in the century after his death – could wait as long for answers to some equally plain questions.

And I am satisfied, myself, that *Raven Travelling* stands as a separate work, linked to the larger cycle but not incorporated in it. The Sapsucker episode, which Skaay positioned as a coda to the second part of the Large Poem, is of interest in this regard. Boas thought it a preposterous intrusion. Swanton, while insisting that it stay, did finally consent to say in a note that it "seems altogether out of place here."[39] In fact, it is handsomely balanced by other episodes elsewhere in the poem. It is also one of the links between Skaay's Large Poem and *Raven Travelling*. More such links occur in sections three and four of the cycle. But the outer movements of the poem – sections one and five – are oriented differently. Both begin with the story of a woman and her superhuman son, and both in due course mention *Hiilinga*, the Thunderbird, instead of alluding to *Xhuuya*, the Raven. Both then evoke a nameless, vengeful deity inhabiting the sky, and both conclude with scenes of mass destruction.

SKAAY'S LARGE POEM
An Outline of the Qquuna Cycle

1 First Trilogy

    1.1 *Nang Ttl Dlstlas* = The One They Hand Along

    1.2 *Simnaasum Nang Awgha Daghiyalaghan* = One Who Acquired a Wolverine for a Mother

    1.3 *Sqaghahl Gujaanggha* = Sqaghahl's Daughter

2 Second Trilogy

    2.1 *Xhuut Stlaay Nang Taaga Ttaagha sta Ttl Ttsaa'astagas* = The One They Abandoned for Eating a Seal Flipper

    2.2 *Xhuuwaji Tlaalgha* = The Man Who Married a Grizzly

    2.3 *Sttluujagadang* = Sapsucker

3 Third Trilogy

    3.1 *Quyaa Gyaaghandaal* = Honored Standing Traveller

    3.2 *Ghudangxhiiwat* = Quartz Ribs

    3.3 *Siixha* = Hoverer [Wiigit's Revenge]

4 *Sghaana Ghuunan Qaas* = Spirit-Being Going Naked

    4.1 *Ll Dawghan·ghalang* = His Younger Brothers

    4.2 *Nang Kilstlas at Tangghwan Llaana Gujaanggha* = Voicehandler & Sea Dweller's Daughter

    4.3 *Sqqaxyaaw* = Varied Thrush

5 *Ghahljuung ghii Nang Dlqiis* = Born through a Wound

    5.1 *Qwiis Jin·ghwas haw Ghuxhagangdalga* = The Sky's Rim is a Raging Fire

    5.2 *Gul Qawgha* = Tobacco Seeds

The first, second and fifth parts of the Large Poem are tied to one another in another way. Each opens with the formulaic phrase *Ll gidaagang, wansuuga* – "There was a child of good family, they say." Each then recounts, in a complex, long first movement, the fall and eventual redemption of someone born and raised in fortunate conditions. The third and fourth parts of the cycle begin with different words – and so they must, because these parts speak of the rise to fortune (and the further metamorphosis) of characters who first seem good for nothing.

The chart on the facing page is a simple table of contents of the five-part cycle. This is a far cry from a structural analysis, but it shows the basic narrative plan. There are four fingers of three joints each, and there is a thumb.

The last two digits of this hand – parts four and five of the poem – are straight by European standards. That is to say, European readers commonly perceive that, in these two portions of the cycle, the subdivisions cohere. This makes it easy to describe them as single movements rather than suites – but they too are flexible, jointed structures, and the boundaries between their constituent episodes are clear.

What does it take to induce that sense of coherence in a reader trained on European narrative? The main requirement, it seems, is a persistent central character. In the fourth and fifth parts of the Large Poem, the individual events are often just as startling, by European standards, as anything that happens earlier in the poem, yet the reassuring presence of a single central character has made it relatively easy for Boas, Swanton and others to accept these sections of the poem as wholes. A reader who learns to listen for *thematic* continuity more than for consistency of setting and of character will find that the earlier parts of the Large Poem are just as integral as the later ones. But this means listening to the poem as something like a large piece of chamber music made from nouns and verbs – instead of reading it as something like a novel that is constantly losing its way.

This mode of attention is not confined to the world of classical music in European culture. It is also how we learn to look at larger plants and animals, and especially at the human body, both in real life and in painted or sculpted form. We see the surface and the outline – often sheathed with clothes – yet in the mind's eye we also see the structure, because we know it well. We know all the possible folds, bends and contortions of which the body is normally capable, and we delight in the work of a painter who can show us that he understands them too. When we see an illegal contortion – a limb out of joint, or a broken bone – we feel sympathetic pain. That is the way experienced listeners hear the myths in an oral culture.

In its lovely glove of words, Skaay's poem has the structure of five fingers, or four fingers and a thumb. If we are experienced listeners, that is enough. We imagine the palm, the invisible bones that join in a wrist; we remember the echoes, allusions and names that link these poems, and the larger poem they make, to the whole body of Haida mythology – a body that every student of Haida literature learns to recognize and imagine, though it is a body that, in its entirety, no one has ever depicted or seen.

Skaay's other major work, *Raven Travelling* – whose form is explored in the following chapters and mapped in appendix 4 – is not a sixth digit nor a forearm that is added to this five-part structure – nor is it unrelated. It is another five-part structure.

It is the other hand.

9 The Shaping of the Canon

Skaay, MOODY AND SWANTON worked together intently for three weeks. They filled thirty pages of Swanton's field notebook every day in the beginning and more than forty pages a day as they built up speed. By early November, Swanton had recorded Skaay's entire extant works – and Moody introduced him to Ghandl before he completed his work with Skaay. Altogether, during five months at Hlghagilda, Swanton transcribed about sixty narratives from a dozen different mythtellers, and more than fifty short songs from an unknown number of singers. Then he went north to Ghaw, where he wrote down another ninety stories told by five more storytellers, and transcribed another fifty songs.

As his letters have told us, Swanton knew he could not do justice to the songs. He had come to the Northwest Coast with nothing but pencil and paper, and he could not write music any more than Skaay or Ghandl could write words. He was right to believe that transcribing the lyrics alone was inadequate, but that was the best he could do, and there are several whole genres of Haida song for which he gives us no example.[1] What obsessed him were the narratives. The 150 of these that he transcribed at Hlghagilda and Ghaw fall into three obvious classes.

(1) There are *qqaygaang* or myths. This is the primary genre of classical Haida literature. Ghandl's poem about the man who married a goose, Skaay's poem about a woman abducted by a spirit-being from the seafloor, and his quick vignette about the

Sapsucker getting his feathers are examples. But Skaay, Sghii-dagits and others liked to weave these individual myths into larger compositions, much as a Haida sculptor might weave many figures and stories into a panel or a pole. So far as we know, no critical vocabulary developed in classical Haida for distinguishing the parts of myths from the wholes.

(2) There are *qqayaagaang* or "traditions." These include the traditional stories of families or lineages and are often, in effect, deeds of land in narrative form. They are episodic, anecdotal tales that frequently record the formation of bonds between ancestors and places. Short motifs familiar from the myths often appear in the *qqayaagaang,* much as literary allusions appear in the writings of historians and jurists in the European tradition – but in the family histories Swanton recorded, these mythical motifs are never extensively explored.

(3) There are *gyaahlghalang*: historical or personal accounts of adventures or notable events. These are often told in the first person, and they so often involve disputes that Swanton classed them generally as "war stories." We should remember, however, that the English word "war" had a different range of meanings in 1900 than it had by 1918 or 1939, and that the Haida word *qaydaw*, which Moody and Swanton routinely translated as *war*, really meant sporadic raids and skirmishes, not the use of heavy weapons nor the mounting of a centralized campaign.

Oral histories, like written ones, vary widely in their literary quality, and the extant body of classical Haida literature includes *gyaahlghalang* of considerable literary interest. Though briefer than Herodotos' account of the Greco-Persian Wars, some of these are histories in his sense. Others belong to a genre almost lost in European literature. They are medicine stories, *sghaagaa gyaahlghalanggha*: tales of vision quests and the spiritual journeys of shamans. Like the myths, they are normally told in the third person, but they are set in historical time.[2]

The words *qqaygaang* and *qqayaagaang* both come from the root *qqay,* to be old (or full or ripe or round). The difference between them is the infix -*aa*-. This changes the mode of the verb, so that it emphasizes a state or a condition over a process or an action. *Qqayaagaang*, it seems, are things that are continuously old and ripe and full – and *qqaygaang* are things that are continuously ripening and refilling. *Gyaahlghalang* is related to the verb *gyaahlgaa*, which means to grow *up* but not to grow *old*.

We know how determined Swanton was to hear every story anyone would tell and to transcribe every story he heard. But we should not think this exhausts the list of literary genres familiar to Skaay and his friends. If Swanton had arrived in Haida Gwaii two decades earlier, or had worked more surreptitiously, or had practiced a less courteous brand of ethnology, the extant body of classical Haida literature would be different than it is.

Potlatch oratory was and still remains a major genre all along the Northwest Coast. Splendid examples have been published in Nootka, Kwakwala and Tlingit,[3] and fine examples in many languages, Haida included, are still to be heard. But the potlatch was illegal in Canada from 1885 until 1951, and Swanton had come to the Islands just when the resident missionaries were reaching the height of their power. Sponsoring a potlatch so the orators could speak would have placed the participants at risk and could have jeopardized the whole of Swanton's program.[4]

The elegy or poem of lamentation was also a familiar – all too familiar – form of literature on the Northwest Coast toward the close of the classical period, but elegies were not performed to order for visiting anthropologists. The most moving example I know of – and surely one of the masterpieces of published Native American oral literature – was spoken into a tape recorder at Yakutat, Alaska, in 1972 by the Eyak elder Anna Nelson Harry.[5] We will see in a moment why Swanton could not hear poems like that in Haida Gwaii in 1900, even if a poet like Anna Harry had been seated by his side.

Most of the adventure tales Swanton heard are autobiographical, and if he had probed for more extended autobiography he might have heard that too. Several Haida and Northern

Wakashan men and women have dictated their autobiographies, mostly in English, since the early 1930s. One of the most substantial of these is the autobiography of Daxhiigang's daughter Florence Davidson. But the earliest such document we have – the autobiography of the Nuuchahnulth elder Saayaacchapis – was dictated in the Nootka language in late 1913 and early 1914.[6]

It has been argued that autobiography is a genre basically alien to Native American literature. And most of the published examples – often heavily rewritten by their English-speaking editors – include a good deal that might never have been said if an anthropologist hadn't asked. This is not the case at all with the autobiography of Saayaacchapis. The entire undertaking looks like his idea, and every sentence seems to have been spoken of the author's own volition – though what he said would not survive as a text if Edward Sapir had not been there to hear it and to write it down. The same is true of the autobiographical tales Swanton heard from Sghaagya.[7] Their author was in charge.

➤   ➤   ➤

There is one more irreparable gap in Swanton's rich Haida anthology. Out of 150 narratives, he did not record one that was told by a woman. He often dealt with Haida women during his year in the Islands. He transcribed songs that women sang, he bought some artworks from women, and he talked to some of them extensively about family history, house names, place names and other matters of mutual interest. But even at Ghaw, where one of his coworkers and teachers was a woman – Mary Ridley of the Kuna Llaanas – he recorded no women's stories or narrative poems.

All of Haida literary history, up until the moment when Gumsiiwa and Sghiidagits, Skaay and Ghandl began to understand how Swanton could be used, is now a reign of silence. It is right that we should ask now why the silence broke for Haida men before it did for Haida women.[8]

Women are far from having equal representation in the over-all record of Native North American oral literature, but their voices are by no means absent altogether. In 1870, at Fort Good Hope on the Mackenzie River, an elderly shaman known to out-siders as Lizette K'achodi sang songs and told stories in the Slavey language[9] to the missionary Émile Petitot and allowed her scandalized and fascinated guest to write them down. In the 1980s, the Tlingit elder Seidayaa taped dozens of long narrative poems and chapters of autobiography which were then tran-scribed by her adopted nephew, the linguist Jeff Leer.[10] I can think offhand of at least thirty Native North American women of literary importance whose works were transcribed, at length, in their own languages, during the intervening century.[11] Yet the general rule – especially in the earlier years – is that male mythtellers spoke more freely to visiting linguists than women did. One important factor – not in itself an explanation – is that most of the linguists themselves were men.

Swanton was physically small and profoundly shy – "an elf of a man," as a larger, more ebullient friend remembered him.[12] Later in life, he described himself as someone who "cordially loathed from the ground up the entire competitive system."[13] He put storytellers at ease, and he listened to what he was told, but he did not, so far as we can tell, press people for information they were reluctant to divulge. In the case of the women he spoke to, that often included even their names. Twenty years earlier an-other elf of a man – the hunchbacked geologist George Dawson, who brought the first camera to Haida Gwaii – had remarked on the reluctance of Haida women to be photographed.[14]

Franz Boas heard a number of stories from women (including Haida women) on the Northwest Coast between 1886 and 1900, but in those years Boas often worked with urbanized and dis-placed people. Boas's Haida teachers were working for wages in Victoria, where village rules of deference and reticence were waived. And Boas recorded their stories only in German or

English. The first woman mythteller on the Northwest Coast to be recorded in her own language was a Kwakwalan elder by the name of Qasalas. She told Q'ixitasu' a story in Kwakwala about a woman who was murdered by her husband and whose four brothers then avenged her death. Q'ixitasu' transcribed this tale at Fort Rupert, probably in the fall of 1900 – just as Swanton was starting to work in Haida Gwaii. Ten years later, a Nuuchahnulth man named Qiixxa, speaking Nootka, told "the same" story – in fact, of course, a very different story built from the same events – to Edward Sapir. There is much to be learned by reading the stories of Qiixxa and Qasalas together – and a detailed comparison of tone and style is not especially difficult in this case, because Nootka and Kwakwala are sister languages.[15]

In 1933 two anthropologists, Kaj Birket-Smith and Frederica de Laguna, met the Eyak mythteller Anna Nelson (later Anna Nelson Harry) in Cordova, Alaska, near the mouth of the Copper River. Their experience casts some further light on the problems facing Swanton in 1900 and 1901. Anna Nelson answered her visitors' questions about linguistic and ethnographic matters, but she left the telling of stories to her husband Galushia. It was clear to Birket-Smith and de Laguna that Galushia had learned these stories from his wife and still often needed her assistance when he told them. Moreover, one of the anthropologists asking for these stories was a woman. Yet household protocol was such that Anna told her stories to Galushia and Galushia told them to the guests.[16] When another thirty years had passed, Anna Nelson Harry agreed to tell her stories directly to the linguist Michael Krauss – but conditions then were different in several respects. Galushia was dead; Anna was living in the Tlingit community of Yakutat with her Tlingit-speaking second husband; Krauss was young enough to be her grandson and was passionately interested in Eyak; and Anna was keenly aware that she was one of the last three or four fluent speakers of Eyak still alive. Most importantly, perhaps, she could whisper as quietly as she pleased – and that was often very quietly indeed – to the impassive ear of Krauss's tape-recorder.

Swanton too had some of these advantages – he was young, and he was passionately interested – but that was not enough. His method of taking dictation still required a degree of public presence on the storyteller's part. The stories he heard were *told* instead of *confided.* Under these conditions, it is inconceivable that Swanton could have recorded the stories of Haida women as fully as he did the stories of men – and unlikely he could have recorded them at all without resorting to subterfuge.

Classical Haida narrative as we know it bears some interesting resemblances to Haida formline painting and carving – and these, so far as we know, were almost exclusively male arts in the classical period. There is proof, as we shall see, that some women knew the mythology just as well as or better than men. And there are women mythtellers now in Haida Gwaii (but there are also, now, several women painters and sculptors). It would be nice to know if there was formerly a distinct women's tradition of narrative art in the Haida language, and if it corresponded in any way to other arts – weaving, basketry and spruce-root embroidery – practiced by women.[17]

In recent years, several women anthropologists[18] have transcribed stories from Haida elders of both sexes, and Haida women elders in the present day seem as open with their stories as the older men. No one has reported any evidence of a separate body of myths told by Haida women and not by men. But the emphases and styles of Haida women mythtellers, along with all the content of women's personal stories and medicine tales, are absent from the record of classical Haida literature.

At Hlghagilda in 1900, someone – we do not know who – said to Swanton, "No one living knows the full story of this island. The last who knew it was an old woman of Ninstints [Sghan Gwaay, one of the southernmost of the major Haida villages] who died some ten or fifteen years ago."[19] More intriguing still is the mysterious unnamed woman with whom Skaay conferred, or said he conferred, before telling Swanton his second magnum opus, *Xhuuya Qaagaangas,* or *Raven Travelling.*

❦   ❦   ❦

The epic of the trickster lies at the center of the oral literature of the Northwest Coast. Swanton recorded many portions and versions of this tapestry of stories at Hlghagilda and Ghaw and tried his best to fit these fragments into wholes. Out of all these pieces, there is one sentence supplied by a woman. Swanton doesn't give her name, but he tells us she belonged to the Stastas family of the Eagle side and in 1900 was living at Hlghagilda.[20] Daxhiigang was also a Stastas from Hlghagilda, and the woman was therefore either Daxhiigang's mother Kkaawquuna or one of his aunts. Because of the way her sentence meshes with the story, it seems quite certain she was present as a listener – and possibly a critic – while Skaay was telling Moody and Swanton his own version of *Raven Travelling.*

Skaay saved this work for last, and when he did begin to tell it, he started near the end, with the bridge leading into what Skaay called the Youngsters' Poem, *Nang hittaghaninas qqaygaanggha.* This is the anthology of ribald trickster tales that Skaay, Ghandl, Haayas, Kingagwaaw and others all apparently regarded as the right way to conclude the poem. The earlier part of the story, which Skaay called the Poem of the Elders, *Nang qqayas qqaygaanggha,* has its own fair share of scandalous, hilarious events, but at the same time it recounts in some detail the basic formation and arrangement of the world. It deals with the separation of sea and land and day and night, the establishment of the seasons, the coloration of the birds, and other essentials. Skaay started with the profane part of the story, Swanton says, "but next morning he said that he had been talking over the proper place to begin with an old woman."[21] Then he started all over again at what is plainly the beginning.

There is, by the way, no other early authority for these two terms, the Youngsters' Poem and the Elders' Poem (or the Young Man's Story and the Old Man's Story, as Swanton understood them). We do not know whether these were Skaay's private terms or everybody's terms or something in between. Neither do we know for certain what they mean. Do they tell us who is expected to tell the story? Or who is expected to be listening? Were they concocted on the spot, as part of the elaborate joke Skaay played on Swanton when he started the story near the end? Or do they point to something present in the myth itself? The Raven is repeatedly reborn in the course of his own story, so it seems that he is older (or at any rate no younger) when his long biography begins than when it ends. But in the early part of the story he is constantly surrounded by changing sets of parents and other elders. In the latter part of the story, he is always on his own. This contradiction can be stated even more concretely. In the Poem of the Elders, the Raven is repeatedly reincarnated as a newborn child. In the Youngsters' Poem, he repeatedly steals the skin of an old man.

➤   ➤   ➤

In addition to Skaay and Ghandl, Swanton recorded a number of very interesting storytellers and poets of lesser skill or with a smaller range. At Hlghagilda alone, there were more than half a dozen of importance. Sghiidagits, the headman of the village, was one. Sghaagya was another. Henry Moody's father, Gumsiiwa, was a third. Tlaajang Quuna (Tom Stevens), the nephew and heir of Daxhiigang's father, was a fourth. A fifth was Xhaaydakuns (Tom Price), a capable sculptor as well as a mythteller, who was headman of the Saahgi Qiighawaay.[22] And there were two who were especially close to Skaay: his friend Kilxhawgins and his family headman, Xhyuu.

Some of these poets are fond of puns and some of them are not. A few sometimes inflate their sentences with adjectives, while the best ones, even in performances that last for hours, never waste a word. Ghandl has a sense of pathos as delicate and exact as we expect from a great violinist. Skaay has a narrative reach equalled by none of the others, and Swanton's transcripts make it clear that Skaay also made the greatest use of dramatic vocal gestures.

We might wonder why the two best poets Swanton met are also the first he recorded at length. The answer, I think, is that the people knew full well who were the poets in their midst, and once Swanton had paid his respects to Sghiidagits, Henry Moody led him directly to the best Haida poets – and maybe the only trained professionals – still alive.

We might also wonder why these poets – Skaay especially, since he was the first – confided their treasures to Swanton so readily. I don't believe, myself, that the answer is money or vanity. I think the credit goes to Swanton's colleague Henry Moody. Moody belonged to a family called the Qaagyals Qiighawaay, of the Raven side. His mother was a sister of Gidansta, the head of that family and hereditary headman of Qquuna, where Skaay was born. Henry, in fact, was Gidansta's senior nephew and heir. He was therefore one of the princes of the vanished Haida world. He brought Swanton to Skaay. And when Skaay dictated his poems, he was speaking them not to John Swanton the anthropologist, but to the future chief of Qquuna, his own ancestral village – even though that village had by then lain empty for twenty years.[23]

It is not altogether inconceivable that Henry Moody made these decisions and arrangements on his own, acting on Swanton's behalf. But I think it much more likely that the guidance came from Moody's father, Gumsiiwa. Moody brought Swanton to Gumsiiwa first of all, and Gumsiiwa dictated the first Haida story Swanton transcribed. He therefore saw how the transcription process worked and may have played a crucial role in determining how it would go. I have a hunch that Gumsiiwa understood how to turn Swanton's presence to advantage, ensuring his son Henry not only a salary but a good postgraduate course in classical Haida literature and culture. If this is how it was, we have Gumsiiwa to thank for sending Henry Moody and John Swanton to Sghiidagits, Skaay and Ghandl.

Swanton cannot have known at this point what was happening to him, even if he realized who was steering his course. In the beginning, he didn't even know the meanings of the words that he was patiently transcribing. He did know, from the outset, that the mythtellers he met were individual human beings, and he took real interest in their differences. So great, nevertheless, was his respect for the work of his earlier teacher that even Swanton never freed himself entirely from Boas's belief that oral literature is essentially independent of individual thought and style.

It is a fact that oral poets very rarely claim to be original. It is also a fact that no two are the same. At the other extreme, modern artists in literate societies rarely claim to be anything less than wholly original. Even those who know they are slaves of fashion, and those who know they are dutiful servants of living tradition, comprehend that this is not what their dealers or agents or publishers want them to say.

Among the 150 narrative poems and stories that Swanton recorded in Haida, many concern the shape and structure of the universe. In many of these stories, we meet a repeating cast of characters: Xhuuya, Nang Kilstlas, Tangghwan Llaana, Tl·laajaat – whose English names are the Raven, Voicehandler, Sea Dweller, Fairweather Woman – and others. The breadth and depth of thought in these stories is enormous. But this thought is almost always expressed in terse and concrete terms. It takes the form of images and events which can be painted, carved or danced as well as spoken.

Line is a powerful force in Haida art – but it is line that shrinks and swells and bends and flexes like a muscle. It forms attachments, like the anchor points of muscles, bones or feathers, and it builds and releases tension, like a bow. It also severs and rejoins itself, forming out-of-round organic hollows, pockets and pools: knots, joints and breathing holes in the tense, motionless current that keeps them alive. That is the nature of line in Haida painting; it is also the nature of *plot* in Haida narrative. Neither the visual art nor the poetry has room for picturesque detail. Their power and complexity demand a sparer form. Yet to anyone who studies the art closely, no two Haida carvers are the same. And no two Haida poets either.

In their last collaboration, Skaay spoke into Henry Moody's ear and John Swanton's notebook a poem that sketches the creation of the present world. It isn't *the* Haida vision of creation; it is Skaay's particular vision, or one of his visions: the one he agreed to spin into words in the final days of October 1900, surrounded by memories of the dead and by the counsel and attention of a few surviving friends. Swanton asked other Haida poets to tell him the same story, and they did. They told him *Raven Travelling* over and over. No two of them are the same.

If Swanton had asked a single poet – Skaay, let us say – to tell the same story again and again, how different would the versions be? For a scientist inquiring into the nature of oral literature, there is no more obvious experiment than that. Boas had conducted such experiments in the 1890s with the Chinook myth-teller Qqiltí[24] – albeit for linguistic rather than literary reasons – and Swanton had studied those texts in writing his dissertation, but Swanton never tried such experiments with Skaay, nor with any other mythteller he met, in any of the languages he worked in, during forty active years as a linguist and ethnologist. That was not his kind of science: not his notion of a healthy way of dealing with the world.

What if he had called on Skaay in a different season or a different year or with a different colleague – the heir-apparent of Hlghagilda, perhaps, instead of Henry Moody, the heir-apparent of Qquuna? Would he then have heard the same ten-hour cycle, the same Big Poem, or a different cycle entirely? That is the sort of experiment that Swanton might have enjoyed, but not one he found time and opportunity to perform.[25]

10 The Flyting of Skaay and Xhyuu

ONE DAY IN LATE OCTOBER, Swanton and Moody arrived at Skaay's home, expecting to hear the opening scene of *Raven Travelling.* Skaay had promised to tell the entire story, or Swanton believed that he had, but the old man took the linguist by surprise. He began *in medias res,* with an episode in which the Raven goes to fight the Southeast Wind. Not until the following morning, after Skaay had talked (or so he said) with the old woman, did Moody and Swanton hear the real beginning of the poem. But Skaay's false start is of considerable interest:

Gyaanhaw gaaysta lla qaagiighans gaatxhanhaw
lla ttsaan hlindalang, wansuuga.
Naaghastagangxhan xhitiit tlgughiidaxhan lla ttsaan hlingas.
Gyaanhaw Ttlaayttlaay lla gii agang kinggwas
gyaan lla lla suudas,   5
«Guuwanu. Dang qqayaghiida.»

Gyaan lla ising ghaawghuhlaangxhan kihljuuwas....[1]

After that, as he was travelling along,
he called out for a crew, they say.
He asked all sorts of birds to join his crew.
Steller's Jay said he was ready,
and he said to him,   5
«No. You're too old.»

That one said again that he was coming.
Then this one grabbed him by the topknot
and gave it a good yank, they say.
And that one's head got long and flat on top, they say.   10
And then he gave up calling for a crew.

The first words, *gyaanhaw gaaysta,* mean "and from there" or "and then, after that." It is not the kind of phrase Skaay uses at the outset of a story. Swanton must have wondered what was going on. And the high incidence of errors (bungled consonants especially) in the text is reasonable proof that the transcriber was confused. But there were others in the room; a conversation must have been in progress just before the recording session began. Skaay's decision to begin here is a joke, not a mistake. And it is a joke we might still try, a century late, to understand.

Skaay lived at Hlghagilda just as he had at Ttanuu, in the house of the hereditary headman of his lineage, the Qquuna Qiighawaay, who was also the hereditary headman of the village of Ttanuu. This headman's name was Xhyuu, "Southeast Wind." *Xhyuu* is the harshest wind that blows in Haida Gwaii, and the wind's name mimics what it signifies. It starts out turbulent and deep (*xh*), whistles up the palate (*y*), and is stretched, backed and rounded at the end (*uu*). Swanton had asked for or been promised the story of the trickster, and Skaay obliged, starting with a yarn in which his house chief's namesake, the Big Wind, plays a central role. The passage quoted above continues:

Then they all went aboard the canoe.
And then they headed off.
They travelled and travelled and travelled and travelled.

They came in front of the Halibut people's town.   15
Hu hu hu hu hu! They crowded down.
«The Raven is going to fight, they say.»
They said that sort of thing as they crowded down.

And then he asked them to come too,
and they agreed.
They stuck themselves like lapstrakes
  to the hull of the canoe,   20
and then they started off.
They travelled and travelled.

At dawn they landed there in front of that one's town.
The Halibut people lay with their heads facing out
flanking the path coming down from the house.
Birds stood flanking the path as well.
They hid behind the halibut.

They waited and waited awhile.
Then, dressed in his fancy hat,
he stepped outside.   30

One of the halibut flipped its tail.
He fell down.
Then the next one flipped its tail.
One by one they flipped their tails
until they had flipped him aboard the canoe.

Then he asked them why they treated him this way.
They said they did it because he blew too hard and long.
Then they let him go, they say.
And then they headed back.
That was Southeast Wind, they say.   40

The last line of this passage rises like a gale: *Xhyuu ahaw ii-jaang, wansuuga.* There is nothing in the transcript to show that Skaay gave it special treatment, but not much effort is required with a line like that to shake the houseboards: *Xhyuuuuu ahaw iiiiijaang, wansuuuuuga.*

Xhyuu himself was in the room while this story of Xhyuu

was being told, and after Skaay had done a couple of short episodes, Xhyuu himself picked up the tale.[2] Skaay stopped – or was interrupted – after telling the opening episode of the Raven's encounter with Xhawsghaana, or Fishing God. Xhyuu then told the second episode, picking up the story just at the moment where the Raven angers Fishing God by helping himself to Fishing God's dinner and Fishing God's wife.

Xhyuu tells with gusto how Fishing God beat the Raven to a pulp and left his pulverized remains under a boulder on the beach at low tide. Then the tide begins to rise. But the Raven's ten spirit helpers come to his aid and roll away the stone. The smell, Xhyuu says, is what enabled them to find him.

Limp and afloat, the Raven is swallowed by a humpback whale. Then he eats the whale from the inside out. The dying creature drifts ashore in front of a town, and people hurry to the beach to cut it up. In doing so, they set the Raven free.

> *Gyaanhaw yaaxhan lla xithlasi.*
> *Gyaanhaw llanagaay gyawgi agang lla dlstlittaahlsi*
> *gyaan nang qqaya naawas*
> *qqal lla dangttlsttas*
> *gyaan ll skuuji llagha lla daangas*
> *gyaan ll qqalghii llagha lla qattsas*
> *gyaan lla ttlaa lla sihlgha naawas.*[3]

> *Then he flew up high.*
> *Then he came down at the edge of the village*
> *where an old man lived.*
> *He pulled off his skin*
> *and pulled out his bones,*
> *and he dressed himself in his skin*
> *and lived in his place.*

With this, Skaay too has been described – or his reflection has been captured for a moment in the iridescent mirror of the old

216

story. The crickbacked poet is portrayed as none other than the Raven, dressed in an old man's hide. His jest has been repaid. But Xhyuu was warming to his task, and he continued with a coda of three episodes – one in which the Raven wanders around with salmon milt hanging out of his nose; another in which, after taking the form of a woman, he transforms shit into people; and a third in which he tries to cook and serve himself for a meal. Xhyuu's wife was also in the house as her husband was spinning out this tale, and after listening awhile, she offered Xhyuu some unsolicited advice on how to shorten the final episode.[4]

In the fall of 1900, Skaay was close to eighty and Xhyuu was in his sixties. John Swanton was 27. We could describe the interaction of Skaay and Xhyuu as nothing more than banter – simply a way of passing the time and making a couple of bucks from a gullible anthropologist young enough to be the older poet's grandson and the headman's youngest son or nephew. That description is fine as far as it goes, but it does not go far enough. In the impromptu mythtelling contest staged by Skaay and Xhyuu there is a structure – just the sort of structure that often seems to spring up out of nothing when skilled musicians jam. Skaay and Xhyuu are telling jokes and spinning yarns, but that is not quite all; they are also working within a tradition as demanding in its way as the Virginia reel, the minuet, the ballad, or the twelve-bar blues.

In Scotland, such a contest between poets is known as a flyting. But the Flyting of Skaay and Xhyuu is different in character from the *Flyting of Dunbar and Kennedy* or other familiar Celtic examples.[5] Classical Haida mythtellers don't inflate their pride or anger artificially, nor do they confess even their subtler emotions directly; they speak through characters and events, the way musicians speak through notes, motifs and chords, and painters speak through colors, shapes and lines.

Kkwaayang, Daxhiigang's wife – who was twenty years his junior – spent half the year at work in the white man's cannery, just as Persephone, Demeter's daughter, spent half the year in

THE FLYTING OF SKAAY AND XHYUU
The Structure of a Jam Session

1 Skaay's Strophe
  1.1 The Raven's skirmish with Xhyuu
    1.1.1   Recruitment of Steller's Jay
    1.1.2   Recruitment of Halibut people
    1.1.3   Defeat of Xhyuu
  1.2 Theft of seal from children
  1.3 Encounter with Fishing God
    1.3.1   Creation of a northern flicker from feather
    1.3.2   Bartering with Fishing God
       1.3.2.1 The Raven gives Fishing God the flicker
       1.3.2.2 Fishing God catches halibut
                  in vomited seawater
       1.3.2.3 The Raven dines with Fishing God and his wife
    1.3.3   Voyage to Flicker Island
       1.3.3.1 The Raven goes ashore alone
       1.3.3.2 The Raven creates flickers from nasal blood
       1.3.3.3 Fishing God goes ashore
2 Xhyuu's Antistrophe
  2.1 Return of the Raven
    2.1.1   The Raven drifts away from Fishing God
    2.1.2   The Raven sleeps with Fishing God's wife
    2.1.3   Halibut feast
    2.1.4   The Raven sleeps again with Fishing God's wife
    2.1.5   The Raven catches halibut in vomited seawater
  2.2 Return of Fishing God
  2.3 Destruction of the Raven

2.4 Resurrection of the Raven

    2.4.1 Assistance from the ten spirit helpers

    2.4.2 Encounter with onlookers

    2.4.3 Whale swallows the Raven

    2.4.4 The Raven eats the whale from the inside out

    2.4.5 Whale drifts ashore

2.5 Reincarnation of the Raven

    2.5.1 Reincarnation as old man

    2.5.2 Old man scares away the fishermen

    2.5.3 The Raven gorges himself on the whale

3 Xhyuu's Coda

3.1 The Raven visits Eagle with salmon milt hanging from his nose

3.2 The Raven in female form

    3.2.1 Marriage to seal hunter

    3.2.2 Loss of labret while stealing salmon roe

    3.2.3 Discovery of masquerade

        3.2.3.1 Tail feathers discovered

        3.2.3.2 The Raven makes imitation people out of shit

        3.2.3.3 Shit-people melt beside the fire

3.3 Search for self-generated food

    3.3.1 The Raven is fed by three animals

        3.3.1.1 Salmon roe from the Dipper's leg

        3.3.1.2 Grease from the flipper of the Sealion

        3.3.1.3 Grease from the flipper of the Seal

    3.3.2 The Raven tries to replicate their feats

        3.3.2.1 Tries to take salmon roe from his own leg

        3.3.2.2 Tries to feed Sealion by roasting his own hand

        3.3.2.3 Tries to feed Seal by roasting his own hand[6]

    3.3.3 The Raven deserted by his friends

hell. Daxhiigang speaks of his love for his wife, his respect for her independence and her power, and his silent fear of losing her, through the image of a kidnapped woman half-transformed into her captor's shape, the dogfish. Ghandl puts his own deeply personal understanding of the mutability of joy into the paleolithic story of a hunter who married a bird he'd come to kill. Skaay uses a mythologized bit of Tsimshian history to say what he has seen of the destruction of the world, and he speaks about the beauty and renewal of that world – and incidentally, perhaps, about the ingratitude of the young – through a story in which the sapsucker is fledged.

Just as the classical Haida poets avoid portraying or praising themselves directly, so they avoid the directly abusive language often found in Scottish flytings. Skaay and Xhyuu are survivors, not combatants: two old refugees from death who have somehow not forgotten how to laugh.

Myth is a language made of timeless, not of momentary, forms. The themes of the Flyting of Skaay and Xhyuu are not concocted for this occasion; they are *original* in a different sense. They are thousand- or ten-thousand-year-old stories put to current use; they renew the present world by rehearsing what is known of how that world came to be.

After giving the well-mannered Dr Swanton a taste of the Raven's character, Skaay began on the following day to unfold another masterpiece, the Poem of the Elders, which is the first and largest part of *Xhuuya Qaagaangas*. He may indeed have talked about the story in the meantime with a woman. Or he may have made that conversation up. Old women who knew the story inside out were surely living in the village. It is likely they were present in the room. So was the Raven, who *is* the story, and who rarely stoops to the truth when a lie would serve.

3

HLGHUNUHL

11 You Are That Too

IN 1942, Swanton's unpublished southern Haida manuscript – including most of the poems dictated by Ghandl and Skaay more than forty years before – arrived at the American Philosophical Society Library in Philadelphia, where it has remained. It was microfilmed as planned, and microfilm copies have found their way to interested linguists in many parts of the world. As manuscripts go, this one is young and appears to be in excellent shape. It is cleanly typed on sturdy paper, and Swanton's ungainly but quite legible corrections are handwritten in ink on every page. Another anthropologist, Theresa Mayer Durlach, borrowed the manuscript from Boas in the 1920s and indexed certain words to underpin her study of Haida kinship terminology.[1] She is responsible for the handwritten line numbers now found in the margin of each page, and for a few sporadic bits of interlinear translation. A conservator has built the manuscript a custom-tailored box, which makes it seem at first that it can never have been any other size. But look more closely and the ravages appear. There are 350 sheets of typescript altogether. They are numbered, with many gaps, from 23 to 813. This is what remains of Swanton's vision of a full bilingual text of the works of Skaay, Ghandl, Sghiidagits, Kilxhawgins, Tlaajang Quuna, Xhyuu, and other storytellers and poets who survived the century of death in southern Haida Gwaii. The pages missing from the manuscript are those that became the printed book. They contained Swanton's brief introduction, his prose translations and a few original texts. They included ten per cent, to be exact, of the texts he had painstakingly prepared for publication. This is all the Bureau of American Ethnology thought worth the trouble of publishing in 1905.

The top page of the manuscript is darkened and a little worn. It has been on the top of the stack for quite some time. The problem is that the top page is page 2 of its particular Haida text. It begins in mid-sentence. Nearly all of Swanton's field notebooks – for Haida and for every other language that he studied – have now vanished, and sometime between 1905 and 1942 – that is, before the microfilm was made – page one of his leftover typescript vanished as well. The first text in the pile is of course *Raven Travelling*: the Elders' Tale as Skaay decided to tell it, at the urging of a woman whose name we do not know and whose very existence is open to question. What is missing from the Philadelphia manuscript is the origin of the world.

In the spring of 1992 I was rooting through some other Swanton papers at the Smithsonian Institution in Washington, DC. The catalogue listed a letterpress book, donated to the archive twenty years before by John Reed Swanton Jr. When I asked for it, I was handed not a letterpress book but an old brown binder full of onionskin. Moments later, I knew that I was holding Swanton's uncorrected carbon copy of the southern Haida texts.[2] I turned some pages to be sure that I was seeing what I was seeing, and several of the words disappeared before my eyes. The desiccated carbon was so fragile on some pages that I could send whole sentences to oblivion with the light touch of a sleeve. But I had not, in my clumsiness, damaged page one. Within an hour, we had photographic copies of the missing page.

With the restoration of page one, we have the Haida text of *Raven Travelling* as Swanton intended to publish it. But in that form it is still a conflation of voices. The voice at the core of the story is Skaay's. But Swanton heard bits and pieces of the tale told by half a dozen other southern Haida poets. Afterward, he took the scraps of narrative that seemed to augment Skaay's, and wherever they seemed to fit, he grafted them on. Happily, he also labelled these additions. They are therefore easy to remove.

In the early 1900s, oral-formulaic poetry was well understood in the hill towns of Bosnia and Montenegro, where it was still widely practiced, but at Harvard and Columbia, Swanton had been taught that all oral poetry was memorized. Homer, he supposed, was not an oral poet but a kind of editor who stitched the short, unwritten songs of others into a larger written whole. Milman Parry, the brilliant young scholar whose study of Greek and Serbo-Croatian oral epic overturned this view, was not born until 1902.[3]

Some of the passages Swanton added to Skaay's poem are lovely in themselves, and they deserve, like the fragments of Parmenides or Pascal, a literary life and reputation of their own. One of them is also quite substantial and intricately formed. It is the Youngsters' Poem as told by Ghandl. That fragment should be read – now that reading is the only form of attention we are really equipped to provide – side by side with Ghandl's other works as well as with the work of his colleague Skaay. But if we strip all these additions away, Skaay's text leaps out with an integrity of its own. And it turns out to be a finely woven five-part structure (mapped in some detail in appendix 4).

Oral narrative poems are like novels, paintings, ballads, blues tunes, fugues. It is neither necessary nor wise for a storyteller to put quite everything he knows about a story into one inflated version, no matter what the medium or the form. Long as they are, even the *Iliad*, the *Odyssey* and the *Ramayana* – even the largest of all poems, the *Mahabharata* – leave many things unmentioned or implied. So does Skaay's recorded version of *Raven Travelling*. The other versions and the supplementary fragments have their value and their place – in the reader's book, in the listener's mind. That does not mean they ought to be inserted into someone else's solo meditation on the themes. Out of shared and newly found materials, every oral poet makes not one but many versions of the poem, and every listener accumulates in time a passive, layered version of his own.

At the top of page one of Swanton's manuscript is a title: *Xhuuya Qaagaangas*. Beneath that is the opening of a poem that lasts about two hours, spoken in the ruins of a culture a century ago by an old man with a crippled back and a beautiful mind.

My translation follows Skaay's voice alone, beginning where quite clearly he began and ending where he stopped. Apart from his banter with Xhyuu on the previous day, this is as much of *Raven Travelling* as Skaay decided to tell to Moody and Swanton. It is also the only complete and continuous version we have, in classical Haida, of the Poem of the Elders: *Raven Travelling*, part one. In the typographic form used here, its length is roughly 1400 lines.

The poem opens as follows:

Aanishaw tangagyangang, wansuuga.
Ll xitgwaangas, Xhuuya aa.
Tlgu qqawgashlingaay gi lla qyaangas.
Qawdihaw gwaay ghutgwa nang qaadla qqaayghudyas,
llagu qqawghaayghan llagha lla xiidas.   5

Aa ttl sghaana qiidas yasgagas ghiinuusis gangaang
llagu gutgwii xhihldagahldiyaagas.
Ga sghaanagwaay ghaaxas lla ttista qqaa sqqagilaangas,
ttl gwiixhan xhahlgwii at wagwii aa.
Ghaadagas gyaanhaw ising ghaalgagang, wansuuga....[4]   10

Hereabouts was all saltwater, they say.
    He was flying all around, the Raven was,
looking for land that he could stand on.
After a time, at the toe of the Islands, there was one rock awash.
He flew there to sit.

Like sea-cucumbers,[5] *gods lay across it,*
putting their mouths against it side by side.
The newborn gods were sleeping, out along the reef,
heads and tails in all directions.
It was light then, and it turned to night, they say.[6]   10

T*hen, when he had flown a while longer,*
  something brightened toward the north.
It caught his eye, they say.
And then he flew right up against it.

He pushed his mind through
and pulled his body after.

There were five villages strung out in a line.
In the one that was farthest to seaward,
the headman's daughter had just given birth to a child.

Then evening fell.   20
They went to sleep.
Then he skinned the child, starting at the feet,
and crawled inside the skin.
He took the baby's place.

Next day, his grandfather asked for the child,
and they passed him along.
Then his grandfather washed him
and pressed the baby's feet against the ground.
He stretched him up to a standing position.
Then he handed him back.   30

Next day he stretched him again
and handed him back to his mother.

He was hungry after that.
They had not yet started feeding him chewed-up food.

Then evening came again,
and they lay down.
As soon as they were sleeping,
he craned his head around.

He listened throughout the house.
They were sleeping, one and all.   40
Then he unlaced himself from the cradle.
He wiggled his way free
and went outside.

Someone who was half rock, living in the back corner, saw him.
While he was gone, she continued to sit there.
He brought something in in the fold of his robe.
In front of his mother, where the fire smoldered,
he poked at the coals.

He scooped out a cooking spot with a stick,
and there he put what he was carrying.   50
As soon as the embers had cooked them,
he ate them.
They slithered.

He laughed to himself.
Because of that, he was seen from the corner.

Then evening came again,
and they lay down,
and once again he went outside.

He was gone for a while.

He brought things in again in the fold of his robe,   60
and then he took them out
and cooked them in the coals.
Then he pulled them out and ate them, laughing to himself.

The one that was half rock watched him from the corner.
He gobbled his food,
and then he lay down in the cradle.

Morning came,
and all five villages were wailing.
He listened to them talking.
There were five towns.   70
In four of them each of the people was missing an eye.

T hen, they say, one of the old people spoke.
     «The headman's daughter's baby is to blame.
I have seen him.
As soon as they are sleeping,
he slips out of his own skin.»

Then his grandfather gave him a marten-skin blanket.
They wrapped it around him.
His grandfather whispered,
and someone went out.   80
«Bring the headman's daughter's chi-i-i-ild outsi-i-i-ide.»

As soon as the people had gathered,
they stood in a circle,
bouncing him up as they sang him a song.
And after a while they dropped him
and watched him go down.

Turning round to the right he went down through the clouds

and struck water.
He cried and cried as he drifted around,
and after his voice grew tired, he slept.   90

W*hile he was sleeping, something spoke.*
   «Your father's father asks you in.»[7]
He looked around.
Nothing was there.
Again, when he had floated there awhile,
something said the same thing.

Again he looked around.
Nothing was there.
Then he looked through the eye of his marten-skin blanket.

A pied-bill grebe[8] *appeared.*   100
«Your father's father asks you in.»
As he said this, he dived.

Then the one we are speaking of sat up.
He had drifted close to a two-headed kelp.
He stood up and stepped onto it.

He was standing, in fact, on a two-headed stone housepole.
Then he started climbing down.
It was the same to him in the sea as it was to him above.
Then he came down in front of a house,
and someone invited him in.   110

«Come inside, my grandson.
The birds have been singing
    that you would be borrowing something of mine.»
Then he went in.

At the back sat an elder, white as a gull,
who asked him to bring him a box that hung in the corner.

When the old man had it in his hands,
he took out five boxes, one inside the other.
In the innermost box were cylindrical things:
one that glittered
and one that was black.   120

As he handed him these, he said to him,
«You are me.
You are that, too.»

On top of the screens forming a point in the rear of the house,
sleek blue beings were preening themselves.
Those are the things of which he was speaking.

Then he said to him,
«Set this one into the water, round end up,
and bite off part of that one.
Spit it at this.»   130

N*ow when the one that we are speaking of came up,*
he set the black one into the water
and bit off a piece of the one that glittered.
When he spat that at the other,
it bounced away.

He did it the other way round from the way he was told,
and that is the reason it bounced away.

Now he went back to the black one
and bit off a piece of it,
and spat that piece at this one.   140

Then it stuck.
And he bit off a piece of the one that glittered
and spat this piece at that one.
It stuck too.
Trees came into being then, they say.

When he laid this place into the water,
it stretched itself out.
The gods swam to it, taking their places.
The same thing happened with the mainland
when he set it in the water round end up.[9]   150

❧   ❧   ❧

That is the first movement of the poem. The essential theme of the second movement – which is three times longer than the first – is the redistribution of hoarded resources: fish, fresh water, and light. Some of the most widely known and oft-repeated stories of Haida mythology – the Theft of Light for example – are included here, in Skaay's laconic style. Like the funeral march from Fryderyk Chopin's second piano sonata and the nocturne from Aleksandr Borodin's second string quartet, the second movement of Skaay's poem has frequently been pillaged for other uses. The sense of familiarity this produces is, of course, mostly illusory. Poetry is what is lost, not in translation, but in paraphrase. Readers who know nothing whatsoever of Haida culture are therefore, in a sense, at an advantage. Those who know a little more than that – beginning with Franz Boas a century ago – have frequently mistaken this portion of Skaay's poem, or even the whole of it, for an anthology of folktales. That is not what it is – though old familiar tales are crucial to the fabric from which it is made.

This excerpt will serve as an example of the character of the second movement:

Gyaanhaw gaaysta ising lla qaagighang qawdi   230
kkyuu kittlxha ttaagi lla qqaawas.
Gyaan gu lla sghaayhlaw qawdi
lla ghansta ga hltanghwa
    sin qqaawda un·ging gandaalttlxhas
gyaan lla at kyaanangasi....[10]

W hen he had walked on further for a while,   230
    he stopped where a trail came down to the beach.
After he had sat there blubbering awhile,
people arrived sprinkled with eagle down,
    carrying gambling sticks on their backs.
They asked him who he was.

«*My mothers and fathers are dead.*
People tell me that your family
and mine are from the same place,
and so I came to find you.»
They told him to come home with them, they say.

And what a place they came to!   240
And they asked him to sit down.
One of the men went back of the housescreen.
He was absent for a while
and wet from the knees down when he returned.

He had just killed a salmon,
and he had it in his hands.
Then they rubbed quartz crystals back and forth,
and the fire started to burn.

They dressed the salmon then and there.
They heated cooking stones,   250
and then they broiled the fish.

When it was cooked,
they sat him down between them.

These people were beavers, they say.
And they were going out to gamble.
They went home again because of him, they say.

Then one of them went to the back.
He brought some cranberries out in a dish.
They ate those too.

One of them went to the back again.   260
He brought out some mountain goat tripes
and they cut three portions off.
They served the largest of these to their guest,
and they said, «Don't go away.
Make yourself at home here.»

Then they put bags of gambling sticks on their backs,
and then they went off.
When evening came,
they returned.
He was still there, sitting where they left him.   270

One of them went to the back again,
and again he came in with a salmon.
They broiled it.
Then they brought in a platter of cranberries,
then mountain goat tripes,
and when they had eaten,
they went to bed.

Next day at dawn,
they ate another three-course meal

and put their sacks of gambling sticks on their backs   280
and once again they went away.

Then he went behind the screen.
What did he find there but a lake!
The salmon trap sat in the outflowing stream.
The trap was shaking like someone who stands in the cold.
It was that full of salmon.

Small canoes were going different ways across the lake.
The points were red with cranberries.
Spring songs and women's songs were sounding on the water.

He pulled out the salmon trap   290
and folded it flat
and set it on the lakeshore.

Then he rolled it up together with the lake
and rolled the house up too,
and put the bundle under his arm.
He climbed into a tree that stood nearby.
He could hold it in one arm.

Then he came down from the tree
and unrolled them again.
He lit the fire,   300
and he went behind the screen.

He brought out a salmon
and cooked it and ate it at once.
Then he put out the fire
and sat there beside it and sobbed and sobbed.

As he sat there with tear stains on his face,

they came back in.
«Hey, why are you crying?»

«The fire went out. That's why I'm crying.»
They spoke to one another.   310
Then they said to him,
«That's how it goes.»

They started the fire,
and one of them went behind the screen
and brought out a salmon.
They sliced it and cooked it and ate it.
Then they ate berries and mountain goat tripes,
and they lay down.

Early next day,
when they had eaten yet another three-course meal,   320
they put their bags of gambling sticks on their backs
and went away.

Then the one whom we are speaking of ran behind the screen.
He brought out a salmon.
He cooked it and ate it.
Then he ate berries and mountain goat tripes.

Then he went behind the screen
and he pulled up the trap and folded it flat.
The same with the house.
Then he set them by the lakeside   330
and rolled them up together with the lake
and put the bundle under his arm.

He climbed a tree that used to stand beside the lake,
and halfway up the tree he sat and waited.

After he'd been sitting there awhile,
someone came.
The house and lake had disappeared.
After looking all around,
that one suddenly looked upward.
Yes! The guest was sitting there   340
with all his hosts' possessions.

The beaver went away then,
and two of them returned.
They went directly to the tree.
They started chewing on the trunk.

When it started to fall,
the one we are speaking of jumped to another.
When that one started to fall,
he jumped to the next, holding his bundle.
When he had jumped many times from tree to tree,   350
they let him go.

They wandered all around, they say.
After they had wandered for a time,
they found another lake.
They settled there, they say.

THE RAVEN HAS AS MANY names as he has voices. Skaay mentions the names rarely, but every time he does so, he appears to be speaking with care. He says *Xhuuya*, "Raven," once, in a syntactical aside, at the beginning of the poem. More than an hour of narrative follows in which the Raven is only referred to as *lla* or *ll*. These are the two forms, active and neutral, or free and bound, of the third-person animate singular pronoun in Haida. Their English equivalents are *he, she, him, her, his, hers*, and (insofar as these are animate) *it* or *its*. Xhuuya, the Raven, is he and she (and sometimes it) who does not need a name. In the entire second movement, though he acts in almost every sentence, he is never named at all.

Later in the poem, like any creature of rank in the Haida world, the Raven acquires additional names. In the third movement he becomes, despite objections from other characters, Nang Kilstlas Hlingaay, or Voicehandler's Heir. Late in the fourth movement, he is called Nang Kilstlas (Voicehandler) proper. In the fifth and final movement, where he finally hosts a potlatch of his own and decorates the other birds, he is nameless once again. But when Skaay's friend Kilxhawgins was amplifying this part of the story, he called the Raven *Wiigit*.[1] This is the Haida form of Wiigyet, one of the Raven's most familiar names in Tsimshian and in Nishga. It means, in those two languages, Big Man or Great Man.

These names are rich in irony, which is rarely a scarce com-

modity where the Raven is involved. It is perverse to call the
Raven anyone's heir when he is misbehavior incarnate, and a
joke to call him Big Man. In Nishga, Tsimshian and Haida oral
literature alike, he is forever using peapods for canoes, or carving
riverboats from elderberry twigs, or giving other proofs that he
has no regard for measurement or scale, whether physical or
moral. The namelessness he suffers in Skaay's poem is only just,
because no name will tie him down, and nameless though he is,
the story cannot shake him off. Nor can the story beyond the
story, which is the world in which it is told.

As the third movement of Skaay's *Raven Travelling* begins, the
Raven has stolen and redistributed most or all of the things that
humans need: light and water, berries and fish. He has placed the
sun and moon in the sky, and in consultation with a dog, he has
settled the shape of the seasonal calendar. He is now evidently on
the mainland, looking across at Haida Gwaii, where the story
soon takes a familiar turn. The third movement is translated in
full in the following pages, with brief interruptions for comment
at the four main structural divisions.

Gyaanhaw qqaagwii sta lla qaagaasi.   620
Naay Kun ghayuwaay aaxhan isis.
Gyaanhaw ghabaghaay lla dangguhlaasi
gyaan lla kkattagihlsi.
Aasing gut lla qaxitgyaalaasi.

Gyaan llanagaay gut lla qinttsigwaangaasi.
Naay Kun llanagaay nang daghagas jaagha qiighaawas.
Gyaanhaw gu ginggang lla singxidaasi.

Gyaanhaw ttl taysdlas ttaahlghahaw
ll qqal ghii lla qaattsas
gyaan lla ttlaa agang qiidadyas....[2]   630

Then he came from up north.   620
   The smoke from House Point village was nearby.
He pulled his headband off
and threw one end of it this way.
He walked across it quickly.

He looked through the cracks into the houses of the town.
The House Point headman's wife had a newborn child.
He waited until evening.

As soon as they were sleeping,
he climbed inside the child's skin
so that he too was newborn.   630

Morning came, and they gave him a bath,
and his father held him.
Later on, his father's sister came to the fire.
They let her take him.

After she had held him for a while,
he grabbed her by the breasts.
«Owhooo!» she said.
«What made you say that, dear?»
«Well! He nearly wiggled out of my lap.»

The headman of the town, they say, was Pierced Fin.   640
His nephew's name was Floppy Fin, they say.

Soon after that, he had a thought, they say.
«Suppose they took the children of the headmen of the village
        on an outing!»
Next day, the village children were taken on an outing.
They brought along their favorite foods.
The one in charge of him that day was his father's sister.

The children played together for a time,
and then the others left.
After they had gone,
his father's sister sat there all alone.   650

He looked around.
Then he dressed in his own skin,
and then he threw his arms around his father's sister.

«Don't touch me!» his father's sister said to him.
«Your father wants to keep my dowry.
Why else am I single?»

Then he went away and changed himself again.
His father's sister cried,
and she was thinking about how she would explain it.
He thought she should forget it   660
as soon as she went home.

Then she went inside,
and her brother looked at her awhile.
«Why do I see tear stains on your face?» he said.
«I caught him eating sand.
That's the reason I was crying.»

Then he headed out along the sleeping sea.[3]
He strung some keyhole limpet shells he found along the beach
and made a pair of rattles.

Then he suddenly went inland.   670
He pulled the mat away from someone's grave[4]
and unwove it at one side.
He tied a row of shells along the hem.
He made the mat into a dancing skirt.

239

Then he called out to the ghost,
«Are you awake?»
The ghost stood up for him.
He dressed it in the dancing skirt.
Then he put the rattles in its hands.

«Walk along in front of the town,» he said.   680
«Halfway along, shake the rattles toward the town.
That will shower them with nightmares.»

It started dancing like a shaman then, they say.
And when it shook the rattles toward the town
the way he told it to,
the people squirmed.
They all had nightmares.

He entered the house at the edge of the village,
yanked the finest-looking woman out of bed
and lay down with her right there.[5]   690
Then he entered the next house
and lay down with another woman there.

He did it over and over again,
and when he reached his father's house
he went to where his father's sister slept
and then he went to bed with her.

There was an elder living in the corner
whose mind was free of nightmares.
She knew him when she saw him.
The headman's son had stepped outside   700
and left his skin behind.

*L*ater on he came back in
  and lay down again in the cradle.
He gave the ghost its own bed too, they say.

*It seems that he had slept with his father's sister
and his own mother, Floodtide Woman, too.*[6]
*This is what they whispered to each other in the town.
Some time passed,
and then they knew.*

Then they chased his mother out of town. 710
*They chased her son away as well.
She was Big Surf's sister,
married among the People of the Strait, they say.*

One of Ghandl's poems confirms that the People of the Strait, the Qqaytsgha Llaanas, were a family of gods – or a pod of killer whales – living at Naay Kun or House Point, the northeastern-most point of Haida Gwaii. Ghandl also gives the same names – Pierced Fin (Hlghan Xhiila) and Floppy Fin (Hlghan Ghaging) – for the leaders of this family[7] though he says not a word of their relationship to the Raven.

Big Surf (Sghulghu Quuna) is a being mentioned often in classical Haida literature. He is the resident killer whale of Ghahlins Kun, "Highflat Point," a large bluff on the northeast coast of Haida Gwaii. This is the most prominent landform seen by coasting paddlers as they travel the eastern route between Hlghagilda and Ghaw. But everything we know about Sghulghu Quuna's sister, Floodtide Woman, the Raven's earthly mother, comes from two versions of *Raven Travelling*: this one, which Skaay told to Moody and Swanton in Haida, and the version that Daxhiigang told to Boas in Chinook Jargon three years earlier.[8] One of the things to be learned from comparing these two versions is that we ought not to expect fixed, consistent genealogies.

241

Haida poets of the classical period, like Greek poets of Homer's and Hesiod's time, were not reciting standardized theology. Each one envisioned the relationships of the gods as he saw fit. Daxhiigang, for example, told Boas that Floodtide Woman was the sister of Voicehandler, not of Big Surf, and he reverses the relationship of Pierced Fin and Floppy Fin. The latter, he says, was Floodtide Woman's husband, and the former was her lover. (That at any rate is how Boas understood him.)

Skaay's friends and colleagues – some of whom were in the house and listening, side by side with Moody and Swanton in October 1900 – knew that as old Skaay unfolded his poem he was not expounding a fixed canon of Haida mythology. He was unfolding his own vision of the world by speaking in mythological terms. Part of the truth of the vision is that it is never the same twice. Skaay and Daxhiigang work like Renaissance painters and Neoclassical composers, constantly reinterpreting inherited materials. There is much shared wisdom but there are no canonical texts in an oral narrative culture. Words are a means of rediscovery and rebirth instead of repetition.

Skaay continues now, from where we interrupted him.

They started out walking then,
    the two of them, they say,
and after travelling awhile,
they came to the foot of the trail across the point.
They saw a silver otter there, they say.

His mother skinned it.
Then she laced the skin into a frame.   720
She stretched it first of all,
and then she scraped it.
Then she hung it up to dry.

As soon as it was cured,

she dressed her son in it.
He was Voicehandler's Heir, they say.

A*fter travelling awhile,*
she arrived with her son at her brother's door.
A little while later,
someone stuck his head out.   730
«Floodtide Woman is standing outside.»

«Mmmmm.
Then she's been up to her old tricks again,»
her brother said.
«A young boy is with her,» said the other.
«Well, well, well! Then ask her in!»

Then he invited the two of them in.
Her brother's wife offered them food.
Later on, her brother said,
«Floodtide Woman, what are you going to call the child?»   740

She put her hand on the back of her neck then
and rubbed it up and down.
«I'm naming your nephew Voicehandler's Heir.»
She spoke the words slowly, pausing between them.

«Well, name him something else!
Word would surely get around
that someone named her child
for a god too dangerous to think of!»

All the while they lived with her brother,
the child slammed the doorflap,9 going out and coming in.   750
«Floodtide Woman, stop that boy
from doing that so often.»

«*Sorry, sir, I can't control him.*»

«*Ahhh! Listen to what she says!*
She lets her own child do
what the gods would be afraid to.»

Another day he slammed the door again
while his uncle was still sleeping.
«*Floodtide Woman,*» *said his uncle,*
«*Stop that shit-assed kid*   760
from doing that so often!»

«*Sorry, sir, I can't control your darling nephew.*»

Then he pooped right there, where he was sitting,[10]
by the fire, near his mother,
on the side that was closest to the door.
His uncle's wife twiddled her lips at him.
«*Isn't he sweet! I'm sure to sleep with my husband's nephew!*»

He heard what his uncle's wife said about him.

Early the next morning he went out.
When he had walked some distance inland,   770
he met some people singing songs and dancing.
«*Hey,*» *they said to him,*
«*What are you doing?*»

«*I'm looking for women's medicine.*»
«*What does that mean?*
Women's medicine? Medicine for women?
Medicine for love, you mean?»
«*That's it. Medicine for love.*»

The singers kept on singing.

244

As they sang, they sucked the spruce gum in their mouths.   780
Then one of them broke off a piece for him.
«This is women's medicine.»
She told him what to do.

«Go around to the right when you enter the house.
Have the gum in your mouth.
When your uncle's wife asks for it,
don't let her have it.
Ignore her! Ignore her!

«Tell her you want what belongs to her husband.
After you get it,   790
give her the gum.»

Then he left the singers.

He went back to the house,
and when he came in,
there was something red sticking out of his mouth.

His uncle's wife said to him,
«Voicehandler's Heir, give me some gum, please.»
He paid her no attention.

He sat with his mother
and said to his mother,   800
«Tell her I want what belongs to my uncle.
After I have it, I'll give her the gum.»

His mother went up to his uncle's wife
and delivered the message.
His uncle's wife gave him something white and round.
Then he let her have the gum.
She chewed it.

245

As soon as she swallowed the juice
the way she felt about him changed,
and he could see that this was so.   810

Later, when his father and his father's brother passed in their canoes,
    he called out to a dog
who was lying near the doorway,
«Voicehandler's Heir would like the tide to fall
and leave his father and his father's brother stranded.»

The dog repeated his instructions.
Then the ebb tide left the creatures high and dry.
They spouted there.
Then he said to his mother,
«Give them water.»   820

Out she went, but not to her own husband.
She poured the water over Floppy Fin alone.
Then the one we are speaking of went to his mother
and told her to pour water on his father.
She pretended not to hear him.

They were going out to buy some humpback whales
from the gods along the outer coast, they say.

After that he came back in
and talked to the dog a second time.
«Now Voicehandler's Heir wants the tide to rise   830
to where his father and his father's brother are.
Go out and say that.»

The dog ran out and said what he had said.
Xuuuuuw!
They were floating again on the ocean.

They were gone for quite a while.
Then they reappeared in their canoes.
He talked to the dog again.
«Voicehandler's Heir wants a share of what they have.
Go out and say that.» 840

The dog ran out and said what he had said.
Something black was pushed across the sea
and up to the edge of the village.
He went out to see what it was,
and what he found was a humpback whale.

This concludes the second major section of the third movement of the poem. We have seen the Raven renamed Voicehandler's Heir by his doting mother, seen him violate with im-
punity the proprieties of life in his uncle's house, and seen him
extort from his uncle's wife some as yet unidentified power belonging to his uncle. We have seen that Voicehandler's Heir, by
words alone, can change the tides, but that he cannot change the
mind of his own mother. And we know a little more about the
way in which the gods, with whom the Raven is now living, can
switch back and forth between the forms of human beings and
the forms of killer whales. We have seen how the dog – an anom-
alous creature who was the only domesticated animal in the classical Haida world – can function as the Raven's agent.[11] And we
have met some spirit-beings called the singers, *sghalanggaangas,*
who sound faintly like the muses of the Haida world – yet nothing whatever suggests that Skaay or any other Haida mythteller
regarded them as his familiars or his sponsors.

Skaay is not yet finished with the themes he has developed in
this section of the poem, but other themes are now called into
play. These themes are drawn into the poem by the gift that the
Raven has extorted from his fathers. I have called that gift, for
convenience, a humpback whale. The Haida word is *kun,* which

properly applies to any food whale, while *sghaana* refers to killer whales alone. Three large species of *kun* visit the waters surrounding Haida Gwaii. These are the humpback, the grey whale, and the right whale. All three are migratory. Most years, they appear in Haida waters in late spring and early fall, roughly May through July and September to October.[12]

Killer whales, *sghaana*, are the primary visible forms of the gods in the Haida mythworld; *kun* are their favorite food. But the relations between the species are interpreted in other ways as well. Skaay's old friend Kilxhawgins told Swanton of a spirit-being or killer whale woman (*sghaana jaat*) who was married to a human being and had a humpback whale (*kun*) for a lover. This is no surprise, Swanton's teachers told him, because "killer whales are always in love with common [humpback] whales."[13]

Late October – the last part of the season when *kun* are normally present in Haida waters – was once the favorite time for boys to go hunting birds with bows and arrows. Late October also happens to be the time when Skaay performed this version of the poem. He continues:

O n the beach, beside the whale,
    he built himself a blind out of evergreen boughs
and shot many different kinds of birds.

Later, a bufflehead[14] *came there to feed.*
He wanted it.   850
He shot it, taking aim above its head,
and then it flew.
Square in the head is where he hit it.

He took its skin and put it on.
Then he thought of waves coming ashore.
The waves began to come ashore then,
and he glided down to the water.
He dived under a wave as it came toward him.

When he had done this many times,
he flapped up on the shore   860
and came out of the skin.

He hung it to dry in the blind.
He made it his, they say.
He put it into a two-headed spruce for safekeeping.

After he had shot many different kinds of birds,
a sleek blue being came to the whale to feed.
It flew down from above.
It ate from the back of the whale.

He took a shot at it.
His arrow passed between its wings.   870
That disappointed him.

He returned to the blind
early the following morning.
After he had sat there for a while,
it flew down out of the sky again.
It was calling.

As soon as it started to eat from the back of the whale,
he took another shot at it.
Again the arrow slipped between its wings.
That disappointed him.   880

He returned to the blind early again
on the following morning.
Soon it came again to feed.

He aimed above it this time,
just as it was lifting off,
and hit it in the head.

Then he went down to the water to get it
and brought it up to the blind.

He skinned it.
Then he wrapped the skin around himself, they say.   890
And then he flew, way up.
He flew around for quite a while.
Then he dived.

He rammed his beak into the rock
out on the point at the edge of town.
He cried as he struck it.
«Ghaaaaaw!»
It was solid, that rock,
and yet he splintered it by speaking.

Then he hung the skin in the blind to dry,   900
and then he stored it,
side by side with the skin of the bufflehead.

Then he left the place, they say.
He went back to the house
and sat with his mother.

In the world of classical Haida literature, hunting birds is
more than a boys' game; it is the fundamental ritual marking a
male's coming of age. Yet the Raven is not bound, by nature or
by culture, to an ordinary cycle of development. His status as an
infant does nothing to deter him from sexual activity. And hunting birds, despite its evident importance, even to him, as a rite of
passage, gives no guarantee of his subsequent maturity. A line
that Skaay will drop a little later in the poem even suggests that,
in the poet's mind, this bird hunt is a vision within a vision or a
dream within a dream. That does not make it any less potent or
less central to the whole.

page 259:
line 971

Dii haw dang iiji, "You are me," says the old man to the Raven early in the poem. And pointing to some sleek blue beings perched on the screen in the rear of the house, *waa ising dang iiji,* "You are that too." We know now that a sleek blue being is a bird, and Skaay will confirm in time that it is a raven. The bird-hunting scene is a ritual, then, in which the Raven kills, skins and impersonates himself. It is indeed a rite of passage: a ritual in which the Raven dons his ancient mask and reattains his most familiar incarnation.

All the more reason, then, to ask a simple question: If the sleek blue creature is indeed a raven, why not call it a raven? Skaay is not a poet distinguished by his love of ornate or obscurantist diction. His stylistic idiosyncrasies – succinctly tailored verbs; precise, archaic nouns; and animate constructions, for example, where others would avoid them[15] – lie in the direction of compression and directness, not of linguistic ornamentation. But his thought is polyvalent and complex. If *xhuuya,* raven, had been sufficient to his meaning, *xhuuya* is all he would have said.

The passage where this thread begins is this:

Gyaan han lla lla suudas, llagi lla xhastliyaay dluu,

Then • thus • him • he • talking-acting • him-to • he • grasping-handing-the • when,

«Dii haw dang iiji.

"Me • here • you • are.

Waa ising dang iiji.»

That-there • too • you • are."

page 229:
lines
121–126

Taj xwaaghiit laalghaay gutgha kunxhaawsi un·guut

Rear-of-house • toward-being • screens-the • together • corner-forming-did • top-along

giina ghuhlghahl stlabdala ganhlghahldaayasi

creature • blue • slim-being-many • jointly-moving-acting-did

lla suudaasi.

he • talking-acting-did.

And this, again, is the working translation:

As he handed him these, he said to him,
«You are me.
You are that, too.»

On top of the screens forming a point in the rear of the house,
sleek blue beings were preening themselves.
Those are the things of which he was speaking.

In these lines images are nested within images as boxes are nested within boxes in the house on the bottom of the sea. The old man who lives in that house is handing the young Raven two roundish objects, one black and one iridescent. Smack in the middle of this action, he makes two rather startling assertions: *You are me,* and *You are that.* Skaay then explains what "You are that" means – and the explanation is more startling still.

One line of the Haida text calls for a detailed examination. That line is: *giina ghuhlghahl stlabdala ganhlghahldaayasi.*

Giina is a simple noun, often best translated as *thing* or *something,* but in other contexts meaning *creature* or *being* or *animal.* It can refer to inanimate objects, or to animate ones, but it cannot, in normal Haida speech, refer to human beings.

The Haida word *ghuhlghahl* corresponds well to the Chinese word *qīng* and the Navajo *dootł'izh,* but not to any single word in English. It covers most of the range which English divides with narrower terms like blue, green, bluegreen, blueblack, purple and turquoise. It is the color of the sunlit, living world: including the blues and indigoes of the sky, the greens and blues of the sea, the summer colors of the mountains, the breathing greens of needles, shoots and leaves, and the iridescent plumage of several species of birds.[16] It is also, like *qīng* and *dootł'izh,* the name of a range of mineral hues. It is clearly distinct from white (which is *ghaada* in Haida) and red (which is *sghiit*), but it impinges on yellow, brown and black. The Haida word for black, *hlghahl,* is also the word for color in general and appears to be the root from which *ghuhlghahl* is derived.

Giina ghuhlghahl by itself is a phrase that could apply to many things. Once in the Large Poem, Skaay uses the same words (in a different grammatical construction) to describe a medicinal leaf.[17] The adjective *stlabjuu* (plural *stlabdala*), which is added in this case, means narrow or slim or limber or lanky or sleek. It means something that is able to slip through.

The working verb in the line is *ganhlghahldaayasi*. The prefix *gan-* tells us that the creatures are acting in concert, and the infix *-daa-* means they are working as active agents. We know then that the slim bluegreen things, the *giina ghuhlghahl stlabdala*, are not, for example, pine needles; they are *giina*, but they are engaged here in joint and willful action. In other words, they are animals. The suffix chain *-yasi* tells us that this verb refers to something specific already identified, and that it operates in a segregated or privileged region of time. That region could be as complex and large as a myth or as simple and plain as an everyday subordinate clause.

Now we come to the root of the verb. That root, standing between the prefix *gan-* and the infix *-daa-*, is *hlghahl*. It means to move around. But it is perfectly homonymous with another verb, often used as an adjective: *hlghahl,* which means to be colored, and in particular to be black.

Not until much later in the poem – toward the end of the third movement – will we learn that these sleek blue (and by inference blackish) beings are definitely ravens. But why call ravens slender and bluegreen when they appear to many people as well-fed, muscular and iridescent black? This question has good answers in the world of natural history, and equally good answers in the world of myth. Skaay has both feet in both worlds, not one foot in each.

It is worth remembering first of all that blackness and iridescence are precisely the qualities of the two objects being given to the Raven – and the sleek blue beings enter the narrative when Voicehandler is actually *in the process* of handing him these things. Skaay overlays the images. Iridescence and blackness –

two qualities embodied in the raven – are qualities the Raven is about to embody in the world. Slimness and bluegreenness, as it happens, are basic properties of the Haida world too.

There is a counterpart to the scene in a story that the poet Kingagwaaw told to Swanton in the northern dialect of Haida, at Ghaw in the spring of 1901. Here a shaman is escorted under the water by *nang xhaada xhatjuu ghuhlghahl,* "a small bluegreen person." There he enters the house of the headman of the sea, who opens a long series of concentric boxes.

Qqal quwanyuuwanani.
Wagyaan ghutgwa ghagwii nang ghaykw xhatjuu gha ttsistattsani.
Ghaa'i gin ttl isdas uu quuyayuwanan.
Wagyaan ghudaay aahaw gin hltalgaay qqaydattsan.
Xhittiit ttsuujuu iijang.

Ll kkuuta lla jinttamjawan.
Lla qquhl nang sghaagas qqawaawan.
Wagyaan aaji xhittadaay uu nang iittlagidas kkuudanan
gha anggha tlaandagangan.
Wagyaan sttlang inggw lla ll qqawudagaangan.[18]

There were very many layers,
and the last box was small, a very small one.
What was in it was immensely precious.
And this box was the nest of something.
That something was a tiny bird.

Its beak was delicate and long.
The shaman sat close by him,
and the headman loved this bird,
and he took care of it himself
and had it sit upon his hand.

The tiny bird in Kingagwaaw's poem proves to be the bird of summer, whose calls cause root plants to sprout and berries to ripen. After he has brought it to the surface of the earth, the shaman places it in a lake, not in a cage. *Suu sttlinguu qqiniit naagang,* Kingagwaaw says: "Summer lives there on the lakefloor."[19]

❧   ❧   ❧

In the early months of life, the feathers of ravens, *Corvus corax,* are dull and brownish black. At first molt, four to six months after they are born, they acquire the new plumage that looks iridescent black to casual observers but proves on close inspection to be rich gunmetal blue. A raven that is slim and blue is a yearling. In the birdhunting scene of Skaay's *Raven Travelling,* the hunter and his prey are both pubescent. Both are already in the throes of transformation when their transformations cross.

The words *Dii haw dang iiji / waa ising dang iiji,* "You are me / You are that too," are spoken only once, yet they echo through the poem. And they are more than a little reminiscent of a phrase, *tat tvam asi,* "you are that," which tolls like a bell through chapter 6 of the *Chandogya Upanishad:*

> *sa ya eşo'ņimā aitad ātmyam idaṁ sarvam,*
> *tat satyam, sa ātmā:*
> *tat tvam asi, Śvetaketo, iti....*

> *What the world is is the exquisiteness of being;*
> *that is the real and the self as well.*
> *You are that too, Śvetaketu....*[20]

The titular speaker of these lines is the sage Uddālaka Āruņi; the person addressed is Śvetaketu, his 12-year-old son. So we have in the Upanishad, as in the Haida poem, a male elder offering instruction in elemental matters to his cocky and pubescent male heir.

Skaay's language is consistently concrete, and the logic by which he links his images is a kinetic, narrative logic. The early philosopher-poets of India, to whom we owe the Upanishads, take far greater pleasure in abstract terms and a static logic of direct association. I believe it would be wrong, however, to conclude that Skaay is less philosophical, in any significant sense of the word, than his Vedic counterparts. He is not, on the evidence, less thoughtful, less articulate, or less in love with clarity and wisdom. It is true, though, that for Skaay, even elemental statements about the nature of knowledge and being require sustaining narrative context.

Even for Socrates and Plato, mythtelling remains an essential part of the philosophical method. For Skaay, it is the only important method: the quintessential vehicle of ethical, metaphysical and epistemological thought. It is easy enough to say that this imposes limitations on Skaay's philosophy, but I am not sure this is functionally true. In *Raven Travelling* and elsewhere, he poses some extraordinary questions and formulates extraordinary insights, all within the bounds of simple paratactic diction, and all within the orbit of narrative form.

Skaay's ingenuity in handling the birdhunting theme is all the more impressive once we understand that he did not invent the episode itself. It appears in other versions of the poem, including the version Daxhiigang told to Boas at Port Essington in 1897. But Daxhiigang starts his story at House Point, where the Raven is already called Voicehandler's Heir, and sends the Raven out to shoot a raven only a few lines later.[21] Skaay prepares the theme much farther in advance, during the scene in which the Raven visits the seafloor, and he locates the actual hunt – in which the Raven kills and skins himself, and dries and stores his skin – at the precise structural midpoint of his poem. It is the third of the five sections forming the third of the five movements that make up the whole.

Two more sections of that movement still remain, and these complete its formal symmetry. Skaay continues:

After a time, his uncle's wife said to her husband,
«Why are you sitting here day after day?
Go out and hunt something.»
That's the way in which she spoke to him.

Then someone brought him his spear and his quiver.   910
He put pitch on his spearhead- and arrowhead-bindings.
When midnight arrived
he set off,
and his seat was empty next morning.

Then the one we are speaking of went through the door
and stepped out of himself.
He put paint on his face
and a pair of skyblankets over his shoulders.

The moment he came back inside
his uncle's wife began to turn her head.   920
They went behind the screen.
A little while later came the sound
of bedrock cracking deep beneath the island.

Then her husband came ashore.
«Mother of my child,» he said to his wife,
«Why was there that sound
we only hear when we make love?»

She laughed,
and then she said,
«Perhaps I was together with your nephew,   930
Voicehandler's Heir.»

At daybreak the next day,
Big Surf was sitting in the firepit.
Feast-rings were stacked on the top of his hat.

There was a globe of seafoam spinning at the crown.

Voicehandler's Heir began to cast his eyes around,
and then he went outside.
He retrieved his pair of birdskins
and dressed himself in two skyblankets.
After that he came back in.   940

There were two knots tied in this one's hair
and a globe of seafoam crowning that one's hat.
It started spinning very fast.

Streams began to flow from the corners of the house.
He put his mother under his arm
and dressed in the skin of the bufflehead
and bobbed around in the swirling water.
He dived and surfaced here and there.

When the water came up to the roof,
he swam out through the smokehole.   950
Then he dressed in his raven skin and flew.

He rammed his beak into the bottom of the cloud.
The water lapped against his tail.
He smacked it with his feet.
«Stop! I'm the one who owns you!»

That was where it ended.
The big waves started to recede.

Then he looked below him.
Smoke rose peacefully from his uncle's place.
Seeing this displeased him.   960
He flew down.

After flying for a time,
he rammed his beak into the housepole,
calling as he did so.
«*Ghaaaaaw!*» *he said.*

«*The foremost headman! Yes, it's you!*
It's going to be yours!»

Like many other nephews in the mythworld, the Raven has staged a medicine fight with his uncle and apparently done well. But he is not called Big Surf's Heir; he is Voicehandler's Heir. His name as well as his character remind us he has other lives to live. In the fifth and final section of the third movement of the poem, he prepares for yet another incarnation, as adopted son of the spirit-being who inhabits, or incarnates, the most prominent mountain in southeastern Haida Gwaii. Qinggi is the name of this mountain and its resident deity, spirit or killer whale.

Skaay continues the poem – and opens this new section – with lines of stark and charged simplicity:

Gyaanhaw hawxhan ll giidas
gangaaxhan ll giidas.
Awung dangat lla qattsas.   970
Gangaaxhan gaaysta lla xhitiit ttsinhlghwaangxidas....

Then he was a child of good family
just as if a child of good family were what he really was.
He came into the house with his mother.   970
Right after that, he actually did begin to shoot birds.

One day he came into the house
and said to his mother,
«*Mother, Qinggi says he is adopting me, they say.*»

Then his uncle said,
«Fools open their yawps! Floodtide Woman,
stop that boy from talking as he does!
That's one thing we're prepared for, an adoption!»

When he had said it several times, they looked outside,   980
and their hearts started hammering, they say.
Ten canoes of people dancing!
Voicehandler's Heir put his two skyblankets on
and pranced back and forth on the rim of the housepit.

His uncle said,
«His talk has brought it to be.
It is just as he described it.
Well, we have plenty of people and food!»

After Voicehandler's Heir had walked back and forth,
he stamped on the ground to the right of the doorway.
The earth split open at his feet.   990
Someone held a drum up from underneath the ground,
and a line formed behind it.

He went to the opposite side.
He stamped there too.
«Dirt itself has turned to human beings.»
Someone lifted up a drum in that place too.

He did it again in the back of the house at one side.
Someone lifted a drum in that place too.
He did it again on the opposite side.
Then there were four lines streaming.   1000

Tsimshian, Haida, People from the Distant Coast, and Tlingit
were singing their songs from his uncle's house.
And while they were singing, his uncle was saying,

«Well, we have plenty of food!»

They arranged themselves in the house,
and a crowd of people gathered near the door
to serve the meal.

Then, they say, Voicehandler's Heir said,
«Go to my sister Sniffing the Wind.[22]
Ask for food on my behalf.»   1010
Then the servants headed off.
Coho and cranberries followed them home.

Then he said, «Go to my sister Calling Raven[23]
to beg on my behalf.»
Sockeye swarmed into the house with the coho and cranberries.

The Creek Woman of Qqaasta[24] *was the next to offer something.*
The Creek Woman of Qqaadasghu[25] *made a contribution too.*
Food reached to the roof of the house.

The feasting went on until dawn.
And the next day again, and the next day again.   1020
When the guests went home, they say,
ten nights had passed.
But actually, they say, it was ten years.

⸱   ⸱   ⸱

Human beings, according to this story, did not make their own way to the surface of the earth for their own purposes. They were summoned to the surface from their place within the earth because the spirit-beings needed them to stage a celebration. Had it not been for the Raven's insistence on arranging his next adoption, the earth might still be home to gods alone, and humans might be lingering in peace or in frustration in or underneath the ground.

Daxhiigang included a similar episode in the version of *Raven Travelling* he told to Boas at Port Essington.[26] There again, four native nations of the Northwest Coast are summoned from the ground in the four corners of the Raven's uncle's house. Boas understood Daxhiigang to be speaking not of emergence but of the actual transformation of earth into humans. Skaay seems to speak of transformation and emergence both at the same time. But when Haayas of the Hliiyalang Qiighawaay told *Raven Travelling* to Swanton at Ghaw in the spring of 1901, he said that four species of birds instead of four nations of humans came, by prearrangement, out of the ground.[27]

These inconsistencies are evidence, again, that we are dealing not with doctrine but with poetry: a superior form of philosophy, perhaps, and perhaps the only developed and systematic form of philosophy that is possible in a truly oral culture. Plato – evidently the first scholar to study the effect that writing has on thinking – is often said to be the first philosopher. He is indeed among the earliest philosophers for whom we have a name and any written record. But Plato is clearly part of an older tradition. He is the last, not the first, known philosopher in Europe for whom the telling of a myth is a serious form of thinking.[28]

In Hlghagilda and Ghaw and Qquuna and Ttanuu, as in the oral cultures of Ephesos and Miletos, Athens and Akragas, there were no canonical versions of the stories. There was instead a fragile continuity of minds and voices nurturing the stories, thinking and telling them differently as circumstances changed. Only days before he told his own *Raven Travelling* to Boas at Port Essington, Daxhiigang gave a different explanation for the presence on the earth of human beings. According to that story – which Daxhiigang told in sculptural as well as verbal form – the Raven found the first human beings on the beach, crouched inside the shell of a cockle or a clam.[29]

13   The Iridescent Silence of the Trickster

THE FOURTH MOVEMENT of Skaay's *Raven Travelling*
opens as the third movement closed: the Raven is outrageously,
perversely well-behaved:

Gyaanhaw ghungghang Qinggi at lla qaadlgang, wansuuga.
Llanagaay gu anggha lla ttlsgidsi gangaaxhanhaw
ll llaaginangas.
Llaga tagaay ghan ll saawas.
Gam lla kidghattsighangas.

Gyaan daghalaygha ising lla llaaginangaasi
ll giɬghu ga tagaay ghan aa.   1030
Ising gam lla taaghangaasi.

Ga kkiiji tsiqida sting isttsaayas....[1]

This is the full fourth movement in English translation:

Then he went with his father Qinggi, they say.
  As soon as Qinggi landed at his town,
he gave a feast.
He tried to make the one we speak of eat.
But he would not accept a morsel.

Qinggi gave a feast again the next day,

to make his child eat.
Again he would eat nothing.

Two greedyguts arrived,
and someone grabbed a storage chest of cranberries.
One of the two greedyguts opened up his maw.
They poured in the whole boxful.
They poured one down the other's throat as well.

Next day, his father gave another feast.
The greedyguts arrived.
Again they poured entire storage chests
     of cranberries into their mouths.

The one we are speaking of ran to the edge of town.   1040
As he was walking there,
cranberries bubbled up out of the swampland.
He plugged the vent with moss.
When another vent formed, he plugged it too.

Then he went back to the house
and asked the greedyguts closest to the door,
«Tell me, how do you manage to eat so much?»
«Sir, don't ask that.
Do you think this is a happy way to be?»

«No, but tell me.   1050
If you tell me, you will eat
at every feast my father gives.
If you don't agree to tell me,
I will plug you up for good.»

«Alright, sir, sit beside me.
I will tell you what to do.
In the morning, take a bath and then lie down.

Rub yourself raw where you feel it most deeply.
By the following day, a scab will form.
You must swallow the scab.»   1060

He followed these instructions.

Then, after sitting there awhile:
«Father, I'm hungry!»
His father gave a feast without delay.
Again the greedyguts arrived.
Again they upended boxes into their mouths.

He couldn't be filled.
He was famished.
Qinggi gave another feast.
Then he gave another and another, day after day.   1070

At last, the one we speak of went outside.
When he kept picking cranberries out of their turds,
they saw who it was,
and they shut the door in his face.

Then he walked away, they say.
He went around behind his father's house.
«Father, let me come in!»
No answer.
They turned him away.

«Father, let me come in!   1080
I can arrange for you to have grizzly bears.
I can arrange for you to have mountain goats.»
He offered his father everything found on the mainland.
«Oh, but my son, their footsteps would keep me from sleeping.»

It was then that he started his singing.

He was banging his head on the house to keep time,
and the house began to give way.
His father came close to letting him in
when that happened, they say.

Then he got up to leave,   1090
and they snatched at the things he was wearing –
black bear and marten, they say.²
After that, he was gone a long time.

Then one day at dawn he was sitting offshore
in a harbor-seal canoe.
He was wearing the hat that belonged to his uncle.
Seafoam was swirling around on the crown.

After seeing his face,
the villagers gathered in Qinggi's house.
And after they talked about what he would do,   1100
Qinggi got dressed.

The villagers wedged themselves into the seams
in the pillar of feast-rings
    on top of the hat that Qinggi was wearing.

When things had stood that way awhile,
the broad and even ocean³ started to rise.
As the water got higher, Qinggi got taller.
That made the one we are speaking of jealous.

Then he sliced his father's hat in two.
Half the villagers were killed.
After that, he was gone for a while.   1110

And then he was there again, early one morning, they say.
«It's Voicehandler, waiting offshore!»⁴

«*Go down and ask him to come in,*» *his father said.*
«*I would like to see his face.*»

They spread out the mats.
Then his companions came in and sat down.
His father offered him food, over and over.
His father was happy to see him.

After the meal, that evening,
his father sat down near the doorway,⁵ they say.   1120
After a time he said,
«*Well, sir, my son,*
could one of your crewmembers tell us a story from mythtime?»

Voicehandler turned to the people beside him.
«*Do you know any stories from mythtime?*»
«*No,*» *they replied.*
He turned to the other side.
«*Doesn't one of you know any stories from mythtime?*»
«*No, we don't.*»

Then he said to his father,   1130
«*They don't seem to know any stories from mythtime.*»
Then Qinggi, his father, said,
«*Really? Not even the story called* Raven Travelling?
Couldn't one of your crewmembers tell me that story?»

Voicehandler cringed at what people would say,
and he stared at the floor.

After a moment, one of his crew
who was swarthy and little and sat at his right,
leaned back and bellowed,
«*Yayaaaaaaaw!*   1140
The village of Qinggi, the mythteller!»

The house was as quiet as something that someone has dropped.

«Yayaaaaaaaw!
A stalk of bull kelp ten joints long
grew just in front of the village of Qinggi, the mythteller.
The gods came out to see it
and died on the spot!»

«Yayaaaaaaaw!
A rainbow scratched its back
right in front of the village of Qinggi, the mythteller.   1150
The gods came out to watch it
and died on the spot!»

«Yayaaaaaaaw!
Last season a reef came out of the sea
in front of the village of Qinggi, the mythteller.
Gull God stood at one end and Cormorant God[6] at the other,
and they tossed the tailflukes of humpback whales back and forth.
The gods came out to watch,
and they died on the spot!»

«Yayaaaaaaaw!   1160
Harlequin Duck and Steller's Jay
staged a race in Qinggi the mythteller's village.
The gods came out to see,
and they died on the spot!»

«Yayaaaaaaaw!
A Raven rattle's ribcage came unlaced and flew around
with long, thin songs coming out of its mouth[7]
a season ago at the home of the mythteller Qinggi.
The gods came out to see,
and they died on the spot!»   1170

«*Yayaaaaaaaw!*
Jilaquns was here a season ago,
doing her weaving in White Quartz Bay,
at the edge of the village of Qinggi, the mythteller.
The gods came out to see
and died on the spot!»

«*Yayaaaaaaaw!*
Plain Old Marten and the other one who outruns trout[8]
chased each other up, down, back and around
at the edge of the village of Qinggi, the mythteller.   1180
The gods came out to see it
and died on the spot!»

          '   '   '

Boas studied over fifty different versions of the Raven story in preparing the elaborate study of Northwest Coast mythology that he published in 1916.[9] Further versions of the story have been published since that time. Skaay's is the only one in which the mythteller toys with a narrative mirror. It is the only recorded version in which one character asks another to tell the very story already being told.[10] This is also the only place in classical Haida literature where we will find the phrase [*nang*] *qqaygaanga llaghaaygaa,* "poet" or "mythteller," and the only mythtext in which one mythcreature turns to another and says, *Gam gwaa qqaygaanga ghan dalang unsatghang?* – "Don't you know any myths?"[11]

The game is not drawn out, as in the corresponding passages of the *Ramayana* and the *Odyssey*. Here the mirror is scarcely raised before the episode explodes in a cannonade of insult, mocking myth and literature alike as mere collections of tall tales. Yet I think this scene is one of the pinnacles of Skaay's art as a mythteller.

Skaay had lived the whole of his long life beneath the shadow

of the trickster in a new and terrible form. Human-looking beings of a sort not mentioned in his version of creation – beings
who must have looked to Skaay like the brothers of John Swanton – had been coming to the Islands all that time, with manners
as reprehensible and hungers as insatiable as those Skaay attributes to the Raven. Like the Raven, they had taken what was offered, asked for more, bribed and threatened in pursuit of what
they wanted, and delivered broken promises, destruction and
death in return. Then came Swanton: small, unarmed, to all ap-
pearances as innocent as a child, yet peculiarly insistent in his
demands. He did not say *Give me all your furs and fish, your housepoles or your souls* – those riches, by and large, were already
taken. He said, *Tell me everything you know; tell me all your stories;
and tell me in particular the story "Raven Travelling."*

Skaay complied. What else should a mythteller do when
asked to tell myths? What else should a mythteller do when offered not just money but assiduous attention and respect – and
especially when his listeners include, besides the strange young
foreigner, the son of an old friend, heir apparent to the headship
of the mythteller's own ancestral village?

Skaay complied – but he also found a way to illuminate the
work in which he, Moody and Swanton were collectively involved. That, I think, is one of his reasons – not his only reason,
but one of them – for raising the mirror, asking the central character in the myth if he would like to take the storyteller's place
and tell the myth in which he appears.

The figure of self-knowledge in Skaay's poem is not like a
dressing-room mirror. It does not answer shape with shape and
eyelash with eyelash in every detail. It is more like a flake of
abalone shell that answers light with light and dances on. There
is no literal portrait of John Swanton in Skaay's poem – just as in
the flyting of Skaay and Xhyuu there are no literal portraits of
the poets who joke with one another as they go. There is only a
flash of light, a wink in Swanton's direction, to show that Skaay

is pondering the presence of the innocent and earnest-looking man who is ravenous for stories and who tells none in his turn.[12]

>   >   >

A hedge, now, against misunderstanding. I have suggested that Xhyuu alludes to Skaay through the figure of the Raven in the skin of an old man, and that Skaay alludes to Swanton and his work, with even greater subtlety, in a scene involving Qinggi and the Raven. These allusions occur as sudden flashes: moments in which the myth itself illuminates the conditions in which it is told. It does not seem to me that the Raven is ever, in a larger sense, a portrait of anyone but himself. And I have said that in an old world new to Europeans, Europeans sometimes play the Raven's part, the trickster's part, the rule-breaker's part. That is not to say that European culture earns the trickster's share of credit, or serves the trickster's deeper purposes, or knows the trickster's trick of being constantly reborn.

Unlike other things that eat, the trickster is not food. In the final section of the flyting, Xhyuu told the well-known yarn in which the Raven watches the Sealion roasting his flipper over the fire. Oil drips from the flipper, and the Sealion offers it to his guests. The Raven later tries to do the same, producing only pain and the stench of burning feathers. Skaay portrays him likewise, as a sponge that sops up stories yet can tell none in his turn. Ask the Raven for a story, you get the trickster's signature: his iridescent silence. From his cohorts you get parodies of stories.[13]

When he arrives at Qinggi's house, the Raven will eat nothing. The trickster is a creature who exaggerates everything he does, and here he is reborn as an aristocrat beyond the reach of ordinary needs. Hunger – his natural condition – is something the Raven must relearn. Ravens do indeed eat scabs as well as dung – though not as a rule their own.[14] And it is evidently part of the trickster's job to reopen and maintain the world's wounds. But what exactly is it that the greedyguts teaches to the Raven?

He teaches him, it seems, to reduce himself to food – though hints of autocastration and masturbation also lurk in these instructions.[15] After he has done as he is told – another atypical trick for the Raven – his hunger is restored. This is the main event in the first scene of the fourth movement. In the final scene, Qinggi – who has moved to the guest's position in the house – asks the Raven not to *reduce* but to *enlarge* himself to food. He asks him to feed others, by telling his own story. This yields the only moment in the poem when the Raven is ashamed.

When Swanton met him at Skidegate Mission, Skaay was living in the house of Xhyuu, the headman of his lineage, the Qquuna Qiighawaay. Years earlier, Skaay lived in the corresponding house at Ttanuu, where the headman of his lineage was headman of the town. It is difficult now to determine how many family headmen Skaay had outlived, but we know of one at least. A headman of the Qquuna Qiighawaay who used the well-known name Gitkuna died in 1877. Twelve months later, at a potlatch honoring Gitkuna and ratifying Xhyuu as his successor, Gitkuna's housepole was removed and a replacement pole was raised. Coincidentally, George Dawson's Geological Survey vessel anchored off Ttanuu on 7 July 1878, and two days later Dawson photographed the village. His crisp glass negative shows Gitkuna's housepole, just before it was removed, and a sculptor working on the new pole destined to replace it.

The photo is reproduced on pages 104–106.

Both the old pole and the new told the same story. Both bore a single major figure: Qinggi, at the moment of his confrontation with the Raven. The smaller figures swarming up the sides of the two poles are Qinggi's villagers, taking refuge in the seams between the feast-rings of his hat.

Skaay was about fifty in 1878. He may or may not, at that young age, have been the senior mythteller living in his headman's house, and therefore may or may not have been asked to tell the story of Qinggi and the Raven when the housepoles were exchanged. It was in any case a story he had ample cause to dwell

Ttanuu, September 1897, looking east from the top of an abandoned house. In the left foreground is the housepole of Xhyuu's neighbor Qalgingaan of the Daaghanga Silgas. Second from left is Xhyuu's own housepole, rising from its frame. Qinggi and the young Raven are obscured by the protruding house-beams, but the beak of the long-billed Raven at the base of the pole is visible at the bottom of the photograph. The third pole from the left is Waanaghan's memorial pole. Fourth and fifth from left are the housepoles of the next two houses, both belonging to members of the Jiigwahl Llaanas. Sixth from left – again in the foreground – is the memorial pole of Xhyuu's uncle, Gitkuna. Another half dozen memorials and mortuary poles can be seen in the rest of the photo, which was taken by C. F. Newcombe.

(Royal British Columbia Museum, PN 5)

on. Skaay lived half his life in a house that told this story to it-self and to the world through its poles.

In the technical system of Haida heraldry, Qinggi is no one's family crest. There is a sense, though, in which Qinggi, more than any other figure, is Skaay's emblem and Skaay is Qinggi's voice. The spirit-being Qinggi, according to Daxhiigang, was once headman of Ttanuu.[16] And when Skaay mentions, just in passing, that the Raven killed off half the population of that vil-lage at one stroke, he knows whereof he speaks. In fact he speaks with great restraint. That *one half,* heard in the light of Haida his-tory, is understatement, not exaggeration.

Skaay's account of this disaster is completed with his usual ef-ficiency. It takes a mere two lines. Directly on its heels comes the final confrontation between Qinggi and the Raven. This is the moment in which the poem stops in its tracks to watch its own reflection. That instant of retrograde motion and stillness is a test of the poem itself and of the poet who is telling it. It is a test of the listener too: a way of asking *Who is telling what to whom?* Are we listening to the poem, or are we characters within it?

"That which is creative must create itself," Keats says.[17] The

FACING PAGE: The remains of Xhyuu's house at Ttanuu, summer 1903. The lowest figure on the housepole – largely obscured by brush – is the long-billed Raven. Above him sits Qinggi with the young adopted Raven, in human form, in his embrace. This Raven is holding a bear cub – one of the animals he offers to Qinggi in Skaay's poem. Qinggi's head is level with the roof of the house. Above that rises his tall hat, along the sides of which the villagers have taken refuge. A third incarnation of the Raven – his familiar avian form – is perched on the top.

Two memorial poles stand in front of the house. The taller of these, bear-ing the figure of the Dogfish, was erected after 1878 in memory of Xhyuu's pred-ecessor, his maternal uncle Gitkuna. The other is a memorial for Gitkuna's own maternal uncle. The figure on that pole (again overgrown by brush) is the Beaver wearing an equally tall hat. Photograph by Arthur Church. (Compare the photo on p 107, taken by Newcombe a year earlier.)

(American Museum of Natural History, Library Services, 106695)

trickster, though, does not create. His arts are transformation and mutation, not creation. He makes nothing until given someone else's form or industry to start with. He cannot tell the story of himself any more than he can make, from scratch, the Islands and the mainland or the sun and moon and stars.

Odysseus, a literary trickster who keeps slipping through the boundaries between history, fiction and myth, can spin out his own story or another's on demand, but even he must cede his present and his future to the gods – and when he hears it from Demodokos in the eighth book of the *Odyssey*, his own story brings tears promptly to his eyes. The Raven of the Youngsters' Poem, that catalog of trespass and adventure, has several Odyssean qualities, including a glib tongue. Here in the Poem of the Elders, his silence is still basic to the text. The Raven's inability to spin out his own tale represents the myth's refusal to give up being myth and turn to literature instead.

Skaay's poem leaves no doubt that he is conscious of his art, but he has no more need than Giotto or Uccello to sign what he has made. His poems are built of images and themes shared throughout the Northwest Coast, yet the poems are his alone. They bear the imprint of his mind, his voice, though not his face or name. The mirror is raised, enough to show that the storyteller knows the story listens to itself, and to its teller and its listeners, as deeply as they listen to the story. But there are no demonstrations of authorial self-importance. There is nothing in the story like Velázquez's outsized portrait of himself that stands behind a glass in the central gallery of the Prado. Those who come to listen to Skaay's story come to listen to the world unfolding in his voice, and not to see themselves, or to be seen, seeing the painting of the painter painting.

14   The Last People in the World

THE FIFTH AND FINAL MOVEMENT of Skaay's poem about the Raven is, like the second, an episodic sequence driven by the trickster's greed. Skaay recounts the Raven's breaches of propriety with obvious amusement but with hunterly reserve, never stooping once in either movement to mention the offending character's name. He does continue naming and locating the places in his poem, mapping mythic space with hunterly precision. But the characters we meet at these locations in the second and fifth movements are not the killer whales inhabiting the landforms. These movements are peopled instead by the archetypal forms of smaller animals and birds.

Throughout the poem, the gods and other mythcreatures seem to be most comfortable in human form – but not perhaps at human scale. Potent beings such as Big Surf and Qinggi, who dominate the third and fourth movements, are large in every way. They live in huge houses, have great powers and are physically immense, or can become so. In the second movement and the fifth, there are occasional suggestions that the scale is Lilliputian. There is a passage in the second movement, for example, where a wild pea pod – known in Haida as *xhuuya tluugha*, "Raven's canoe" – is put to the use its name suggests.[1] Here in the fifth movement, canoes are made from rotten sticks, and spruce cones serve as crewmen.

We begin, once again, where we left off:

Gyaanhaw sta lla qaaydang wansuuga. 1183
Ll qaagighang qawdihaw
Kunji llanagaay ghansta la qaattlxhaayang wansuuga.

Waaxhitgu tluwaay gayttlginggingasi.
Sqanttal giihaw ttl xhawgingas.
Gaasa ghan ttl jilaadasi.

Gyaanhaw gii agang lla qya guda qaawasi
gyaan agang lla sqanttala ghiihldas. 1190
Gyaanhaw ll guhlsghaang wansuuga.
Gyaanhaw gaasigaay lla qquhldagwang qawdihaw
ll kkuuda llagha ttl dangsqattlhlas....[2]

T*hen he went away, they say.*
When he had travelled for a while,
he came to Facedown Town, they say.

A fleet of canoes was bobbing offshore.
They were fishing for flounder.
The bait they were using was salmon roe.

Right away he wanted what he saw
and started acting like a flounder. 1190
Then he went under the water, they say.
When he had been stealing the roe for a while,
they pulled out his beak and hauled in the line.

Back in the village, while they were getting ready to gamble,
they looked at his beak and passed it around.
They handed it one to another.
The one we are speaking of looked at it too.
«Oh,» he said, «it's a scoop for mashed salmon roe.»

He went back of the house
and called the Saw-whet Owl.[3]   1200
He stole his beak
and took it for his own
and gave the Owl something worthless to replace it.

Later on, they went fishing again,
and again he went under the water.
When he had stolen some more of the roe,
a hook went through his beak again, they say.

The one who hooked him hauled him in
and came ashore   1210
and gave him to his child,
and they skewered him for roasting.

When his backside started cooking,
he could hear himself thinking, they say.
«*Why don't they run to the edge of the village for something?*»

They ran outside right after that, they say.
They left the child sitting there alone.
At that moment, he put on his skin
and flew through the smokehole.

The child started crying for its mother.
«*Mommy! My dinner is flying awaaaaay!*»   1220

He never left the town, they say.
And early one morning they started in cooking, they say.
The Crow brought out bark cakes and cranberry sauce.[4]
He set out enough for them all.
They asked even the one we speak of to join them.

He refused to come, they say.
«Not on your life!
You're serving plain old pussytail mussels!»⁵
Then he asked the Eagle to see what it was
they were actually having. 1230

The Eagle returned
and said they had bark cakes with cranberry sauce.
«Well, cousin, tell them I'm coming.»

The Eagle said, «His highness is coming.»
«Not on your life!
We're serving plain old pussytail mussels!»

Before they had even started eating,
he headed toward the woods, they say.
He made ten canoes from hunks of punkwood
and filled them with spruce cones for crewmen. 1240
He put flowerstalks of dunegrass
*   in the crewmens' hands for lances.*

The fleet rounded the point,
and he walked by the tideline, pointing, they say.
«Iixyaaaaay! How can it be?
Canoes rounding the point!
And they bristle with crewmen!»

They dropped their food and flew away, they say.
Then he entered the house
and gorged himself on the bark cakes.
Down on the beach, the canoes kept arriving. 1250
They washed up on shore in a heap.

This concludes section one of the fifth movement. The sticks and cones transformed to warriors and canoes have served the trickster's purpose and are sticks and cones once more. So was there ever really any transformation, or was it hallucination instead? Is this nothing but a yarn about the origin of scarecrows? Like the word-shamans, thought-musicians and conscious artists they are, Skaay and Ghandl often raise such questions. Ghandl likes to leave them hanging in the air. Skaay, who is in love with larger structures, likes to plunge on with the action, and he does so here.

T hen he left the place, they say.
  And as he was leaving,
he picked up his sister, they say.
He left his sister with his wife.
Then, they say, he set off by canoe.

He asked the Junco to serve as his steersman
and took him aboard.
He also took a spear.

The things he had come for were sprawled on the reef   1260
over top of each other.
As soon as they drew alongside,
the Junco went mad.
He brought the Junco back, they say.

Then he asked the Steller's Jay to be his steersman,
and they headed out together.
As soon as they drew alongside,
the Jay started shaking and flapping his wings.
Whoever tried to do it failed.

Then he painted the face of a bracket fungus   1270
and seated it in the stern.
«Look alive there, and backpaddle
as soon as we come alongside,» he said.
When they drew alongside,
the fungus nodded his head.[6]

The one we speak of speared a large one and a small one,
and he brought the two of them home.
He went ashore there
and called his wife to come
and put one of them on her.   1280

Then he put the other on Siiwas,[7] his sister.
She started to cry,
and he said to her,
«Yours will be safe, my darling.»

    Firearms arrived in Haida Gwaii before Skaay was even born, and he was not yet middle-aged when smooth-bore muzzle-loading muskets were abandoned for faster, more accurate breech-loading rifles. It is certain nonetheless that he was trained by men who vividly remembered the older methods of hunting, and who valued the habits of thought and spiritual discipline those older methods involved. Skaay's poetry is rooted in that world, where the only modes of travel are walking and paddling (two actions so nearly at par in the Haida world that they share a single verb) and where the only weapons used are those a hunter can make for himself from local materials.

    The dugout and the paddle and the spear, the stone knife, shell knife, bow and arrow, deadfall, snare, and the fishhook, fishclub, fishing line and bone harpoon are working works of art, not the products of assembly lines and factories. No two such tools are the same. None, as a result, is just a tool, and none works by purely material means. In such a world, there are no dumb animals and no inert materials. Everything that is has ears and voices, and every word a human being speaks is overheard.

Skaay's stories are addressed to other human beings. They are spoken, nonetheless, in the knowledge that the animals and plants and killer whales are listening. His earthy, wary, sly, patrician voice and narrative demeanor are not those of a poet cut adrift from the urgent march of history. This is more than just the voice of an old man spinning out the tales of a vanished world in a half-forgotten language, listened to by no one but a few old cronies, a wide-eyed anthropologist, and the one young Haida in his pay. It is the voice of one who knows that the living world as a whole – one particularly thoughtless and distracted species partially excepted – hears and weighs his every word.

Even here, in recounting the preposterous adventures of the Raven, the Junco and the Jay, he avoids ever naming the quarry outright. His reticence not only suits the joke; it is the way a hunting story should be told. We learn in time, without anyone ever quite having to say so, that the Raven and his cohorts have been out to hunt for *kaw,* that is, vaginas.

Incest, theft, profanity, remarriage and other antics naturally follow the Raven's distribution of feminine genitalia. Haphazard though it seems, this chaos – or rather Skaay's account of it – is skillfully arranged. It leads us to the final scene, set at the small island of Xhiina, south of Ttanuu.

T̲hen he tucked his sister under his arm
and headed off with her.
Siiwas planted ⟨ her tobacco seeds ⟩[8] at Xhiina.

When they matured,
he stood on the leeward side of Xhiina   1350
and called a lot of other birds to join him.

They went to get wood for the potlatch, they say.
They came back with it quickly.
When they had brought only a little,
he asked them to stop.
After that they began to get hungry.

Then he called certain other beings to come.
When they gathered on the water there in front of him,
he dressed himself in something frayed and dirty.
Then he spoke across the water.   1360
They couldn't make him out.

They sent for Porpoise Woman then.⁹
She said, «However would you get along without me?
He wants you to pelt him with abalone and sea urchin.»
They bombarded him with these,
and then he ate them.

Now, since the house was too small,
he held the potlatch out-of-doors, they say.
All the great spirit-beings he invited
came in their canoes.   1370

He pierced the noses of many different birds.
The Eagle asked to have his pierced as well.
The Eagle pestered him and pestered him about it,
so he pierced his carelessly, they say.
That is why the Eagle has his nostrils pointing up, they say.

Then the one whom we are speaking of went out in his canoe.
He came to where the sea was boiling.
He loaded herring into his canoe.
Then he dipped them with the bailer
and tossed them toward the shore.   1380

«*Not even the last people in the world*
will find where you are hiding.»

▸   ▸   ▸

This final episode of Skaay's *Raven Travelling* has puzzled many
readers who perceive the architectural power and beauty of earlier parts of the poem. What do planting tobacco, throwing food,
and piercing the Eagle's nostrils have to do with one another?
That is a question any nineteenth-century Haida – young Henry
Moody, for example – could have answered in a flash.

The potlatch – a ceremonial and invitational feast and property exchange – is a central institution in all the indigenous cultures of the Northwest Coast. And despite the fact that Canadian
federal law forbade the potlatch for more than sixty years, it remains an important institution to this day. English has but one
name for all such ceremonials,[10] while the Haida, Tlingit,
Tsimshian and Nishga languages have evolved an abundance of
terms. The kind of potlatch mentioned here is known as
waahlghal in Haida. Ghandl explained in some detail the procedure for *waahlghal,* and Swanton copied down his words, pre-
serving in the process an excellent example of a rarely studied
genre: Haida oral expository diction.[11] A much briefer description is contained in the letter Swanton wrote to Boas from
Vancouver on New Year's Eve, 1903, summarizing all he had
learned at his final meeting with Henry Moody:

At the waahlghal *potlatch,... when a man built a house, adopted an-*
other chief's son, etc., the secret society novices belonged to his wife's
clan and so did those who were tattooed or whose ears, nose and lips
were pierced. The novice's companions, on the other hand, and those
who did the tattooing, piercing, etc., were of the same clan as the man
potlatching. At a waahlghal *potlatch the property was given by a man*
to the people of his own clan, but a certain amount of this property
was obtained by him from members of the opposite clan through his

wife. So the initiation of persons in his wife's clan, the tattooing of them, etc., were by way of payment for the property so received.[12]

Planting a new tobacco patch all but presupposes building a new house, and completion of the house is the occasion for a *waahlghal* potlatch. Such a potlatch has particular significance for those *on the other side* (Eagle side in this case). It serves as an occasion for public alterations to the person: the assumption of new names, receiving of tattoos, or piercing of the septum, lip or ears. All such quantum leaps in personal identity require publication and acceptance. The venue for this public confirmation is the *waahlghal.* The most momentous changes of this kind – like the Raven's adoption by Qinggi – warrant ceremonials of their own. For the rest, someone else's feast must serve. But to ensure that honor flows in both directions, there must be reciprocity between the sides. That is why symbolic alterations of the self must be performed, at the request of those on one side, by persons on the other. One who celebrates a major change himself (a new house, for example) serves as an agent of change for many others, and his services are paid for in the currencies he spends: chiefly courtesy and food.[13]

It is all there in the poem – except that everything the Raven lays his hand or beak or claw on turns to mockery. He asks for help in bringing in the roofing – but stops the workers moments after they've begun. Does it suddenly occur to him that these are services he has to pay for, or is his house so tiny that one load of bark is all he needs? Skaay later tells us outright that the house will not accommodate the guests: it doesn't fit the potlatch held on its behalf. Sooner or later we have to wonder if the house is really there – or whether it is any more substantial than a fleet of spruce-cone warriors in rotten-wood canoes.

Play-acting at least is one of the Raven's skills, and he exercises it here, dressing like a beggar to demonstrate his poverty and speaking in princely metaphor to demonstrate his rank while he asks for gifts of food from the richest beings in the sea. Porpoise Woman translates the Raven's arcane metaphors into metaphors of a more familiar kind. Then, it seems, the gods themselves are drawn into the comedy. They take Porpoise Woman literally and respond by throwing food.

Greedy though he is, the Raven has been charged in this scene with edible energy, and before the poem can end, he must give that energy away. He does this in his final potlatch gesture, hurling herring toward the waiting hands of unborn human beings.

Skaay's closing is abrupt, but it parallels an earlier deft move, in which the Raven leaves another major legacy to people not yet born. After stealing the light from its miserly owner, the Raven discusses the arrangement of the seasons with a dog. Then he acts out his decision.

> *Gyaanhaw qungaay ttiiji lla qqudlayaasi.*
> *Lla hiljindi qawdi*
> *lla xhasgithlaasi.*
> *«Gam ghutguhl xhaaydaghaay xhan*   615
> *dang qing xattasghangghasang.»*

> *Gyaan qungaay lla ghaytqqamaalaas.*
> *Gyaan lla ghaytqqaysgithlaasi,*
> *sindlgu llaana ising.*[14]

> *Then he bit off a part of the moon.*
> *He chewed it for a while*
> *and flung it upward into place.*
> *«Not even the last people in the world*   615
> *will see how you are stuck there.»*

> *And he dropped the moon and shattered it*
> *and threw the pieces upward into place –*
> *the one that lives inside the daylight too.*

The poem's ending harks back strongly to these lines, which conclude the second movement, and through them to the ending of the first. It was there, in another fit of biting and throwing, that the Raven created the mainland and the Islands: homes for the newborn gods who, a thousand lines later, come full-grown, in their canoes, to the final, crazy potlatch.

➤   ➤   ➤

Swanton's hope, as he has told us, was to transcribe every story, or every mythic episode, told in Haida Gwaii. But you can no more record all the stories in a mythology than you can write down all the sentences in a language. A mythology is not a fixed body of stories; it is an open set. It is a narrative ecology: a watershed, a forest, a community of stories that are born and die and breed with one another and with stories from outside.

The mythteller's calling differs little from the scientist's. It is to elucidate the structure and the workings of the world. Myths are stories that investigate the nature of the world (whereas novels, for example, more often look at questions of proprietary interest to human beings alone). A genuine mythology is a systematically elaborated, extended, interconnected and adaptable set of myths. It is a kind of science in narrative form.

Science too is an ecology of ideas. Science, in fact, is a kind of mythology in computational form. Where science is in fashion and mythology is not, it is widely claimed that science is "true" and mythology "false." This claim proves, on close inspection, less a theorem in science's defense than a partisan slogan. Both science and mythology *aspire* to be true, and both for that reason are perpetually under revision for as long as they are alive. Both lapse into dogma when these revisions stop. Where they are healthy, both mythology and science are as faithful to the real as their practitioners can make them, though it seems to be an axiom that neither ever perfectly succeeds.

Unlike the characters of history, fiction or legend, the creatures of myth are as a rule elemental. Sometimes they are said to be immortal, sometimes not. They exist, in either case, in a timeframe outside normal mortal bounds. They form a set of propositions or presumptions on which the intricate constructions of the mythtellers come repeatedly to rest. They are as fundamental, in their way, to mythic descriptions of the world as the members of the periodic table are to chemical analysis.

The Raven, for example, is as mutable and complex as plutonium or sulphur, air or blood, but he is also elemental in this sense. He is a limit beyond which the mythology he lives in does not reach. His status in the mythworlds of the North Pacific Rim is something like the status of the law of gravity in Newtonian mechanics. Within those worlds, he is a confirmed and universally accepted theorem: not a new hypothesis but a useful explanation for both old and new events. New events are useful to mythology just as they are to science. They bring further revelations of the nature of old, familiar elements, and further confirmations of old, established theorems, as well as new discoveries and hypotheses that alter and supplement the old. It was that sort of living mythology, not a bundle of ossified stories, that Skaay unfolded to his listeners in October 1900.

In the third movement of Skaay's *Raven Travelling*, the Raven has one adoptive uncle (Sghulghu Quuna, or Big Surf); in the fourth movement he has another (Qinggi). But Big Surf's sister, his adoptive mother, calls him Voicehandler's Heir. This points to a third uncle. Once, near the close of the fourth movement, after he has killed off half of Qinggi's people, the survivors call him simply Voicehandler. But who is the previous owner of this name? Skaay assumes we know. Swanton went looking for clarification and got it from Gumsiiwa, Henry Moody's father.

It is not clear now what the circumstances were in which Gumsiiwa answered Swanton's question. The ten sentences Swanton transcribed on that occasion may be the only extant scrap of one of Gumsiiwa's own performances of *Raven Travelling*

– or they may be Gumsiiwa's only extant short poem and the best surviving comment on Skaay's larger one. Those ten sentences form, in either case, one of the small jewels of Haida oral literature.

Early in *Raven Travelling*, Skaay speaks of an old man white as a gull who lives on the floor of the sea. Sleek blue beings –

TEN SENTENCES
Gumsiiwa of the Xhiida Xhaaydaghaay

Nang Kilstlas nagha ghahaw tadl tsigha'awaaghan.
Sing qqalghada ll qaaxuhls
gyaan ll kindagaangas.
Sta lla xitkkudahldattsasi
gyaan gagu lla qqawghaawas guxhan lla qqawgaangas.   5

Gyaan nang qqayas taaydyas
     gam llagwii qiixhaghanggaangas.
Qawdi ising ising ll qaaxuhls
gyaan kindagaangas
gyaan sta lla kkuughwittsaasi
gyaan ll qqawgaangas.   10

Gangaang lla suugang qawdihaw
ghaatxhan ll skujuudayasta lla kyanangas:
«Jaa, gaasintlaw daa suuganggang?»

«Aa, kilstlaay, gam haw hla guudangang ghii suughanggangga.
Sghaana qiidas tsiiyahlingaay gaawung diigi suuwus.   15
Ghaagaanhaw hl suugangga.»

Gyaan han lla lla suudas,
«Hla tlguhlghaasang.»[15]

---

ravens, they turn out to be – perch on the screens in the back of his house, and when the Raven comes to visit, the old man speaks his riveting words: "You are me. You are that too." According to Gumsiiwa, it was this old man who set the poem into motion. He is the one who thinks, and thus creates, the story that the storyteller tells. And he did so for a reason.

[Hlghagilda, autumn 1900]

Loon was living in Voicehandler's house.
She left the house at daybreak
and repeatedly she called.
Then she flew back in
and sat back down where she usually sat. 5

The old man lay there,
*   not looking up at her.*
She left again,
and then she called repeatedly,
and then she came back in
and sat back down. 10

When she kept saying the same thing,
the one who was lying by the fire said,
«Tell me, why do you keep talking?»

«Well, sir, I'm not just talking to my own ears.
The spirit-beings tell me that they have no place to live. 15
That's the reason I keep talking.»

Then he said to her,
«I'll make some.»

Next thing you know, according to Skaay, some kind of light or mirage or reflection appears in the sky. The Raven flies in that direction, passes through the clouds, and steals the skin of a newborn child. Sometime later, still wearing that skin, he is invited by a pied-bill grebe into a house on the floor of the sea. It is Voicehandler's house, Gumsiiwa says. On this view, the Raven is more than just an archetypal trickster who blunders through the universe. The Raven is the horny, greedy, adulterous, incestuous, shit-disturbing and irrepressible *logos*. He is Voicehandler's way of fulfilling his promise to the Loon.

➤   ➤   ➤

Appendix 4, page 430, is a thematic map of Raven Travelling. On page 198 is an outline map of the Large Poem.

Skaay's *Raven Travelling* is a complex work, like his nameless Large Poem, which is briefly mapped in chapter 8. The Large Poem is well over 5000 lines – four times the length of *Raven Travelling* – and the Large Poem appears to belong to a later era of mythtime, but the two works have intriguing things in common. Their matching shape, like two five-fingered hands, is only the beginning.

The first movement of *Raven Travelling* plots relations among the three essential realms: terrestrial, celestial, and most significant of all, submarine. So in its own way does part one of the Large Poem. (Part one of the Large Poem is Skaay's first trilogy, summarized on pages 118–120.) The second movement of *Raven Travelling*, like the second trilogy of the Large Poem, is concerned with the distribution of terrestrial resources. The third major segment of both works is occupied largely with shamanic combat and the assumption of hierarchical roles. In *Raven Travelling*, this is where the Raven shoots and skins the raven, cuckolds his uncle and predicts his own adoption. In the Large Poem, it is where Quyaa Gyaaghandaal (Honored Standing Traveller) learns his name and takes up his position at the bottom of the sea, bearing the weight of the pole that holds all of Xhaaydla Gwaayaay in position.

The fourth movement of *Raven Travelling* is the story of the Raven's relations with Qinggi. This is the one place in the poem where the Raven is called by the title Voicehandler (Nang Kilstlas). Earlier in the poem, Skaay refers (or lets his characters refer) to the Raven as Voicehandler's Heir, but only here in the fourth movement does he use the name in its full and simple form. The corresponding section of the Large Poem is a rich and complex story of the relations between Naked God and Voicehandler. This is the only place in the Large Poem where anyone mentions Voicehandler's name.

Raven Travelling concludes with a tale that involves the Raven and two women: his second wife and his sister. Cloud Woman, the second wife, appears and quickly vanishes again, but not before she furnishes tobacco seeds, which the Raven's sister plants. That act of planting brings the poem to earth and begins the final cadence; nothing else remains except the Raven's crazy pot-latch and his last fling: a quick distribution of herring. The final segment of the Large Poem is once again the story of a hero and two women – mother and wife in this case, and the hero loses them both. In the final lines, a third woman appears. Cloud Woman is her name, and what she does is bring tobacco from the mainland and plant it in the Islands.

This is a superficial sketch of some of the more obvious thematic and structural parallels between *Raven Travelling* and Skaay's Large Poem. There are others which could be charted in great detail, along with the countless thematic and structural differences. These two large works of art are not mere variations on each other, but they have more than enough in common to testify, I think, to an established sense of literary structure. Is that sense of structure Skaay's alone? Or is it evidence of old and shared conventions, resembling (for example) the once widely shared conventions of sonata form, the Baroque suite, or the five-act Elizabethan drama?

Hundreds of large columnar sculptures – known in Haida as

gyaaghang and *xhaat*, and in English as housepoles, memorial poles and burial posts or mortuary poles – stood in the Haida villages two centuries ago. In museum collections around the world, about sixty of these poles can still be seen – some intact and others cut into sections. A few specialized collections hold the rotted, charred remains of at least a dozen more. These, and the hundreds of poles still visible in early photographs, make it possible to study in detail the conventions of nineteenth-century Haida sculpture, and with patience to recognize the touch of certain individual artists, even when we cannot learn their names. Themes and figures are endlessly repeated, as in European art, and yet no two poles are identical. There are subtle poles and crude poles, complex poles and simple poles, deeply carved and shallow poles. The silent chorus of the whole reveals the conventions which give strength to the works of lesser apprentices and resilience to the works of greater masters.

We have, of course, no photos of the works of oral literature spoken in the houses that once stood behind these poles. Swanton's published and manuscript anthologies, large and wonderful though they are, lack the time-depth and the breadth of the photographic record of the sculpture. The photographs – starting with George Dawson's, made in 1878 – give us glimpses of hundreds of pieces of sculpture made when Skaay was still a young man, and some that must have been carved before he was born. There is every reason to think that the traditions of Haida oral literature were as widely shared and as rich as those of Haida sculpture.

STANSING

15 A Knife That Could Open Its Mouth

THE CLASSICAL AUTHORS of the European tradition are people whose personal lives we know little about. There are some, like Sappho and Sophocles, for whom we have authentic-sounding names, places of residence, and real or approximate dates. Others, like Homer and Hesiod, are nothing but names for the shadows cast by their works. Their voices are as clear and unmistakable as the song of the winter wren or the hermit thrush, but the voices are the only proof we have that their owners might exist. Our inability to see them is more than a function of temporal distance. We are separated from them not so much by time as by events: invasions, revolutions, plagues, and the erosive tides of greed and unconcern which reduce human memory to delusion and written records to dust. And we are separated from them by the character of classicism itself. They are artists far more interested in what they can perceive than in perceptions they create. They ask not *Who am I?* but *What is this?*

Invasions, plagues and revolutions separate us now from Skaay as well. The decades since his death have been in some ways as destructive as the centuries between ourselves and Aeschylus. But Skaay is not in any case a poet who would leave us a wide biographical trail or a confessional self-portrait.

The nameless Large Poem and the version of *Raven Travelling* that Skaay dictated in the fall of 1900 give us not a scrap of biographical detail, but they tell us a great deal about the mind of the man who composed them. There are two shorter documents that tell us something more about his background and the facts of his early life. Both of these, again, are texts recorded by John Swanton. One was spoken by Skaay himself. The other – a fragment of autobiography in which Skaay makes a cameo appearance – was spoken by one of his oldest friends.

Early in his stay in Haida Gwaii, Swanton made it a habit to ask not only for myths (*qqaygaang*) but also for family histories (*qqayaagaang*). He evidently hoped in the beginning to record such a story for each surviving lineage. In the end, he got stories of this kind for five families only. The brevity and fragmentary nature of these stories came as a surprise to him, and perhaps he soon stopped asking. Skaay, whose family was the Qquuna Qiighawaay, was one of the people he approached for such a story. In response, he got a tale like no other Skaay had told.

Typical endings

experiential:
-(g)an(i)
inferential:
-(a)ghan(i)
habitual:
-(g)in/-(g)iini
putative:
-(g)ang
definitive:
-(a)s(i)

Time past is multifaceted in Haida. There is a *past experiential,* used when speaking from personal knowledge (*I saw him,* etc). There is a *past inferential,* for stating knowledge gained at second hand (*My mother was born in Ttanuu,* etc). There is also a *past habitual* (*I always used to go,* etc). But the forms we meet most frequently in southern Haida mythtexts are the *putative past* and the *definitive past.* Putative verbs we have met before. They are used when acts are talked, thought or asked about (*Where did he go? He went, they say,* etc). The definitive past is used where time is self-enclosed. It is often found in subordinate clauses, and for Ghandl and Skaay it is the fundamental storytelling mode.

Throughout the Large Poem and *Raven Travelling,* Skaay uses the definitive and putative past. Throughout his family story, he uses past inferential verbs instead. The implication is that he accepts these events as part of historical rather than mythological time. Not all Haida speakers, and not all Haida poets, are concerned with this distinction. Skaay's grammatical decisions and maneuvers are not dictated simply by language or culture. They are grammatical choices inflected by personal style.

Many elements familiar from the myths reappear in Skaay's family story, but the major themes and characters are different. The myths are poems about mythcreatures. At the center of this poem are human beings. The principle theme is the link between people and place. The result is not only a poem; it is a narrative deed of land and declaration of title.

As further proof that this is a poem concerned with history more than with mythtime, a piece of distinctly historical hardware – a pocket knife – appears in the opening lines.

Ttlxingas llanagaay haw ghaghudaayaghan.
Gaaydluuhaw gu sttiqagaghan.
Gaaydluuhaw Dattsikilstlas gujaanggha Jaat Sttaghagaxhiigans
   sqawqquudaxung daghaayaghan.
Dluuhaw Tsixhudalxa gu Jaat Sttaghagaxhiigans kkutwaalaghan....[1]   4

[i]

The village of Ttlxingas[2] was still inhabited,
   but the sickness had come by that time.
Boss Wren's daughter, Thunder Walking Woman,
   owned a knife that could open its mouth.
And Thunder Walking Woman died at Ttsixhudalxa.[3]
They said that something had carried her off   5
because of the knife that could open its mouth.

They paddled Thunder Walking Woman's body back to Ttlxingas.
Then they said that the knife that could open its mouth
   belonged to Disease,
and they paddled it out to the middle.
They fastened feathers to the knife and let it sink.   10
By way of the knife that could open its mouth,
they claimed the sea.

[ii]

Later, Ttaagyaaw took up hunting with dogs,
and while he was out with one of the dogs,

a black bear attacked him.
It tore off his scalp.

They tracked him and found him and carried him in,
and they laid out his body.
With that, they claimed the land as well as the inlets.

Then the Daaghanga Sils family paid them one copper shield
for rights to the inlet: 20
a copper shield matched against the knife.

He was Waanaghan's son.[4]
He was killed at Kkyal.[5]

And a Qaagyals Qiigha woman
     gave the Qquuna Qiighawaay a copper shield,
renewing rights to the inlet, because of the knife.

    [iii]

Skilttakingang too started hunting with dogs.
At Hlghaay[6] *his dogs started barking.*
As he started toward them,
he fell on the rock.
The whole of his lower leg was open to the bone.   30
He died there.
Again they claimed the ocean and the inlets and the land.

The Daaghanga Sils family paid another copper shield
     to confirm their ownership of Ghaahlins
and the Qaagyals Qiigha woman paid another copper shield
     to confirm her ownership of Qana.

They claimed all the islets too.
There was no land not already spoken for.

[iv]

A long time later, Waanaghan settled there again.
Ttawgwaghanat, his daughter, was born
when they were living there at Qquuna.

Then Ttawgwaghanat went to Hlghaay.
A woman of the Saw-Whet Owl family travelled with her,   40
and a Daaghanga Silga woman too.
On the way, they capsized.

Both Ttawgwaghanat and the Owl woman drowned.
Then there were tears and tears and more tears.
Sending them food by way of the fire,[7] *there in the house,*
they claimed the sea and all the Islands.
All of them belonged to the Qquuna Qiighawaay.

[v]

After Waanaghan died,
when another Waanaghan lived in his place,
Gitkuna was born.   50
Gitkuna built the house he called Gutkwaayda.
He married a Qqaadasghu Qiigha woman.

He was seal-hunting once, out at Gwaaya.
He was creeping toward some seals on the beach
    with his harpoon,
and a small killer whale, a pinto, with two sharp dorsal fins,
swam up just beyond the seals.
It was handsome.
He harpooned it.

Writhing from the wound,
it thrashed across the ocean surface, spouting.   60

At Xhiihlaghut it dived.

The hunters left at once in their canoe.
When they came abreast of Gwiighal,[8]
the open sea beyond them was thick with killer whales.
They were somersaulting over the canoe.

Gitkuna looked toward the south.
The sea was thick with killer whales.
And he looked toward the north.
It was the same there too.

The roof planks of the sea flew toward them   70
and landed right beside them.
The crossbeams of the sea stood up on end
and fell in their direction.
The rafters of the sea fell close to them as well.

After paddling a long time at top speed,
they came ashore at Gwiighal.
They brought the canoe up high above the driftwood.
By then the killer whales were doing tailstands
    even on dry land.

Soon Gitkuna's crewmen said,
«We'd better think of something.»   80

Big killer whales were spyhopping right there in the cove.
They offered them tobacco.
When they put another offering
    of calcined shell with the tobacco,
a bat[9] *scooped up the shell and the tobacco in its jaws.*
Then the biggest killer whales moved out to deeper water.
Then the gods went back beneath the sea.

As soon as Gitkuna got home,
the doctors started diagnosing him.
They told him not to go to sea for four years.
Xhiihlaghut's son was the one he'd harpooned.   90

The doctors told Gitkuna and his father
that the gods were still discussing him:
whether to let him climb up something and slip
or let something collapse on him
or perhaps just to let him capsize.

Four years at most, the doctors told him,
and then they were certain to come for him.

From that time on, he took nothing from the sea.
From that time on, he hunted nothing.

Then Skilantlinda brought him a message: 100

    Hovering near you I see
        something that shudders.
    For that I will shatter
        something you love.

After that, they made him a coffin.
He kicked it away with his foot,
and it fell to pieces.
After that, Gitkuna lay down.

While he was still in bed,
a silver otter swam into Qquuna harbor.
Right away, he asked his father
to say that no one else could have it,   110
and his father gave the order.

Gitkuna took a crew of three men,
and they chased it.
First he tried to shoot it in the harbor.
Then it led him out to sea.
The mist closed in on him at once then.

And then they beat the drums for him at Qquuna
and pounded on the beach logs.

After two days and nights of steady fog,
dawn broke calm and clear.   120
Some went out to search in the direction of Lake Inlet.
Others went to search for him toward Rock Point.[10]
His paddle was the only thing they found.

Again they talked about the sea.
Again they talked about the land.

    [vi]

Not long after that, Gitkuna's father died.
Ghwaahldaaw was his successor,
and Gwaahldaaw's son was Tlghakkyaaw.

They had a fishcamp then at Gwaaya,
and the children used to play there.   130
One day a bunch of them went there.
They picked on the auklets[11]
and pulled out their feathers and laughed.

After they had done this quite some time,
they made their way down to the foot of Headman Anjusghas.[12]
They lowered Tlghakkyaaw into one of the crevices.
He knocked leaf-barnacles[13] loose with his digging stick

and handed them up to the others.

After a while, he tried to climb out.
His head was trapped between the rocks.   140
The tide was rising.

They went at once to tell his parents,
and his parents gathered face paint, furs and feathers,
and went to where he was.

Then they built a fire,
and all the time they were feeding it what they had brought,
they were talking and talking to Headman Anjusghas.
They asked for their son to be released.

When the goods had all disappeared,
the crevice enlarged   150
and they pulled out their son.
The cliff had started closing around him
because he made fun of Anjusghas's auklets.

Later, they went out again to get birds.
They went after the auklets again,
and pulled out their feathers and threw them away.
They laughed at them.

Then they went out to the rim of the cliff in a bunch.
Tlghakkyaaw slipped.
He fell off the cliff.   160

Something caught hold of him part way down.
«Don't move!» they told him.
He moved,
and he slipped once again

and went straight to the bottom.

When the children came home with the news,
his father instructed them not to come into the house.
Then the other children's parents
    started making payments to his father.
They gave him a pile of moose skins.[14]

And then they constructed his coffin.   170
They built him a four-legged death-post –
the one with the tree growing out of it now.[15]

After that, the other children kept away
    from the children of the Qquuna Qiighawaay,
because they had paid them.

    [vii]

Before this, powers started coming
    to a woman of the Qquuna Qiighawaay.
When she started to doctor,
she called on her father
to tie a dancing skirt around her.
He did as she asked.

A god was speaking through her.   180
He promised her ten whales.
After she had fasted for a time,
she went outside,
and something near her spluttered.

When she looked,
what she saw were California mussels.
Those were the spirit forms of the whales.
She said they would be in the mouth of the creek at Hlghaay.

After ten nights passed,
they went there to look. 190
Humpback whales floated there,
a string of them.
They found ten whales there at the mouth of the creek.
The vertebrae are still where you can see them.

Then she insulted a god, they say,
over redleaf seaweed, they say.[16]

Someone came into Gutkwaayda.
«Something is moving on Turn-of-the-Tide Island,»[17] *he said.*
«Aiyeee! Aiyeee!»
Then she went out, 200
and she called,
«Who is it? Who's crossing over?
You stay out of here!»

Then they paddled out and looked around.
There was nothing to be seen.
But as soon as they returned,
they wept in Gutkwaayda.
She had insulted one of the spirit-beings, they say,
and so she died.

So it comes to a point.[18] 210

It is easy to mistake this tale as nothing but a kind of family scrapbook or a photograph album in narrative form. It explains itself at once in some respects, even to outsiders – but where is the logic in the sequence, and where is the aesthetic satisfaction of the form?

The moral thrust of the major episodes is clear. So is the sense of tragedy that prevails from beginning to end. Skaay reminds us over and again that the world is not just a place to live; it is a web of living beings more intelligent and powerful than we are. Treat what exists with disrespect, and what exists will take revenge. This double vision of the world reaches a peak in the storm scene near the middle of the poem. The sea, like any other country, is both a home to its inhabitants and also those inhabitants themselves. As Gitkuna and his crew cross the surface of the sea after angering its people, it is likened to a house whose roof is ripped to pieces by the wind. In the same breath, the whole sea is personified. The waves themselves are seen as killer whales.

But where is the family in this so-called family story? And why is what purports to be the story of a matrilineal family so concerned with the relations of father and child? Why are there seven episodes instead of six or eight or five or ten? And why does Skaay choose to tell the episodes in this order, leaping back and forth in time? Many of these questions answer themselves nicely when we plot the genealogies involved.

Skaay does not, of course, recite the family tree. He selects just the nodes and forks he needs to form a repeating relational pattern. Five quintessential, invisible women of the Qquuna Qiighawaay form the backbone of the story. (These women are represented by the five black circles down the middle of the chart on the facing page.) Not one of them is named nor even once directly mentioned. But to anyone thinking in matrilineal terms, they are present by implication, as mothers of the seven Qquuna Qiigha children whose stories we are told. Beneath the surface structure of seven separate episodes is a deep structure of five narrative segments, arising from these five women's marriages. Skaay treats their five husbands differently. We learn the personal names of all except the last (the one who ties a shaman's dancing skirt on his equally nameless daughter), but we never learn what families they belong to. We only know that, as husbands of women of the Qquuna Qiighawaay, they must all belong to families of the Raven side.

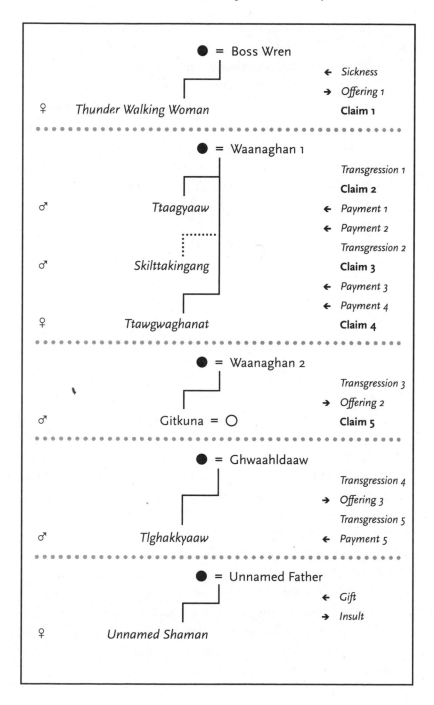

At the center of the poem – third among the five underlying segments – is the story of Gitkuna. It is told at greater length and in more intricate detail than the others. It is also the only place in which a marriage in the other direction (Eagle man to Raven woman) is mentioned. Skaay says nothing about children in connection with this marriage. They belong to another family, and their story, if they have one, is not for him to tell. As for Gitkuna's wife, she is treated like the other married women in the poem. We learn which family she belongs to, but we do not learn her name.

page 299:
line 52

Interwoven with this pattern of relations is the pattern of events. Deaths, offerings, payments, and claims to land and sea are interlaced with a series of transgressions (harpooning the young killer whale, mistreating the auklets, and hunting bears with dogs: an enterprise that always brings disaster in classical Haida literature).

The final episode, Skaay tells us, is a flashback. The first word of section 7 of the poem is *kun·ghastahaw*, which is to say "earlier on" or "before this." Exactly how much earlier, Skaay of course declines to say. Does the story of the shaman who insults a god actually precede and so in some way retroactively explain all six other episodes? I do not know. But by leaving it till last, Skaay gives it extra resonance; he also gives his narrative a balanced symmetrical form. The cycle of five transgressions is flanked by a story of death by disease at the beginning and a doctor's fatal error at the end. On the surface of the story there are seven central characters symmetrically arranged according to gender: FMMFMMF. Beneath this is the pattern of the offspring of five sequential marriages.

page 304:
line 175

Skaay's evident delight in his own language as he tells this story is yet another sign that it is not just a string of family anecdotes. When he tells us, for example, that the shamans have eavesdropped on the gods and are making their report to Gitkuna and his father, Skaay says:

Sghaana qiidas ll xhansgu ga kilhlas
ttl sghaaga ll ghungha gi at lla gi suudagangaghan,
lla ttl dlgwiixhahling
at gwiighang lla ttl xhayxhahling
at lla ttl xhastlxhahling.

page 301:
lines
91–95

The doctors told [Gitkuna] and his father
that the gods were still discussing him:
whether to let him climb up something and slip
or let something collapse on him
or perhaps just to let him capsize.

Whether Skilantlinda was one of these shamans, I do not know, but the riddle he pronounces is again very subtly composed. Swanton gives no indication that Skaay sang it, but the pattern of the speech sounds is song in itself of a kind:

Dang gwadi giina
hl qingakkiigha
gyaan giinaga dang kkuugha
hl qaaytgustlasga.

page 301:
lines
101–102

Hovering near you I see
something that shudders.
For that I will shatter
something you love.

❯ ❯ ❯

Skaay does not appear in his own family story, but Swanton recorded an aside that tied him to it in a way. When he was a child at Qquuna, Skaay said, he had no playmates from families other than his own. The other families in the town held aloof – and they demanded that their children do the same, as claimed in the poem – because those families had payed reparations to

page 304:
line 173

the Qquuna Qiighawaay, Skaay's family, for the death of the youngster Tlghakkyaaw.[19]

The only other scrap of information we possess concerning Skaay's early life is provided by his friend of many years, Kilxhawgins, the historian of Ttanuu.

Kilxhawgins was a native of Ttanuu, and Skaay had moved there as a young man. For reasons now unclear, the people of Ttanuu then mounted a raid on the mainland. Their target was a town now known as Klemtu, in the fjord called Klemtu Passage. Both Haihais and Tsimshian people fish, hunt and trap in this vicinity, and Klemtu has been home in recent centuries to people of both groups. (It appears on the map on page 23 under its Haihais name, Lhṁdu.)[20]

As Kilxhawgins tells the story,

Gaaydluu ttl ttlghudi ttlghudi qawdi
ttl tludawgan.
Qquuna Qiighawaay, Jiigwahl Llaanas waaygyaan
    Qqaadasghu Qiighawaay ising.
Gaaydluu siigaay gu gagi ghaaljuugani.

Gitgyagas ghan ttl aaxhanaghilaay dluu 5
ttlagi singgadlan·gan.
Tlugha stansingxha guugha haw ttl iijin....[21]

When we had readied ourselves and readied ourselves,
    we set off.
We were Qquuna Qiighawaay and Jiigwahl Llaanas
    and Qqaadasghu Qiighawaay.
We spent the night at sea.[22]

We had nearly reached Gitgyagas[23] 5
when the dawn broke over us.
We were together in eight canoes....

Some days of preliminaries follow: a feast, a fast, the purgative drinking of seawater, and extensive consultation with the shamans to ensure propitious timing. When the chosen day arrives, the first order of business is careful reconnaissance. Then the assault begins.

Gha ttalang giijisghaagani.
Qqandagaay ising tljigiilgan.
Gangaaxhan ttawjighaay ttl giixidani.   190
Hu hu hu hu hu!

Nagaay ghii ttl xhundaalgani.
Gaaydluuhaw gul gwa hl qaagan.
Nagaay ghii ttl qqawxhanggangagiini
    ttl xhaldaang gada dlghagani.
Giina wadluuxhanhaw ttl giigan....

In we went.
Those offshore came in as well.
They started right away to take the fort.   190
Hu hu hu hu hu!

We poured into their homes.
I myself was only looking for tobacco.
Others took the ones they found in the houses captive.
They took all sorts of things.

Then came a shout:
«The father of Iihljiwaas is hit!»
And then we ran for the canoes.

I stumbled on a corpse
as I passed between the houses.   200
The man behind me stopped to chop the head off.[24]

I slithered down the slope to the beach on my rear end.
Others had the boats offshore already.
I was glad to get aboard.

Gyaagujang²⁵ had taken someone's storage box.
After he had taken it outside
and was bending down beside it,
they shot him.
He was wounded,
but we were able to bring him aboard.   210

Half our men were trapped there in the fort.
Then three were on their feet in Reef Canoe.²⁶
One of them started loading the muskets.
Then they attacked again.

Skaay was their steersman.
All the time he was guiding them in,
he was firing.

They reached the fort.
They got all the way up there
and started back down.   220
Then they were fired on,
from the same place as before.

After that, they made their way out.
So they escaped.
The others held their fort again.
We came away with only a little property.
We left behind the corpse of a man from Ttanuu.

Then we all pulled back.
Gitkuna's canoe and his son's canoe were silent.

The others were singing for joy.   230

Then a boat came by with a mat for a sail.
There was one person aboard.
Gitkuna took him prisoner.

He said there were more people down the inlet.
Gitkuna said we should capture them.
No one agreed.

Then we burned tobacco for the dead man from Ttanuu.
And Gitkuna said to the one of the Paddler family
who had taken the dead man's head,
«Cousin, let me have his severed head.»   240

He tossed it to him then and there.
That is why ⟨when someone has some loot
*   we want to share⟩ we say,*
«He cut off someone's head!»

When we came to open water,
a big canoe went by.
We chased it –
but oh! the men of Ttanuu were tired of paddling.

And then we came back to Ttanuu.

So it comes once again to a point.   249

I cannot date this raid precisely, but my guess is it occurred in the 1850s, when Skaay was in his twenties. The Gitkuna who figures in the story (namesake of the earlier Gitkuna who harpooned the killer whale) died as an old man in 1877, leaving his names and position to his nephew Xhyuu.

Swanton put this tale last in his published collection of southern Haida texts and allowed himself a footnote in response to
Skaay's appearance in the story:

*Owing to his conduct at this time, he claimed to be numbered among
the "brave men." I esteem it fortunate that this old man's life was
preserved.*[27]

This is the one published statement that leaked through
Swanton's mask of ethnographic objectivity to attest to his relationship with Skaay. The mask is soft, of course, and quite trans-
parent. Every page of Swanton's Haida work proves, in its mute
way, his admiration for and gratitude to his teachers. But only in
this footnote did those emotions rise to an audible whisper.

The dangers of the raid on Klemtu were no doubt real enough
– but in fact, throughout Skaay's lifetime, the most dangerous
thing that any Haida could do was simply to stay home, awaiting
the next wave of smallpox or of measles. The shell layer at
Qquuna – over 2 m deep – is evidence that the site had been inhabited for a thousand years or more when Skaay was born
there, around 1828. More than 400 people lived at Qquuna in the
early nineteenth century, but by 1880 it was empty, and so it has
remained. Ttanuu, which was home to more than 500 people in
the early 1800s, shrank and was replenished over the years by
survivors from Qquuna, Hlkkyaa, Hlqiinul and elsewhere. Skaay
was one of these arrivals. But by 1887 the population of Ttanuu
was less than a hundred. These survivors – Skaay again among
them – abandoned the village and built a new town at the old site
of Qqaadasghu. Births continued; deaths continued to outpace
them. In 1897, Skaay and 67 others were alive to move to
Hlghagilda, which by then had been rechristened Skidegate
Mission.[28] Qquuna, Ttanuu and the other villages those 68 survivors came from had been home to more than a thousand.

16 The Historian of Ttanuu

IF HIS MEMORY and the missionary's records can be trusted, Kilxhawgins the historian was born in Ttanuu in 1837. He belonged to the lineage called Qqaadasghu Qiighawaay, "the Descendants of [the village of] Qqaadasghu," of the Raven side. When he moved from Ttanuu, with other survivors of the smallpox, around 1887, to the old, empty village site of Qqaadasghu – a distance of some 25 sea miles – he was abandoning the place on earth he loved above all others, and returning, in the hope of a fresh start, to the place from which his family claimed its origins.

He was baptized twice, on 22 November 1891 and 13 March 1892, and gave his age on both occasions as 54. There is no reason to think he was "converted," any more than Skaay was, though Kilxhawgins had a different cast of mind than his old friend: an historian's mind more than that of a mythteller.

Kilxhawgins was not so widely travelled as Herodotos, and he did not have the luxury, if that is what it is, of writing down his thoughts or reading other people's records. But he was, like Herodotos, passionately interested in why and how things happen. He is noticeably interested in the deeds of women as well as those of men, and in the moral weight of deeds, yet he is perfectly content in every case to state the facts as he understands them and leave the moral judgments to be rendered by his hearers. Spiritual skill and spiritual leverage interest him as much as political finesse, but he is always on the lookout for straightforward explanations, and quite prepared to question the relation of causes and effects. He purports, like Herodotos, to have no style, and therefore speaks a language of beautiful simplicity. And he has like Herodotos a deep sense of the tragedy, the humor and the curious persistence of all-too-human history.

He is interested, like every good historian, in everything: in words, food, events, the magic of machinery and the routes to spiritual power. And he knows, like any good historian, that history is not made out of dates and generalizations but out of perishable, luminous details. He was an initiate of a spirit-dancing society imported from the mainland,[1] and he seems uncannily well informed about the visions and activities of shamans he had known. He may also have been vain about his age or looked older than his years. A missionary gave him, at the age of 54, the name Abraham Jones, and gave his wife Tsatskiila the name Sarah.[2]

If his age was recorded correctly, Kilxhawgins was a decade younger than Skaay, and was 63 years old in November 1900, when he began dictating history and memoirs to Henry Moody and John Swanton. He could in that case still have been a youngster at the time of the Klemtu raid, in which he and Skaay were both involved. In that event, his claim that he "was only looking for tobacco" while the others were attempting to take slaves may be as true as it is coy.

page 311:
line 193

After the four major mythtellers – Skaay and Ghandl from the south, Kingagwaaw and Haayas from the north – Kilxhawgins is the classical Haida author who survives in greatest bulk. His extant works total 3000 or 4000 lines.[3] His compass is wide but it is centered, resolutely on southern Haida Gwaii, and in particular on the village of Ttanuu.

One day toward the end of 1900, he started to tell Moody and Swanton of a feud between the people of Ttanuu and the people of Hlghagilda. He often calls the latter Hlghaayuu Xhaaydaghaay, the People of Skidegate Inlet. This is a reminder that the people of Ttanuu must fight alone, while the people of Hlghagilda have the neighboring towns as allies.

Ttsidalang naawdihaw
Hlghaayuu Xhaaydaghaay Ttanuu gha qaydaawang wansuuga.
Gyaanhaw ghagu ttl ghiitgandyas.

Qquuhlgha haw ga jaada sghunxhan
  kunaan gi qa'in·ghaawang wansuugang.
Jaadaay wagi qaadyasi qquuhlga   5
ttsaanuwaay ising waagha yuughudyasi....[4]

In the bow-and-arrow days,
the People of the Inlet were preparing
    to attack Ttanuu, they say.
So they were scouting.

Near the village, there were women out alone
    digging lupine roots,[5] they say.   5
Close to the place where they were digging,
the women built a fire.

When the cooking stones were heated
and the lupine roots were steaming,
the warriors started peeking
    at the women from the trees.

Then the lupine roots were done,   10
and then they were done to perfection.
And all the while they were peeling them,
the women cried wahaaywan!

When the meal was prepared,
the warriors came for it, they say.
They took the women prisoner.

When they returned with them to Hlghagilda,

317

they were shouting the cry of delight
   they had captured, they say.
After that, they said wahaaywan!
whenever they did anything.   20

The news reached Ttanuu,
that they had captured the cry of delight.
And four canoes of warriors left Ttanuu
   to raid Hlghagilda, they say.

They landed west of Guuhlgha[6]
and took cover.
After they had hidden there awhile,
a canoe went by beneath them with three men aboard.
The one in the middle was fair in complexion and fat.
His hair was hanging loose.

The paddlers passed behind a point.   30
Then they launched the best of their canoes
and chased the other.
And they came up close behind,
and they were watching.

One of those farthest forward drew his bow
and shot beyond them.
When his arrow hit the water just ahead of their canoe,
the three men turned and looked astern.
Then, they say, the warriors said to one another
   it was Daghas.[7]

Then they pulled up alongside,   40
and then they killed them.
They cut the throat of Daghas first.
Then they did the same to both his crewmen.

318

At Ttanuu, they put the three heads up
  on poles on the stockade, they say.
Then the Jigwahl Llaanas, so they say, had a new cry of delight:
  Never Look Astern!
And when they heard that in Hlghagilda,
they cringed, they say....   47

In a mind inured to watching the world's wars on the evening news, this account may raise some questions. Were the Haida of earlier days really such passionate lovers of language that a war could be ended in the north with a ten-line poem and another war started in the south simply by stealing a single word? A nonsense word at that? We have Sghaagya's report as an eye-witness in the first case, and Kilxhawgins's authority as historian of his people in the second. It may be too that wars between the European nations, and gang wars in America, have been started and settled for less. But we should not misunderstand what Kilxhawgins has in mind when he dwells on the stolen word and appears to forget the kidnapped women. This is classical Haida reserve. Those women were his grandmothers and aunts. He has everything to lose and nothing whatever to gain by further talk of their misfortune or by mentioning their names.

Kilxhawgins stopped himself at this point for some reason. Later that day, or the following day, he picked up the story again:

Asgaay sta gaghiit qawdihaw
ising Ttanuu at Hlghagilda xhaaydaghaay
  gutghii tlu'iijingaxidaghan.

Gyaanhaw Ghaay Ttawjis gu Hlghaayuu Xhaaydaghaay ttl skidas.
Gyaan ghan ttl guuthlghahlxidyaay atxhan
Kwagyans xhaaydaghaay kkwaayindaayang wansuugang.   5
Gyaanhaw gi ttl ttlghadasi.
Gam ghaghang qqal xhakkat·tlghangasi....[8]

After some time passed,
    the people of Ttanuu and the people of Hlghagilda
       began to paddle back and forth again.

Then the Inlet People came to Blood Fort.
As soon as they began to disembark
Kwagyans[9] counted them, they say.   5
Then they laid them flat
without anyone's skin being scratched in return.

After they destroyed them,
⟨when they counted them again,⟩   8a
one youngster was missing.
They launched a canoe   10
and searched for him.

He'd swum away.
He was crouching by the tideline
    on the point beyond the fort, they say.
They found him there, they say.

He begged for mercy there, they say.
So they called it Beg-for-Mercy Cove.
And then they killed him too, they say.
They named it Blood Fort for all the blood that flowed.

Some time later, a Daaghanga Silga woman
    who was married to a Ghangxhiit man[10]   20
brought food up to her family at Ttanuu, they say.

She found Ttanuu an empty shell, they say.
After slaughtering the people of Hlghagilda at Blood Fort,
the people of Ttanuu became afraid.
So they had left the town, they say,

and they were camping out at Ttaahldi.[11]

The woman decided to sleep in the woods
    close to Ttanuu, they say.
Two slaves were travelling with her,
and one of them said they should sleep in the woods, they say.
He said that he could hear the sound of crewmen   30
whom he couldn't see, they say.
«Take us away,» he said to his mistress.
«Last night, people came here in canoes!»
She wouldn't believe him, they say.

They headed for a place not far beyond the village.
As they paddled toward a smooth beach,
there dead ahead of them, men started launching a canoe.
They spun in their seats and paddled away.
The others chased them ashore, they say.

Her crewmen ran for their lives,   40
and she remained behind alone.
And she refused to let them take her.
She rested her head on the gunwale.

«Get on with it,» she said. «Cut off my head!
It doesn't interest me to be imprisoned.
Neither does it interest me to run away.

«Get on with it then! Cut off my head!
Right here, my brother used to say,
yours were easiest to sever.»
She drew her hand across her throat   50
as she was saying this, they say.

And then they took her head, they say.

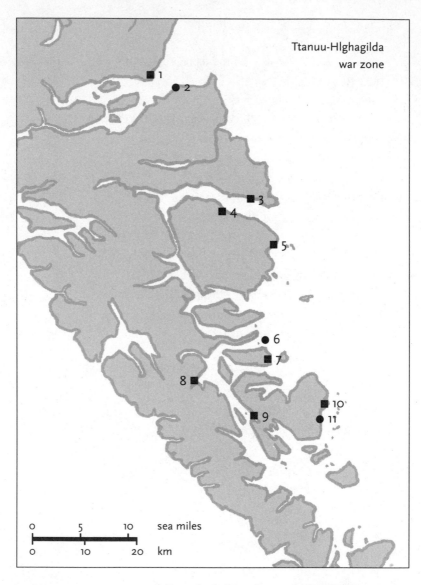

Ttanuu-Hlghagilda
war zone

sea miles

km

1 HLGHAGILDA
2 Kun·ghaay
3 Hlqiinul
4 Qqaadasghu
5 Qquuna

6 Qqaaxhada Ttaawji
(Dogfish Fort, on
Tsiiskaay Island)
7 TTANUU
8 Ttaahldi

9 Xhuut Ttsiixwas
(Seal Beach)
10 Hlkkyaa
11 Ghaay Ttaawji
(Blood Fort)

And those who were with her
escaped to the forest, they say.

They heard about it at Ttaahldi,
where they were camping.
Then they clustered together like people besieged,
sleeping in one house.

Afterward, the Inlet People launched a fresh assault.
Across from where they landed,   60
someone had begun to fall a tall redcedar
     to make a new canoe, they say.
Then he left it and paddled away.

The raiders asked the eldest one among them,
« When you have started falling a cedar,
    how is your mind during the night?»

« The days run together –
    the same as they do when the woman
    you have dreamed of sleeping with agrees.
He'll be back very early in the morning.»

They chose three men to spend the night there, they say.   70
He returned very early in the morning.
They killed him.
Then they went to sea.

After that they ambushed
a group of people paddling from Ttaahldi.
One of that bunch hoisted himself up
     into an overhanging tree, they say.
He alone escaped.
They killed the others.

All that autumn and on into winter
the raiders were swarming around them.   80
There was not one single day of freedom.

One of those whose sister was beheaded near Ttanuu
was in need of a canoe, they say.
Ginaaskilas[12] gave him a five-fathom unfinished hull.

He and his younger brother worked on it.
When they had just about finished,
Ginaaskilas decided to keep it, they say.

Alder said to Kkwiidangaay, the younger of the two,
«Cut through the hull.[13]
If he says a word about it,   90
I will kill him.»

So he cut clear through.
They pretended not to notice.
Then there was one canoe fewer, they say.

*A***ll winter long, no one went out in any direction.**
Finally, some of them went to sea for meat,
and they came home safely, they say.
By then they could see that spring was beginning.

Then Alder and The Grandson,[14] the two of them together,
went to raid Hlghagilda again, they say.   100

Some who stayed behind
felt the world lose its balance then, they say.
The ground was trembling,
thunderclaps were sounding overhead,
and there were landslides.

A Qqaadasghu Qiigha woman named
    The Lady with the Buck Teeth
used to keep two pair of horseclam shells
    and mallard oil and male mallard feathers.
She set the shells out
and filled them to the brim with heated oil.

Then she set the feathers on the rims,   110
and then she talked to them, they say.
«Oh-oh-ohhh, your mallard oil might spill.»

It stopped then.
She believed that it had stopped
because the things she used had warded it away.

As the warriors arrived in front of Hlghagilda,
those who stayed behind broke camp, they say.
They were loaded up
and riding there at anchor in the creek mouth.

Some time later, listening within themselves,   120
they started on their way, they say.
They camped that night at Seal Beach,¹⁵ they say.
They lay there all night wide awake, they say.
Amasaan and his relations were on guard, they say.

They moved again on the following day.
After they had travelled for a while,
they camped at Little Black Cod, they say.

When the two canoes of warriors disengaged,
the ones who stayed behind could feel the danger pass.
They broke their fast then,   130
but all they ate was forest food and mussels.

Then Ginaaskilas went out to scout the headland.
West Coast Cloud and a Qqaadasghu Qiigha woman[16]
got a slave to take them out in that direction.

As they were on their way across,
they met the warriors.
Two scalps dangled from the stern of each canoe.
And they told her what had happened.

«We found Hlghagilda an empty shell.
But at first we didn't go into the houses.»   140

They pulled back right away, they say,
and hid their boats just seaward of the town.
Then they went back and looted Hlghagilda.
They found a cache of sixty crates of oil
and split them into pieces with an axe.

And one of those whose sister was beheaded
while she was still alive
slit the throats of four youngsters
who were practicing with fishing spears, they say.

So the women preceded them shouting the victory.   150
People paddled over from the hideout
where Ginaaskilas was making his inspection.
And they shouted, «Iixhyaaa!
Alder and The Grandson found Hlghagilda an empty shell!
The booty they took overflows their canoes!»

Their voices swelled up with pride,
and they paddled toward a large canoe
they noticed coming toward them.

When they came a little nearer,
they could see that it was Ganxhwat's Gull Canoe.[17]   160
They spun their own canoe around
and ran to land.
Alder and The Grandson beached their boats there too.

Then The Grandson's boat started drifting with the wind.
With the Inlet People bearing down upon them,
Kiijaay swam to the drifting canoe.
Instead of bringing her to windward,
he snatched the pair of scalps
and swam back with them to shore.

He danced along the tideline   170
with the scalps between his teeth.
«Hello there! Eagles of the Inlet! How wonderful to see you!»

I will interrupt Kilxhawgins at this point, to say that a day-long battle was fought at this location, using bows, arrows, spears and wooden armor. After hours of fighting, one person was killed on each side, and both parties withdrew. Then, the historian says, the people of Ttanuu passed another year as refugees in their own country, living in one fort and fish camp after another. They ended up at *Qqaaxhada Ttaawji*, Dogfish Fort – on a small, steep islet called Tsiiskay,[18] just north of Ttanuu.

This fort was the best of all, they say.   254
They cut away the brush
and pitched their camp there.

Ginaaskilas owned a string of scoter bills.[19]
He draped the palisade with them, they say,
because someone's canoe was approaching.
But he had too few.   260

Another woman had ten of them,
and he gave her a slave in exchange for them.
The going rate for one was twenty muskrat skins, they say.[20]

In the following year, they all set out from Dogfish Fort
to mount another attack on Hlghagilda.
Up the inlet from the town,
as they landed their canoes,
someone spotted them, they say.

The People of Hlghagilda bore down on them at once.
They shot at them.   270
They wounded one, they say.

They went ashore behind Kun·ghaay.[21]
There the Jigwahl Llaanas retreated into the trees.
They left the wounded man.
He lay in the canoe.

As Taayhlgwaay was going ashore,
he turned around and hollered.

«Hey! Skilghatgwans! Try to get ashore!
Sit in a hollow tree in the woods!
If I get to Hlqiinul   280
and can borrow a canoe,
I'll paddle back to get you!»

The wounded man responded with a nod.
«Sure you will,» he said, they say.

The Inlet People broke up their canoes, they say.
Not a long time after that,
the wounded man signalled them with smoke

to come and take his head, they say.
And then they paddled over from Hlghagilda
and took his head.[22]   290

The Jigwahl Llaanas made their way by land around the point.
They had no food,
and they were cold at night, they say.

After a time, they saw a sea otter coming ashore.
They built a fire for it there
and cooked it in a pit.

After it was done,
they set it in front of Ginaaskilas.
He said, «You set this here
in front of me to eat.   300
But I am not about to eat it.
The sand might see me if I did.»

Then they continued.
They hobbled into Hlqiinul.
Then they began to pay Taayhlgwaay,
but he would not be shamed
into doing what he said he would, they say.

They borrowed a canoe from people in Hlqiinul
and paddled it to Qquuna, they say.
Someone paddled them from there to Dogfish Fort.   310
They stayed there quite a while.

When autumn came again,
they camped again at Ttaahldi.
After they finished gathering food,
they moved to Dogfish Fort again.

329

After that winter was over
and spring came again,
a pale fell out of the front of the palisade.
Then the same thing happened again.

*Gwiisukuunas*²³ *called his nephew then*
    and this is what he said: 320
«Headman's son, the women can go wherever they please.
The madness is flat on its back.
The madness is over.»
At that moment it ended, they say.

It was then that the leader Ginaaskilas died.
Right after Qaayjit succeeded him as leader,
they settled again at Ttanuu, they say.

This is the end of the history.   328

In the last line – *Haw tlan asgaay gyaahlghalangaay ghiilga* –
Kilxhawgins names the genre to which his work belongs. This is
gyaahlghalang, not *qqaygaang* nor *qqayaagaang.* It is history, not
myth or family tradition: perpetuated memory of events, not a
narrative statement of law, either natural or human.

➤   ➤   ➤

Sghaagya of the Yaakkw Gitinaay, who recited to Swanton the
Kyaanusili peace poem, had spent a lifetime in such feuds –
though in Sghaagya's and Kilxhawgins's time, the bows and
arrows, spears and slatted armor had given way to store-bought
firearms. Sghaagya himself is not perhaps, to purists, a perfectly
classical Haida author. He tells his tales in a relatively modern,
colloquial tongue, but he is not without his own form of eloquence. One of his stories closes with these words:

Gaaysta gut ttl ghudanggaangghandixhan
dii dlquuna ghyahlgaay dluu.
Sttiqayuuwanaay dluu
Xhaayda Gwaaygha xhaaydaghaay hayluwaay dluu
tlan gut isdaxidani.
Dluuhaw dlayghiidani.[24]

They were still trying to kill one another
when I was growing up.
When the great sickness came
and the people of Haida Gwaii were disappearing,
it started to end.
There was peace then.

This incidentally is the earliest recorded use of the modern name *Xhaayda Gwaay* (Haida Gwaii), "Islands of the People," in place of the classical *Xhaaydla Gwaayaay*, "The Islands on the *xhaaydla*," or "The Islands on the Boundary between Worlds."

17   Chase What's Gone

W HY AREN'T THERE MORE works of poetry and history, on the scale of Skaay's and Kilxhawgins's, in the annals of Native American literature? In fact, there are many such works, in dozens of Native American languages. Still we ought to ask, why aren't there more? It is a question probably best answered by Kilxhawgins's favorite method: example instead of deduction.

In March 1902, while Swanton sat in his Washington office typing the Haida texts of Skaay's and Ghandl's poems, his colleague Alfred Kroeber was on the Colorado River, listening to another epic poem, spoken in a Yuman language: Mojave. From his base in Berkeley, Kroeber made a number of short trips to the Mojave country between 1900 and 1905. On this occasion, his guide and translator Kwatnialka (Jack Jones) took him across the river to the Arizona side, just north of Needles, California, and a few kilometers inland. There in the village of Ah'akwinyevai, Kwatnialka and Kroeber met an old man known as Inyokutavere, "Chase What's Gone." At Kroeber's request, he began to tell a story. He spoke for six days, three or four hours a day, pausing every few sentences for Kwatnialka to translate. Fifty years later, Kroeber appeared to remember him vividly:

He was stone blind. He was below the average of Mohave tallness, slight in figure, spare, almost frail with age. His gray hair was long and unkempt, his features were sharp, delicate, sensitive.... He sat indoors, on the loose sand floor of his house, for the whole of the six days I was with him, in the frequent posture of Mohave men, his feet beneath him or behind him to the side, not with the legs crossed. He sat still whether reciting or awaiting his turn; but drank in all the Sweet Caporal cigarettes I provided. His housemates sat about and listened, or went and came as they had things to do.[1]

The story, said Inyokutavere, had come to him in a dream, and as he told it, he dreamed it once again. Kroeber was struck, though, by the difference between this and the other Mojave dream-poems he had heard.

There is no magic or supernatural ingredient in the tale, beyond such occasional deeds as the Mohave believed living members of their tribe were able to perform or experience: sorcery, charming, omens.... As regards its content and form, it might well be history.

At the same time there is nothing to show that any of the events ... did happen, or that any of the numerous personages named ever existed.... In short, the story is pseudohistory. It is a product of imagination, not of recollection; and therefore an effort at literature.... It can in effect be characterized as a prose epic.... It is also a secular epic: it contains neither mythology nor ritual elements, just as it is without trace of metrical or other formally stylized language....

Some of these statements – that Inyokutavere's epic was prose, and that it contained no formally stylized language – seem immensely unlikely on other evidence, but they are statements we can now neither contradict nor verify, because Kroeber recorded nothing more than his own condensed and edited version of Kwatnialka's rough translation. Kwatnialka, Kroeber says,

allowed the old man to proceed – for perhaps five to ten minutes – until he had as much as he could remember, then Englished it to me. With omission of repetitions, condensation of verbiage, and some abbreviating of words, I nearly kept up with him writing in longhand.

This procedure is typical of the methods used by most of Swanton's predecessors, many of his contemporaries and even by a number of his successors. The results – no matter how articulate or well-intentioned the scholar who produces them – have no literary substance whatsoever. They tell us only what the alien listener noticed and thought he understood. But what we need to know – what we always need to know – is what the poet actually said.

There are some other basic facts we will never learn about this performance, or any other performance, of Inyokutavere's epic poem. We will never, for instance, know how long it was nor how its author thought it ought to end. After six days of dictation, Inyokutavere was by no means through, but Kroeber was expected back in Berkeley. He promised to return to hear the rest of the tale – and some months later he did return, but by then Inyokutavere was dead. Kroeber looked for others who might be able to finish the epic, but in doing so he learned "that no Mohave could 'continue' the narration of another."[2] The people knew what the scholar should have known – and surely did know but was not prepared to admit. They knew that no two people's dreams or poems are quite the same. Another Mojave poet by the name of Pamich told Kroeber a different kind of poem in March 1903 and explained it as follows:

I was a baby boy [still in the womb] when I dreamed this singing. It was given me by the Ravens. Now I am a man but have not forgotten it. I dreamed it before I ever was born. If I had been born when I dreamed it, I would have forgotten it. No, I did not learn it from other Mohaves, and I did not hear any of them sing it. In fact, no one else sings like this, for it was I that dreamed it myself.[3]

This again is Kroeber's summary of Kwatnialka's on-the-spot translation. There is no original we can check for basic accuracy, nuance or inflection. Kroeber came back every year for five years to the Colorado River to hear what the Mojave had to say, but his methods never changed. He took down many words and names but not one text, not even one full sentence, in the language.[4]

Literature can survive certain kinds of transformation and compaction. The words of Lǎo Zi and of Shakespeare have survived, in their way, extensive changes of pronunciation. The verse of Sophocles and Pindar has survived, after a fashion, not just conversion into writing but also – in the interests of conserving precious parchment and papyrus – many centuries of storage and recopying in the outward dress of prose. Much literature survives, to some degree, even the traumas of careful translation. But the process of compaction and translation to which Kwatnialka and Kroeber subjected Inyokutavere's poem is something else again. The literary quality and even the basic literary character and nature of the poem will remain unknown to us forever. So would the quality and character of the *Iliad* or *Beowulf* or the history of Thucydides or the speeches of Martin Luther King – or J.S. Bach's sonatas and partitas for solo violin – if they were filtered in this way, with all the repetitions stripped out and everything else reduced to a hurried paraphrase.

In the same years that Kroeber was paying his annual calls on the Mojave, another anthropologist, Clark Wissler, was making annual visits to the Blackfoot country in northwestern Montana and southern Alberta. There he worked with a native speaker of Blackfoot, David Duvall. In 1909, Wissler and Duvall published their *Mythology of the Blackfoot Indians*. Introducing that book, Wissler tells us proudly what he has done:

The usual method was to record literal oral translations, which were in turn rendered with some freedom, though the translator's idiom has been retained wherever feasible.... In narration the Blackfoot often repeat sentences at irregular intervals, as if they wished to prevent the listener from forgetting their import. Naturally such repetitions were eliminated in the translations....[5]

335

Wissler and Duvall had the confidence of many if not all of the old people they met. If they had simply written down what the mythtellers told them, and had published the results, with or without Duvall's translation, we could thank them for bequeathing us a literary resource of inexhaustible value. Instead, we have 150 pages of quite polished but derivative English prose. This prose is courteous, respectful and pleasant to read, but it bears no more resemblance to the style of the unnamed Blackfoot mythtellers speaking to Duvall than Robert Graves's *The Greek Myths* does to the style of Aeschylus. This is a fact Clark Wissler was reluctant to admit but not a fact that he was blind to:

While texts will be indispensable for linguistic research, the present condition of Blackfoot mythology is such that its comparative study would not be materially facilitated by such records. Each narrator has his own version, in the telling of which he is usually consistent; and, while the main features of the myths are the same for all, the minor differences are so great that extreme accuracy of detail with one individual would avail little.... This variable condition may be interpreted as a breaking-down of Blackfoot mythology, but there is another factor to be considered. Myths are told by a few individuals, who take pride in their ability and knowledge, and usually impress their own individuality upon the form of the narrative. Thus it seems equally probable that the various versions represent individual contributions, and in a certain sense, are the ownership-marks of the narrators....[5]

Wissler knew, it seems, exactly what was happening. He knew that every mythteller he met had an identity and style of his own, the same as any European painter or composer. But that isn't what he wanted. He wanted to make continental contrasts and comparisons. Wissler worked most of his life for the American Museum of Natural History in New York. He was Boas's successor, in fact, as head of that museum's Department of Anthropology. His literate and polished versions of Blackfoot oral poems resemble in some ways the glass-encased exhibits of Plains Indian culture found in many institutions of that kind. It is not just that the texts are deliberately truncated; it is that they have passed into other hands with other allegiances. Fidelity to the world from which they come is no longer as important as the ease with which an impatient and alien public can compare and contrast them with the items in the next case, summarizing yet another culture. Literature is left with little to say in a world thus reduced to "them" and "us." Kilxhawgins the historian, with his love of direct quotation and accumulating detail, and his lifetime of attention to one corner of the world, is perhaps a better scientist than Wissler, and in any case an eloquent reminder that the subject, not the student nor the teacher, must ultimately reign.

Reducing all Blackfoot versions of a myth to a single stereotypical version is no different, after all, from conflating all Italian paintings of the crucifixion into a single consensual scene. What do we lose if we do so? We lose, first of all, the *reality and power* of the myth that is portrayed. It shrinks to a cartoon. Secondly, we lose the *history* of literature and painting. We lose the content of the myth, and we lose all the learning and insight, perception and wisdom, that the myth has been used to convey. Textual standardization, like political and doctrinal and commercial standardization, is the antithesis, not the culmination, of culture.

As luck would have it, a Dutch linguist, Christianus Cornelius Uhlenbeck, arrived in Browning, Montana, from Leiden in the spring of 1910. He and his student Jan de Josselin de Jong spent the next three months taking direct dictation in Blackfoot. In the following year they returned for three more months to do the same. Between 1911 and 1914, they published three volumes of Blackfoot texts. Uhlenbeck and another of his colleagues later supplemented these with a two-volume Blackfoot-English dictionary and a substantial Blackfoot grammar. The translations published side-by-side with Uhlenbeck's and Josselin de Jong's Blackfoot texts are considerably rougher than the paraphrases published by Wissler and Duvall. But thanks to these Dutch scholars and their Blackfoot colleague Joseph Tatsey, we know what Blackfoot poetry was like in the early years of the twentieth century. We know the mythtellers' styles and their names. The texts cry out for retranslation – but endless retranslation is quite feasible in this case, just as with the Greek and Latin classics, because original texts have been preserved. The rest is paraphrase: a fraudulent form of silence.

❦   ❦   ❦

Thanks to the historian Kilxhawgins and his listeners, Henry Moody and John Swanton, we also know a tiny bit about the life of the Haida poet Skaay. We know that he cannot have been a cripple all his life. Sometime in the middle nineteenth century he steered the lead canoe in an abortive mainland raid. Did his fellow warriors hear some early versions of his poems? Or did he speak them to the trees and to the waves, in the somber days of winter, as the smallpox carried off his family and his friends? Or did he dream their subtle structures only later, when a crippled back confined him to the village? These are questions it is now too late to answer. They are questions all the same that we must not forget to ask.

TLIIHL

18   A Blue Hole in the Heart

THE ORAL LITERATURE that Swanton heard at Ghaw
differs in many ways from what he heard at Hlghagilda, and it is
tempting to ascribe these differences to nineteenth-century
events. The shrunken Haida metropolis of Ghadaghaaxhiwaas
had a permanent Hudson's Bay post by 1869 and was then well
on its way to becoming the mission town of Masset. It had a permanent resident missionary from 1876 – seven years earlier than
Hlghagilda – and the movement of holocaust survivors into
Masset from the outlying villages was earlier, swifter and more
direct than the corresponding migration to Skidegate. Influential
family heads in northern Haida Gwaii found it worth their while
to be baptized well before their counterparts in the south.[1]

Yet the southern Haida towns were not without exposure to
the general store, the church and other fashionable trends. Victoria, the new colonial capital,[2] was 500 sea miles south of Hlghagilda, but in the 1850s and 1860s many Haida made the voyage
every year by ocean-going dugout. An independent trading post
opened at the old southern village site of Quughahl, near
Qquuna, in 1869 – the same year as the first Hudson's Bay post
at Ghaw. And Amos Russ (1849–1934), who claimed to be the
first Haida convert to Christianity, was a native of Hlghagilda,
preaching to his neighbors and his friends as early as 1870.

The striking difference between northern and southern Haida
literature at the end of the nineteenth century may have more to
do with cultural geography than with degrees of colonial pres-

sure. It may depend in part upon historical events that are now entirely hidden from view. It may also depend in part upon the land itself.

Southern Haida Gwaii is an indissoluble tangle of land and sky and sea: in Swanton's words, "a ragged chain of mountains half submerged in the ocean."[3] Northern Haida Gwaii is broad, full of muskeg, low hills and tall Sitka spruce. By the standards of the Coast Range, it is flat. The southern village sites were not only smaller than Ghaw, they were far more self-protective and secluded. A shallow, narrow inlet and short, well-hidden trails pierce the mountains of southern Haida Gwaii, surreptitiously linking the villages on the relatively sheltered east coast with those a world away – though sometimes only a kilometer away – on the open Pacific. The links are there, and they were used. Yet every southern Haida village had its own light and weather. Each one was – and though the houses have long vanished, each still is – a world of its own.

Trade, intermarriage and other relations between the northern and southern villages were continuous, but the differences in dialect are great. It is, in fact, chiefly out of courtesy that northern and southern Haida are described as two dialects rather than two close but separate languages. By 1900, north and south had clearly known centuries of diverging cultural growth.[4]

Swanton's judgment of the literary differences, in 1901, was this:

Although greater in number, and, if anything, more satisfactory from the point of view of linguistics ... [the northern texts] are less gratifying from a purely ethnological standpoint, being shorter and also showing more evidences of missionary influence.... This influence does not so much operate to introduce foreign elements as to reduce the length of the stories and deprive them of some of their old significance. There also appears to be less respect for myths among Masset than among Skidegate people, and when this happens more liberties are certain to be taken with them.[5]

Proving the truth or falsity of that evaluation – because of the large body of evidence involved – would require a sizeable book in itself, but to me Swanton's judgment on this point seems essentially correct. The fact remains that in his big anthology of northern Haida literature – about forty stories told by Kingagwaaw, nearly as many again by Haayas, and at least a dozen more by lesser artists – there are some probing and beautiful works: enough indeed to fill a book, and a better book than literary advocacy or analysis would make.

We can look at one of those works here. But in fairness we need something we have not heard yet with which to compare it.

       ➤   ➤   ➤

One of the poems that Ghandl told to Swanton in November 1900 concerns a class of beings called the *Tluu Xhaaydaghaay*, the Canoe People. These are spirit-beings who, it seems, circumnavigate the Islands in all seasons and all weathers, appearing ashore wherever a shaman provides them a route.

Ghandl had a name for his poem, but Swanton had some difficulty writing that name down. It was probably *Qqaadaxwa ga Jihlghiidalgins,* "Those Who Stay a Long Way out to Sea." The performance Swanton heard seems to me peculiarly foreshortened. It begins at what appears to be a beginning, but not with what sounds like an opening phrase. Then without any thematic development, it plunges to the center of the action. Whatever the cause of its odd shape, it is a poem of enormous intensity. The text as we have it opens as follows:

Gyaanhaw ttl tlaahlghu
xha ghuudlagha lla gandaxitghaawang, wansuuga.
Ttl gandaalghu qawdihaw
lla gi yaananga ghiihlghwas.

Gyaan nang tldaghawa stala ghayhlgahlda gu   5
lla ganhlina ttl xhaghaawang wansuuga.

Gyaanhaw xhagaay llagha xhiidaxha tlgaay llgaay ghii llagha
  ganhlgahlghuwaasi.
Llagha sqqiinan hlghugaangang, wansuuga....[6]   8

A nd then there were the ten of them
  who went to hunt with dogs, they say.
And after they had travelled for a while,
the mist settled in.

And they came to a steep cliff,   5
and they clambered up it, they say.

And then their dogs ran back and forth on the ground below,
squawking up at them like gulls, they say.

And then they built a fire on top of the cliff.
The one they called the brainless one   10
fed his hunting bow to the fire, they say.
And when it had vanished completely,
it lay in plain sight on the ground below.

Then he fed himself to the fire as well.
For a while he burned.
Then he vanished completely
and stood in plain sight on the ground below.
And he called to his elder brothers to do the same.

«*Come on, do what I did.*
I suffered no pain.»   20
So they started to feed themselves to the fire.
And one by one, as soon as they vanished,
they stood on the ground.

When they put in the next to the eldest,
his skin shrivelled up and his eyes bulged.

342

This was because he was frightened, they say.
But after he vanished,
he stood with the others below.

Then the eldest did the same.
That cliff is called The Tall Thin Rock, they say.   30

Then they set off, they say.
After they travelled a ways,
a wren sang to one side of them.
They could see that it punctured
    a blue hole through the heart
of the one who had passed closest to it, they say.

They went a ways further
and came to the head of Big Inlet,7 they say.

And they went a ways further.
A falcon's feather floated there in front of them.
They tied it into the hair of the youngest, they say.   40
They tied it with skin from the throat of a mallard.
It made him look handsome.

Then they came to a seasonal village.
One house in the middle had roofplanks.
They stayed there, they say.
They gathered their food from the beds of blue mussels
    at one end of town.
And the brainless one played with the mussels.

He was trying to spit them as far as he could.
Soon the others were egging him on, they say.
One of them climbed on top of the house   50
and held out his cape, away from his shoulder.

After a while he looked at the cape.
It was covered with feathers.
It is said they did not understand
that this was a sign they had broken their fast.

They walked through the town,
and they found an abandoned canoe, they say.
It was covered with moss.
Nettles grew over it too.
They cleaned it and patched it.   60
The brainless one made them a cedarbark bailer.
He carved a perching songbird on the handle.

Then they tied some feathers into another one's hair.
The brainless one got in the bow with a pole.
And one of them lay on his back in the stern.
They went down the inlet, they say.

And they went for a ways,
and they came to a town
where a drum was sounding.
A shaman was calling his powers.   70

The firelight came through the doorway
        and all the way down to the shore.
They landed below it.

The bow man went up for a look,
and as he came near:
«Here, the Spirit Who Handles the Bow Pole is coming ashore!»
This made him embarrassed.
He returned to the canoe.

Another went up for a look,

and as he came near:
«Pierced by a Wren[8] is coming ashore!»   80
He looked at himself.
He was punctured and blue.
This made him embarrassed.
He backed away.

Another went up for a look,
and when he came near,
he also heard the shaman speaking.
«Now the Spirit Who Holds up the Sky while He Travels
    is coming ashore!»
He went back too.

Then another went ashore,   90
and a voice said,
«Well now, the Spirit Who Runs on the Water
    is coming ashore.»

Another went up for a look,
and when he came near:
«Here is Swimming Puffin Spirit coming ashore.»
He was embarrassed as well,
and he backed away.

Then the next one went ashore,
and a voice said,
«This is Falcon Feather Floating on the Water
    coming ashore!»   100
He took a close look at the shaman.
He saw that shaman's clothes were the same as his own.
He too backed off.

Yet another went ashore,

and when he came near:
«Well now, Necklace of Clouds is coming ashore!»
And he also backed off.

The next went ashore,
and as he came near:
«Now Spirit with the Bulging Eyes is coming ashore!»   110
Then he remembered
that something had happened to him, they say.

Another went ashore.
When he came near the doorway:
«Well now, the Spirit Who Lies on His Back on the Water
*   is coming ashore.»*
He went back to the canoe.

Then the eldest came up for a look,
and when he came near:
«Now the Spirit Half of Whose Voice Is the Voice of the Raven,
who's in charge of the canoe, is coming ashore.»   120

And the eldest one said,
«It's true: we have turned into spirits.
If that's how it is,
we should be on our way.»

They took some of the village children aboard,
and they stuffed them into cracks in the hull of the canoe.
From one end of town,
*   they gathered some grass to make nests.*
They arranged it around themselves
where they were sitting.

Then they headed for the open coast, they say.   130

When the one with the pole pushed them off,
the wood turned red wherever he touched it.
He moved the canoe by himself with only the pole.

As they travelled along,
they found feathers afloat on the sea.
They put them in a painted box and saved them.
Flicker feathers were their favorite,
and they saved them above all.

They came to another town,
and they beached the canoe.   140
Not far away, a woman was crying.
They brought her aboard.

When this woman's husband came in from his fishing,
he saw someone's arms embracing his wife.
He threw live coals on the hands,
but his wife was the only one there,
and the only one screaming.

She is the one who was sitting there crying.
They took her aboard, they say.

They opened the cracks in the hull,   150
and they stuffed in her hands.
That cured her, they say.
They adopted her as their sister
and gave her the seat reserved for the bailer.

Then, they say, they arrived off Qaysun,
and Fairweather Woman,
      the headwater woman of Swiftcurrent Creek,
            came out to meet them.

«Hello, my brothers. I'll give you directions.
The eldest brother sits amidships.
He's in charge of the canoe.
His name will be
    Spirit Half of Whose Voice Is the Voice of the Raven.   160

«Half the canoe should be Eagle
and half of it Raven.
Half of the dancing hats should be black
and half of them white.

«Next will be the one whose name is
    Spirit with the Bulging Eyes.
Next will be Pierced by a Wren.9
Next, the Spirit Who Holds up the Sky while He Travels.
Next, the Spirit Who Runs on the Water.
Next, the one named Swimming Puffin Spirit.
Next, the one called Necklace of Clouds.   170
Next, the Spirit Who Lies on His Back on the Water.
Next, the Spirit Who Handles the Bow Pole.
He will set the course of the canoe.
He will take you wherever you go
to give power to people.
And the next to the youngest
    will be Falcon Feather Floating on the Water.

«Your sister, who sits in the stern,
will be called the Spirit Woman Who Keeps Bailing.

«Now, my brothers, take your seats in the canoe.
Go to Charcoal Island.   180
He's the one who paints the spirit-beings.
He will paint you.

«*For four nights you will dance in your canoe.*
Then you will be finished with your changing.»

Four years is what she meant, they say.

That one also gave them clothes.
He dressed them in dancing hats
    and aprons with puffin-beak rattles.
Then he wrapped a skin of cloud around the whole canoe.
Inside the cloud, he assigned them their seats
and built them the nests that they sit on.[10]   190

Then it was finished.
This is where it ends.

,   ,   ,

The formulaic opening is missing, but here we have the formulaic closing phrase that Ghandl likes to use: *Haw tlan ll ghiida*: "Here finished it [animate] becomes."

Some four months later and 100 km north, Haayas, the headman of the Hliiyalang Qiighawaay, told Swanton "exactly the same" story – which is to say, a wholly different story based on the same subject. In doing so, of course, he produced a very different work of art: a wholly different poem with precisely the same plot.

Despite my hunch that it is shorter than it might have been, the poem we have just heard remains in my opinion one of Ghandl's finer works. Haayas's poem on the same theme is slower, more prosaic, but also, in my view, a fair example of Haayas at his best. Ghandl and Haayas are very different poets, who at their best or otherwise make different kinds of poems – different in style, different in pacing, different in focus, and incidentally different in dialect.

This is Haayas:

Qqanan ttaygha ttl naangan dluu
nang sghwaansing xha qaadaghaayagan.
Xhaay ll ghaanga tlaahlangi.
Sandlan sghwaansingaay gyang xhaadagaay ahl ll istiidaghwan.
Ttl xha qaadaghawan.   5
Jaasilang ising ll isdaghawan....[11]

When they camped at the mouth of the Tallgrass River,[12]
one of them had hunting dogs.
Ten were in his kennel.
He left one morning with his people.
They went to hunt with dogs.   5
They took their sisters with them too.

The ground was flat.
They had not gone far
when the dogs caught wind of something.
They chased it.   10
When they had killed it and lighted a fire,
the day was ending.

They cooked it,
and they ate it,
eating their fill.
It was fatter than black bears usually are.
They did not give a thought to this fact.

It was different from black bear,
and its hair was matted in strands.
They gave not a thought to the matter.   20
And then it was night.
They lay down.
At daybreak the one who hunted with dogs looked up.

350

Then he looked around.
He saw steep cliffs
walling them in on all sides.
He roused his companions.

They all sat up.
They looked everywhere around.
They saw steep cliffs walling them in on all sides.   30
They saw no escape,
and they were unhappy.

One of them said,
«Let's build a fire.»
They did as he said.
They had no idea what else they should do,
so they kindled a fire.

They did it —
but not for the sake of preparing a meal.
They did it for nothing   40
except to have fire to sit by.
They saw no way out.

They were talking it over,
and one of them said,
«Let's put a dog into the fire.»

They agreed, one and all.
«Put black bear fat in the fire first.»
And they did what was said.
They put black bear fat in the fire.
It started to burn.   50

Then they hobbled one of the dogs.

They put it in too.
When it had burned completely away,
they looked up above.
They saw the same dog
walking around at the top of the cliffs.

They said, «Let's tie the legs of all of the dogs.
Let's do the same with them all.»
So they hobbled the dogs.

They had nine dogs left,   60
and when they had tied them,
they put them, one by one, into the fire.
As soon as each was burned away completely,
they saw it again at the top of the cliffs.

They put all ten of them into the fire.
And then up above, at the top of the cliffs,
they could see them.

The one who hunted with dogs said,
«Put me in the fire too.»
He said it again,   70
and they did as he told them.

Much as they loved him,
they knew that a spirit-being had trapped them,
and so they consented.
They fed him to the fire
as he told them they should do.

He burned completely away.
They looked up above.
They saw him again,

walking around with the dogs. 80
Up until then, they had been weeping.
But now they could see him,
walking around with the dogs.

Another one said the same thing:
«Tie up my hands and my feet
and put me in the fire.»
And they did as he said.
They put him into the fire.

After he burned completely away,
they looked up above. 90
They saw him again,
walking around with the one who hunted with dogs.
After that, they were happy.

They understood
that they were not simply going to die.
Then another spoke up.
«It is not good to tie each other up,» he said.
«We would be happier
if we walked into the fire.»

And they did what he said. 100
They stepped into the fire
without being tied.

All of them walked, one after another, into the fire.
All of them escaped,
and they were happy.

Then they came back to the camp.
They landed.

They saw that the people had left
the mouth of the Tallgrass River.

The one who hunted with dogs said to launch the canoe,
and they did so. 110
They went in pursuit of their friends.
They were now just as happy
as they had been unhappy before.
They were happy because they were freed
from the cliff that enclosed them.
That's how it was as they paddled along.

When they came in sight of Ttii,
they sang paddling songs.
They sang out so the others would hear them.
Even so, the village gave no sign. 120
Even so, they continued their singing.

When we're closer to town,
they will hear us, they thought,
so they kept up their singing.
Even so, the others heard nothing.

They came up in front of the town.
Even so, no one paid them the slightest attention.
Then they spoke to one of their number.
«Older brother, go ashore.
Ask why it is they don't notice us,» 130
they said to one from among them.

He did what they said.
He went up to the others
and talked to them.
They paid him no attention.

354

When he entered the house,
he rattled the doorflap.
No one there in the house looked toward the door.

He walked between them
and went to the rear of the house.
In the rear of the house sat his friends and his wife   140
    with the head of the household.
He sat down among them.
His wife and the headman said to each other,
«What has come over us?»
Then the one who had just come ashore understood
that he and his brothers had turned into gods.[13]

Then he stood up
and went back the way he had come.
As he stepped through the door
he had tears in his eyes.   150

He returned after a moment to the canoe.
Before he had reached them,
they started to question him.
«Why don't they see us?» they said.
They spoke without leaving their seats in the canoe.

«We have turned into gods,» he responded.
At last the crewmen knew what had happened.
The one with the hunting dogs said,
«Let's go back where we were.»
The crew did as he said.   160
They agreed.
They went back where they'd been.

They arrived at their campsite.

The place did not please them at all.
They pulled up in front of it.

One of them stood in the bow with his pole.
The leader said to him,
«Bring us about,»[14]
and he did as he said,
but not one went ashore.   170

They said to each other,
«Wait, we could try the village again.»
All of them said,
«Let's go there now!»
And then they admitted their feelings.

By then the canoe had drifted a little.
The leader spoke to the one in the bow.
«Bring the bow around toward the village.»

As he brought them about with the bow toward the village,
just as he said,   180
they arrived in front of the village.
But earlier, they had paddled a long time.

«Why is it we paddled a long time to the village before,
and now, by bringing the bow around toward the village,
we come up in front of it?»
They asked this of one another.

«Really, we've turned into gods,»
they said to each other.
They had really turned into gods.

«Let's name one another,»   190
they said to each other.

356

They were ready to do it at once by speaking in turn.

They said, «First give the bow man a name.»
And they gave him a name.
«His name will be
     Spirit Who Handles the Bow Pole.»
That's what they named him.

They were ready to name the ones amidships too.
And they gave them names.
«His name will be the Spirit Who Keeps Bailing.»
That is another name that they used.   200

Soon the whole crew had been named.
They named each one of their sisters too.
«This one's name will be Clear Sky Woman.»
«One will be Myth Woman.»[15]
«One will be Cloud Woman.»
«And one will be called
     Woman Carrying Something Important.»[16]
Soon they finished naming one another.
Each of them was named by all the others.

A short time later, though,
     they talked about the meaning of the names
that they had given one another.   210

«Cloud Woman, every time they see you
it is going to be calm.»
They told Cloud Woman that,
and she was glad.

«Clear Sky Woman, through you
     they will look for bright weather.»

«*Myth Woman, it will be through you
    that the last people listen to the myths.*»
[*They told*] *her this,*
[*and she agreed.*]¹⁷   218a

«*When they say your name,
    Woman Carrying Something Important,
    they will know that you are not alone.*»   220
That is what they told her.

«*You there at the bow, next time a flesh-and-blood person
        dances like a shaman
    you will let him know your name.*
I am the Spirit Who Handles the Bow Pole,
you will say.»

«*Spirit Who Keeps Bailing, you as well.
    A shaman will ask you your name.*
I am the Spirit Who Keeps Bailing,
you will tell him.

«*I, you will say,*
    am one of the ones who come by canoe.
    Some time ago we went hunting with dogs.   230
    *Let them know how it was
    that we turned into gods,*»
    they said to him then.

*He agreed.
He said what they told him.
He spoke through a shaman.*

*Then people came to know their names.
But without that shaman,*   240

it never would have happened
that the people learned their names.

More than that, the people learned
the way they died.
So their friends' minds were guided by the shaman.
They came to understand
how the one with the hunting dogs died.

No one had known
what had become of them.
That one shaman was the only one   250
who said that he had heard them
tell the story of themselves.

After he had spoken,
this was a story they couldn't forget.
They repeated it night after night to each other.
For that reason, moreover, they never forgot it.

And it has become the myth of the one with the hunting dogs.
This is the end.   258

‛   ‛   ‛

It is worth examining Haayas's ending:

Lla kihlgustuu   253
gam aaji gyaahlingaay da ttlaa qqiisgatghanggaangan.
Singya qwan gut aaji gutga ahl ttl gyaahlindagaangani.
Ahluu gam da ttlaa qqiisgatghanggaangan.

Haw ttlaa gu nang xha qaadaghaayas ahl
*   qiigaangaay ghiidang.*
Haw tlan ghiidang.

The last two lines are in the present tense. Everywhere else, Haayas relies on past inferential forms of the verb – as if he were giving a history lesson. This is part of his style, all of a piece with his easy tone. Haayas tells even *Raven Travelling* using forms of the verb that suggest a secular history.

The closing formula, since it lacks an animate pronoun, also implies that to Haayas the story is not an animate being. In the previous sentence, nevertheless, he plainly tells us he regards it as a *qqiigaang*, the northern dialect form of *qqaygaang*. To its author, this is myth instead of history. It is told with the assistance of Jaatahl Qqaygaanga, Myth Woman, who lives within the story though she may not say a word. But what the spirits tell the shaman, and what their human friends then tell to one another, is what Haayas calls *gyaahling*, the northern form of *gyaahlghalang*. The story within the story – which is the whole story except for a sliver of frame – is taken for history. The story of the telling of that story is nonetheless a myth.

If history adheres to events as understood or as reported – which it does in the traditions of Haayas and Kilxhawgins and of Gibbon and Herodotos alike – what does myth adhere to? To the history of history? To the fact of repetition? A myth is a pattern of meaning that reproduces itself: a pattern that refuses to stop meaning, or in other words refuses to die out. Myth is easily confused, in certain cultures, with advertisements, slogans, placebos and so on: things that have no reproductive power and no resonance or meaning of their own but are resolutely pushed to appear as if they did. A myth in Haayas's sense is not the same as history; it is the sense that history makes. It is resonant, meaningful pattern. "Myth" in the journalist's sense is something else: repetitious explanation or assertion, printed on the surface of the fabric but absent from the weave.

19   The Prosody of Meaning

Reduced to their lyrics alone, the Haida songs Swanton transcribed are extremely brief – usually longer than a haiku but never as long as a sonnet. When we read them instead of hearing them, or speak them instead of singing them, our standards of judgment are bound to be askew.[1] But even in this form, they sometimes offer up a glimpse of their economy and power. That power is cloaked in extraordinary subtlety and reserve.

For almost every song transcribed, Swanton learned the family ownership but not individual authorship.[2] Song composition seems, however, to be a genre in which the northern artists excelled. Swanton took down less than half as many songs at Ghadaghaaxhiwaas as he did at Hlghagilda, but – to judge from the words alone – most of the best songs came from northern singers. This, for instance, is a lullaby belonging to the Hliiyalang Kun Llanagaay, a northern family of the Raven side:

> *Aagwa naanang tlgaa guut*
> *diinang kuyandalaanii.*
> *Waghan sttagha kujawaanii.*
> *Gam hla kunggingang ang.*[3]

> *My child strides*
> *through the land of his grandmothers.*
> *Therefore his foot is precious.*
> *Don't keep crying.*

Sghaagya and Kilxhawgins may at times give the impression that death was taken lightly in the old Haida world. There is evidence aplenty that it was not. But death is treated by some Haida artists with a subtlety so great it is easily missed. This is the full text of a mourning song, owned by the women of another northern family, the Sttlinga Llaanas of the Raven side. It is a song to be sung on the death of a warrior:

> *Hakkun dang gudans kkyangu*
> *gam qayt tlakkala gha*
> *dii dang qqawdang uuja?*[4]

> *If that was your plan,*
> *why didn't you seat me*
> *in the shelter of a tree?*

This peacemaking song is equally reserved. Swanton understood it to be common property, but it too was sung in the northern dialect and is probably a northern composition:

> *Yaahl dii taadas dluu*
> *qqinang dii unsatsgaayanduu.*
> *Haw tlsiinuut*
> *dagang hl suuga.*[5]

> *If the Raven had eaten me,*
> *I would not recognize myself.*
> *Now for the first time,*
> *for my own sake I am singing.*

Without a doubt, this is a kind of Haida poetry. But far too many students of Native American literature – linguistically skilled professionals like Boas and linguistically innocent amateurs alike – have assumed that songs were the only genre of

Native American literature in which poetry might lurk. Others, including Kroeber, after looking in vain for familiar acoustic furniture – rhyming couplets, pentameters, and so on – have announced *ex cathedra* that Native American poetry doesn't exist.[6]

Boas, whose opinions on these issues often wandered back and forth, was hampered first of all by temperament. "Boas is so highly inhibited a nature," wrote Sapir, "that he has always preferred to show that a thing might not be so than to suggest that it might be."[7] He was also hampered by two assumptions. Boas thought that poetry was a synonym for verse, and that every work of literature, oral or written, was either verse or prose.

Aristotle, Philip Sidney, Percy Shelley, Charles Baudelaire, Gerard Manley Hopkins, T. S. Eliot and a considerable number of others could have unconfused him on the first point. "It is not ryming and versing that maketh a Poet, (no more then a long gown maketh an Advocate...)," Sidney says. "One may be a Poet without versing, and a versefier without Poetrie."[8] But Eliot's discussion of the problem – published in 1930 with his translation of Saint-John Perse's prose poem *Anabase* – is couched in language Boas might have found less easy to ignore.

"There is a logic of the imagination as well as a logic of concepts," Eliot says. "It would be convenient if poetry were always verse – either accentual, alliterative, or quantitative; but [it] is not." One reason we frequently misjudge these simple facts, Eliot tells us, is our poverty of terminology: "we have three terms where we need four: we have 'verse' and 'poetry' on the one side, and only 'prose' on the other...."[9]

Verse and its associated conventions – alliteration, rhyme and other patterned forms of artful wordplay – are very old conventions in Indo-European languages and cultures, reaching back to the early Vedas and beyond.[10] But verse in the strictly acoustic sense of the word does not play the same role in preagricultural societies. Humans, as a rule, do not begin to farm their language until they have begun to till the earth and to manipulate the growth of plants and animals. Songs are sung throughout the world, by many species in addition to our own. But in hunter-gatherer cultures the larger forms of poetry lack musical accompaniment, both overt (harp or lyre, for example) or covert (in the form of embedded metrical pattern). The reason is quite simple: poetry and music in such cultures are not two separate arts with separate outer forms. Both are at home in the speaking of myth. *Myth is that form of language in which poetry and music have not as yet diverged.*[11]

This does not mean that hunters have no poetry; it means that following the poetry they make is more like moving through a forest or a canyon, or waiting in a blind, than like moving through an orchard or a field. The language is often highly ordered, rich, compact – but it is not arranged in neat, symmetrical rows.

Prose in the equally strict sense is a later development still: the linguistic equivalent not of gardening, herding and farming but of roadbuilding, surveying and systematic mapping. It is limited, on the whole, to cultures that possess not only agriculture but metallurgy and writing.

There is a reason, nonetheless, why verse and poetry so often coexist – and the thinness of our critical vocabulary is not the only reason why the terms are easily confused. Verse is language set part way to music. It is language that is gesturing or reaching – unsuccessfully as a rule – back toward myth, where poetry and music are one in the same.

Boas's second problem with terminology – his belief that every instance of literary language must be either verse or prose – may be equally endemic to the European tradition, but poets and some critics have seen through this false hypothesis as well. It is the literary counterpart of the stalwart Newtonian view that all matter must be solid, liquid or gas. Present-day physicists agree that the vast majority of the matter in the universe is actually in none of these three states, and a few recent literary critics – Northrop Frye among them – have admitted that much literary language is neither verse nor prose. Frye recognized a third important state of language whose principal component "is neither the prose sentence nor the metrical line, but a kind of thought-breath or phrase."[12]

Frye's ideas were not available to Boas, but Gerard Manley Hopkins, Ezra Pound and others could have helped him with the problem. Hopkins, in some lecture notes he wrote in the 1870s, also distinguishes three states of literary language. These are (1) prose; (2) *"figure of spoken sound, which in the narrower sense is verse"*; and (3) "beyond verse…, *figure of grammar.*"[13]

Poetry is a kind of content, or a quality of content, and verse is a kind of form. In India, where the mnemonic value of verse has long been recognized, even lawbooks have been versified. In nineteenth-century France, where the social acceptability and the orderly beauty of verse became a positive disadvantage to poets such as Baudelaire and Rimbaud (and to a different kind of poet named Flaubert), poetry was taught to dress as prose. In aboriginal North America, neither verse nor prose, in the narrow sense, played any major role, but neither poetry nor talk was hampered by the absence of these modes.

Thematic or visionary coherence is prominent in myth, acoustic coherence in verse, discursive and syntactical coherence in prose. Thematic patterns, like syntactic and acoustic ones, can be microscopic, macroscopic or both.[14] But the patterns are primarily composed of things like predicates and images, not of things like syllables, pitches and stresses. In classical Haida poetry, as in the poetry of most preagricultural peoples, *what there is to count* is almost always *what there is to think about*, not *what there is to hear.*[15] This is poetry in which noetic prosody underlies – and far outreaches, as a rule – the prosody of sound. (And so it ought to underlie the visual prosody – typography in other words – inevitably added in transcription and translation.)

In works such as the Kyaanusili peace poem, what there is to think about fuses very nicely with what there is to hear. The prosody of meaning leaves its imprint in the prosody of sound, but the prosody of sound does not *come loose* from the prosody of meaning – as it must before a repertoire of meters or of verse forms can arise in any literary culture.

Hopkins's notes contain another very useful piece of advice, which is that "We must not insist on knowing where verse ends and prose (or verseless composition) begins, for they pass into one another." The states of literary language – verse, prose, and however many others there may be – are not mutually exclusive. Matthew Arnold was not wrong (nor even cruel) to call Alexander Pope's verse a splendid example of prose. A composition in verse calls attention to its own acoustic pattern, and a composition in prose to its own syntactic and logical flow. This does not prohibit any work from doing both at the same time, nor from being thematically patterned as well. Many if not most works of literature partake in some degree of the nature of vision, verse and prose. To say that a work is one or the other of these is as a rule only to point to its most conspicuous or highly developed feature. From the discursive point of view, the poems of Skaay and Ghandl can be described as associative prose. They are also, if you like, free verse – unmetered rhythmical phrases – from the metrist's point of view; and they are well-paced, shapely periods when studied with the ears of the rhetorician. But to sense their true dimensions, we must grasp another aspect of these poems: the one from which we start to hear the silent music of their images and themes.

To understand the songs, we need to hear them sung. To understand the myths, we need to hear them told. We also need to think them through, and to think them in conjunction with each other. If we also insist on the perspective of the connoisseur of language, we will not go altogether unrewarded. The songs, the myths, the family traditions, and the histories as well, contain the sorts of literary jewels that are coveted where poetry is memorized and read as well as listened to. The Kyaanusili poem is one superb example. The riddle Skilantlinda poses to Gitkuna is another. A third closes the first story in Skaay's Large Poem:

pages 166–167; pages 301 & 309

366

Diidaxwa llanaa gi at qqaadaxwa llanaa gi
    ttl qiixhagangdal qawdi gu dluu,
qyanggagaay dluu,
lla ttl ghastlgayang wansuuga.

page 98:
lines
594–596

To the landward towns and the seaward towns
    it was equally far,
they could see that it was,
when they put him over the side, they say.

Another sumptuous example is a stanza about birdsong that occurs near the beginning of Ghandl's "Those Who Stay a Long Way out to Sea":

Gyaanhaw sta lla gandaxitghawang wansuuga.
Ll gandaaldighu qawdihaw
dattsi ll dagwulgi hlkyaaghwas.
Gaayguusta nang dldajiyas kkuugha gu
    ll ghuhlghahl xhiihlsuu
lla qingghawang wansuuga.

page 343:
lines 31–35

Then they set off, they say.
After they travelled a ways,
a wren sang to one side of them.
They could see that it punctured
    a blue hole through the heart
of the one who had passed closest to it, they say.

I cite these passages for pleasure. I also cite them to show that poetry, even by the narrowest, most hidebound definition of the term, is a quintessential part of aboriginal American tradition. It would not be hard to gather an anthology of passages like this in fifty other Native American languages. But an anthology like that would still misrepresent Native American oral poetry by cutting it to fit colonial, literate expectations. Until we start to hear and see the kind of poetry inherent in the larger works from which these excerpts come, we stand little chance of understanding Native American intellectual and literary traditions – or of understanding poetry itself in more than ethnocentric terms.

➤   ➤   ➤

Liú Xié, a Chinese critic writing fifteen hundred years before our time, saw literature as landscape and the other way around. Sun and moon and mountains and rivers, he says, are the *wén* of *dào.*[16] They are, that is, the literature and culture of the Tao, the message-bearing legacy and wisdom of what-is.

The myths exist, most mythtellers say, independently of any human culture. We learn them from the others: other animals, the trees, the creeks, the ground. But wherever they are told in the words that humans use, they are told by individual human beings. Learning how to hear the telling of a myth means learning how to hear the myth itself and how to hear the one who tells it. Myth, like music, speaks when someone with the skill is willing to perform. It also speaks, like music, *on behalf* of the performer. For that to happen, the performer must step back instead of forward, and let the myth itself say what it can about the world. Rarely, but once in a while, a mythteller speaks of this process directly.

One day in March 1928, in the village of Husum, Washington, close to where the White Salmon River empties into the Columbia, a Sahaptin-speaking shaman known as Shláwtxan[17] began to tell a story. *Áw iwachá tíin,* he said: "Now there were people." *Iwachá tíin cháw ílkwash,* "There were people without fire." As Shláwtxan soon explained, the people without fire were the people of the earth. Led by their headman-in-waiting, the Beaver, they went to steal fire from the people of the sky.

Two human beings were listening intently as the tale continued to unfold. One of the two was a young anthropologist, Melville Jacobs. He had studied, like John Swanton, with Franz Boas, and he was busy, just as Swanton would have been, writing down what the mythteller said. When the story reached what was plainly a conclusion, Shláwtxan pronounced the conventional formula, *Íkunik iwá wat'ít'aash,* "So goes the myth," which certified its close. Then he kept right on talking to Jacobs, and Jacobs kept on writing. What Shláwtxan said that day sheds light, I think, on all the indigenous literatures of western North America, and in its way on literature worldwide:

> *Míniknash aníya ínk wat'ít'aash?*
> *Cháw ínk.*
> *Anamún itxánana tiichám,*
> *mún itxánana tíin,*
> *kúuk pá'anakwa tíinan tiichámnan.*   5
>
> *Kúuk itxánana k'pínk anak'pínk iwachá tíin*
> *k'pínk itxánana kákya,*
> *itxánana waykáanash,*
> *itxánana iwínat,*
> *itxánana tmaanít,*   10
> *itxánana xnít.*
>
> *Tł'áaxw k'pínk kwnínkat ittáwaxna wat'ít'aash.*
>
> *Cháw íchlaksim tiichámpa,*
> *anakúłk iwshá tiichám.*
> *Kwnák tł'áaxw tinxtínx tíin,*   15
> *kúushxi sínwit,*
> *kúushxi tkwátat.*
>
> *Anamíł íchi iwachá tíin.*
> *Cháw qúyx tamánwit,*
> *tíin itxánana tamánwitki.*   20

Ittáwaxna {ínk} tíin íchi íkuuk,
kúuk ikwítamsh kumánk,
anak'pínk shín kumánk ittáwaxshamta.

Kúuk k'pínk iyíkshana wat'ít'aashnan,
kú k'pínk ipxwísha íchi íkuuk.   25
Íkunik ittáwaxnima tiichám kú wat'ít'aash
    kumánk íchi íkuuk.

Áw cháw-wíyat tł'aaxw k'pínk iwátsha wat'ít'aash.

Áw ínk xwísaat,
kúmash watísha tł'áaxwsimk'a,
wiyáanakwanisha wat'ít'ash.   30
Íxwinam páyikshata ínk shiix.
Áwmash ní cháw-wíyat tł'áaxw wat'ít'ash
    íchnak tiichámpa,
        Xwálxwaypam tiichám.

Kúnam áw páyksha.[18]

How did I make the myths?
    I didn't.
After places came to be,
after people came to be,
the people and the places were destroyed.   5

Those who were previously people
turned into birds and furred animals,
turned into fish,
turned into elk and deer,
turned into fruit trees and berry bushes,   10
turned into root plants.

Those are the ones from whom the myths come.

Not just here in this place,
but in every place there is:
all the different kinds of people,   15
differing languages,
differing foods.

There were that many kinds of people here.
Rather than the white man's law,
people lived by their own law.   20

People came to be here then,
and they have been here since,
the ones who will continue being born here.

They were listening to myths back then,
and they are thinking of them still.   25
The land and the myths have grown together this way
*   from then until now.*

Now almost all those myths are disappearing.

I am old now,
telling you the whole of it,
leaving the myths behind.   30
Even so, you will keep on hearing me clearly.
Now I have given you almost all the myths
*   of this country,*
*   the Klikitat country.*

That is what you hear now.

20 Shellheap of the Gods

THERE IS A PROVERB widely known on the Northwest Coast, though you will hear it much more often now in English than in Haida or Tlingit or Nishga. In southern Haida it is this: *tlgaay higha ttlabju'waaga;*[1] in English: *the world is as sharp as a knife.* That, at any rate, is now the standard English form, which came by way of a German translation from Tlingit,[2] made in the early 1890s by Franz Boas. If we translate the Haida literally, the saying seems a little less dramatic but a little more precise. *Tlgaay,* "the earth" (or the ground, or the place); *higha,* "straight up"; *ttlabju'waaga,* "is shaped like a woodcutter's wedge or the head of an axe."

There is also a story – or a folktale, you could say, because no literary version has come down to us – that enshrines and elucidates the proverb:

A man once said to his careless son: The world is as sharp as a knife. If you don't watch out, you'll fall right off. His son replied that the earth was wide and flat; no one could fall off. And as he kicked at the ground to show how solid and reliable it was, he ran a splinter into his foot and died soon after.[3]

Other Haida proverbs are preserved in the literary amber of Swanton's Haida texts. I am fond, myself, of this one: *Gam nang qqangas gidaayga kkuuxu gutgwiiga qanaatgangghanggang:*[4] "A pauper does not wear his marten skins fur-side out."

The status of such proverbs in the context of mythology is something like the status of clichés in conversation and of well-tried formulae in science and mathematics. The rule $a = \pi r^2$ for finding the area of a circle, as an example, is useful and evidently true, but it ceases to be interesting as science. It is not *in itself* a rule flexible enough for creative application to new situations. For that we need a theorem of greater scope – at once more simple and more complex. That is to say, in the kind of science that is called mythology, we need not just a proverb but a story.

> > >

Skaay's headman, Xhyuu, was baptized once at least, but Xhyuu, like Skaay, had no apparent liking for his Christian name and no love for the trappings that went with it. He let himself be known to English-speaking visitors as Kloo, a vague approximation of his favorite Haida name, and he preferred the English title Captain to the more conventional Chief. He was young when he succeeded his uncle Gitkuna in 1877 at Ttanuu, and evidently he was still in his early sixties when he and his wife were drowned in Hecate Strait. Newcombe sailed unexpectedly into Hlghagilda in time to hear the missionary hymns that were sung at their joint funeral on Thursday, 27 August 1903.[5]

Xhyuu, when Swanton met him, was the headman of a devastated lineage or clan and of a singularly beautiful but empty and disintegrating town. He was also, on the evidence, a thoughtful and articulate Haida statesman. When Swanton asked him to tell stories, he told two. One concerns a selfish headman who is ousted by a younger and more conscientious person.[6] The other concerns the fate of Qquuna, Xhyuu's and Skaay's ancestral village.

In the fall of 1900, Qquuna lay as empty as Ttanuu. So did Hlkkyaa, the third major village in the area. Xhyuu had never lived there, but Hlkkyaa is the town from which his title, Xhyuu, the Southeast Wind, descends. It will be useful, as Xhyuu unfolds his story, to remember these facts and several others. One is that Xhyuu's lineage is on the Eagle side. The Eagle is his crest, his emblem, just as it is Skaay's. Another is that while a Haida village headman is usually a man, he is known as *llaana awgha*, "town mother."

Under the Haida aristocracy's old rules of matrilineal succession, a man cannot inherit either property or position from his father. These must come to him instead from his mother's brother. Well in advance of his own death, a man in a position of some trust (the headman of a village or a lineage, for example) might bring his chosen nephew into the house to begin the transfer of knowledge and power. The legacy did not pass in one lump. Names, responsibilities and privileges, including permission to sleep with the uncle's wife, passed little by little to the nephew, beginning well before his uncle's death and continuing for some time after.

Xhyuu was, in some degree at least, Skaay's former student as well as his protector and his prince. This is the opening of his poem about an uncle, a nephew, some eagles, and the village in which he and Skaay were born:

> Qquuna llanagaay haw ghaghudaayang wansuuga.
> Gyaan gu nang llaana awghaasi naatgha haw
>   hlawatugwaanggangas.
> Llaga ttsiidalangaay ghudaay qwaan·ghiihlsi.
> Gyaanhaw ghaatxhan qaang jaagha qqaatgu
>   hlawxaw lla xhaghaaghas.
> Gyaanhaw ll ghaxhii lla qyaangang wansuuga....[7]   5

In the translation, I have marked what seem to me the five main sections and the four-line coda of the poem. But there is every reason to think the story was told as a living whole, whose hard, articulating skeleton of thought lies usefully enmeshed and properly concealed in the muscles of the voice, beneath the seamless skin of words:

The village of Qquuna existed, they say. [i]
   The nephew of the one who was the town mother
     whittled all the time.
He made a lot of boxes full of arrow shafts.
Once upon a time he threw some shavings in the fire
    just in front of his uncle's wife.
And then he saw between her legs, they say. 5

Then he went outside where they were gambling.
His uncle sat there too.
A northern flicker browsed overhead a little later.
The red of its tail feathers flashed.
And then he said, 10
«Ha! That's a lot like what I saw
    inside the house a moment ago.»

When he spoke those words,
his uncle was ashamed.

Then his uncle had a redcedar felled,
and they roughed it out for a canoe.
Then they gathered pitch
and put it in the cedar.
Then they heated it
and set the nephew into it, they say.

Then they paddled him out to sea 20
and set him adrift.
Then he started weeping,
and he wept until he slept.

Then the north wind blew. [ii]
   When he had drifted for a while,
he washed ashore at Shellheap of the Gods.
He lay there in the sunshine,

and it softened up his bonds.

Then he started walking,
and he reached a town, they say.   30
Nighttime came,
and he peered inside the houses.

After peeking for a while,
he looked inside the town mother's house
where a woman sat alone behind the screens
that were shielding one corner.
She was beautiful.
He kept on looking at her.

Then they went to bed,
and then he went to her.   40
The woman said,
«Who are you?
I am promised by my father
        to One Whose Mother's Brother Warmed Him by the Fire
                and Abandoned Him at Sea.»

«That would be me,» he said to her.
They slept with one another then.
As he was lying there beside her,
her father overheard.

When morning came, her father said,
«We'll see who was talking with my child.»
Then he called to her,   50
«Say there! Who sneaked in the way a spirit-being would?
I promised my daughter
        to One Whose Mother's Brother, So They Say,
                Abandoned Him at Sea.»

«*Father, he's the one, he says.*»
«*Bring your husband down to breakfast then, my dear.*»
  Then she brought him out,
  and his wife's father offered him some food.

  After he had stayed in that vicinity awhile,
  he told his wife that he was thinking
  about going back to see his uncle's town.
  Then his wife reported the news to her father, they say.   60

  Her father told his son-in-law to go and get a box
  that sat by the back wall.
  When he brought it to her father,
  he pulled five boxes from within it
  and started lifting out the skins of eagles.

  He gave him one of these
  with white mixed in among the darker underfeathers.

  Then the young man left the house
  and got inside the skin
  and he flew at something that moved in front of the house.   70
  He was like an expert flier.
  Then he flew down.

S *oon he was looking down on his uncle's town.*   [iii]
  Then he perched at Qquuna Point.
From there he watched his uncle's town.

  Soon, they say, some children crowded round him.
  Boys shot at him with target arrows.
  Every time they took a shot
  he perched a little lower down, they say.

He shrank himself within the skin.   80
He was continuously changing
as his father-in-law had taught him.
That is why the older man had given him
    the skin with speckled underfeathers.

Soon they stopped the boys from shooting
and the men began to shoot at him instead.
With every shot they took,
he perched still lower down.

Soon, when a crowd of them had gathered,
he grabbed one by the head, they say.
Then, when he flew up with him,   90
another grabbed his feet.

When he lifted that one too,
someone grabbed his feet as well.
When they had all seized one another's feet,
he flew away with the whole town.

Then he flew them out to sea
and dropped them there.
They say they all turned into little islands.
And the village of Qquuna then was an empty shell.

Then he flew back up from there, they say.   100

When he was in the other town,   [iv]
    they put their skins on every morning
and perched on something long in front of the town.
After they discussed what they were going for,
they all flew off at once.

Evening came,

and they flew back again together.
They brought in many things:
    humpback whale tails, white-sided dolphin,
        porpoise, halibut, red snapper, and spring salmon.
Whatever they could think of,
they could hunt.   110

One day he told his wife
he wanted to go hunting alongside them.
Then his wife's father offered him a different one.
He gave him one belonging to a youngster.

Then he put it on
and flew to sea with them
and brought back a spring salmon.
His father-in-law was pleased with him.

Dawn broke,
and his father-in-law warned him: 120
he was not to touch the long thing in the water
    just off Qquuna Point.

Then one day when he went out with them
he saw a humpback whale
and took hold of it, they say.
It was not beyond the power of his wings.
Then his wife's father liked him even more.

Dawn broke,
and his father-in-law told him
how they hunted all throughout the Islands.
Then when he sat with the others in front of the houses,   130
he could see with his own eyes
where the saltwater fish and the sea mammals live in the ocean
    all the way down to the toe of the Islands.

O ne day he flew down.
and flexed his talons at the long thing in the water.   [v]
When he did that for the second time,
he grabbed it.
He tried to fly up with it.
It shrank beneath the water
and began to pull him under.

Another eagle grabbed his wingtips.   140
That one too was drawn under,
and another grabbed his wings.

From up at the head and down at the toe of the Islands,
    where they had gone,
the moment they saw him
they started to fly.
They flocked together just above him.
From high up in the town they were watching him too.

They kept disappearing,
each one clinging to the pinions of another,
while it continued pulling them down.   150
Then the ones in the town came down in a flock.
It pulled them under too.

Then his father-in-law and his wife put on their skins.
After his father-in-law got ready to go with the rest of them,
and his wife got ready to go too,
his wife's grandmother put on her skin.
She sharpened her dulled claws on a whetstone.

All the while she was doing so, she said,
«Hai hai, hai hai, hai hai!
How did my grandchild's husband come to have talons?   160
Hai hai!»

She was very old, they say.

Soon she flew down
and grabbed hold of her granddaughter.
After flying in place and tugging awhile,
she saw one of them come to the surface.

When she saw yet another one come to the surface,
something cracked at the root of the island.
Then she flew up with the string of them.
What had pulled them down came up with them.   170
A geoduck god[8] is what it was, they say.

So the town was repeopled, they say.
And he started to hunt for food for his father-in-law
just the way he did before.

*

But the village of Qquuna is empty, they say —   [coda]
because what happened then
keeps happening, they say.

And so it ends.   178

➤   ➤   ➤

Xhyuu did not become a master of the art in a class with Ghandl
or Skaay, but he had learned – from Skaay and no doubt others –
how to think in mythic terms. His transitions are sometimes less
than graceful, like Sghiidagits's, and yet he understands the use
of subtle cues to link contrasting scenes. He also knew, as a
mythteller must, how to *see* the myths he told. Newcombe and
others admired his skill as a public speaker, and his rhetorical
abilities are evident, even in the silence of transcription. The moment when the eagles converge on Qquuna Point from the
length and breadth of Haida Gwaii is one such instance:

page 380:
lines
143–147

Gwaays ghutgwaaxhit at gwaays kun·gwaaxhit
        ttl iijaangas sta
lla ttl qins gangaaxhan
lla ttl xidaawxidas.
Ll siiyagha sghun ngaahlgahldyaasi.
Llanagaay sta ising lla ttl qinttahldyaasi.

From up at the head and down at the toe of the Islands,
        where they had gone,
the moment they saw him
they started to fly.
They flocked together just above him.
From high up in the town they were watching him too.

Xhyuu was something I believe to be quite rare in the present world: a civic leader with a well-developed sense of how literature functions and how it can be used. He understood, practiced and supported the art of oral literature in much the way that European princes have occasionally practiced and sustained the art of music. The myths he agreed to perform for Swanton are not numerous or long, but he told them in a way that proves he knew the telling of a myth can be a form of meditation: a method of reflection on the nature of the world and on events as they unfold. Amid the ruins of his culture he remained Skaay's patron, and when the chance arose, he became one of Swanton's first collaborators and hosts.

He was also, I suspect, one of Swanton's unseen sponsors and protectors. Without the active if tacit approval of Sghiidagits, Xhyuu and Gumsiiwa – the three senior statesmen in Hlghagilda as the twentieth century dawned – Swanton's precious parcel of manuscripts would never have left Haida Gwaii intact.

S<small>WANTON DID</small> what Alfred Kroeber, Clark Wissler and most other North American anthropologists of the period failed to do: he took dictation and he published, in substantial bulk, what the mythtellers he listened to actually said. But he did not allow himself to publish or preserve, as Kroeber did, portraits of the oral poets he knew. Swanton mentions Skaay's crippled back but once in passing – only in a confidential letter – and he never breathes a word of Ghandl's blindness. He spent years studying the language and the visions of these poets, yet he left us nothing that compares with Kroeber's quick and lively sketch of Inyokutavere. Nor did he leave us an account of how it was in the fall of 1900 just to hear a Haida poet speak to a Haida audience, with no one slowing the pace to take dictation.

The closest thing we have to such a record comes from a sport hunter and game conservationist by the name of Charles Sheldon, who spent some weeks in Haida Gwaii in the fall of 1906. Sheldon, like several Haida hunters remembered by Kilxhawgins, had an itch for taking heads – though by the rules of Sheldon's culture, the heads had to come from other species, and always from the largest and most splendid individuals in sight. Sheldon had come to Haida Gwaii to look for *Rangifer tarandus dawsoni*, the Dawson caribou, found only in these islands. A few were still alive in 1906, but all Sheldon saw was stale dung and recently shed antlers. The last known Dawson caribou was shot on Sunday, 1 November 1908, with the express intent of stuffing it and putting it on show in the British Columbia Provincial Museum.

During most of his stay in Haida Gwaii, Sheldon employed a young bilingual Haida named Robert Brown as his assistant and interpreter. The Haida who impressed him most, however, was an older man from Ghaw whom he calls Glower. In November 1906, Glower and his family and friends were fishing for halibut near the abandoned village of Qang, a short day's paddle west of Ghaw. Sheldon and Brown were in the bush, and on Wednesday, November 7th, they hiked out to Qang (Kung, as Sheldon spells it), intending to join Glower and the others.

Though it rained all night, the following day was clear, and we took down the shelter, made up our packs, and plunged into the dripping salal, travelling directly east. In six hours we reached the beach not far from Kung, and after cooking supper went over to Glower's house to spend the evening. In his large house, ten or twelve Indians – men, women and children – were sitting around a fire in the center eating some crabs which had just been boiled. Dried halibut was hanging on all the walls and fresh ones were hung to dry on poles above the fire. Glower and his wife were seated at one end of the fire, apparently presiding over a feast....

Glower assumed some dignity as my host, and after listening to my experience in trying to find a caribou, began to talk in the clucking Haida language. Soon he quite forgot my presence and launched into excited speech accompanied with violent gestures. The others sat around him in a circle, listening in rapt attention for two hours, and responding to his climaxes with grunts of approval. From Robert I learned that he was relating a mythical tale....[1]

So far as we can judge from Sheldon's summary, the tale Glower was relating is one of which no other record survives: one of the works of Haida oral poetry that Swanton did not manage to transcribe, despite his efforts to get everything. There is no such thing, of course, as a fully documented oral literature.

384

Oral poets of the caliber of Skaay can never have been common in any century or culture. Anthropologists like Boas, Swanton and Sapir met one if they were lucky, sometimes two if they were blessed, in any given Native American nation, even at a time when many wholly oral aboriginal communities were more or less intact. And because of the methodical, deliberate and continuing extermination of wholly oral cultures – the oral poet's only natural habitat – poetry and poets of that kind are now as rare as Dawson caribou were in 1906.

Detailed accounts of what oral poets actually do – as distinct from raw transcriptions of their poems – are extremely rare as well. There are a few fine analytical accounts, by literate outsiders, of certain kinds of oral composition,[2] but rarest of all is the outsider who has asked an oral poet to reflect on his own art.

Most of the oral poetry that finds its way to written form emerges, necessarily, from cultural collisions or assaults. In Periclean Athens, ninth-century England or twentieth-century North America, what oral poets have to say is written down because the world in which they live is being invaded by writers and writing. And with writing come the kinds of social values and the kinds of institutions – political, educational, religious and commercial – that the written word sustains. Almost every oral poet or historian whose work we can now read has lived and worked in just such difficult conditions – because these are the conditions under which works of truly oral literature are finally stuffed and mounted.

We might therefore stand to learn a thing or two about the art and the predicament of Ghandl, Skaay and others from another oral poet who lived and worked in another world. It is a long way from Haida Gwaii to Ireland, and from a world of dugout canoes and killer whales to a world of wheeled carts and oats and cattle, but the momentary leap may be worthwhile.

Like Henry Moody (Nang Gayhildangaay Yuuwans) and Daxhiigang (Charlie Edenshaw), Séamus Ó Duilearga is a man whose double life made one name and identity impractical. His

British colleagues knew him not as Séamus but as J.H. (James) Delargy. He was introduced as such in London on 28 November 1945 when he addressed the British Academy on the subject of Gaelic oral literature. There he spoke at length about the skills of his teacher Seán Ó Conaill, the *scéalaí* (mythteller) of Cillrialaig, on the coast of County Kerry.

Seán Ó Conaill and Ghandl lived in different corners of the globe, but they have several things in common in addition to their species and their gender. They were born perhaps a year or two apart, each in an old, south-facing but exposed island village off the northwest coast of a large continent: close to 53° N latitude, though measurements of that kind were quite meaningless to them both. Their villages had both retained a language, a tradition of oral literature, and an ancient way of life despite the British empire and despite the best intentions of the church. Both these villages depended first of all on fish, but both had acquired the potato from British or Spanish imperial sources – though not at the same date.

It is true, of course, that the English claimed authority in Ireland long before they did in Haida Gwaii, and that in these two places, even before colonization, the world was differently worked. Ghandl's house and fire were of wood; Ó Conaill's house was stone and his fire was peat. Agriculture, pastoralism and metallurgy are old traditions in Ireland. The land has been deforested for centuries as a result. Yet Ó Conaill had remained far more a fisherman than a herdsman or a farmer. Writing too is an old Irish institution, but one in which Ó Conaill had no part.

When Ó Duilearga tried to tell the British Academy something about Ó Conaill, he began not with the man but with the landscape:

It is a lonely, wind-swept place where man has formed here and there out of the rocks and boulders and rough mountain land a crazy quilt of tiny fields to grow his oats and rye, hay and potatoes. Past the houses the rocky road winds like a ribbon along the side of the hill to reach here at journey's end the last of all inhabited places on this edge of the known world....

Seán Ó Conaill, when I met him for the first time in 1923, was seventy years of age. His family had lived in the same place for at least five generations.... His pedigree was as follows: Seán the son of Dônal, the son of Muiris, the son of Séathra. He had a local reputation as a story-teller in a parish where there were many story-tellers and tradition-bearers. He had never left his native district except on the memorable occasion when he had gone by train to the famous fair at Killorglin, and walked home again! He had never been to school, was illiterate so far as unimaginative census officials were concerned, and he could neither speak nor understand English. But he was one of the best-read men in the unwritten literature of the people whom I have ever known, his mind a storehouse of tradition of all kinds.... He was a conscious literary artist. He took a deep pleasure in telling his tales; his language was clear and vigorous, and had in it the stuff of literature....

One of the finest tales I wrote from him was a version of Aarne-Thompson 425;[3] this he had learnt fifty years before at the house of a kinsman in a village a few miles away. It was late, he told me, when he left his neighbour's fireside, the night was very dark, and the familiar pathway across the hills seemed rougher than usual. Seán was repeating the tale he had learnt as he made his way homewards, and so intent was he on his task that he stumbled and fell full length into a mountain stream that ran across his path. "But," said he to me, "I didn't mind. I had my story!"...

In Seán Ó Conaill's youth story-tellers were quite common in the district, but as he grew older the old tales were not so much heard as formerly. Finally, there came a time when it was but rarely that he had an opportunity himself of practising his art in public. So, lest he should lose command over the tales he loved, he used to repeat them aloud when he thought no one was near, using the gesticulations and the emphasis, and all the other tricks of narration, as if he were once again the centre of a fireside story-telling. His son, Pats, told me that he had seen his father thus engaged, telling his tales to an unresponsive stone wall, while herding the grazing cattle. On returning from market, as he walked slowly up the hills behind his old grey mare, he could be heard declaiming his tales to the back of the cart! In this way he kept a firm grip on stories which he had not told to an audience for over twenty years; and when I began to visit him for the dual purpose of learning Irish and writing down his stories, I found that he could re-peat these tales to me without hesitation.[4]

⟩   ⟩   ⟩

In the early 1850s, when Seán Ó Conaill was born in Cillrialaig and Ghandl of the Qayahl Llaanas in Qaysun, the latter village was decidedly the larger. It consisted of some 18 houses with a to-tal population on the order of 300.[5] When Charles Newcombe visited the site in 1901, he found 15 poles still standing, but only two houses that were more than barren frames, and not a single permanent resident. The habitable houses contained the simple furnishings of a seasonal fishing camp: wooden cooking boxes, cooking stones and tongs, ladles, stone tobacco mortars, the long lines of stretched, smoked kelp stipe used in deepwater jigging for black cod, and the stone hammers and anvils used for working the scrap-iron hooks. Newcombe's guide on this trip was Xhaayda-kuns, hereditary headman of another abandoned village, Sghan Gwaay, near the southern tip of the Islands. Xhaaydakuns told Newcombe that in the 1840s, the male population of Qaysun had mounted a raid against a Haihais or Heiltsuk village on the main-land. On the voyage home, in Tsimshian waters, the raiders were attacked, and three or four canoe loads of men – which could eas-ily be half the adult males of Qaysun – were killed or enslaved.[6] The village was still weak from this disaster when gold was dis-covered in the area in 1852.

Gold brought not only Europeans but new Haida residents as well, chiefly from the neighboring village of Tsaa'ahl. The Euro-peans did not stay, but hard on the heels of the gold rush came the smallpox epidemics of the 1860s. In the 1870s, Qaysun and Tsaa'ahl were abandoned.

Ghandl remembered both these villages well, and he was able to list for Swanton the names of former houses and their owners, as well as the houses built by refugees from these two towns in the new village of Xayna, near Skidegate Mission.[7] But Ghandl was a poet and a thinker as well as a refugee himself. Like many displaced artists, from Xenophanes to Stravinsky, he wanted to talk less about the ruins left behind than about the mental landscape he had managed to bring with him. Out of that, he was able to rebuild, if anyone cared, a civilization. In addition to the large body of narrative poetry he dictated to Swanton, he spent many hours answering the anthropologist's questions. As he did so, he unfolded a vision of the universe. Many of the statements on cosmology anonymously paraphrased and quoted in Swanton's book about the Haida[8] – as if they were fixed Haida doctrine or nationwide consensus – are actually portions of Ghandl's personal vision.

Swanton followed the standard practice of anthropologists in his time when he treated Ghandl's personal philosophy as a representative or stereotypical view. Yet we know that Swanton was aware of Ghandl's thoughtfulness, his knowledge, and the intensity of his vision. Those are the very reasons why Swanton came to question him time and again, and eventually to turn him into unofficial spokesman for the Haida on questions of cosmology and metaphysics. If those conversations had been taped or fully transcribed, we might have not only Ghandl's poems but his philosophical dialogues.

In August 1901, at the end of Swanton's year in Haida Gwaii, he returned briefly to Hlghagilda to gather up his gear and take his leave. It was Ghandl that he sought out then for some final hours of discussion. Swanton had some questions about the nature and relations of the gods; Ghandl had the answers. Though almost all of Swanton's field notes have vanished, his notes from these last conversations with Ghandl do survive, and they provide, in faded graphite, a fragmentary glimpse of an extraordinary mind.[9]

Blind mythtellers are figures of myth themselves, of course. They are figures of history too. They are frequent in the record of oral poetry all around the world and of Native North American oral poetry in particular. Two reasons for this are obvious. The first is that blindness – especially in hunter-gatherer society – markedly reduces the temptation to pursue most interests *other than* poetry. The second is that smallpox and measles – two virulent causes of blindness as well as of death among Native Americans – swept repeatedly over the continent in the century before its oral literatures began to be transcribed.

Side by side with Ghandl's works we can read, for example, those of the sightless Chipewyan poet Ekunélyel, transcribed at Great Slave Lake in 1863 by Émile Petitot. Ekunélyel was the first indigenous poet north of the Rio Grande who dictated a body of work to a European linguist – and he is still, like Ghandl, waiting for the wider recognition he deserves.

Another blind poet of obvious importance is Kanyátaííyo' (John Arthur Gibson), an Onondaga mythteller and orator living in southern Ontario, who dictated texts to several ethnographers up until his death in 1912. Yet another is Casa Maria, a Jicarilla poet who dictated stories to Pliny Goddard near Dulce, New Mexico, in 1909. Another is Isidor Solovyov, a blind Aleut singer and mythteller, who spoke at length to the Lithuanian ethnographer Waldemar Jochelson in 1909 and 1910 on Unalaska Island. Then there is the Nuuchahnulth orator Saayaacchapis, sighted in his youth but blind by 1913, when he dictated hours upon hours of stories, speeches, songs, and autobiography to Edward Sapir. Two more of Ghandl's peers are the sightless poets Kâ-kîsikâw-pîhtokêw and Nâh-namiskwêkâpaw, transcribed in Cree near Battleford, Saskatchewan, by Leonard Bloomfield in 1925.[10] If we had a transcript of his words, instead of just a précis, we could add the blind Mojave poet Inyokutavere to this list as well.

If literary history were history instead of wishful thinking, these names and others would be known as the names of important North American authors. We could then begin to ask some simple questions. We could investigate, for starters, what it is that Native American oral poets, speaking hundreds of different languages in hundreds of different cultural traditions and physical environments, have in common, and what if anything sets them apart from poets in other oral or literate traditions. We could ask what the blind poets, the poets of the mountains, or the poets of the plains, or the poets of coastal villages, or the poets of horticultural societies like the Iroquois and the Hopi, have in common with each other, and with poets living elsewhere in similar conditions. We could also start to ask how literate poets living now in North America measure up against some of the distinguished oral poets who preceded them.

Comparative literature is the infant among the humanities and the one that has, I think, contributed least to the simple necessity of cross-cultural respect and understanding. When and if it comes of age, Skaay and Ghandl will quite naturally be read in direct comparison with other Háida poets and with the best classical mythtellers in many other Native American languages – Bill Ray in Kato, Hánc'ibyjim in Maidu, Qqiltí in Chinook and Kathlamet, François Mandeville in Chipewyan, Weyiiletpuu in Nimipu, Kâ-kîsikâw-pîhtokêw in Cree, Chiishch'ilíts'ósí in Navajo and Kootye in Kawaiko, just to name a few. And of course they will be read in direct comparison with mythtellers, poets and artists in other traditions worldwide.[11]

Qaysun, 1901. Photograph by C.F. Newcombe.

(Royal British Columbia Museum, PN 59)

22 How the Town Mother's Wife Became the Widow of Her Husband's Sister's Sons

IN DAXHIIGANG'S DRAWING of the Dogfish Woman, the white forms are as tense as the black forms, and just as carefully shaped. The negative shapes and the positive shapes are modelled with equal precision. And in the poems of Skaay and Ghandl, the silences, the intervals of reticence, are as carefully formed as the statements. What the mythteller says is rarely more than half of the story. We have to listen to his sentences, and also to the silences his sentences enclose. Learning how to do this, especially when we come as strangers to the stories, takes a little time.

Ghandl is a master of those silences: the conceptual and visionary counterparts to rests in music. They are particularly audible, I think, in a work he called *Naadalang tlaahlinggiisghwaansingghu haayludaayagan nang at qqaygangaay*: "The Story [or Poem or Myth] of One Who Got Rid of Nine of His Nephews."

Enjoying the poem as a work of oral literature will be a little easier, of course, if we already know the story, as any Haida listener would. And it so happens that we do, because Xhyuu of the Qquuna Qiighawaay, Skaay's headman and patron, has recently told it. Ghandl's version of the story is longer. It runs for some 300 lines – not that lines are what we hear. Rather, the mind makes some 300 turns as it dances its way through the story, and these turns take the form of some 300 predicates. For those who wish to follow the language closely, the first 35 of these lines are printed here in Haida with a very literal English gloss.[1]

*O*ne who was the mother of a town kept starting to arrange
      to let his nephews take his wife, they say.   1
Then he led them out and they were gone forever more.
He said he had some firewood he wanted brought inside,   3
and they were gone forever more.

He said he had some bark² and some cormorants as well,   5
and then he sent them out with nets,
and they were gone forever more.   7

He did it over and over again,   8

Nang llaana awgha haw naadalang jaaghang
Someone • town • mother-of • here • nephews • wife-his
      iinaghihldaxidang, wansuuga.   1
        conjugal-become-cause-began • there-said-is.
Lla ghalqaaydisi kkyahl waaghii gawsghwaananggangasi.   2
He • leading-going-ahead-did • whenever • thataway • gone-altogether-repeatedly-was.
Ttsaanughaalanga lla daghan ll suuwus lla dawdaasi   3
Fire-cook • he • possess • same-he • said • he • gather-cause-did
gyaan waaghiixhan gawsghwaananggangasi.   4
and • thataway-indeed • gone-altogether-repeatedly-was.

Qquuji at kkyalu lla daghaghaawang ll suuwus   5
Bark • and • cormorant • he • possess-distantly-did • same-he • said
gii lla axhadaaghadaasi.   6
for • he • net-set-cause-did.
Waaghiixhan gawsghwaananggangasi.   7
Thataway-indeed • gone-altogether-repeatedly-was.

Han lla istagandixhan   8
Thus • he • doing-continuing-indeed

until nine of them had disappeared, they say.   9
And the youngest one began to understand.

The youngest started to bathe himself, they say.   11
When he had bathed himself awhile, he grew strong.
Anything he squeezed   13
just shattered in his hands.
If he twisted the limb of a spruce,   15
he pulled it clean out of the tree.

When he became extremely strong,   17

---

tlaahlinggiisghwaansingghu haaylaawang, wansuuga.   9
ten-minus-one-many • vanish-had • there-said-is.
Gyaan ll dawghan·gha ghan unsatdaahlsi.   10
And • same-them • younger-sibling-of • about • understanding-bit-by-bit-was.

Gyaanhaw agang lla ginggaxidang, wansuuga.   11
And-then • self • he • bathe-began • there-said-is.
Agang lla gingga qawdi ll dagwiyaaghihls.   12
Self • he • bathe • awhile • same-he • strong very-became.
Giinaxhan lla giijighuhldas   13
Things-indeed • he • grasp-if-did.
gyaan ghii lla tlhlgangas.   14
then • throughout • he • hand-break-did.
Qayt tlaaji ising lla tluuhisghuhldas   15
Spruce • limbs • also • he • hand-twist-if-did
gyaan lla dangttsabstagangas.   16
then • he • pull-suddenly-out-did.

Ll dagwiyaaghihljihliigaay dluu   17
Same-he • strong-very-becoming-extremely-the • when

he started making things, they say.   18

He made a pair of hard, sharp wedges.   19
Then he got a giant mussel[3] shell.
He made it into a razor.   21
And then he got a weasel skin,
and then he got a feather.   23

Then he took a lump of wet clay   24
and shaped it with a pocket in the middle.
He shaped it so that he could go inside.   26

---

giinaxhan lla tlghuhlghaxidang, wansuuga.   18
things-indeed • he • hand-make-began • there-said-is.

Ttlu kku sting lla ghihlgiidaas.   19
Wedge • sharp • two • he • become-continue-caused.
Gyaan sgunskaxhawa qqal ising lla istas.   20
And • alone-living [= *big California mussel*] • shell • also • he • got.
Lla ttlkkiighahlsi.   21
He • flat-sharp-make-did.
Gyaan tliga qqal ising lla istas   22
And • weasel • skin • also • he • got
gyaan hltangghu ising.   23
and • feather • also.

Gyaan hlkkyan tsaanaay ising lla tlqqajighiyaalas   24
And • forest • tidewater-the [= *mud*] • also • he • hand-lump-squeeze-hard-did
gyaan qaahli lla xhiihldaasi.   25
and • inside • he • hole-cause-did.
Ghii qattsas dluu lla ghiidaasi.   26
Into • enter-could • when • he • into-cause-did.

Then he bathed himself again   27
and he sat on the top of the house.

After he sat there for a while,   29
his uncle came outside, they say.
When his uncle discovered him up there
his uncle hurried back inside.   32

His uncle was envious, they say.   33
His uncle sent someone out to call his nephew in.
And then he came, they say.   35

Gyaanhaw gingghang lla ginggadas   27
And-then • likewise • he • bathe-did
gyaan naay un·gu lla qqaawusi.   28
and • house-the • top-on • he • sit-did.

Ll qqaawu qawdi   29
Same-he • sitting • awhile
ll qaagha qaattlxhagwagang wansuuga.   30
same-he • maternal-uncle of • go-toward-outward-did • there-said-is.
Lla ghii lla qiixhagaay dluu   31
Him • into • he • examining-the • when
Ll stiihlttsas.   32
same-he • return-hurry-did.

Ll qaagha sttiigangaayang wansuuga.   33
Same-he • maternal-uncle-of • sick-continuously-being-was • there-said-is.
Llaghan ll qaagha llaghan ghaghuyaang ghattlxhagwadas.   34
Him-for • same-he • maternal-uncle-of • him-for • in-bringing • rushing-outward-caused.
Gyaanhaw gha lla qaaydang wansuuga.   35
And-then • in • he • went • there-said-is.

He went inside,
and his uncle spread a mat for him.
When he had offered him some food, he said,
«Nephew, you are the one who should marry my wife.»
That night, he slept with her, they say.   40

Next day his uncle said,
«Nephew, I have firewood out back.
I want it brought into the house.»

He hid the wedges in his clothes.
His uncle led the way.
He walked along behind.

His uncle pried open a dry tree.
He braced it with something.
Then his uncle dropped his own wedge down the crack, they say,
and told his nephew to go get it.   50

He went inside the tree to get the wedge, they say.
His uncle knocked the brace out,
and the crack snapped shut, they say.
And then his uncle was delighted.

«Look at that!
That's the end of the one who intended to marry my wife.»
He heard his uncle say it.
Then his uncle walked away.

Then he pushed his wedges through, they say,
and broke open the tree.   60
Then he stepped out
and split it into pieces.
His older brothers' bones were there inside.

398

He stomped on half of it and scattered it around.
He carried the rest of it home on his shoulder
and threw it down in the house.

That was his uncle's power, they say.
And then again he slept with his uncle's wife.

Next day his uncle said to him, they say,
«Nephew, come with me.   70
We'll get some cormorants.
I own some that are perching over there.»

He took along the weasel skin and feather,
and went hunting with his uncle.

At the top of a tall cliff a log was sticking out.
From there his uncle dropped the net.
The cormorant was trapped in it.
And his uncle said to him,
«Now, nephew, your turn.»

When he stepped out on the log,   80
his uncle pushed him over.

He tucked himself inside the feather,
and then he floated down.
He heard his uncle singing,
«Look at that!
That's the end of the one who intended to marry my wife.»
And his uncle went away.

Then he dressed in his weasel skin
and climbed back up the cliff.
He dropped the net again, and again, and again.   90
He caught the whole flock of cormorants.

After catching all of them,
he tore the nets to shreds
and scattered all the pieces.
He dragged the cormorants back
and dragged them into the house.
Those were his uncle's powers, they say.
⟨*And again he slept with his uncle's wife.*⟩   97a

The next day he went to get bark with his uncle, they say.
He hid what he had made.
He walked behind his uncle.   100
⟨*His uncle built a fire there*   100a
to steam the bark, they say.⟩⁴   100b

When the bark had cooked awhile,
his uncle picked some up.
He reached out to take some too,
and his uncle pushed him in.

Then he tucked himself inside the clay container he had made.
He didn't feel the burning,
but he heard his uncle singing,
«*Look at that!*
That's the end of the one who intended to marry my wife.»

When his uncle went away,   110
he came back out.
He pushed away the bark
and scattered it around
and carried the rest of it home on his shoulder
and tossed it down in the house.
That too was his uncle's power, they say.
And again he slept with his uncle's wife.

The next day again his uncle said,
«*Nephew, come with me.*
I have some cockles.[5]
I want them brought up to the house.»
Then he went with him.
He took along his mussel-shell knife, they say.

The cockle opened its mouth.
His uncle told him to get it,
and when he went to get it,
his uncle pushed him in.
And again his uncle was pleased.
«*Look at that!*
That's the end of the one who intended to marry my wife.»

When his uncle went away,
he cut the muscles of the cockle
so the shell fell open.
He scattered half of it around
and lifted the rest of it up on his shoulder
and threw it down in the house.
He had killed his uncle's powers, they say.

Then his uncle spread out the skin of a black bear.
He invited him to sleep there, they say.

And when he did fall asleep there,
his uncle picked him up
and put him in a box.
He tied it with cords.
He took him far out to sea, they say.
And then he put him overboard.
And again his uncle was pleased,
and he paddled home.

120

130

140

A fter drifting awhile,
    he felt himself washing ashore.
When he was just getting ready to burst the box,   150
he heard two women speaking lovely words to one another.
One was saying,
«Cloudwatcher, a box has washed ashore.»
And he heard her,
and he did not burst the box.

The two women lifted up the lid,
and they helped him out.
Cloudwatcher's elder sister said,
«I'm the one who saw him first,
and I'm the one who is going to marry him.»   160

Then they took him home.
They took him into their father's house,
and they treated him well.

When they had offered him something to eat,
he went outside.
He walked through the town for a while,
and then he went into the middle house.

Eagle skins were hanging there.
He took down one with lovely feathers,
and then he put it on.   170
He moved his wings.
He almost sailed through the doorway.
He stopped himself by grabbing onto the frame.
He took the skin off right away.

Then he went back to the house of his father-in-law.
His father-in-law was saying,
«It's funny. My skin tickles,

just the way it does when there is someone else inside.»
He was the mother of the town, they say.

Next day early in the morning, he heard an eagle scream.   180
He went outside to look, they say.
There was something set up in front of the house.
Eagles were perched on it in a row.
They were calling each other
and sharpening their talons.
Then they went out hunting.

Later in the day, they came back in.
Some of them were carrying spring salmon.
Others were carrying red snapper.
Others had humpback whale.   190

Again the next day, early, he heard them
    calling in front of the house.
He told his wife he wanted to go hunting too.

She spoke to her father, they say.
And her father said,
«My dear, I will lend your husband
one I used to wear when I was young.»

He brought out a box.
He pulled out one with lovely feathers,
and he gave it to his daughter,
and he said to her,   200
«Tell your husband never to go near
    the little thing sticking out nearby.»

Then he went out with them, flying.
He brought in part of a humpback whale.
He flew home ahead of all the others,

and they brought in many kinds of things.
His father-in-law was pleased with him.
Then they cooked the whale.

When the food was served,
they led in an old woman, shaking with age.
They said to her,   210
«Drink whale broth, old woman.»
And she did that very thing.

He flew with them again the following day.
He was starting to get used to it.
And he brought in the jaw of a whale.
In his other claw, he carried a spring salmon.

He flew home ahead of them all.
They brought back many kinds of things.
And again when they served the whale,
they brought the old woman in,   220
and she drank the whale broth.

Next day, when he went out with them again,
he touched whatever it was that was sticking out.
And he grabbed hold of it, they say.
He flapped his wings awhile, holding steady.
Then it drew him down beneath the waves.

Another eagle seized his wings.
When that one too was about to go under,
one of them carried the news to the town,
that he had done what he had done.   230

As she sharpened her dulled talons,
the old woman said,

«*What is it, what is it*
my grandchild's husband has hold of?»

Her wings were like dry branches.
She flew low.
She flew there crookedly.
She teetered through the air.

There were five of them still above water
when she arrived.   240
When the last was just going under,
she grabbed hold.

After she flapped her wings for a time,
she started to pull them back up to the surface.
They came up in a line.
The thing he had hold of broke loose at the bottom.
He brought it up with him, they say.

They said, «*Put it way, way out,*
away from where people will go for their food.»

He took it way out to sea, they say.   250
Then he picked up a spring salmon and part of a humpback whale.
He flew back with them in his talons.
He had killed the thing that frightened them, they say.
It was a horseclam god,[6] *they say.*

*L*ater on, when he had lived with his wife for a while,   [iii]
  he went to see his uncle's town, they say.
He flew there dressed in the skin of the eagle.
He perched for a while at the edge of the town,
and he saw his uncle come out of the house.
Then he flew away.   260

The next day, early, he flew there once again.
He picked up a humpback whale
and dropped it in front of his uncle's house
while the people were still sleeping.

Then he perched on a dead tree at the edge of town.
After a while, someone came out.
He called them to the whale, and they came.
His uncle claimed the whole thing for himself.
He stood up on top of the whale.

Then the eagle flew.   270
He flew around above his uncle.
They laughed at him.
«He is thinking of whale meat,»
they said.

And again he perched on the tree.
He sat there awhile,
and once again his uncle claimed the whale.
He stood there and declared it.

Then the eagle flew a second time.
He grabbed his uncle by his overgrown topknot 7   280
and carried him away.

After he had carried him awhile,
his uncle knew the eagle was his nephew.
«Nephew,» he said,
«Take me back.
You'll be the one who marries my wife.
I will give you the town.»

When they had flown some ways further,

he said the same thing to his nephew once again.
And when they had flown further awhile,   290
his nephew dropped him in the open sea.

Then he flew landward.
He went to his uncle's town.
There he married his uncle's wife.
He came to own the town, they say.
His uncle too became a god in mid ocean, they say.

So it ends.   297

           ➤   ➤   ➤

Myths are doorways between realms. The journey between worlds is one of the most basic mythic themes. Gilgamesh, Persephone, Eurydike and Orpheus, Odysseus, Cuchulain, Christ, Mohammed, Satan, God and countless other named and nameless creatures of the mythworld make such visitations. Some of the best-known have no other role to play, no other duty to perform, except to make these journeys that connect and yet keep separate the worlds within the world.

But each performance of a myth involves another journey, where the visitor is us. Through the doorway of the story, we, the listeners, step into other worlds beside, behind, within our own.

Both in the myth and out of it, the reason for such voyages is learning, not by rote but by experience. *That is why the myths take mythic form.* Knowledge is digested when experience occurs, and in order for experience to happen, a story must unfold.

The story that unfolds in Ghandl's poem is full of well-known themes, as a sentence may be full of well-known words. A story is, in fact, a sentence: a big sentence saying, or revealing, many things that a full list of its components cannot say. Here there are themes that are familiar in many Native American literatures. Some of them, again, belong to a lexicon of images that

407

is close to worldwide. One is the theme of the hero who is cast adrift in a box and thereby travels between worlds.[8] Another is the theme of the old shaman who subjects potential sons-in-law to a series of lethal tests – though here of course the sons-in-law are nephews. Another is the theme of the group of brothers who are killed, one by one, in competition with some adversary, until the last of them succeeds.

Often in such stories the successful hero finds his brother's bones, spits medicine upon them and restores the dead to life. Ghandl chose not to include a resurrection scene in this poem. Only one brother out of ten lives long enough to fill his social role and so (by implication) to bear children. One out of ten is a Haida literary convention – but it is also the rate of survival Ghandl and Skaay and Xhyuu and Sghiidagits had experienced first hand.

Ghandl doesn't resurrect the nine lost brothers – but unlike Xhyuu, he does redeem the town.

Both poets work with mirror images. In Xhyuu's poem, the chain of eagles rescued from the sea is answered by the chain of human beings who are dumped there. In Ghandl's poem, the uncle, like the clam, is carried out to sea. The uncle's career as a shaman is ended, and his new life as a spirit-being begins. Like those who hunted bears with dogs, the uncle may start now to work through other shamans. Ghandl does not say. He tells us only that the last surviving nephew does indeed finally take his uncle's wife and assume his uncle's place as headman.

Why the difference between Ghandl's poem and Xhyuu's? The great anomaly in Ghandl's own life, after all, is his survival. He is there, while others aren't, to tell the story. And he is not the headman of a wholly vacant town.

˚   ˚   ˚

Readers of European classical literature are likely to notice a certain resemblance between the poem of the Nine Nephews and a larger and more famous work: the *Odyssey.* In both we have a hero – a survivor – who is washed up on an island and effectively reborn: re-equipped by the headman of the place after forming an alliance with his daughter. In both we have a pack of murdered suitors. And in both we have a problem of succession which the re-empowered hero solves when he comes home to take revenge. Both works end with a striking act of dislocation. In the case of Ghandl's poem, the hero plants his uncle far at sea. In Homer's poem, the hero plants his oar far inland. And both these heroes – the Tenth Nephew and Odysseus – are powerfully identified with eagles.[9]

There are differences, of course. In the matrilineal system of the Haida aristocracy, where a succession is involved, the suitors must be brothers of the hero, and the hero is expected to marry his own aunt. In patrilineal Greece, this cannot happen. Telemakhos cannot succeed his father by marrying his mother. (Other myths remind us what would happen if he tried.) And there is no real succession in the *Odyssey*. Odysseus returns and so succeeds himself. To that extent, he plays a double role, counterpart not just to the tenth nephew but also to the uncle in Ghandl's poem.

Matrilineal succession is not, of course, a guarantee of overt matriarchal rule. It can be quite the opposite. The passive strength and visibility of Penelope, the prize, in Homer's poem, and the voiceless anonymity of her counterpart in Ghandl's, throw light on outward social norms – and literary norms – in the two cultures. It is fair to say, however, that for its own time and place, neither is a realistic portrait of a normal woman's life.

Other differences between the poems are linked to the difference in length. Ghandl's is 300 rather short lines long and highly economical. The *Odyssey*, at 12,000 hexameters, is rich in picturesque details, flashbacks and delays. Allowing for all that, it is still possible to map one poem against the other in intricate detail. There are features repeated in parallel, features augmented, diminished, inverted. If the two poems' skeletal structures are treated as musical themes, it is easy to show, step by step, how either one can be transformed into the other.

What such comparisons depend upon, however, is not the myths themselves; it is the ways in which the myths are worked and handled by these particular artists. If we put Xhyuu's work in place of Ghandl's, for example, though parallels continue to exist, the elegant relations disappear; the web of transformations vanishes. I venture to think that if we practiced comparative mythology in honest terms – working with full original texts instead of summaries in translation – we would find that the whole system of comparison disintegrates unless the human element is fully factored in. We cannot compare two myths in the abstract. All we can ever compare are embodiments, versions, performances of myths. If these performances are summaries, we are certain to learn more about the summarizer's mind than we do about the people and the cultures who provide him the material he condenses and reworks.

❦   ❦   ❦

As usual with Ghandl's work, the poem of the Nine Nephews has some vivid human touches. When, for example, the tenth nephew washes ashore,

page 402:
lines
150–155

Ghudaay ghaal lla sttakkabdastlxidyaay dluu
ga jaada sting gutgha kihlguulas lla guudangas.
Han siiwusi,
«Yan·ghaqattsi, ghuda gayttsisghaawaghan.»
Gyaan lla guudansi,
gyaan gam ghudaay lla sttakkabdasghangasi.

When he was just getting ready to burst the box,
he heard two women speaking lovely words to one another.
One was saying,
«Cloudwatcher, a box has washed ashore.»
And he heard her,
and he did not burst the box.

That moment of hesitation, when the young man waits for an invisible woman to rescue him rather than rescuing himself, brings us eye to eye with the central figure in the poem. In the middle of his story, he is waiting just as we are to find out what comes next. There are similar moments not only in the *Odyssey* but in secular literature too, where the gods are not permitted to appear. There is the moment, for example, when Emma Bovary arrives in the big house along with many other guests and for the first time in her life is confronted with a formal dinner. Then, Flaubert says, *Madame Bovary remarqua que plusieurs dames n'avaient pas mis leurs gants dans leurs verres*: "Madame Bovary noticed that some of the ladies had not put their gloves into their wineglasses." From that one laconic sentence, a world of complexity unfolds, just as it does from Ghandl's couplet, *Gyaan lla guudansi, / gyaan gam ghudaay lla sttakkabdasghangasi*: "And he heard her, / and he did not burst the box."

We learn from Flaubert's sentence that, in the world Emma Bovary has entered, ladies all wear gloves to formal dinners, that wineglasses are set at all the places, and that a lady is expected to decline the implication of equality by placing her long gloves in the longstemmed glass, like limp cloth flowers, leaving the men to drink the wine. We also learn that several of the ladies at this dinner are prepared to break the rule. Emma is therefore faced with a choice. How she responds is, in its way, beside the point. Flaubert, like the first-rate anthropologist he is, allows himself and us to see that these are the facts, and we are all the richer for that, whatever course Emma Bovary may choose.

Guests may come to dinner far more often than young marriageable males wash up on the beach, gift-wrapped in bearskin and encased in a wooden box, but the woman in Flaubert's novel and the man in Ghandl's poem are both arriving on unknown shores. Both confront decisions they have never made before. Like Odysseus washed ashore on Skheria, the island of the Phaiakians, in the fifth book of the *Odyssey*, the man in Ghandl's poem has power and good fortune that ordinary humans like Emma and Charles Bovary are denied, but he does not know where he is, and when he hears a well-bred woman's voice he chooses to hang back: to find his course by letting it find him. His tendency to overreach will surface later on, when the eagles have adopted him and warned him not to touch the spirit-power of the clam.

The old woman who saves him is drawn, it seems to me – like the swineherd and the old nurse Eurykleia in the *Odyssey* – with particular affection.

page 405:
lines
235–238

Ll xiyaay llagha hlqawxawaagas.
Ll xitsghaayas.
Lla ga ghaxiidangas.
Tlghitxhan ll xitstaaxyanggwaangas.

Her wings were like dry branches.
She flew low.
She flew there crookedly.
She teetered through the air.

She is not Ghandl's invention. She plays the same essential role in the story as Xhyuu told it – and also in a version that Daxhiigang told to Boas at Port Essington in 1897. At Ghaw in 1901, Kingagwaaw took up the same theme, in the midst of a different story, and spoke of a pillar of eagles rescued by an elder – woman or man he did not say.[10] But here in Ghandl's poem, the old woman has a vividness and stature that no one else confers on her. I have a hunch – though of course I cannot prove – that she is based on some particular old woman Ghandl knew.

❧   ❧   ❧

In the Gemäldegalerie in Berlin is a small canvas (69 × 86 cm) painted by Andrea Mantegna, probably at Padua toward the end of the 1450s. The theme is the Presentation at the Temple (that is, the Virgin Mary's presentation of her baby to the priest). The figures in the foreground – Mary, the Christ child, Joseph and the old priest – are drawn with a half-Gothic stiffness that confines them to the world of the myth. But there are two more figures in the painting. Thanks to a bout of inspired research by the art historian Wolfram Prinz, we can be reasonably sure, half a millennium after the fact, who these two are. The man in the far right background, craning to get a look at the central characters of the painting, is plainly Mantegna himself, and the woman on the far left, who is looking rather abstractedly out of the frame, is almost certainly Nicolosia Bellini: Giovanni Bellini's sister and Andrea Mantegna's wife.[11]

The comparison and contrast of Mantegna's *Presentation at the Temple* with another painting of the same scene, made by Giovanni Bellini at nearly the same time, is a familiar kind of exercise for students and professionals alike in the art history of Europe.[12] The comparison and contrast between Ghandl's "One Who Got Rid of Nine of His Nephews" and Xhyuu's poem on the same theme could be an equally standard topic in Native American literary history. It could – except that scholars who have worked in these two fields have worked on entirely different presumptions. In the one case, the humanity of the artist and his subject has been glorified. In the other, with a few remarkable exceptions, the humanity of the artist and the subject has been utterly forgotten when not actually denied.

Mantegna's picture is not odd. There are hundreds of such Renaissance frescoes and paintings in which incidental characters come suddenly alive. They turn and look out of the frame or peer across at the main action with a frankness and intensity that seems to guarantee the painter knew their faces and their foibles and their names. Once in a while we are lucky enough to learn their identities too. Even when we don't, their palpable humanity gives body to the myths. By their presence in the picture, they link the worlds of myth and everyday. That is not to say they erase the essential distinction between the two; they remind us instead how easy it is to cross the all-important barriers established by the frame around the myth and by the frame around the painting. Something similar occurs when Skaay and Xhyuu see one another in the myths, and when Ghandl catches the figure of someone he knew – one of his grandmothers or aunts, perhaps – in the net of the poem, and there in the midst of the myth, he can offer to that real and living woman, or her memory, a conjured cup of whale broth.

APPENDICES

Appendix 1

Haida Spelling and Pronunciation

S EVERAL DIFFERENT SYSTEMS of spelling coexist in the pages of this book. This appendix explains in some detail the system I have used throughout for writing Haida. This is not the only system now in use, and the differences among the various systems are explained in appendix 2. The systems I have used for other Native American languages are explained more briefly in appendix 3.

Haida vowels are short and long, like vowels in Greek, Latin, Arabic and Hebrew. Short vowels are written once (**a**, **i**, **u**) and long vowels twice (**aa**, **ii**, **uu**). The sounds are approximately these:

a	ranges from the *a* in English *distant* to the *a* in English *art*	**i**	as in English *sit*
		ii	like *ea* in English *seat*
aa	like *a* in English *father,* but lengthened: *faaarther!*	**u**	like *oo* in English *wood*
		uu	like *oo* in English *food*

The diphthongs **aw**, **ay**, **aaw**, **aay** are likewise short and long. Haida *aw/aaw* = *ou* in English *ouch*, and Haida *ay/aay* = *i* in English *right*. Haida vowels are mutable in length, like Hebrew vowels, instead of fixed, like vowels in Greek, so syllable length in Haida is migratory, much like stress in English. For example, the long vowel in the word *llaana* (meaning dwelling or dweller, people or town) shrinks when the long definitive suffix is added: *llanagaay* (*the* people or *the* town).

In Haida as in English, French, German, Italian, Polish, Portuguese and Spanish, some basic consonants are represented by digraphs (pairs of letters). Two others are represented by trigraphs. A midpoint is used, as in Catalan, to separate letters that would otherwise form a digraph. (In Catalan, two adjacent but separate *l*'s are written *l·l* to show that they are different from the *ll* digraph. In Haida, *n·g* means *n*, then *g*, and not the sound *ng*.) *Sh* and *th*, however, are never digraphs; they always represent the separate consonants *s* or *t* followed by *h*. (The initial sounds in English *ship, this* and *thin* do not occur in Haida.)

The consonants are **b, d, dl, g, gh, h, hl, j, k, kk, kw, l, ll, m, n, ng, q, qq, s, t, tl, ts, tt, ttl, tts, w, x, xh, y** and the glottal stop, written as an apostrophe ('). The sounds represented by *gh* and *xh* are different in the northern and southern dialects. In northern speech, *xh* often simply disappears, while *gh* drops from the uvula into the pharynx. On the few occasions where I wanted to distinguish northern from southern *gh,* I have written the former as a single, rounded open quote (').

The letters have roughly the same value in Haida as in English, with the following additions, clarifications and exceptions:

dl voiced alveolar lateral affricate, much as in English *ad lib*

g voiced velar stop, as in English *get,* but voiced more lightly than in English

gh uvular *g* (voiced uvular stop), like Tsimshian or Tlingit *g;* but in northern speech, a pharyngeal stop

hl voiceless alveolar lateral fricative, like the Navajo *ł,* Icelandic *hl* or Welsh *ll*

j voiced palato-alveolar affricate, as in English *judge*

kk glottalized *k,* like the Tlingit or Navajo *k'*

ll glottalized *l*

ng velar nasal, as in English *wing*

n·g *n* followed by *g* (= *ng* as in English *Wingate*)

n·gh *n* followed by *gh* (uvular *g*)

q uvular *k* (voiceless uvular stop), like the Arabic *qâf,* the Hebrew *qôph,* Tlingit *k̲,* or the *q* of Inuktitut

qq glottalized *q*

tl voiceless alveolar lateral affricate, like Navajo *tł* or the *tl* in English *exactly*

ts voiceless alveolar affricate, as in English *its;* also often palato-alveolar, like *ch* in English *cheese*

tt glottalized *t,* like the *t'* of Hausa, Tlingit and Navajo

ttl glottalized *tl,* like the Tlingit *tl'* or Navajo *tł'*

tts glottalized *ts,* like the Tlingit or Navajo *ts'*

x voiceless velar fricative, like Russian x, the Arabic *khâ,* the *ch* in German *Bach;* or palatal, like the *j* in Spanish *hijo* or *ch* in German *ich*

xh voiceless uvular fricative, like *ch* in Scottish *loch*

' glottal stop, like the catch in the midst of English *oh oh!*

' smooth pharyngeal stop, like Arabic *'ain* or Hebrew *'ayin* (northern counterpart to southern Haida *gh*)

A short vowel followed by a voiceless consonant (', *h, k, kk, q, qq, s, t, tt, ts, tts, x, xh*) is usually pronounced with a lowered tone.

Labials in general seem to have the status of resident aliens. The labial nasal *m* occurs in the negative particle *gam* but rarely otherwise, except in Nishga and Tsimshian loan words. The labial stop *b* is rare and not distinguished from *p*. The labialized stop *kw* is only found in loan words. Alveolars may be in the midst of slow mutation or collapse. Swanton had a hard time distinguishing *dl* from *tl*, and syllables which closed with a voiceless alveolar stop (*t*) in Skaay's time almost always close with a voiced stop (*d*) in modern Haida speech.

Haida words in which the first written letter is a vowel or *w* routinely begin with a glottal stop. Out of laziness and a dislike for extra apostrophes, I leave this initial stop unwritten. The literary quotative *wansuuga,* for example – a frequent and crucial word in classical Haida literature – could by a more fastidious scribe be written *'wansuuga* or *wwansuuga.*

To summarize:

- *doubled vowels are long;*
- *doubled consonants are glottalized*
  (that is, they are pronounced with a glottal stop superimposed);
- *the two consonants written with* h (gh *and* xh) *are uvular*
  (that is, they are pronounced deep in the throat).

Appendix 2

Haida as a Written Language

T HE LOGBOOKS and memoirs of European sailors who visited Haida Gwaii late in the eighteenth century contain sporadic efforts to spell some Haida words and names in the Latin alphabet. The first attempts to write continuous Haida text were made by missionaries: Charles Harrison and John Henry Keen. Toward the end of the nineteenth century both men published incomplete translations of the Bible into Haida and attempted to write grammars of the language. But Franz Boas and John Swanton were the first literate outsiders to listen to the language and its literature as subjects of serious interest in their own right. Swanton was the first who tried to write and analyze the language in a systematic way. After five years of unremitting labor, he knew that he had barely scratched the surface.

Swanton wrote and later typed his Haida texts in a phonetic script that Boas had developed for use across the continent of North America. In representing Haida vowels, it is more complex and more fussy than it needs to be. In representing consonants, it is accurate for everything except the glottal stop, but typographically it is cumbersome.

More recent works meant for a scholarly audience use a standard international or American phonetic alphabet. Robert Levine's incomplete but useful southern Haida grammar (1977) is an example.

In the last two decades, many attempts have been made to create a simpler system specifically for Haida. The alphabet used in Jeff Leer's grammar and Erma Lawrence's Alaskan dialect dictionary (1977) is modelled on a system developed earlier, and still in common use, for writing Tlingit. John Enrico's Haida alphabet and my own are both attempts at further simplification.[1] My system differs from Enrico's chiefly in the simplified marking of glottals and in eschewing the use of 7 for the glottal stop, *c* for the fricative *x*, and *r* for uvular *g*.

FIVE SYSTEMS OF HAIDA SPELLING

Bringhurst 1999	Enrico 1995	Leer 1977	Levine 1977	Swanton 1903–1912
a	a	a	a, ʌ	a, â, ä, A, ạ
aa	aa	aa	a, e	ā, a′, e
b	b	b, p	b	b, p
d	d	d	d	d
dl	dl	dl	λ	L., ḷ, l̓̆, ˥
g	g	g	g	g
gh	r	g̲, ĝ	ğ	g·, g̲
hl	hl	hl	ł	Ł, ł
i	i	i	i	i, î, e, ê
ii	ii	ii	i, e	ī, i′, ē, ei
j	j	j	ǰ	dj
k	k	k	k	k
kk	k'	k'	k̓	k!
l	l	l	l	l
ll	'l	'l	l	l
m	m	m	m	m
n	n	n	n	n
ng	ng	ng	ŋ	ñ
q	q	k̲	q	q
qq	q'	k̲'	q̓	q!
s	s	s	s	s
t	t	t	t	t
tt	t'	t'	t̓	t!
tl	tl	tl	ƛ	L, ̣
ttl	tl'	tl'	ƛ̓	L!, ̣!
ts	ts	ts, ch	c	tc, dj
tts	ts'	ts'	c̓	tc!
u	u	u	u	u, o
uu	uu	uu	u	ū, u′, ō
w	w	w	w	w, u, o
x	c	x	x	x., x̲
xh	x	x̲, x̂	x̌	x
y	y	y	y	y, i
'	7	'	ʔ	-
‘	G	g	ʕ	ε, ‘

The writing systems used in the early days by Harrison and Keen ignore essential features of the Haida language, but nothing much is written in their alphabets except translations of the Christian scriptures. All the remaining systems, from Swanton's to the present, are similar enough, and empirical enough, that a reader who has learned any one of them can switch in a few minutes to any of the others. But fluent speakers of Haida are few, and no two speakers' speech is quite the same; different linguists hear sounds differently and make different suppositions about grammar; and editors have followed different paths in their attempts to bring consistency to classical and recent Haida texts.[2] For the serious student of Haida it is therefore not enough to learn the different alphabets in use. One must also learn how each writer uses the system (or the systems) he or she prefers.

This is not quite so hopeless or so onerous a task as it may sound. Haida spelling is roughly where English spelling was in the Elizabethan age. The alphabet itself is close to being standardized. Spelling is less consistent – and is likely to remain so unless a common system is politically imposed. But aleatory orthography did not prevent the reading and writing of English in Malory's or Shakespeare's time, nor the reading and writing of French in the age of Rabelais and Montaigne.

Swanton started taking texts within days of his arrival in the Haida country, learning the language as he went along. His published and unpublished Haida texts – edited in solitude, with nothing to consult except his notebooks and his memory – inevitably veer back and forth between phonetic and phonemic information (that is, between the idiosyncratic, highly variable speech sounds that he heard and the idealized, meaningful noises that these speech sounds represent). Every later student of Haida oral literature has been humbled by the magnitude and quality of the work performed by Swanton and his Haida colleagues, and at the same time has struggled with the maze of inconsistency it presents.

Eighty years after Swanton made his transcripts, John Enrico began the mammoth task of re-editing them all, in close collaboration with the eldest, most fluent and most knowledgeable speakers he could find: Laala Ttaaghwaay (Kathleen Hans) and Gidahl Qaa'anga (Hazel Stevens). Only a small portion of these re-edited (or as Enrico likes to say, *re-elicited*) texts have been published to date,[3] but they come much closer to rigorous consistency than Swanton's.

I have found Enrico's texts immensely helpful, and I wish I had had access to them all. Nevertheless, they represent editorial priorities different from my own. While many undoubted errors – slips of the tongue and of the pen – have been corrected through reelicitation, the style of Skaay, Ghandl and other oral poets of a century ago has also been reformed, in some degree, to match the speech of a later age, and of speakers who are not oral poets by vocation.

Leaving Swanton's text precisely as it stands is not an attractive option. Like any manuscript produced under difficult conditions, it cries out for correction of obvious errors. And there is nothing to be gained by retaining its perversely complex script. It is a record of the words of poets who could neither read nor write, and *the form in which it is written* therefore merits no special historical privilege. The question is: how do we restore the text using Skaay and Ghandl themselves, not later speakers, as benchmarks? At what point does the process of restoration and correction turn to a process of normalization and modernization?

The revision of Swanton's texts undertaken by Enrico, Laala Ttaaghwaay and Gidahl Qaa'anga is invaluable, regardless whether one treats it as a new and definitive edition, or a commentary to be used in interpreting the old, or a tool to be used in preparing an edition yet to come. Another of its values, incidentally, is the further light it throws on Henry Moody's huge contribution to Swanton's work. We know how Moody and Swanton worked together to achieve the original transcription. The word-by-word reinvention of the text by Enrico and his colleagues has revealed a good deal about the further contribution Moody made when he and Swanton first went back to translate and correct the raw transcription.

The passages of Haida quoted in the present book fall, as a rule, somewhere between the Swanton manuscript and Enrico's revised and corrected versions. My aim is not a perfectly consistent text but one securely rooted in a single authorial voice and historical time. As the Haida language continues to change, the voices Swanton heard are bound to seem increasingly archaic, artificial and literary (or in less charitable terms, plain wrong) by contemporary standards. I have attempted to correct the texts with reference to *themselves*, but not with reference to any linguistic data outside them. And apart from the orthography itself, my impulse, for better or for worse, has been to change as little as possible.

The question of precisely how to treat the texts is not, of course, entirely a question of philology. If we retain the older view that Native American oral literature is really communal production, and deny the fact of individual authorship, then a text that is edited by committee may claim to be better in principle than texts dictated and transcribed by individuals, no matter what their talents; and a text that is periodically brought up to date, reflecting current notions of grammar and phonology, may claim to be better in principle than any text that is fixed in historical time. If we accept instead the primacy of the individual voice, then a text that is faithful to that voice, not a text with communal sanction, is what we will prefer.

Insofar as the mythtellers are artists, insofar as they are shamans, insofar as they are faithful to their visions and their dreams, they stand apart from the community they serve without ever ceasing to serve it. That was the predicament of the finest Haida carver I have known; I think it was the predicament of the finest Haida poets I have read. And I imagine this dictates in some degree the kind of life their works can lead, later, in our midst.

Others can choose differently, of course. The surviving Haida texts can be edited many times, like any other classical texts, with varying aims in mind, and they can circulate in many competing editions, so long as there is anyone prepared to hear and read them.

Appendix 3

Spelling of Other Native American Languages

IN AN EFFORT to set Haida oral literature and the Haida language in context, I have often mentioned names, words or phrases in other Native American languages and have quoted a few texts in other languages as well. Where a script is in popular use among native speakers, I have usually adopted it with little or no change. This means using several different symbols for some phonemes – but that is a complication we already take for granted in the languages and literatures of Europe. The spelling systems used are outlined here. While none of these descriptions is complete, they should suffice to make phonemic sense of any phrase or text or name appearing in this book.

For ARIKARA, I use a system based on that of Douglas Parks. Long vowels are written double. The apostrophe represents a glottal stop. The letter *č* is pronounced like *ch* in English *cheese*. The acute marks *stress*, not tone. Arikara is rich in devoiced vowels and semivowels, which Parks writes as capitals. I write them with a ring diacritic instead, as is usual in Cheyenne. Thus *å* is devoiced *a*, and *ñ̊* is devoiced *n*.

For further reference, see Parks 1991.

For BLACKFOOT (Siksika), I use the alphabet developed by Donald Frantz and Norma Russell. Long vowels are written double and long *consonants* are likewise. The acute accent signifies a *high tone*. The apostrophe represents a glottal stop, and *h* is a voiceless uvular fricative, like Navajo *h* or Haida *xh*.

Further reference: Donald G. Frantz, *Blackfoot Grammar* (2nd ed., Toronto: University of Toronto Press, 1995); Donald G. Frantz & Norma Russell, *Blackfoot Dictionary of Stems, Roots and Affixes* (2nd ed., Toronto: University of Toronto Press, 1995).

CREE has its own syllabic script, but here I have used an equally familiar Latin-based orthography instead. The letter *š* is pronounced like *sh*
in English; *c* represents a sound which varies from English *ts* to *ch* to *j*;
the *h* is a voiceless glottal fricative. Long vowels are marked with a circumflex. Thus Cree *â* corresponds to Haida *aa*, etc.

Further reference: Ellis 1995: 371–554; Freda Ahenakew, *Cree
Language Structures* (Winnipeg: Pemmican Press, 1987).

For HEILTSUK, my alphabet is based on the one developed by John Rath
for the Heiltsuk Cultural Education Centre. The uvulars are *ǧ, q* and *x̌*.
Consonants followed by *v* (*kv, k'v, qv, q'v*, etc) are labialized (pronounced
with rounded lips). The *c* = *ts*. The *lh* is a voiceless lateral fricative (like
Haida *hl*). Glottalized consonants carry an apostrophe. High tone is
marked with an acute. The unglottalized resonants *l, m* and *n* can be
vowels as well as consonants and can therefore carry tonal inflection.

Further reference: John C. Rath, *A Practical Heiltsuk-English Dictionary with a Grammatical Introduction*, Mercury Series 75, 2 vols. (Ottawa:
National Museums of Canada, 1981).

For HOPI cited here, I use the Hopi nation's standard
system. Long vowels are written double. The apostrophe is a glottal
stop. Hopi *q* corresponds to Haida *q*, but Hopi *k* is palatal: farther forward in the mouth than the normal *k* of Haida or English. Hopi *v* at the
beginning of a syllable is bilabial, as in Spanish; at the end of a syllable, it is devoiced to sound like English *f*. Hopi *r* at the beginning of a
syllable is retroflexed; at the end of a syllable, it too is devoiced; the resulting sound is a kind of tuneless whistle.

Further reference: *Hopìikwa Lavàytutuveni: A Hopi Dictionary of the
Third Mesa Dialect* (Tucson: University of Arizona Press, 1997).

For HUPA, my orthography is based on the one developed by Victor
Golla for the Hoopa Tribal Council. But I write long vowels by simple
doubling, where the Tribal Council system uses a colon. (So I write
shaan instead of *sha:n*, etc.) Hupa *ł* (called a *barred* L or *fricative* L) is a
voiceless lateral fricative, like *hl* in Haida and *ll* in Welsh. Consonants
followed by apostrophes are glottalized. The apostrophe in other positions indicates a glottal stop.

Further reference: Victor Golla, "Sketch of Hupa, an Athapaskan
Language," *Handbook of North American Indians*, vol. 17 (1996): 364–389.

For KARUK (Karok), I use a system recently developed for the Karuk nation by William Bright. Doubled vowels are long, and the apostrophe is always a glottal stop. There are no glottalized consonants. The digraphs *ch* and *sh* are pronounced as in *Cheshire*. The acute signifies *high tone*, the circumflex a *falling tone*. It is customary in Karuk to write the tonic accent only on the first mora of a long vowel, where in Athapaskan languages it is usual to mark deflected tones on both moras. (Karuk *ée* therefore corresponds to Navajo *éé*, and Karuk *âa* to Navajo *áa*.)

William Bright, *The Karok Language* (Berkeley: University of California Publications in Linguistics 13, 1957) uses Bright's older orthography but remains the basic reference.

For KAWAIKO (Laguna Pueblo Keresan), I have used, with regret, a simplified writing system based on the Boas texts (Boas 1925–8). Long vowels are written double and glottalized consonants are marked with an apostrophe. Tone, in this simplified orthography, is not marked.

For KWAKWALA, I use an updated version of the U'mista Cultural Centre orthography. The a̱ is a blunt central vowel, like *a* in English *sofa* or *u* in English *but*. Uvular consonants are g̱, q and x̱. A consonant followed by *w* (*gw, g̱w, kw, k'w*, etc) is labialized (pronounced with rounded lips). The voiceless lateral fricative, corresponding to Haida *hl*, is written *ł*, as in Hupa. The lateral affricates are *dl, tł* and *t'ł*. The glottalized consonants are *k', k'w, 'l, 'm, 'n, p', q', q'w, t', t'ł, t's, 'w* and *'y*. (Note that the apostrophes *follow* the stops [*k, p, q, t*], *precede* the glides and resonants [*l, m, n, w, y*], and are written *in the middle* of the affricates and labials.)

Neville J. Lincoln & John C. Rath, *North Wakashan Comparative Root List*, Mercury Series 68 (Ottawa: National Museums of Canada, 1980) is very helpful but uses a different orthography.

In writing LAKHOTA, I follow the usage of David Rood and Allan Taylor. For the few words included in this book, it is enough to know the following. The apostrophe represents a glottal stop, and the letter *š* is pronounced much like English *sh*. Nasal vowels are marked with a nasal hook. (Thus, for example, *ą* is a nasal *a*, like the first vowel in French *français*. The uppercase form of *ą* is *Ą*.) Stress is marked with an acute.

Further reference: David S. Rood & Allan R. Taylor, "Sketch of Lakhota, a Siouan Language," *Handbook of North American Indians*, vol. 17 (1996): 440–482.

LUSHOOTSEED, like other Salish languages, is customarily written in a subset of the American phonetic alphabet. The vowels are *a, i, u* and *ə*. The latter symbol (called a *schwa*) represents a bland, stressless vowel like the *e* in English *happen*. The *c* is an alveolar affricate, like English or Haida *ts*. The *č* is like *ch* in English *cheese*, and the *š* like *sh* in English *ship*. The *ł* is a voiceless lateral fricative, like Kwakwala or Hupa *ł*, Haida *hl*, and Heiltsuk *lh*. The *q* is a voiceless uvular stop, like *q* in Haida and Kwakwala. The gelded question mark (*ʔ*) signifies a glottal stop. Glottalized consonants (*c̓, č̓,* etc) are written with a superposed apostrophe. Labialized consonants (*gʷ, kʷ, q̓ʷ,* etc) are spoken with rounded lips and written with *w* superscript.

MILUK is written here with an orthography based on that of Hupa. The *ts'* is glottalized *ts,* and *x̌* is a voiceless uvular fricative.

For NAVAJO, I use the standard alphabet of Young and Morgan. An apostrophe following a consonant means that it is glottalized; in other positions, the apostrophe represents a glottal stop. The *ł* is a voiceless lateral fricative, like *hl* in Haida, and the voiceless lateral affricate (Haida *tl*) is written *tł*. The Navajo *t* is usually pronounced as an affricated stop, *tx*. The *h* is pronounced as a velar fricative (*x*) at the beginning of a syllable but as a glottal spirant (*h*) at the end. High tone is marked with an acute accent; long vowels are written double; nasal vowels, which are frequent, are written with a nasal hook. In the word *'asdzą́ą́,* for example, the first vowel is short, oral and low; the second is long, nasal and high. In the word *nóogał,* the first vowel is long, oral and falling. (It starts on a high tone and ends on a low tone.)

Further reference: Robert W. Young & William Morgan, *The Navajo Language* (2nd ed., Albuquerque: University of New Mexico Press, 1987), and *Analytical Lexicon of Navajo* (Albuquerque: University of New Mexico Press, 1992).

In NISHGA (Nisga'a, Gitksan) and its sister language Tsimshian, long vowels are written double, glottalized consonants are written with apostrophes, and uvular consonants are underlined. Nishga *ü* and *üü* are high unrounded central vowels. The *ł* is a voiceless lateral fricative, corresponding to Haida *hl*. Note that Nishga includes both velar and uvular voiceless fricatives (*x* and *x̱*). Tsimshian, by contrast, has only the latter, which is written with a simple *x*. Thus:

Nishga g̲ = Tsimshian g̲ = Heiltsuk ǧ = Haida gh;
Nishga k̲ = Tsimshian k̲ = Heiltsuk q = Haida q;
Nishga x̲ = Tsimshian x = Heiltsuk x̌ = Haida xh.

Further reference: Lonnie Hindle & Bruce Rigsby, *A Short Practical Dictionary of the Gitksan Language* (Moscow, Idaho: Northwest Anthropological Research Notes 7.1, 1973) and Marie-Lucie Tarpent, ed. *Hańiimagoońisgum Algax̲hl Nisg̲a'a: Nishga Phrase Dictionary* (New Aiyansh, BC: School District 92, 1986).

NOOTKA, the language of the Nuuchahnulth people, is written here with an experimental system based on that of Haida. Doubled vowels are long. The digraph *hh* represents pharyngeal *h*, like Arabic *ḥâ* or the *xh* of *northern* Haida. The apostrophe is a glottal stop. There is also a pharyngeal stop, resembling Arabic *'ayn* (the sound represented in phonetic script by ʕ). This is written here as a turned, rounded comma or single open quote ('). The uvular fricative is written *xx* instead of *x̲* or *xh*. All other doubled consonants are glottalized. There are six labialized consonants: *kw, kkw, qw, qqw, xw, xxw*. These are like their counterparts (*k, kk*, etc) but pronounced with rounded lips. Thus Nootka *qw* = Kwakwala *qw* = Heiltsuk *qv*. There are two vowels, *e* and *ee*, not found in Haida, and there are several additional consonants:

ch as in English *cheese*	*p* same as in English
cch glottalized *ch*, like the *ch'* of Navajo and Tlingit	*pp* glottalized *p*
	sh as in English *ship*
m' glottalized *m*	*ww* glottalized *w*
n' glottalized *n*	*yy* glottalized *y*

A midpoint is inserted when required for clarification of digraphs (in the word *'uts·hhintlmihhsa*, "wishing to marry," for example).

Sapir & Swadesh 1939 is an excellent introduction to the language but uses a different orthography.

OJIBWA, like Cree, has a syllabic script of its own, but here I have used a roman orthography instead. This is modelled on the common system as refined by John D. Nichols. Long vowels are written double, and the glottal stop is marked by an apostrophe. The digraph *sh* has the same sound as in English, and *zh* sounds like *z* in English *azure*. Vowels followed by *nh* or *n'* or *ny* are nasalized.

427

Reference: John D. Nichols & Earl Nyholm, *A Concise Dictionary of Minnesota Ojibwe* (Minneapolis: University of Minnesota Press, 1995).

PAWNEE names are spelled here using an orthography developed by Douglas Parks. Long vowels are written double, glottalized consonants are followed by an apostrophe, and the apostrophe alone represents a glottal stop. The letter *c* represents the affricate *ts*.

A useful reference, now in some ways out of date, is Parks's *Grammar of Pawnee* (New York: Garland, 1976).

For SAHAPTIN, two practical alphabets (known as the Yakima and Warm Springs systems) are currently in use. I have followed the Yakima system.

The barred *i* (*i*) is a short high central vowel, like the first vowel in English *bitter*. Long vowels are written double. Glottalized consonants are written with apostrophe. The apostrophe in other positions marks a glottal stop. The *ł* is a voiceless lateral fricative, like Navajo *ł* or Haida *hl*. The voiceless lateral affricate is accordingly written *tł*, as in Navajo and Kwakwala, rather than *tl*, as in Haida. Sahaptin *tł'* corresponds to Navajo *tł'*, Kwakwala *t'ł* and Haida *ttl*. The uvulars (corresponding to Haida *q* and *xh*) are written with underlines, <u>k</u> and <u>x</u>, as in Nishga. The digraphs *sh* and *ch* are pronounced as in English *ship* and *cheese*. The acute marks *stress*, not tone.

Further reference: Bruce Rigsby & Noel Rude, "Sketch of Sahaptin, a Sahaptian Language," *Handbook of North American Indians*, vol. 17: Languages, edited by Ives Goddard (Washington, DC: Smithsonian Institution, 1996): 666–692.

For TLINGIT, I follow the eccentric but well-established system of Naish and Story. An apostrophe following a consonant means that it is glottalized. Underlined consonants are uvular. (Thus, for instance, Tlingit <u>k</u> = Haida *q*, Tlingit <u>k</u>' = Nishga *q*' = Haida *qq*, and Tlingit <u>x</u> = Haida *xh*.) Doubled vowels are long, but long *e* is written *ei*, long *i* is written *ee*, and long *u* is written *oo*. The acute accent signifies high tone and is written on the first mora only of long vowels and diphthongs. (Thus *é* is high short *e*, and *ée* is high long *i*.) The combinations *ch* and *sh* are pronounced as in English *churlish*. Note that there is no phoneme in Tlingit corresponding to the plain *l* of English and Haida. The Tlingit letter *l* = Tsimshian and Navajo *ł* = Haida *hl*. An interliteral period (as in the word k̲oo.éex') is used instead of an apostrophe as the sign of the glottal stop.

Further reference: Gillian Story & Constance Naish, *Tlingit Verb Dictionary* (College: Alaska Native Language Center, 1973); Story & Naish, *Tlingit Noun Dictionary*, 2nd ed., rev. by Henry Davis & Jeff Leer (Sitka: Sheldon Jackson College, 1976); and the extended introduction to Dauenhauer & Dauenhauer 1987.

Note that a different orthography – not at present as widely known, but certainly no less satisfactory – is used in Nyman & Leer 1993 and in several other recent publications.

In TSIMSHIAN, as in Nishga, long vowels are written double, glottalized consonants are followed by apostrophes, and uvular consonants (g̲ and k̲) are underlined. Tsimshian *x*, however, is always uvular, corresponding to Haida *xh* and the x̲ of Nishga, Kwakwala and Tlingit. The *ł* is a voiceless lateral fricative, corresponding to Haida *hl*. Tsimshian *ü* and *üü* are short and long high unrounded central vowels. The *ẅ* is a velar glide: a semivowel, like *w* or *y*, but pronounced farther back in the mouth and with unrounded lips.

The writing system has been simplified since these works were produced, but they remain the best reference sources available: John Asher Dunn's *Reference Grammar for the Coast Tsimshian Language*, Mercury Series 55 (Ottawa: National Museums of Canada, 1979) and *A Practical Dictionary of the Coast Tsimshian Language*, Mercury Series 42 (Ottawa: National Museums of Canada, 1978).

UTE (also known as Chemehuevi or Southern Paiute) is rich in voiceless vowels, geminated consonants and other complications, but for the few Ute words that are mentioned in this book, it is necessary only to know the following. Long vowels are written double. The apostrophe represents a glottal stop. Ute *g* is the phoneticians' gamma (ɣ): a voiced velar fricative, resembling the *g* in Northeast German *sagen*, the Arabic *ghayn* or the γ of modern (not classical) Greek. The *ğ* and *x̌* are uvular fricatives – the former voiced, the latter not.

Volume 10 of Edward Sapir's *Collected Works* (1989f) includes a good Ute-English dictionary and grammar as well as a body of texts, first published in 1930. More recent aids include Talmy Givón, *Ute Dictionary* (Ignacio, Colorado: Ute Press, 1979) and *Ute Reference Grammar* (Ignacio, Colorado: Ute Press, 1980).

Appendix 4

The Structure of Skaay's Raven Travelling:
The Poem of the Elders

1 CELESTIAL REBIRTH: *Raven as Xhuuya*   *[Name 1]*

    1.1 Rebirth   *[Flood 1]*

        1.1.1 Rebirth in the sky world   *[Rebirth 1]*

        1.1.2 Steals half the eyes of the sky people

        1.1.3 Expulsion

    1.2 Adoption beneath the sea   *[Adoption 1]*

        1.2.1 Invitation from the Grebe

        1.2.2 Descends the two-headed stone housepole

        1.2.3 Gift of the two sticks

            1.2.3.1 Nest of boxes

            1.2.3.2 Sleek Blue Beings   *[Mirror image 1]* ◄

            1.2.3.3 Gift and instructions

    1.3 Creation of land from the flood   *[Biting & chewing 1]*

2 REDISTRIBUTION: *Raven as nameless*   *[Nameless 1]*

    2.1 Encounters with proto-humans   *[Humans 1]*

        2.1.1 The Haida

        2.1.2 The Seaward People or Mainlanders

        2.1.3 The Ghangxhiit Xhaaydaghaay

    2.2 Theft and dispersal of fish

        2.2.1 Contest with spring salmon

        2.2.2 Theft of lake, house & fishtrap from the Beavers

        2.2.3 Dispersal of fish

            2.2.3.1 Raven unrolls the lake

            2.2.3.2 Wooing of Jilaquns   *[Marriage 1]*

            2.2.3.3 Installs new house & wife in the Islands

3.3 The Raven shoots bufflehead & raven   *[Mirror image 2]* ◄
   3.3.1 Shoots & skins bufflehead ⎫
   3.3.2 Tries & fails to shoot raven   ⎬ *[**midpoint of story**]*
   3.3.3 Shoots & skins raven ⎭
3.4 Second Flood
   3.4.1 Cuckolding of uncle
   3.4.2 Maternal uncle's flood   *[Flood 2]*
   3.4.3 Reversal of the flood
3.5 Creation of human beings   *[Humans 2]*
   3.5.1 Arrival of visitors for adoption feast   *[Adoption 3]*
   3.5.2 Creation of the four peoples
   3.5.3 Food from the Headwater Women   *[Potlatch 1]*

4 COMING OF AGE: *Raven as Voicehandler*   *[Name 3]*
4.1 Eating of scabs
   4.1.1 Refuses to eat
   4.1.2 Seeks instruction from fat people
   4.1.3 Eats scabs to produce insatiable appetite   *[Scab 1]*
   4.1.4 Eats dung
   4.1.5 Expulsion from village
4.2 Third Flood
   4.2.1 Attempts to blackmail Qinggi
   4.2.2 Mounts assault on Qinggi's house
   4.2.3 Floods Qinggi's town   *[Flood 3]*
      4.2.3.1 Flood begins
      4.2.3.2 People climb Qinggi's hat
      4.2.3.3 Half of townspeople lost
4.3 Mythtelling contest
   4.3.1 Return of the prodigal son
   4.3.2 Qinggi asks for *Raven Travelling*   *[Mirror image 3]* ◄
   4.3.3 Jibing at Qinggi, the Mythteller

5 INDEPENDENCE: *Raven as nameless*   *[Nameless 2]*
5.1 Encounter with the flounder fishermen
   5.1.1 Loses beak
   5.1.2 Borrows beak from the Saw-whet Owl
   5.1.3 Capture by fishermen

Appendix 5

Haida Village Names

Swanton listed 126 Haida towns in his *Contributions to the Ethnology of the Haida* and added three more in an unpublished supplementary note.[4] A few of the names on his list appear to be duplicates. Many others are the names of seasonal camps, seldom inhabited year around. But several major village sites are missing from the list. Archaeologists and mythtellers agree that Haida villages moved from time to time. Perhaps as few as ten or twenty permanently populated sites endured throughout the whole of the classical period – yet it is likely that, at any given time within that period, fifty villages or more were actually inhabited, while fifty to a hundred other named, familiar sites were lying fallow. In the 1980s, George MacDonald mapped 21 village sites and assembled early photographic evidence for all but one of these. Newcombe's maps, museum reports and field notes confirm the precise location of dozens more.[5]

The names of more than sixty Haida villages appear in the extant classical literature. That is only about half the number of village names mentioned to Swanton by his teachers in the course of conversation. The literature also includes the names of many points, creeks, mountains and islands in Haida Gwaii, and the names of many geographical features and towns in the Tlingit, Nishga, Tsimshian and northern Wakashan country as well. Close study of the poetry therefore requires a substantial gazetteer.

The following list is confined to major villages whose names occur in the text of the present work and, for cross-reference, those that are illustrated in George MacDonald's *Haida Monumental Art.*

In this book, I use the old Haida form – the literary form – of the village names. And all my spellings – even of the names of northern towns – are in the southern dialect.

Bringhurst	Swanton	Colonial	MacDonald
Daadans	Da'dens		Dadens
Gawjaaws	Gaodja'os	Drum	Lina
Ghadaghaaxhiwaas *	ᵋatē'was **	Masset	Masset
Ghawkkyan	ᵋa'ok!ian	Howkan	
Ghiijaaw	ᵋīdjao	Mission Hill	Idjao
Hlghagilda	Łg.agî'lda	Skidegate	Skidegate
Hliiyalang	Łi'elañ		Hiellan
Hlinqwan	Łî'nqoân	Klinkwan	
Hlkkyaa	Łk!ia'	Windy Bay	
Hlqiinul	Łqê'nul	Cumshewa	Cumshewa
Kasaan	GAsān	Kasaan	
Kunji	Ku'ndji	Dogfish Bay	
Kunxhalas	Ku'nxalas		Kunhalas
Kkaykkaanii	K!aigā'ni	Kaigani	
Kkyuusta	K!iū'stA		Kiusta
Naay Kun	Nā-iku'n	Rose Spit	
Qang	Qañ	Kung	Kang
Qayju	Qai'dju		Kaidju
Qaysun	Qai'sun	Gold Harbour	Kaisun
Quughahl	Qō'g.ał	McCoy's Cove	
Qqayaang	Q!ayā'ñ		Kayang
Qqaadasghu	Q!ā'dASg.o	New Clue	
Qquuna	Q!ō'na	Skedans	Skedans
Saqqwaan	Saqoâ'n	Sukkwan	
Sghan Gwaay	Sg.Aˈngwa-i	Ninstints	Ninstints
Sqay	Sqa-i		
Sqiina	Sqē'na		
Tiiyan	Tī'an		Tian
Ttanuu	T!anū'	Clue, Kloo	Tanu
Ttii	T!ē		
Ttsaa'ahl	Tc!ā'ał	Gold Harbour	Chaatl
Xayna	X.A'ina	New Gold Harbour	Haina
Yan	Yan	Yan	Yan
Yaa'ats	Yats	Yatze	Yatze
Yaakkw	Yā'k!ᵘ		Yaku

* *Ghaw* for short.
** Also often ᵋatᵋaiwas, romanized by later writers as *Uttewas*.

Appendix 6

A Short Pronouncing Glossary of Haida People and Places

Daxhiigang 1839–1920. Sculptor. Born at Hlghagilda, later lived at Ghaw and Port Essington. As headman of the Stastas lineage of the Eagle side, 1894–1920, he was known as Iidansaa. Christened Charlie Edenshaw. Husband of Kkwaayang. [*Da* rhymes with *ma* and *pa*; *xhii* rhymes with *see*; *gang* as in English, except that the *ga* is like *gua* in *guard*. The *xh* is like *ch* in *Bach* but deeper in the throat.]

Ghandl *c.* 1851–*c.* 1920. Poet. Born at Qaysun, moved to Xayna, then to Hlghagilda. Qayahl Llaanas lineage, Eagle side. Christened Walter McGregor. [*Gh* like *g* in *good* but deeper in the throat; *andl* as in *and less.*]

Gumsiiwa *c.* 1840–*c.* 1915. Poet; headman of the village of Hlqinul and of the Xhiida Xhaaydaghaay, an Eagle lineage. Christened Job Moody. Father of Henry Moody. [Vowels as in *could see ya*. *G* and *m* as in English *gum*.]

Haayas *c.* 1835–*c.* 1905. Poet; headman of Hliiyalang and of the Hliiyalang Qiighawaay, Eagle side. Moved from Hliiyalang to Ghaw in the 1860s. Christened Isaac Haias. [*Haay* like English *high*; *as* as in *ascent*.]

Kilxhawgins *c.* 1837–*c.* 1910. Historian. Born at Ttanuu, moved to Qqaadasghu, then to Hlghagilda. Qqaadasghu Qiighawaay lineage, Raven side. Christened Abraham Jones. [*Kil* as in *kill*; *xhaw* rhymes with *how*; *gins* as in *begins*. The *xh* is like *ch* in *Bach* but deeper in the throat.]

Kingagwaaw *c.* 1846–*c.* 1920. Poet. Born and raised at Yan, moved to Ghaw. Ghaw Sttlan Llanagaay lineage, Raven side.

Christened Walter Kingagwo. [*Kinga* rhymes with *sing-a* in *sing a song*; *gw* as in *Gwen*; *gwaaw* rhymes with *how*, and the vowel is drawn out.]

Kkwaayang   *c.*1858–1926. Wife of Daxhiigang. Born and raised at Ghaw. Yaakw Llaanas lineage, Eagle side. [*Kkwaay* is like *choi* in *choir*, but the vowel is extended, and *kk* is *k* with a glottal catch; *ang* as in British *anxiety*.]

Sghaagya   *c.*1830–*c.*1905. Warrior, trader and autobiographer. Born and raised at Ttsaa'ahl. Moved to Ghaw, then to Hlghagilda. Yaakkw Gitinaay, Eagle side. Christened Richard. [Rhymes with *dawg ya*. The first vowel is longer than the second; the *gh* is a hard *g* deep in the throat.]

Sghiidagits   *c.*1840–1902. Headman of Hlghagilda and of the Na Yuuwans Xhaaydaghaay, an Eagle lineage, 1892–1902. Christened Philip Jackson. [Rhymes with *Frieda sits*. The *gh* is a hard *g* deep in the throat. The *g* in *gits* is also hard but light and forward in the mouth.]

Skaay   *c.*1827–*c.*1905. Poet. Born at Qquuna, moved to Ttanuu, then to Qqaadasghu, then to Hlghagilda. Qquuna Qiighawaay lineage, Eagle side. [Like English *sky*, with the vowel drawn out.]

Xhyuu   *c.*1840–1903. Headman of Ttanuu and of the Qquuna Qiighawaay, Eagle side, 1887–1903. Born at Qquuna, lived at Ttanuu, Qqaadasghu and Hlghagilda. [Rhymes with *you*. *Xh* is like *ch* in *Bach* but deeper in the throat.]

▸ PLACES ▸

All map numbers here refer to the map and list of villages on pp 24–25.

Haida Gwaii   "Islands of the People." [Rhymes with *sighed a sigh*.] (Note that this is not precisely a Haida name; it is the standard English derivative of the modern Haida *Xhaayda Gwaay*, which is itself a reduction of the classical Haida name *Xhaaydla Gwaayaay*.)

Xhaaydla
Gwaayaay   "The Islands on the Boundary between Worlds." [Rhymes with *I'd a dry eye*. The *xh* is like *ch* in *Bach* but deeper in the throat; *dl* as in *ad lib*.]

437

Ghaw — "Inlet." Now as in the past, the largest Haida village. Map N° 1. Full name *Ghadaghaaxhiwaas,* "White Hillside"; now called Masset. Broadly, also the southern Haida name for northern Haida Gwaii. [Rhymes with *how*; the *gh* is a hard *g* deep in the throat. (In Skaay's dialect it is, but as explained in appendix 1, the pronunciation is different in Ghaw itself.)]

Hlghagilda — "Pool of Stones." Village near the mouth of Hlghayu Qaahli (Skidegate Inlet). Map N° 10. Now Skidegate. [Rhymes with *saw Hilda*; the *hl* is a voiceless (tuneless) ʟ; the *gh* is a hard *g* deep in the throat; *gilda* as in *gild a lily.*]

Qaysun — "Sea Lion Place." Village on the outer coast. Map N° 82. Ghandl's birthplace. [Vowels as in *high wood. Q* is like *k* but deeper in the throat.]

Qinggi — "Always Looking." Mountain. Map N° 40. [*Qing* is like English *king*, but the *q* is deeper in the throat than *k*; *gi* like *gui* in *guillotine.*]

Qqaadasghu — Old village on Qquuna Gwaay. Map N° 27. Rebuilt in 1887 by survivors from Ttanuu. Home of Skaay, Xhyuu and Kilxhawgins from 1887 to 1897. [Rhymes with *Gaawd asked you,* emphasizing and Arkansizing *God. Qq* is like *k* but deeper in the throat and spoken with a glottal catch; *gh* is like *g* in *good* but deeper in the throat.]

Qquuna — "Edge." Village on Qquuna Gwaay ("Edge Island," now called Louise Island.) Map N° 28. Skaay's birthplace. [Rhymes with *soon-a* in *soon ashore. Qq* is like *k* but deeper in the throat and spoken with a glottal catch.]

Ttanuu — "Eel Grass." Village on Ttanuu Gwaay. Map N° 33. Home of Skaay, Xhyuu and Kilxhawgins for most of their lives. [Rhymes with *canoe. Tt* is *t* with a glottal catch.]

Xayna — "Sunshine." Village on Xayna Gwaay ("Sunshine Island," now called Maude Island) in Hlghayu Qaahli (Skidegate Inlet). Map N° 15. Home of Ghandl and his family from *c.* 1875 to *c.* 1895. [Rhymes with *sign-u* in *sign up. X* is like *ch* in *Bach.*]

Notes

> NOTES TO THE PROLOGUE >

1 *Le Cru et le cuit* (1964), ouverture: *Nous ne prétendons donc pas montrer comment les hommes pensent dans les mythes mais comment les mythes se pensent dans les hommes, et à leur insu.*

2 "Canadian Fate and Imperialism," Winnipeg: *Canadian Dimension* 4.3 (1967): 24. The essay is reprinted in Grant's *Technology and Empire* (Toronto: Anansi, 1969). Two decades later Northrop Frye, in a lecture entitled "Levels of Cultural Identity" (1993: 168–182) went to some trouble to contradict this assertion, though here too the language smacks unhappily of "them" and "us."

> NOTES TO CHAPTER ONE >

1 For preference I have used native place names in this book. When a standard reference is required, I use the names from current marine charts published by the Canadian Hydrographic Service. These are indexed in the relevant coast pilot (Canada, Dept. of Fisheries & Oceans 1991). A partial list of Haida village names and their colonial equivalents is given in appendix 5, p 434.

2 The name Haida Gwaii is probably a 19th-century coinage, and the spelling fits none of the systems now in use for writing Haida. It has been ratified, however, by the Council of the Haida Nation and is now in widespread use.

3 George Dawson transcribed the name in 1878 as "Skatz-sai," and gave the puzzling translation "angry waters" (Dawson 1993: 52). Newton Chittenden, a real-estate promoter hired by the provincial government to visit Haida Gwaii in 1884, heard it as "Scotsgi" (misprinted "Seotsgi" in Chittenden 1884: 68). But the name was current well before that. John Boit, a 21-year-old ship's captain from Massachusetts, met a Haida he called "Scorch Eye" on 20 June 1795 and killed him the following day (Boit 1794–6: folio 7r). A belated census made in 1901 by Charles Newcombe confirms that Sqaatsigaay was one of the names of the headman of the Qayahl Llaanas lineage (Newcombe n.d. 1: v 38 f 1).

4 The baptism is recorded in the old church ledger for Skidegate, Gold Harbour and Clue (Crosby et al. n.d.: 48). Gold Harbour in this case means New Gold Harbour, or Xayna, and Clue means New Clue, or Qqaadasghu.

5 Details are given in Boyd 1990 & 1994 and in Galois 1996. Postcontact epidemics with a serious effect on the Haida population include at least the following: smallpox 1775–6, smallpox or measles *c.* 1810–11, measles and influenza 1848, smallpox 1862–3, measles 1868.

6 Swanton never mentions this important fact. It is remembered nonetheless by Gidahl Qaa'anga (Hazel Stevens) of Skidegate, who was born in 1901 and listened to Ghandl when she was a child. See Enrico 1995: 10. Where congenital resistance is low and vaccines are not available, blindness is a common side effect of smallpox, measles, diphtheria and other infectious diseases. These three in particular plagued aboriginal peoples of the Northwest Coast during the 18th and 19th centuries.

7 Many people less dedicated than Swanton have doubted that such a process can work, but it very often has, and has sometimes produced better results than the tape recorder. According to William Bright, it was formerly the custom of Karuk mythtellers to tell stories to children one sentence at a time for verbatim repetition. Such procedures may have been in wide use in North America before the European invasion. Albert Lord's *Epic Singers and Oral Tradition* includes some pertinent remarks on the effects of dictation as compared with normal performance or audio recording, based on Lord's experience with oral poets in Bosnia and Montenegro (Lord 1991: 45–48).

8 The original text of the poem is in Swanton n.d.2: folios 354–358.

9 The sweet inner bark (phloem) of pine trees is an important springtime food for people living off the land across most of North America. The pine phloem eaten on the Northwest Coast comes from the lodgepole or shore pine, *Pinus contorta*, called *ttsaahl* in Haida. After the outer bark is removed, the phloem is scraped from the tree in long, thin strips, like luminous linguine.

   Charles Newcombe's extensive unpublished notes (Newcombe n.d.6) remain a vital documentary source on Haida botany. They are supplemented now by the extensive research of Nancy Turner.

10 *Zostera marina*, called *ttanuu* in Haida and eelgrass or seagrass in English, is a submarine plant of the pondweed family, Zosteraceae. People eat the lower parts of the plant – rhizomes, stems, and the bases of the leaves. Geese appear to like the upper leaves as well.

11 *Trifolium wormskjoldii*, which grows in tidal meadows, is the common clover in the Haida country and possibly the only indigenous species. The rhizomes are important food for shorebirds, deer and human beings. In Haida these rhizomes are called *naa* and the whole plant is *naahlqqaay*, "naa-branches."

12 Readers familiar with ravens will recognize this behavior. It is documented superbly in Lawrence Kilham's *The American Crow and the Common Raven* (1989). Another informative work on avian intelligence is Alexander Skutch, *The Minds of Birds* (1996).

13 Swan Maiden stories from elsewhere in the world are summarized in a number of sources – e.g., Dixon 1916 for Oceania and Kleivan 1962 for the North American arctic – but original texts with identifiable authors have been published very rarely. Around 1910, on the island of Ambae (formerly known as Aoba) in Vanuatu, two men named Guero and Taï dictated stories on this theme in the language now called Northeast Ambae. These are published, with French translation, in Suas 1912: 54–60.

  Barbara Fass Leavy's recent study *In Search of the Swan Maiden* (New York University Press, 1994) is typical of studies in the field. Works by Europeans (e.g., Ibsen) are treated as the works of individuals. Works from elsewhere in the world are treated as if composed by a committee of the whole – and even that imaginary committee is not always very carefully identified. Leavy quotes, for example (p 59), Swanton's synopsis of Ghandl's "swan maiden" story and attributes it to a tribe she calls "the Jesup of North America." Jesup, however, is not the name of any Native American nation; it is the name of a philanthropist, Morris Jesup, who subsidized a program of research directed by Franz Boas at the American Museum of Natural History. Results of this research – including two of Swanton's books about the Haida – were published as a 30-volume series called *The Jesup North Pacific Expedition.*

14 Keith Basso's essay "Speaking with Names" (Basso 1996: 71– 104) is a fine case study of this phenomenon. It illustrates how stories can be usefully called to mind, in Apache culture, by quick but pointed reference to the places where they occurred.

15 There is a damaged early replica of the edited version, now in the Art Institute of Chicago.

> NOTES TO CHAPTER TWO >

1 If we letter the objects in the order of acquisition, we can write this transformation in these terms:

$$(A) \cdot (B)(C^2)(DEFGH) \cdots (I) \rightarrow (BD) \cdots (AE)(IF) \cdots (GH)(C^2),$$

where A = *marlinspike*; B = *oil*; C^2 = *pair of wedges*; I = *mouse skin*, etc. The parentheses represent the grouping of objects, or in a musical sense the *phrasing* of images. The dots represent degrees of delay or suspense or disjunction.

2 Analogous scenes appear in many contexts, not only in the literatures of the Northwest Coast. In the story of creation that Yellow Brow dictated in Crow to Robert Lowie in Montana in 1931 (Lowie 1960: 210–215), the bear gives claws

instead of getting them. Later they are used, in a surprising move, to make the dancing prairie chicken's wings.

3 Bogoraz was a skilled linguist and dedicated revolutionary, born in the Ukraine in 1865. He was jailed in 1886 for his political activities, and his career as an ethnologist began when he was banished to Siberia in 1890. From 1901 to 1904 he was in New York at the invitation of Franz Boas. He published extensively in Russian under his own name and also under the pseudonyms N.A. Tan and V.G. Tan. In English, he more often used the name Waldemar Bogoras.

4 Bogoras 1918: 38–40. Other stories told by Rumyantsev appear on pp 48–49, 52–58, 67–69 & 72–73 of the same volume. There is more Yukaghir material in Jochelson 1900 & 1926.

5 Swanton's translation is in Swanton 1905b: 264–268. Snyder wrote his study, *He Who Hunted Birds in His Father's Village*, in 1951, when he and Dell Hymes were roommates at Reed College. It was published only in 1979. Paraphrased and plagiarized versions of the poem do of course exist (the first such is probably the version in Edward S. Curtis's *The North American Indian* [vol. 11: pp 168–171; Seattle: Curtis, 1916]), but these have not supplanted the original.

▸ NOTES TO CHAPTER THREE ▸

1 The Haida certainly grew tobacco in precolonial times, and they began to grow potatoes at a very early date – possibly before the documented beginning of the fur trade. The tobacco question is addressed in Turner & Taylor 1972.

2 "Cultural Anthropology and Psychiatry" (1932), in Sapir 1949: 515. The same passage is quoted, with relevant excerpts from other authors, in Kroeber & Kluckhohn 1952: 126.

3 "The Ethnological Significance of Esoteric Doctrines" (1902), in Boas 1940: 314.

4 Several spellings of Edenshaw's names are still in use. The Haida form, Iidansaa, is from Tlingit *iitinashu'*, "leaving nothing behind," a term that refers to the face of a calving tidewater glacier. The spellings Edensa, Edensaw and Edenshaw are frequent in the secondary literature. One of the earliest spellings was *Edenshew*. Gwaayang Gwanhlin (Arthur Edward Edenshaw, Daxhiigang's uncle and mentor) had a nameplate with that spelling fixed beside the house-pole of the house he built at Ghadaghaaxhiwaas about 1875. But *Edenshaw* is the form chosen by Gwaayang Gwanhlin's son, Kihlguulins (Henry Edenshaw). Kihlguulins was a schoolteacher by profession, and his advice on matters of this kind held sway in the community. That was the form adopted by Swanton. (Boas, not Swanton, is responsible for the spelling *Edensaw* in Swanton's 1905 *Ethnology*.)

"Tahayren," a form that appears from time to time in the tertiary literature, was Marius Barbeau's attempt to spell Daxhiigang.

The shipboard meeting with Daxhiigang is reported in Swanton's letter to Boas, 23 September 1900 (Dept. of Anthropology Archives, AMNH, New York).

5 Original in the Dept. of Anthropology Archives, AMNH, New York.

6 Swanton 1908a: 273.

7 Original text on folios 490–493, Swanton n.d.2. Swanton's translation is in his ethnology, Swanton 1905a: 94–95. There is a discussion in Kane 1998: 46–51. John Enrico has recently re-edited the text; this is published, with his translation, in Enrico 1995: 160–168. The identity of the storyteller is confirmed in the Haida typescript and in Swanton's letter to Boas dated 30 September 1900, though in a later letter (14 October) he mistakenly attributes the story to Henry Moody instead of his father Job.

8 The name Gumsiiwa or Cumshewa has been a subject of confusion among scholars since Swanton first recorded it. Ghandl made it clear to Swanton that the word was connected with the coming of white traders (Swanton 1905a: 105). Someone else – possibly Gumsiiwa himself – also told him, correctly, that it was Heiltsuk in origin. But it does not mean "rich at the mouth of the river," as Boas supposed (Swanton 1905a: 105 n 1). The root is Heiltsuk *q'vémxsiwa*, which means someone or something that stands out or protrudes. For close to two centuries, this has been the Heiltsuk term for white man. The Heiltsuk were active intermediaries in the fur trade, especially in the 1830s, when the only Hudson's Bay post in the area lay in their domain – and Heiltsuk now includes such cognates as the verb *q'vémxsiwak'ala*, "to speak English." There is evidence, however, that "Gumsiiwa" was in use as a headman's name in Haida Gwaii when the first Europeans arrived. Its precontact meaning – and the metaphor behind its early use as a name for Europeans – may be visible in the Tsimshian noun *umksiwa*. This word means European or Caucasian; it also means driftwood.

9 The red chiton, *sghiidaa*, is a leathery looking mollusk, *Cryptochiton stelleri*, widely known in English as a gumboot. The suffix *-gits* is a diminutive, meaning little, plain or ordinary. Its use here, in the headman's ceremonial name, is affectionate and ironic, and it is often used in a similar way in naming some of the creatures of Haida myth.

10 This tale is translated, in part, in chapter 5 and discussed in chapter 6. See appendix 3 for details of the spelling of Tsimshian names.

11 Skaay appears, in his various guises, on pp 1, 87, 88 & 94 of the church ledger for Skidegate, Gold Harbour and Clue (Crosby et al. n.d.). His age on 13 March 1892 is given as 64. No reason is given for his multiple Christian names, but it is clear from the officiating clergymen's cross-references that all these names belong to the same person. An undated note on the first page of the ledger implies that he was dead by 1916, at which date he would have been 88 or 89.

12 This was Rev. John Henry Keen's *The Gospel According to Saint Luke in Haida* (London: British & Foreign Bible Society, 1899). Daxhiigang showed his copy to Swanton, who reported it to Boas on 23 September 1900. (The letter is now in the Dept. of Anthropology Archives, AMNH.) Keen also translated the Gospel of John (1899), the Acts of the Apostles (1898) and excerpts from the *Book of Common Prayer* (London: Society for the Promotion of Christian Knowledge, 1899). His predecessor Charles Harrison had published a translation of the Gospel of Matthew in 1891.

Keen's translations may owe their merit chiefly to the help of Daxhiigang's cousin Kihlguulins (Newcombe 1906: 149). But Swanton was impressed by Keen's "very considerable ability" as a linguist and by "his great superiority to other missionaries in the region when it comes to matters of this kind" (Swanton to Boas, 23 November 1903; now in the Boas papers, APSL, Philadelphia). Keen's 1906 Haida grammar bears this statement out, though it was soon superseded by Swanton's own (far from perfect) grammar of 1911.

13 Original in the Dept. of Anthropology Archives, AMNH. This letter is quoted at greater length on p 173.

14 Original on folios 102–111, Swanton n.d.2.

15 By far the best documentary source on Haida ornithology is the extensive list of bird names dictated by Tlaajang Quuna (Tom Stevens) of the Naay Kun Qiighawaay (Newcombe n.d.4). But the legendary blue hawk or blue falcon (Haida *skyaamskun*) does not appear in that monument of Haida science. The word is clearly related to the Tsimshian word *sgyaamsm*, meaning kestrel or merlin – but the name that Tlaajang Quuna gave for the kestrel was *dawghatl-xhayang*. This was evidently his name for any small hawk or falcon, since he used it also for the sharp-shinned hawk. Sharp-shins breed in Haida Gwaii; kestrels and merlins do not.

16 Swanton's interpolation, evidently in consultation with Skaay himself (1905b: 151, 171 n 8).

17 Haida *gwaaykkya*, Latin *Veratrum viride*, also known in English as cornlily. This is a highly toxic plant widely used on the Northwest Coast as a ritual purgative. (It is not at all the same as the edible cornlily of eastern North America, *Clintonia borealis*.)

18 Halibut hooks were of wood (usually alder), with a bone or (after European contact) metal barb lashed on with spruce-root twine. The scraps Skaay has in mind could be of these materials. Another possibility is devil's club (*Oplopanax horridus* in Latin; *jiihlinjaaw* in Haida). This potent plant was used to purify the hooks when they were baited. Even mundane substances like bits of twine might work if they had come from well-used hooks, because of the enormous ritual energy that fishermen in Haida Gwaii and elsewhere on the Northwest Coast expended on the tackle used for halibut.

19 Sea-cukes (sea-cucumbers, *ghiinuu* in Haida) are edible holothurians, especially those of the species *Parastichopus californicus*. These are the food of the poor, and Wealth Woman is commonly met collecting them. (See also pp 469–470: note 5 to chapter 11.)

20 Grease (*taw*) is edible grease or thick oil, usually from eulachon. It is eaten like mayonnaise with dried berries or fish. It appears here only in the metaphor, *gudaagha taw lla gutgaystlghaayang*, "he poured grease into [her] mind."

21 Warm saltwater is drunk as a purgative before important undertakings.

22 This again is *sghiidaa*, the big, leathery mollusk known to biologists as *Cryptochiton stelleri*. It is the creature for which the headman Sghiidagits was named.

23 The implication is that a year has passed.

24 Haida armor was generally made of wooden slats and hide, but Swanton understood this armor to be made of copper. It has thus become customary to identify the younger son's wife as Xaalajaat, Copper Woman. If that is who she is, this is her only appearance in extant Haida literature. Copper, *xaal*, is not mentioned until later in the poem (p 96, line 533).

25 Master Carver, Watghadagaang, is the nonhuman embodiment of artistic skill in painting and woodworking. He lives in the forest, not in the sea. The literal meaning of his Haida name is "Maker of Flat Surfaces."

26 The birthing stake – a handhold for the woman in labor – was widely used on the Northwest Coast.

27 This is not as odd as it may sound. The urine of healthy humans is a sterile fluid, chiefly water, ammonia and carbonic acid. It makes an excellent biological cleansing agent, useful in treating insect bites and wounds. A bath in a grandparent's urine – so long as the donor is free of disease – is therefore not just a ritual honor for the child but a perfectly defensible obstetric procedure.

28 My interpolation.

29 Swanton n.d.2: folio 111. The postscript is spoken in something approaching Skaay's style, but Swanton says it was Moody who added it (Swanton 1905b: 172 n 22). So it appears that Moody was learning what Skaay had to teach.

▸ NOTES TO CHAPTER FOUR ▸

1 MacDonald 1983, which is the best available source on classical Haida architecture, includes a village plan and historical photographs of Ttanuu. The house of Skaay's family head is Tanu 5 in MacDonald's census. Henry Joseph Muskett, who travelled to Haida Gwaii with Charles Newcombe in 1902, made detailed measurements of the structure and recorded them in his diary (Muskett 1902) as follows: groundplan 50′ × 53′ [15.25 m × 16 m]; height 23′ [7 m]; widths of

top terrace 10′ and 6′ [3 m & 1.8 m]; width of second terrace 4′9″ [1.45 m]; height of steps 2′4″ and 2′6″ [71 cm & 76 cm]. The headman's house at Qquuna, by contrast, was 40′ × 44′ [12 m × 13.4 m] and 15′6″ [4.7 m] at the ridgepole. Another house more typical of the village at large was 34′ [10.4 m] square and 12′3″ [3.75 m] high at the ridgepole.

2 See MacDonald 1983: 18, 142–144; Blackman 1972. MacDonald calls the house "Monster House," but its Haida name was simply *Na Yuuwans*, "Big House." Its builder was Wiiha of the Sghajuugahl Llaanas.

3 Daxhiigang's daughter Florence Davidson told Margaret Blackman that the housepit in her grandfather Gwaayang Gwanhlin's house at Kkyuusta was ten tiers deep (Blackman 1982: 66), but this again is hyperbole, just like Skaay's, unless tier is meant as a unit of measure. The pit was indeed "ten steps deep" – about 1.8 m – but there were not ten steps in the sidewalls. See MacDonald 1983: 189–190. James Swan measured this house in 1883, about a decade after Gwaayang Gwanhlin and his family had moved out of it. He found it 48′ [14.6 m] square, 11′6″ [3.5 m] high at the corners and 16′6″ [5 m] at the ridgepole (Swan 1883a: entry for 9 August).

4 Swan 1883a: entry for Thursday, 6 September. Swan wrote 13 totemic columns [housepoles], but 20 can be identified from turn-of-the-century photographs. I think the 13 is therefore likely to be an error for 23. Much further information, including a map of the village based on the 1968 archaeological survey, appears in MacDonald 1983: 88–100.

5 Chilkat blankets are well documented and illustrated in Cheryl Samuel's *The Chilkat Dancing Blanket* (1982). There is a brief discussion of their iconography, in relation to Haida sculpture, in Bringhurst & Steltzer 1992: 66–67. Skyblankets are widely known to contemporary weavers as Raven's Tail blankets, a translation of their Tlingit name. Samuel 1987 is a study of these robes.

6 See Samuel 1987: 94–103.

7 Lévi-Strauss 1979 traces the sculptural image of projecting eyes up and down the Northwest Coast.

8 Sapir & Swadesh 1939: 162. In Sapir & Swadesh 1955: 314, Saayaacchapis recounts to his grandson Hiixuqqin'is a speech that culminates with the words *Yyuuqwaaqa hhawwihlmis qasnaak cchushaa*, "Wealth also has keen eyes."

9 The houses in question are MacDonald's Tanu 8, 10 and 11, all belonging to members of the Qqaadasghu Qiighawaay. For photos, see MacDonald 1983: 95–96. Pole 10 is now in the Smithsonian Institution, Washington, DC. The remains of pole 11 are in the Royal British Columbia Museum, Victoria, and a replica of this pole, carved in 1966 by the northern Wakashan sculptors Henry and Tony Hunt, now stands in the museum courtyard. People unfamiliar with Haida tradition have often misconstrued this figure as "the weeping woman of

Ttanuu," but early Haida interpretations are unanimous in regarding it as the image of a submarine old man.

1 Such terminology is frequent, not only in the languages of the Northwest Coast, but in Native American languages generally. In Nootka, for example, mythtellers use the nouns *hhaakwaatl* and *hhawwihlatl*. The former means wellborn daughter; the latter means an equally fortunate young male. In the plains language Arikara, a favored child is called *piiraasštawi'u'*. (The use of this term is well explained in Parks, 1991, vol. 3: 96–97.) But the prejudice is not universal. To the Miluk- and Hanis-speaking mythteller Hets'miixwn (Annie Miner Peterson) of the Oregon coast, the Miluk term *heededik'yilga*, "rich person's child," was a venemous curse. (See Jacobs 1939: 111 &c.) Recent Haida thought on questions of rank and status, and some of the language currently used, is discussed in Marianne Boelscher's *The Curtain Within* (1988).

2 If we translate *wansuuga* into the Siouan language Lakhota, for example, we have a choice of at least four common forms: the "major quotatives" *ške'* and *škeló'*, the "minor quotative" *keyápi'*, and its short form *ke'* (all from *keyá*, "to say"). Each form has a rhetorical weight of its own.

    In the Caddoan language Arikara, the basic quotative is the simple prefix *wi-*, but there are fuller forms – single words and whole clauses and sentences – conveying the same concept as *wansuuga*; an example is the Arikara word *nootihwáči*. This is the distal plural indicative form of the verb *waaka*, "to say," which is in English "there [or then] they say."

    In Navajo, an Athapaskan language, the counterpart to *wansuuga* is *jiní*. This word peppers the performances of most Navajo mythtellers because it means "he said" and "she said" as well as "they say." In the works of Navajo mythtellers, a sentence containing dialogue often ends with the doubled verb *jiní jiní*. This phrase has nine or more distinct potential meanings, but it is usually understood in the sense of the Haida *ll suugang wansuuga*, "he/she said, they say." In Arikara the same effect is achieved by adding the quotative prefix *wi-* to the verb "he said," giving the form *witiwaáko'*, "is-said-to-have-said."

    The Lakhota and Navajo forms, like *wansuuga* in Haida, normally come at the end of a clause or sentence. *Yaw* and *pu' yaw*, the corresponding expressions in Hopi, have a different rhetorical weight because their usual place in the sentence is at the beginning. Ute, like Hopi, is an Utaztecan language, and Ute mythtellers use the cognate forms *ya'a*, *ya'agw* and *yaxwaang*. These are enclitics, which means they must follow something – but usually what they follow is the first word in the sentence.

    In classical Kwakwala, the quotative is *'la*, a verbal form that is usually absorbed in a larger introductory word or phrase. Examples include *we la'lai*, "so they say it goes"; *laem'lai*, "and as they say it goes"; and *hiem'lawis*, "and then as they say...."

Nootka and Kwakwala are sister languages, but their quotatives function quite differently. A Nootka sentence begins, as a rule, with the major verb, and *wansuuga* is rendered by the verbal suffix *-we'in*. Thus for example *Hluchnaakwe'in Qu'ishinm'it* = "Woman-have-saidheard Raven-descendant." This means "The mythcreature Raven had a woman, it is said," which means in its turn, "The Raven was married, they say."

In the Algonquian language Cree, *wansuuga* is expressed as *itwâniwan*, and in its sister language Ojibwa as *giiwenh*. Both of these are independent verbs which can be placed almost anywhere the speaker wishes, but Cree and Ojibwa mythtellers use the quotative very sparingly as a rule. So does Homer, in whose language *wansuuga* = φασί, another enclitic (*Iliad* 2.783, 4.375, 6.100; *Odyssey* 1.189, 3.188, 6.42, etc).

The role of quotatives in oral literature is discussed in Lee 1938, Mishler 1981 and Chafe & Nichols 1986.

3 The link between these disparate perspectives is explored in Northrop Frye's wise essay "The Koine of Myth" (Frye 1990: 3–17).

4 Kootye's recorded works constitute the bulk of Boas's *Keresan Texts* (1925–28). For a close analysis of the opening formula, see Boas 1923. Gyiimi's extended closing formula is in Boas 1925–28, vol. 1: 26 & vol. 2: 38. The spelling system used here for Kawaiko (Laguna Keresan) is explained in appendix 3.

5 The Dutch lingust Cornelius Uhlenbeck transcribed a substantial number of stories by Káínaikoan in 1910 and 1911. Uhlenbeck 1912 includes 17 of these, along with several others to which Káínaikoan contributed episodes. The Blackfoot text as quoted here has been respelled by Donald Frantz. Appendix 3 describes the system used.

6 Harrington 1930: 131, 140, 145, 147, 161, etc. The text as printed here has been respelled by William Bright. The orthography is outlined in appendix 3.

7 The plant invoked in line 4 is *Brodiaea congesta*, an edible lily (a relative, therefore, of onion, leek, asparagus and camas) growing in the Klamath River country. The young shoots and corms, called *ataychúkinach* in Karuk, are harvested in spring and the mature plants, called *tayiith*, in midsummer.

8 The stories of Tahseench'e' (Emma Frank) are still in manuscript (Sapir n.d.2) though all have now been edited by Victor Golla and are awaiting publication in Sapir's *Collected Works*. One brief example, including this closing formula, is published in Golla & Silver 1977: 17–25. The orthography used here is outlined in appendix 3. "Bluestone" is Sapir's translation, supplied with the information that this was the hardest rock known to the Hupas. According to Golla, it is therefore probably serpentine.

9 Another formula Swanton heard but did not retain in his edited Haida texts is *Lla tl siittiiji*, "It [animate] is partly finished." This, he says, is a formula the

mythtellers used to interrupt a story that was too long to tell at a single sitting. (See Swanton 1905b: 270 n 6.)

10 There is nothing inherent in any Haida noun to show that it is animate or inanimate, nor are there any clues in most forms of the verb. There is nothing, that is, which corresponds to the intrinsic distinction of animate and inanimate in Ojibwa. But Haida has no direct *inanimate* pronouns. When speaking about anything inanimate, a fluent speaker leaves the pronoun out – and adjusts her speech as need be to eliminate confusion. The subject's inanimate character, in other words, can only be inferred from what the speaker *doesn't* say.

11 Boas met an exceptionally skillful Tsimshian mythteller in Victoria, BC, in 1886. He did not record the name, the lineage nor even the gender of this artist, but he preserved German versions of five of the stories he was told. One of these (Boas 1888: 232–241) is a complex story in four movements. Movements 1, 2 and 4 correspond to the three-movement story Sghiidagits told to Swanton in October 1900.

12 The Haida text is in Swanton n.d.2: folios 556–561. For Swanton's translation, see Swanton 1905b: 336–340. There are many published versions of the first major theme – that of the woman who married a bear. One of the best was dictated in Tlingit by Yeilnaawú of the Tuḵ.weidí at Teslin, Yukon, in 1972 and 1973. Text and translation are in Dauenhauer & Dauenhauer 1987: 166–193, 369–380. Unpublished texts include a version dictated in Tsimshian in the 1930s by Herbert Wallace, the hereditary headman of the village of Kitsiis. This was transcribed by the Nishga ethnographer Gwüsḵ'aayn (Beynon n.d.: text 5). For a comparative study of earlier versions, see Boas 1916: 835–845.

13 The name as Swanton heard it is Saghadila'u: a curious name in part because it seems to mix the consonants of the northern and southern dialects of Haida. This ensures at any rate that the name will sound exotic in any Haida context. The root, I believe, is the Tsimshian verb *dzagmdaawł,* to go across or go ashore. (Boas 1888: 232 n 2 proposes an alternate spelling and etymology.)

14 Delousing the head was a normal task for a spouse or lover. The easiest way to deal with the lice as they are found is to bite them between the front teeth.

15 The implication is that the two halves of her body ground themselves to froth on the whetstone as they struggled to rejoin.

16 Sea otter pelts are usually brown or black, though white facial fur is not uncommon. The rare individuals whose coats are entirely blond or silver are called in Haida *quu ghaada,* "white sea otter," or simply *giina ghaada,* "white creature." The white coloration develops with age and is not, as Swanton thought, a sign of youth. But the role of the silver otter in Northwest Coast mythology is complex. Skaay mentions these creatures several times (chapters 12 and 15 include examples), and in 1938 the Tsimshian mythteller Henry

Reeves dictated a story to Gwüs_k_'aayn in which "a big white sea otter" ('*wii moksgm płoon*) plays a leading role. White sea otters (*mikmoksgm płoon*), according to Reeves, are "messengers of the sea otter headman" (*haydzisga sm'oogidm płoon*), and the big white otter is "the sea otters' slave" (*łałuungida płoon*). The full text is in Reeves 1992.

17 So as not to mar the pelt. Deerhides in this pristine condition – called in Navajo *dook'áák'ehii*, "those with no arrow wound" – are often mentioned in Navajo oral poetry. There is no information on comparable uses of sea otter skins in Haida Gwaii – but no sea otter had been seen in Haida Gwaii for half a century before Swanton arrived.

18 In ordinary life, killer whales have only one dorsal fin each. In the Haida myth-world they may have as many as five.

19 A tall, steep headland in Portland Inlet, near the mouth of the Nass River. In Haida metaphysics, every mountain – or every mountain fronting on the sea – has its deity in residence, who can also take the form of a killer whale. It is interesting that the Tsimshian word for mountain, *sga'niis*, resembles the Haida word *sghaana*, meaning deity, spirit or power as well as killer whale. An etymological connection between the two words is unlikely, but the assonance cannot have gone unnoticed in a world where many people spoke both tongues.

20 Lamas is a steep, straight fjord about a mile wide and 30 miles long, near the boundary between the Nishga and Tsimshian territories. It is shown on modern charts as Work Channel, close north and east of the port of Prince Rupert. In Swanton's translation (1905b: 338) the women in this underwater world are digging wild clover roots. The Haida manuscript says nothing of the sort, so it may be that Swanton accidentally dropped a line of Haida when typing up his notes. Other mythtellers say these women are really geese, for whom clover roots are, of course, an appropriate food. (See for example the version told by Kihltlaayga at Ghaw in the spring of 1901, in Swanton 1908a: 495–500). I have not located Gyadiigha; because of the probable corruption of this sentence, I am not even sure it is a place name.

21 This is where we learn the protagonist's name – and though Sghiidagits does not say so, it appears to be where the protagonist himself first learns it too. Nanasimgit is a shortened form of Gunanasimgit, which is the Haida adaptation of the Tsimshian name Ganaxnox Sm'oogyit. This means "spirit-power headman" or "spirit-power aristocrat." (The literal meaning of *sm'oogyit* is "real person" or "genuine person." This is the conventional Tsimshian term for a headman or for any member of the upper class.)

22 Isniigahl is a mountain – I am not sure which one – in the region of Portland Inlet, which leads to the mouth of the Nass. The Haida name may be a corruption of the Nishga *gyisidaawł*, "downstream." Sghiidagits calls the son of this mountain (that is to say, the son of the spirit-being who lives in the mountain)

Gitgidamttsiixh. I think this name is derived from the Tsimshian *gidiganiitsk,* meaning Northwest Wind.

23 *Tsuga heterophylla,* the western hemlock (*qqang* in Haida), is one of the dominant trees in the lowland coastal forest. The wood is neither hard enough nor durable enough to find much use in Haida architecture or sculpture, but the phloem is an important food, the branches are used to gather herring roe, and the dead trees are a useful source of firewood. A tree that dies before it falls is, of course, especially prized, because the wood is dry the moment it is cut.

24 When Moody and Swanton were working through the transcript of this story and drafting their translation, Moody insisted that three lines be inserted here:

> *Gyaghangaay qaaji hlghunwalaaghani.*
> *Kilgatxhadlaayaghani.*
> *Ll qiijugighugaangang wansuuga.*

> *The housepole had three heads.*
> *It gave the alarm.*
> *It was always watching, they say.*

It is certain that Moody had heard the story before, and perhaps he had been learning to tell it himself. But these lines are not in Sghiidagits's style and do not belong in his version. (See Swanton n.d.2: 561; 1905b: 340 n 8.)

25 Ttadlat Ghadala, "Outruns Trout," is a mythname of the Swallow, who is said to be the fastest of the birds, just as Plain Old Marten or Crummy Old Marten (Kkuuxu Ginaagits) is said to be the fastest thing on land. The two often appear in the myths as a pair. But Sghiidagits said earlier that Plain Old Marten was the one Nanasimgit left in charge of his canoe. This looks like a mistake, though the canoeman may be just a surface person – an unusually fast surface person – named for the creature of myth who is mentioned here. "Plain Old Marten" has roughly the same tone as "plain old mink" or "plain old diamonds." The same diminutive suffix, *-gits,* appears in Sghiidagits's name as well.

26 The names translated Mainland Mouse and Mainland Weasel are Hlgiiyuttsin and Hlkumaaksihl. They are found nowhere else in extant classical Haida literature and are clearly of mainland origin. *Wittsiin* is Tsimshian for mouse, and *maksiił* is Tsimshian for weasel. The prefix in both cases probably comes from the Tsimshian diminutive *łgu.* In myth and daily life alike, the normal Haida words for mouse and weasel are quite different: *qagan* and *ttlalgaa.*

27 Swanton n.d.2: folio 561.

28 Skaay makes sparing use of the particle *wiiyadhaw* – the southern form corresponding to *wiidhaw.* Sghiidagits, in this story, says *wiidhaw* once, and sometimes twice, in almost every narrative sentence, though he never utters the word when he is representing dialogue. Apart from the Nanasimgit triptych,

there is only one more page of Haida narrative which Swanton credits to Sghiidagits (Swanton n.d.2: 601; 1905b: 356). I do not know when this page was dictated, nor under what conditions, but the style is noticeably different from that of the Nanasimgit narrative.

29 The organic nature of number in Native American philosophy is the subject of an interesting essay by J. Peter Denny (Denny 1986).

▸ NOTES TO CHAPTER SIX ▸

1 The three Haida mythtellers identified in *Indianische Sagen* are "Old Kaigani," Wiha [= Wiiha], and Johnny Swan. Wiha is identified more precisely in Boas's notes as Johnny Wiha of Skidegate. Swan was a Skidegate man as well.

2 Benedict 1935, vol 1: xxix.

3 Most of this material is now in a single folder of manuscript, Boas n.d.1.

4 For a summary of archaeological research on the Northwest Coast, see Matson & Coupland 1995.

5 Kkwaayang was born about 1858 and died in 1926. She was known in English as Isabella. The family name, Yaakw Llaanas, means "those amidships" in a canoe, from Haida *yakw,* "middle," but it has further associations. *Yaakw* in Tsimshian means potlatch, from *yaa,* "to give away."

6 The early history of the salmon canning industry on the British Columbia coast is outlined in Blyth 1991. Daxhiigang's daughter's recollections of this time are summarized in Blackman 1982: 57. For a portrait of Port Essington seen through the eyes of an adventuring colonial, see R. Geddes Large, *The Skeena: River of Destiny* (Vancouver: Mitchell Press, 1981): 28–43.

7 Boas left a fairly detailed account of these sessions, in the form of several letters to his wife (see Rohner 1969: 223–231).

8 Boas 1927. The book is based on a series of lectures Boas delivered in Oslo in 1925, after Daxhiigang's death.

9 Daxhiigang spoke Chinook Jargon poorly in Boas's opinion. But the fact that it was no one's native language did not prevent it from having a literature. See Hymes & Zenk, "Narrative Structure in Chinook Jargon" (1987).

10 Swanton 1905b: 138–146, 186–187, 247–250, 273–276, 316–317, 320, 363; 1908a: 623–624, 755, all reproduced from Boas n.d.2. Boas wrote to Swanton on 10 February 1906, saying: "I am sorry that you did not let me see the proofs of the traditions told to me by Edensaw which you printed in your Bulletin. I had never written them out for publication, and I think I should have made some alterations in the English. I might also have added a few remarks." [Quoted from Boas's carbon copy, APSL, Philadelphia.]

11 Many of these drawings – still at the AMNH, New York – are reproduced in Swanton 1905a. They include figures 7 and 8 on Swanton's plate xxi, figures 1–6 on plate xxii, figures 2–4 on plate xxiii, and figure 19 on Swanton's p 144.

12 Boas n.d.2: 23; compare Swanton 1908a: 755.

13 *Facial Paintings of the Indians of Northern British Columbia* (Boas 1898a). Though Boas did not intend it as such, this brief book became entirely a study of Daxhiigang's painting. It is in fact the first book devoted to the work of any Native American artist, and the first book devoted to the work of a Canadian visual artist in any cultural tradition.

14 The annotations on the drawing are as follows.

IN BOAS'S HAND ON THE FRONT: *Tattooing of / Yak^wlānas / Git'î'ns [of] Skidegate / Q'onaqē'wē [i.e.,* tattoo design representing a figure used in heraldry by the Yaakw Llaanas, Gitins of Hlghagilda, and Qquuna Qiighawaay].

IN SWANTON'S HAND ON THE BACK: *2 Gytins stole this tattooing from the Q'ōnaqēowai who in return stole Raven from them. There was nearly a fight over this but they were evened up by counter movements. So each has both. Edensaw's wife's family Yak^wla'nas has it too. This dogfish was a woman. The figure inside is the human form of the other. Dogfish is sister of NEñʌdasʟ'as (see story).*

Swanton's notes are repeated in more dignified prose, but without additional information, in his ethnology (Swanton 1905a: 142). The phonetic spelling in his notes shows that his source was a speaker of northern Haida – possibly Kihlguulins (Henry Edenshaw), but also possibly Daxhiigang himself. (Daxhiigang was born in the south but acculturated to northern speech.)

The Gitins of Hlghagilda were a large family amalgamated from (or divided into) four branches. The dominant branch in the later 19th century was Na Yuuwans Xhaaydaghaay, the Big House People. The headman of this family, whose hereditary name was Sghiidagits, served as headman of Hlghagilda.

The subject of the squabble Swanton mentions is, of course, not a particular work of art nor its particular design – which is freely created in each instance by the individual artist. The subject of the dispute is heraldic copyright. Families, and sometimes individuals, claim exclusive rights to use and display, as heraldic crests, any and all works of art in which certain figures are represented. These rights, while jealously guarded, are also sometimes shared, through gift or sale, with other individuals, or assigned in perpetuity by one family to another.

Daxhiigang, as a member of the Naay Kun Qiighawaay of the Raven side, claimed no right whatever to the heraldic use of the Dogfish or the Dogfish Woman, but he was perfectly free as an artist to represent these figures, and to sell or give away his representations. He was also free to put them to use in appropriate contexts: namely, in articles representing his wife and children, all of whom were members of the Yaakw Llaanas.

The importance attached to heraldic use of the Dogfish can be estimated in part from the large exterior sculptures standing at Qquuna and Hlghagilda in the 1880s. At Qquuna, four of the 50 poles in the village (two housepoles, one memorial pole, one mortuary pole) carried images of the Dogfish. Three of the four belonged to members of the Qquuna Qiighawaay. At Hlghagilda, Dogfish had become the rage. The image appeared on 12 of some 65 poles then standing. Nine or ten of these belonged to members of the Gitins of Hlghagilda. Another belonged to a man who was married to a woman of this family. The last belonged to the only white man living in the town: a retired whaler named Charles Jefferson of Newburyport, Massachusetts, who had built a Haida house and married one of the village headman's daughters.

At Ttanuu in the same years, only one pole bore the image of the Dogfish. It was raised in 1879, in memory of a recent headman, both of the village and of the Qquuna Qiighawaay. Other figures were more in fashion at Ttanuu. One of these (shown in the photos on pp 108–109) was the long-eyed god of the sea, whom Swanton heard described as the Dogfish Woman's brother. (The poles of these three villages are catalogued in MacDonald 1983: 38–54, 78–100.)

15 Swanton 1905b: 70. Swanton knew Giikw by his Christian name, Edward.

16 See Sapir & Swadesh 1939: 62–67.

17 Beynon n.d.: text 95. A related story, also told by Arthur Lewis, is summarized on pp 469–470: note 5 to chapter 11.

18 MacDonald (1983: 40) gives the date as 1898. This is contradicted by the missionary ledger (Crosby et al. n.d.), recording the death of the elder Sghiidagits on 19 October 1892.

19 Houses 13, 14 & 15 in Swanton's list (1905a: 286), corresponding to houses 17, 18 & 19 in MacDonald's (1983: 48–50).

20 In MacDonald's catalogue, these poles are Skidegate 18x1, 18x2 and 18x3. The newest can be dated from photographs. It does not appear in Dawson's photos, made in 1878, and it looks brand new in a photo made by Edward Dossetter in 1881 (AMNH neg 42264, reproduced in MacDonald 1983: plate 43). The suggestion that the pole was raised in 1881 for a woman who did not in fact die until 1892 (MacDonald 1983: 49) seems to be based on a misunderstanding.

21 The model is now owned by the AMNH, is reproduced and discussed in Swanton's ethnology (Swanton 1905a: 130 & plate VII.2). (Note however that in Swanton's discussion, all references to plates VII.1 and VII.2 are reversed.)

22 These are conveniently tabulated in Boas 1916: 840–845.

23 The letter in which this accusation is made is quoted at length on p 173.

24 Chafe 1981 is a useful study of differences between Native American ritual language and the language of conversation. Similar differences can be found between Haida narratives transcribed in 1900 and those recorded in recent

decades. The recent texts are, as a rule, far simpler, shorter, and stylistically more informal or relaxed. For examples, see Eastman & Edwards 1991, Haldane 1986 and Hamilton 1986. More extensive Haida texts have been recorded in recent years by John Enrico, Marianne Boelscher and others, but these remain unpublished. (There is some discussion in Boelscher 1988.) The rather forlorn state of Haida lyric in the late 20th century is documented in Enrico & Stuart 1996. The author of all the texts in Eastman & Edwards 1991, incidentally, is Lillian Pettviel. These are the only published Haida texts dictated by a woman.

Similar stylistic shifts are apparent in many postclassical Native American texts. Carlson 1977 includes examples in Nitinaht and Kwakwala. Phinney 1934: vii–viii is a brief but insightful discussion, by a native speaker, of the same phenomenon in Nimipu.

25 Details of Swanton's life are recorded in Kroeber 1940, Nichols 1940, Fenton 1959, Steward 1960, and in Swanton's own brief, unpublished autobiography (Swanton n.d.7), from which the quoted passage comes.

26 Yeats 1920: 298–299. The essay is actually dated 14 October 1914.

27 Swanton 1928: 30–31.

28 Kroeber 1940: 1.

29 Farrand (1867–1939) was by training a physician and psychologist, not a linguist. He published among other things a study of Salish basketry and a synopsis of the oral literature of the Salish-speaking Quinault. In 1900, at Boas's urging, he tried transcribing texts in Alsea (a language then still spoken by a few survivors on the northern Oregon coast), but he soon gave up. His work with the Quinault mythteller Bob Pope and with unnamed Chilcotin and Heiltsuk mythtellers was conducted entirely in English. After a time he gave up anthropology for administration. His few Alsea texts were later edited and published by Leo Frachtenberg. (The results of these adventures appear as Farrand 1900 & 1902; Boas 1916: 883–888; and Frachtenberg 1917 & 1920.)

30 An alternate spelling of Qqiltí is Q'iltí. The initial consonant is a glottalized voiceless uvular stop, like the *qq* in Haida. Stress falls on the second syllable.

31 Boas to his parents, 16 July 1890, in Rohner 1969: 122.

32 Boas's transcriptions from 1890–1894 are indeed the only substantive records of Shoalwater Chinook and Kathlamet. In the century since, the neighboring oral literatures have been studied very fruitfully by Edward Sapir, Melville Jacobs and Dell Hymes. The results are published in Sapir 1989f, vols. 7–8; Jacobs 1958–9, 1959, 1960; and Hymes 1981.

33 This was published as Swanton 1900.

34 The BAE functioned from 1879 to 1964. Swanton was the first, and for a long time the only, trained ethnologist it employed. Judd 1967 gives additional detail.

35 Original in the Dept. of Anthropology Archives, AMNH, New York.

36 Typed copy in the Dept. of Anthropology Archives, AMNH, New York.

1 "Tres cuadros del vino," in Ortega 1957–83: vol. 2: 57–58: *Los dioses son el sentido superior que las cosas poseen si se les mira en conexión unas con otras.... Decir que no hay dioses es decir que las cosas no tienen, además de su constitución material, el aroma, el nimbo de una significación ideal, de un sentido. Es decir que la vida no tiene sentido, que las cosas carecen de conexión.*

   Velázquez, Ortega goes on to say, "is *our* painter. He has prepared the way for our age, freed from gods: a bureaucratic age in which, in place of Dionysos, we speak merely of alcoholism." But it is possible that Ortega, in the midst of his brilliance, is wrong on one basic point. Velázquez, he says, "is a complete atheist, a great infidel. With his brush, he sends the gods flying." This may be a description less appropriate to what Velázquez actually did than to what his patrons and admirers wished him to do.

2 Compare, for instance, the stone sculpture of the Northwest Coast (Duff 1975) with Polynesian stone sculpture, and the narrative poetry of the Haida with that of the Ainu (translated in Philippi 1979). Needham & Lu 1985 is a wide-ranging, scholarly synopsis of Asian/American cultural resemblances, but its primary foci are China, Mexico and Peru. It has much of interest to say about metallurgy, bark cloth, the blowgun and the sweet potato, but little to say about art and nothing at all about oral literature.

3 For examples of the literary analogues, see Petitot 1888; Bogoras 1910, 1917, 1918; and Jochelson 1908, 1926. (Some of the limitations and defects of these sources are analyzed in Chowning 1962.) On circumpolar visual art and cultural geography, a convenient reference is Fitzhugh & Crowell 1988. There is more than ample evidence of cultural connections between Siberia and the Northwest Coast of North America. (The stories by Ghandl of the Qayahl Llaanas and Ekaterina Rumyantsev, juxtaposed in the first chapters of this book, are one example.) This does not, of course, prove that the Haida or other Native Americans are descended from Asian immigrants.

4 Many of the recorded masterpieces of Native North American oral literature have never been published, though many of the manuscripts have been micro-filmed. For manuscript materials, the most important finding aids are Freeman 1966, Kendall 1982 and the catalogue of the National Anthropological Archives, Smithsonian Institution, Washington, DC.

5 Swanton to Boas, 4 December 1900. Original in the Dept. of Anthropology Archives, AMNH, New York.

6 Swanton n.d.2: folios 25–27.

7 The northern Wakashans include the Haisla, Haihais, Henaaksiala, Heiltsuk, Uwikeeno and Kwakwalan or Kwakiutl. In older writings, the Heiltsuk are of-ten called the Bella Bella, while Haisla, Haihais, Henaaksiala and Uwikeeno are often all considered, wrongly, as Kwakiutl. The Nuxalk, in earlier writings, are usually labelled Bella Coola. Uwikeeno is often spelled Oowekeeno.

The name "Kwakiutl" remains even now a subject of confusion and dispute. Strictly speaking, it is the name of only one subgroup (just as Holland, strictly speaking, is the name of only a portion of the Netherlands). Some writers have therefore adopted the indigenous term *Kwakwaka'wakw,* which means speakers of Kwakwala. This is assuredly correct – just as it is correct to call the Germans *Deutsche* and the French *Français* – but *Kwakwaka'wakw* seems to me a term unlikely to survive as is in English. "Kwakwalan" is a practical substitute.

8 The concept of visual language in Northwest Coast art is explored in Bring-hurst & Steltzer 1992. For more, see Holm 1965 and Holm & Reid 1975.

9 The Uwekyala language is spoken by the Uwikeeno, the Heiltsuk language by the Heiltsuk and the Haihais, and the Haisla language by the Haisla and Henaaksiala (or Kitimaat and Kitlope) nations. Speakers of the Nootka lan-guage are nowadays known as Nuuchahnulth or West Coast People.

For examples of Nuxalk oral literature, see Boas 1898b (in English only) and Davis & Saunders 1980 (Nuxalk and English). For Haisla oral literature, see Robertson 1990. For Heiltsuk, see Boas 1928 and (in English only) Boas 1932. For Uwekyala, see Boas 1928 and Walkus 1982. (Though its title does not say so, Boas 1928 includes texts in two languages, Uwekyala and Heiltsuk. All, however, were edited with Heiltsuk as a reference.) There is a rich selection of Kwakwala texts in Boas & Hunt 1905 & 1906, and in Boas 1910 & 1935–43. Much of the best classical southern Wakashan literature is still in manuscript, but fine examples are contained in Sapir & Swadesh 1939 and 1955.

10 Boas's *Tsimshian Texts* (1902) are actually in the Nishga language, while his *Tsimshian Texts, new series* (1912) are indeed in Tsimshian. Philip Latimer, the older of the two principal speakers of the 1902 Nishga texts, appears to be per-fectly fluent, but he was a native speaker of Tsimshian who had married a Nishga woman and was living in the Nishga town of Kincolith. Using him as a phenotype of the Nishga mythteller is analogous to relying on a native speaker of Swedish as a source for oral literature in Norwegian, or choosing a native speaker of German as a source for oral literature in Dutch.

A literary mix-up of major proportions is also superimposed on this lin-guistic one. The texts published in Boas's *Tsimshian Texts,* new series (1912), and (in English translation only) in the Tsimshian section of *Tsimshian Mythology* (1916), were supplied to Boas by the Tsimshian writer Henry Tate (c. 1850–1914). But Tate wrote most or all of his texts in English and translated them into Tsimshian, not the other way around. Boas was dissatisfied with Tate's sys-tem of spelling and therefore had some of the stories read aloud from Tate's manuscript by Archie Dundas, another native speaker, so that he, Boas, could retranscribe them. *Tsimshian Texts, new series* thus consists of texts that were written by Tate in English, translated by him into Tsimshian, redictated with changes, and retranslated by Dundas and Boas back into English. *Tsimshian Mythology* pp 58–392 consists again of texts written by Tate in English and translated by him into Tsimshian, but here they are presented in English only. The published text is Boas's edited version of Tate's original, with occasional reference to Tate's Tsimshian translation. For more, see p 464 n 33 and the studies of Ralph Maud (Maud 1989; Tate 1993 with Maud's introduction).

The Nishga ethnologist Gwüsk̲'aayn (William Beynon, 1888–1958) is a more dependable source than Tate, and several texts recorded by him have been published in recent years (see Bennet & Gasin 1992, Brown 1992, Marsden 1992 and Reeves 1992). Most of Gwüsk̲'aayn's work nonetheless remains in manuscript – and many of his manuscripts were cut, quite literally, to pieces by Marius Barbeau, who was his principal employer.

Another brief but useful collection of Tsimshian texts – transcribed by Boas himself – is published in Schulenburg 1894: 183–193. Some of these were dictated by a man called Matthias, from Max̲łaqxaała (Old Metlakatla), others by a woman from Port Simpson whom Boas knew as Mrs Lawson.

11 Tlingit oral culture fared comparatively well in the 20th century, and the best sources are recent ones. Tlingit texts from the classical period, however, are scarce. See Swanton 1908b, Dauenhauer & Dauenhauer 1987 and 1990, and Nyman & Leer 1993. For Eyak oral literature, see Krauss 1982.

12 *The Black Canoe* (Bringhurst & Steltzer 1992) chronicles the progress of a form through several different materials (or the repeated reincarnation of a form) by tracing the development of a single large piece of Haida art.

13 All three vowels are pronounced: *Nadéné*.

14 Edward Sapir, Heinz-Jürgen Pinnow and Joseph Greenberg, among others, have argued that Haida is part of Nadene. Opponents of this view include Robert Levine, Michael Krauss and Jeff Leer. Sapir was singularly brilliant, and his normal method of studying a language was not to sift through missionary wordlists or other suspect data but to find a native speaker and start talking. That insistence on direct sensory contact with the language is one of the things that made him a great taxonomist. But Sapir had only a few days' real experience with Haida, and his views were therefore tentative at best. (See Sapir 1921b, 1949, & 1989f, vol. 6; Pinnow 1985, 1985–6; Greenberg 1987: 321–331; Levine 1979; Krauss 1979; Leer 1991, and also Haas 1969: 98–107.)

The best defense to date of the thesis that Haida is part of Nadene is probably the one published in 1994 by Greenberg's younger colleague Merrit Ruhlen. This lists 324 comparisons, of which 202 include Haida. About half of these are spurious. Some are words we know to be late borrowings; some compare incomparable elements; many are based on corrupt information. There remain about a hundred plausible looking cognates in the list, and others could easily be added. This is enough to warrant further research, though it is not by any means proof of Ruhlen's claim, that Haida is part of Nadene or that Nadene is part of a larger superphylum called Dene-Caucasian.

15 A large and sometimes acrimonious body of writing has grown up around this issue. The theory of three linguistic groups is presented in Greenberg 1987. It is defended and extended in Ruhlen 1987, Ruhlen 1994, and Greenberg 1996. Rankin 1992 and Golla 1996 are two of the more civil critiques of Greenberg's data and his methods.

16 The old view that Yukaghir is a relative of Chukchi and Koryak now has few adherents. Björn Collinder classifies it instead as part of the Samoyed branch of the Uralic family, and thus as a distant cousin of Finnish, Estonian, Lapp and Hungarian. Others have argued that Yukaghir is just as solitary as Haida, Ket or Basque. See Collinder, *An Introduction to the Uralic Languages* (Berkeley: University of California Press, 1965): 30.

17 These statements are true even within the synoptic classification system of Greenberg and Ruhlen. Tsimshian, in their system, belongs to the phylum called Amerind, Haida to the phylum Nadene, Yukaghir to the phylum Uralic-Yukaghir, English to the phylum Indo-Hittite, Yoruba to the phylum Niger-Kordofanian, and the Chinese languages to the phylum Sino-Tibetan.

18 Sapir, *Collected Works* (1989f), vol. 6: 134. There is further information in Victor Golla's editorial note, pp 138–139 of the same volume, and his edition of the full correspondence (Golla 1984). The manuscript dictionary is Sapir n.d.1, in the APSL, Philadelphia. Working independently, Robert Shafter prepared a similar document, published in 1952 as "Athapaskan and Sino-Tibetan," IJAL 18: 12–19.

19 Swanton calls Sghaagya by his Christian name, which was Richard. One of his autobiographical tales is published in bilingual form (Swanton 1905b: 104–109). The Haida texts of the remainder are in Swanton n.d.2: 649–720, with translations in Swanton 1905b: 364–400. Sghaagya dictated two brief myth texts (Swanton 1905b: 44–47; n.d.2: 583–587 and 1905b: 348–351), but he is at his best as a raconteur instead of a mythteller. In his essay on the Haida language, Swanton analyzes one of Sghaagya's shorter texts in considerable detail (Swanton 1910: 277–281). The author's Haida name, incidentally, can be found in Swanton n.d.2: folios 653, 654, 719 and 1905b: 367, 368, 398. These are the occasions in which Sghaagya speaks of himself in the third person.

20 Swanton n.d.2: 696; cf. 1905b: 385.

21 The term Sghaagya uses here is *aahljaaw qagaan*, "disaster song." Enrico & Stuart, in their detailed study of northern Haida music, found no surviving examples of the genre. (Enrico & Stuart 1996: 47.)

22 Swanton n.d.2: 700. For the context, see Swanton 1905b: 384–389.

23 A person's fathers, in the old Haida system, are all the male members of the father's lineage who belong, more or less, to the biological father's generation.

24 There are recordings of Tlingit oratory on wax cylinders dating from 1899 (now published in Dauenhauer & Dauenhauer 1990: 156–161, 325–329). Boas's transcriptions of oratory in Kwakwala may go back as early as 1894. There are also plenty of fraudulent imitations. Some of these are dealt with in Rudolf Kaiser's excellent study "Chief Seattle's Speech(es)" (1987).

25 Julien Ttsinnayinen dictated a story in Chipewyan to Émile Petitot at Great Slave Lake in September 1862. It is published, with others told in 1863 by Pacôme Kkraykhraa, Ekunélyel and François Beaulieu, in Petitot 1888. These seem to be the oldest securely dated texts in Native Canadian literature.

26 The sapsucker of the Northwest Coast is *Sphyrapicus ruber,* the redbreasted sapsucker, but the coastal birds have striking bright red heads. Locally, they are often called redheaded woodpeckers – a name that ornithologists reserve for *Melanerpes erythrocephalus* of central and eastern North America.

27 Swanton n.d.2: folio 166. The northern Haida mythteller Kingagwaaw treats the Sapsucker theme in his own way as part of his version of *Raven Travelling* (Swanton 1908a: 324–325).

▶ NOTES TO CHAPTER EIGHT ▶

1 Original in the Dept. of Anthropology Archives, AMNH. All letters cited in this chapter come from the same archive except where noted otherwise.

 The mention of long stories of wars between the towns remains a puzzle. All the so-called war stories Swanton recorded are short, and none was told by Skaay. But a mythological war provides the culmination of Skaay's first three-part suite (summarized on pp 118–120). I wonder whether Swanton misinterpreted a reference Skaay made to that story – or whether Skaay was talking of another set of stories Swanton never got to hear.

2 Jean Low's brief biography of Newcombe (Low 1982) is informative regarding Newcombe's English background but inaccurate concerning his activities in Haida Gwaii and his relations with Henry Moody and John Swanton. For the later period, Cole 1995 is more dependable and thorough. Swanton and Newcombe did not apparently meet until shortly after Swanton's arrival in Hlghagilda, but Newcombe had known Franz Boas since 1894 and had worked with Henry Moody since 1895. It was probably on Newcombe's recommendation that Swanton sought out Moody on his arrival in Haida Gwaii.

3 This letter is now in the C.F. Newcombe papers, British Columbia Archives, Victoria. The view of Homer that Swanton had imbibed at Harvard in the 1890s was the Neoclassical view, defined two centuries before by the English classicist Richard Bentley (1662–1742). In Bentley's estimation, the *Iliad* and the *Odyssey*

were "loose songs … not collected together in the form of an Epic Poem, till Pisistratus's time." Elias Lönnrot (1802–1884), the compiler of the *Kalevala*, acted on this theory and claimed in turn that Homer had been a compiler and editor like himself. Henry Wadsworth Longfellow (1807–1882), who borrowed Lönnrot's meter for *The Song of Hiawatha*, did much to reinforce this teaching at Harvard as well. The proposition that Homer was a scribe has repeatedly been challenged by people acquainted with living traditions of oral epic. It was challenged, for example, by the Russian scholar Vasilii Radlov (1837–1918), who knew the oral epics of the Kirghiz, and by the Slovenian scholar Matija Murko (1861–1952), who knew the rich tradition of Serbo-Croatian oral epic – a tradition sustained in the 20th century chiefly by Bosnian Muslims. But no such insight into Homeric practice was current in Harvard Yard until Milman Parry taught there in the 1930s.

4 The monetary details are laid out in Swanton's letters dated 30 September and 14 October 1900 (the same letters quoted in part on pp 69, 75 & 173).

5 The Kaigani country is the southern part of Prince of Wales Island in Alaska, to which several hundred Haida migrated during the 18th and 19th centuries, and which is Haida country still. The name is an English simplification of the Haida Kkaykkaanii, short for Kkaykkaanii Llanagaay, "Crabapple Town." This is the name of a Haida village (empty at present) on what is now called Cape Muzon, the southern tip of Dall Island, Alaska.

   The Tongass is the rest of the southern part of the Alaska panhandle: the domain of the T'angaas division of the Tlingit. (That at any rate is what Tongass meant to Swanton; now it is also the name of the US National Forest covering most of southeastern Alaska.)

   The mouth of the Copper River, at the top of the Gulf of Alaska, is the old northeastern limit of Eyak territory and thus a convenient northern boundary for the cultural province of the northern Northwest Coast.

6 Boas's replies to Swanton's letters of this period are evidently lost.

7 In the northern dialect, *gh* is swallowed, becoming a pharyngeal instead of a uvular stop, and the *x* is dropped altogether, so that the name Ghadaghaa-xhiwaas elides to 'At'aaywaas. (See appendix 1.) Maasit Gwaay, the source of the English name Masset, is an island near Ghadaghaaxhiwaas, on the west side of the entrance to Masset Sound. Haayas of the Hliiyalang Qiighawaay told Swanton it was once the site of a fortified village (Swanton 1908a: 773).

8 One of Haayas's poems is analyzed in Hymes 1995.

9 John Work (1791–1861) was a factor with the Hudson's Bay Co. His Haida population figures were published by Dawson in 1880 (= Dawson 1993: 165). James Swan counted 65 houses in the village in 1883, of which four were new and unfinished and ten were old and unoccupied. A year later Newton Chittenden reported only 40 inhabited houses and the frames of several more. These numbers

are broadly confirmed by George MacDonald's more recent archaeological survey. (See Swan 1883b: 17, 61; Chittenden 1884: 19; MacDonald 1983: 132–133.)

10 Sinhlagutgaang (1852–1922) was known in English as Amy Edenshaw.

11 Original and transcript in the Dept. of Anthropology Archives, AMNH.

12 Inverness was a cannery on the Tsimshian coast between Prince Rupert and Port Essington – south of the present Port Edward, at a place known in Tsimshian as Wilaqłootk. It was built in 1876 and for a short time was the only cannery upcoast of the Fraser River. Kkwaayang, Daxhiigang's wife, was one of its first seasonal employees. She worked there and at other canneries most summers for four decades.

13 The BAE had its offices in the old Adams Building, 1333 F Street, until it moved to the Smithsonian Building on the Capitol Mall in 1910.

14 Swanton n.d.7.

15 This is one of the themes of Swanton's very brief "Concordance of American Myths" (Swanton 1907).

16 Original in the APSL, Philadelphia.

17 See Swanton 1905b: 195–200; Enrico 1995: 136–151.

18 Swanton 1905a: 72; 1905a: 182 n 1; and 1905b: 110 n *a*. In his handwritten notes, made while talking with Henry Moody in Vancouver in December 1903, Swanton refers to *Nang Ttl Dlstlas* or "One They Hand Along" as story 2. Story 1 in that case can only be *Raven Travelling*. (Swanton n.d.1: vol. 2 insert.)

19 After Holmes's death in 1933, Swanton was prevailed upon to write the required obituary essay for the National Academy of Sciences' *Biographical Memoirs*. He performed this task with diplomatic courtesy, speaking at length of Holmes's enthusiasm for drawing and his "irrepressibly artistic taste," but passing in almost perfect silence over his unproductive nine-year term as Chief of the BAE and his later stint as Director of the US National Gallery.

20 Newcombe made notes of his own on a conversation he had with Henry Moody in Victoria on 23 December 1903 (Newcombe n.d.1: v 38 f 1), and on 30 December he wrote to Boas reporting the Swantons' unexpected visit. Whether Moody and Swanton met in Victoria as well as Vancouver remains unclear. Swanton's original notes from these sessions have survived, again by accident, because they were tucked into the back of an earlier field notebook (Swanton n.d.1: vol. 2). The letter of New Year's Eve, written on Hotel Badminton stationery, is in the Dept. of Anthropology Archives, AMNH.

21 Why the best Tlingit mythteller Swanton met was known as Deikinaak'w (Tlingit for "Little Haida") remains to be explained. The Ḵookhíttaan or Box House People are a subdivision of the Kaagwaantaan clan of the Eagle side

(Wolf side) of the Tlingit, based in the Sitka region. The Kaasx̲'agweidí were a family of the Raven side (Crow side), based at Wrangell and vicinity. Léek's son, K̲aadashaan, was headman of the Kaasx̲'agweidí at the beginning of the 20th century and Swanton's host at Wrangell in 1904.

Léek and her son both told stories during that visit, but Swanton transcribed only the words of the son. Léek appears in retrospect to be much the better mythteller, but all we have on which to base this shaky judgement are the English summaries published in Swanton 1909.

In 1910, Swanton did transcribe some original texts from a woman named Selina Williams Langley, a speaker of Koasati. The originals of these are still in manuscript (Swanton n.d.5 & 6). English paraphrases are published, without ascription, in Swanton 1929: 166–213.

22 The difference in page count, between 1500 and 400, is of course the difference between interlinear notebook pages and densely typeset prose. As a rule, when I speak in this book of the length of a Haida text, I mean its length in the typographic form used here, where every clause is treated like a verse line. In that form, Swanton's Skidegate texts fill about 800 pages.

23 In addition to Haida and Tlingit, the list includes Alabama, Atakapa, Caddo, Catawba, Cherokee, Chickasaw, Shoalwater Chinook, Chitimacha, Choctaw, Creek, Hitchiti, Kitsai, Koasati, Lakhota, Natchez, Tawasa, Tonkawa, Tunica and Wichita. Most of these are Siouan, Caddoan and Muskogean languages, spoken in the central and southeastern United States.

24 Swanton to Boas, 16 August 1903. Original in APSL, Philadelphia.

25 Kroeber 1940: 3.

26 Boas believed, for example, even in 1938, that Skaay's *Xhuuya Qaagaangas* consisted of "unrelated episodes" (Boas et al. 1938: 597).

27 "Mythology and Folk-Tales of the North American Indians," (1914, reprinted in Boas 1940: 451–490).

28 Notably in his 1917 charter for the newly founded *International Journal of American Linguistics* (reprinted in Boas 1940: 199–210) and in his essay "Stylistic Aspects of Primitive Literature" (1925, in Boas 1940: 491–502).

29 Swanton to Boas, 31 March 1905. Original in APSL, Philadelphia.

30 Boas to R.W. Brock (Geological Survey of Canada), 14 May 1910. Copy in APSL, Philadelphia. The letter is in response to an inquiry from Brock, who was looking for someone to head the Geological Survey's newly created Division of Anthropology. Boas recommended Edward Sapir, who was indeed given the job.

31 See Hyatt 1990.

32 Boas was in southeastern British Columbia in August 1914 taking texts in

Kutenai, but he did no work on the coast. On this trip, working with the skill-ful Kutenai mythteller known as Pałnapi or Barnaby, Boas finally tried using an intermediary listener, as Swanton had described to him in 1900. But Boas disliked this way of working and quickly gave it up. He demanded instead that Barnaby speak to him directly but slowly enough for transcription.

33 Q'ix̱itasu' worked with Boas for 45 years, from 1888 until 1933. His mother, Ansnaq, was Tlingit and his father, Robert Hunt, was a Scot, but he was raised at Tsax̱is (Fort Rupert), and Kwakwala was his mother tongue. Boas taught him to write it phonetically in 1893. (See Canizzo 1983; Berman 1996.)

The decade-long collaboration between Boas and Henry Tate began in May 1903 and ended with Tate's death in April 1914. It was conducted entirely by mail – the two men never met – and it produced the immense study *Tsimshian Mythology* (1916). This is among many other things the first book-length study of the work of any Native American author and the first book-length study of the work of a Canadian author in any language or tradition. It has the same un-sung historical importance as Boas's *Facial Paintings* of 1898. (See p 453 n 13.)

The beginnings of the Tate/Boas relationship are documented by a letter from Tate to Boas dated 2 May 1903 and Boas's reply dated 13 May. [The orig-inal of Tate's letter and a carbon of Boas's are in the APSL, Philadelphia.] The problems that arose are apparent in letters they exchanged two years later. On 22 May 1905, Boas wrote as follows:

My *dear Mr. Tate,*

I received your letter of May, and also the 112 pages of the Tkamshum story, for which I thank you very much....

In reading over the Tkamshum story, which is very interesting,... I notice that often the words that you use in this English translation are just the same as the words which I used in my Nass River stories, and which George Hunt has used in his stories from Fort Rupert. It also seems to me that you write the English first, and the Indian afterwards between lines.

I should like it much better to have the stories told in just the same way as they are told by your people.... I would therefore beg to ask you, in writing the follow-ing parts of the story, to write your Tsimshian first, just as your old people are in the habit of telling the stories, and then to write the English between the lines, and not to follow my example or that of George Hunt....

P.S. *Please be sure to write in the future your Tsimshian first, and then the English translation between the lines.*

Tate replied on 6 July, in his finest copybook hand:

Dear Sir

I received your letter of the last mail, and I am so very sorry for you have not believe at my history of Tk̲āmshim beginning. It because I have with me a three very wises men Chief Neāsh-ya-ganāit and then two others Gilashgilāsh, and also E. Maxwell. These three olden men they are full wisdom. The Chief was knew the beginning of Tḵāmshim history right to the end.... So I believed that my people knows very the history of Tḵāmshim than any other Indian round about us. So I don't want to by or as the Naas history or Geo. Hunt. I will go by the history of My peoples....

[Again, the carbon of Boas's letter and the original of Tate's are in the APSL, Philadelphia. Txaamsm – or Tḵāmshim in Tate's spelling – is one of the Raven's Tsimshian names.]

Tsimshian was Tate's first language, but missionary schooling had considerably affected his sense of values. It is clear from the surviving manuscripts that he did indeed often write the English version first, rough though it is. Boas did not hide the problem (it is declared on the first page of his preface to *Tsimshian Mythology*), but he also may not have appreciated its scope. Tate's recent editor, Ralph Maud, appears convinced that the English precedes the Tsimshian in almost every case.

Tate's extant manuscripts are now divided among the APSL in Philadelphia; the NAA in Washington, DC; and Columbia University in New York. Boas 1908 is a close analysis of one of Tate's Tsimshian texts. The English version is in Boas 1916: 113–115.

34 See for example Boas 1940: 452, 200 & 492. These statements date from 1914, 1917 and 1925.

35 The fruits of Sapir's work with Tony Tillohash – including the important "Song Recitative in Paiute Mythology" – are in Sapir's *Collected Works* (1989f), vol 10. The stories of Saayaacchapis and Qiixxa remain largely in manuscript, but see Sapir 1989f, vol. 4: 451f, and Sapir & Swadesh 1939 & 1955. Charlie Mitchell and Chiishch'ilíts'ósí are in Sapir 1942 and the forthcoming *Collected Works*, vol. 15. (Chiishch'ilíts'ósí also worked with Berard Haile and is the source of Haile 1943.) For Nick Tumaka and Leo Zuni, see Bunzel 1932 & 1933; Benedict 1935, vol. 1: xxix–xliii; Tedlock 1983: 37–39, 184; and Parezo 1992. (Benedict, to preserve the anonymity of living mythtellers, referred to them not by name but by number. Leo Zuni is number 6, Nick Tumaka number 7.)

In addition to taking his dictation, Sapir wrote three character studies of Saayaacchapis: two in prose and one in verse. These are collected in Sapir 1989f, vol. 4: 450–456, 481–506 & 507–510. For a biography of Tillohash, see Sapir's introduction to the texts (Sapir 1989f, vol. 10: 319–320), the supplementary note supplied by Catherine Fowler and Robert Euler (Sapir 1989f, vol. 10: 779–784), and Fowler & Fowler 1986.

36 Boas's carbon copy of this letter is in APSL, Philadelphia.

37 Original in APSL, Philadelphia.

38 Details are in Butler 1983.

39 Swanton 1905b: 187.

1 The 106 lyrics Swanton transcribed were eventually published as *Haida Songs* (Swanton 1912). Enrico & Stuart 1996 is a detailed study of recent Haida song in which music and text are examined together.

2 Many if not all Native American languages have convenient terms for distinguishing between myths on the one hand and historical narratives, comic tales or personal reminiscences on the other. This does not guarantee that precise distinctions are always possible or even desirable. In Cree, for example, the names of the different literary genres are, for the most part, parallel to the names of the genres in Haida – but Cree mythtellers often deliberately interchange or combine the terms that theoretically distinguish myths from secular stories. There are published examples in the stories Kâ-kîsikâw-pîhtokêw told to Leonard Bloomfield in Saskatchewan in 1925, and in those Simeon Scott told to Douglas Ellis at James Bay in the 1950s. (See for instance Bloomfield 1930: 1, 110, 130, 267; Ellis 1995: 2, 8, 58, 391 n 1. For a wider discussion of literary genres in Cree, see Ellis 1995: xix–xxxvi.)

3 There are many examples in Sapir & Swadesh 1939 and 1955, and in Dauenhauer & Dauenhauer 1990.

4 Conflicting dates are often cited for the onset of government suppression of the potlatch. Cole & Chaikin (1990: 14) report that the subject was discussed in the Canadian federal cabinet during 1883 and the law enacted by Parliament on 19 April 1884, with effect from 1 January 1885. But the potlatch was suppressed by different means in different areas. Among the Haida, Nishga and Tsimshian, its suppression came primarily through missionary pressure, and the work was largely done in many areas by the time the law was passed. On the central coast the situation was different. Cole & Chaikin tell the story in some detail.

5 The recording was made, transcribed and translated by Michael Krauss. The poem is published in Krauss's *In Honor of Eyak* (1982): 155–157, and in Anna Harry's voice on the accompanying tape.

6 Margaret Blackman's *During My Time* (1982) is in fact a biography of Florence Davidson, based on her elicited and recorded (but unpublished) autobiography. Blackman's opening chapter includes an interesting discussion of the role of autobiography in Haida culture. The published portions of Saayaacchapis's autobiography are in Sapir & Swadesh 1939: 128–177.

7 The Haida text of these tales is in Swanton n.d.2: folios 649–720 & Swanton 1905b: 105–109. Swanton's translation is in 1905b: 104–108, 364–400.

8 The relative silence of women on the Northwest Coast in the early 20th century is not an unfamiliar scholarly theme. It is touched upon, for example, in De Laguna 1972: 444, 521; Kan 1989: 55, 61–62; Blackman 1982: 28.

9 K'achodi (or Khatchôti) spoke the Big Willow dialect of Slavey, often called Hare. Her works are published in Slavey and French in Petitot 1888: 257–463.

10 Nyman & Leer 1994 is a volume of Seidayaa's stories with Leer's translation.

11 Some examples: Toby Riddle, transcribed in Klamath by Albert Gatschet in 1877; Kaagigeepinäsihkwä, transcribed in Ojibwa by William Jones about 1904; Gwìsgwashaán, transcribed in Takelma by Edward Sapir in 1906; "Mrs Molasses," transcribed in the Chilula dialect of Hupa by Pliny Goddard in 1907; Imkyánvaan, transcribed in Karuk by John P. Harrington about 1928; Caastawirahiika', Cakarikuseeriku' and Ctaaharitkari', transcribed in Pawnee by Gene Weltfish in 1928–29; Selina Williams Langley, transcribed in Koasati by Swanton in 1929; Victoria Howard, transcribed and acoustically recorded in the Clackamas dialect of Kiksht by Melville Jacobs in 1929–30; K'amaxalas and 'Man'manliqalas, transcribed in Kwakwala by Q'ixitasu', probably in 1930–31; Hets'miiẍwn (Annie Miner Peterson), transcribed and acoustically recorded in the two Coosan languages, Miluk and Hanis, by Melville Jacobs in 1933–4; Weyiiletpuu, transcribed in Nimipu (Nez Perce) by her son Archie Phinney about 1932; Chona Dominguez, recorded in Cahuilla by Hansjakob Seiler in 1955; Anna Nelson Harry, recorded in Eyak by Michael Krauss in 1963–72; Agnes Edgar, recorded in Nuxalk by Philip Davis & Ross Saunders in 1967; Stikûstâhkáta and Stičiišáxkûx, both recorded in Arikara by Douglas Parks in the mid 1970s; Sóena'hané'e, recorded in Cheyenne by Wayne Leman in 1975; and Grace McKibben, recorded in Wintu by Alice Shepherd between 1975 and 1982. Sources for the study of all these are listed in the bibliography.

12 Fenton 1959: 664.

13 Quoted in Fenton 1959: 666.

14 Journal entry for 23 August 1878, published in Dawson 1993: 70.

15 Qasalas's story (both transcript and translation) is in Boas 1910: 400–413. The transcript and translation of Qiixxa's story are in Sapir & Swadesh 1939: 76–81. Other works on the same theme are listed in Boas 1916: 849. As mentioned in note 11 above, Q'ixitasu' transcribed stories by two other Kwakwala-speaking women, K'amaxalas and 'Man'manliqalas. These are in Boas 1930, vol. 1: 246–250 & vol. 2: 241–246, and 1935–43, vol. 1: 17–23, 58–61, 219–227 & vol. 2: 15–21, 59–61, 209–218. Qasalas and K'amaxalas also recounted some of their dreams to Q'ixitasu'; these are in Boas 1925: 6–9, 16–17, 20–21, 38–39.

Judith Berman (1991, 1996) has rightly described Q'ixitasu' as a literary figure: one who wrote after talking with his sources far more often than he took direct dictation. Nevertheless there is a great range of voices in his work. In many instances the tone, the pace, the phrasing, even the dialectal inflections, as well as the bare plot, appear to come from the original narrator.

Between 1947 and 1953, Gwüsk'aayn recorded stories from several Nishga and Tsimshian women: Dorothy Brown, Mary Clayton, Helen Clifton, Agnes

Haldane and Emma Patalas. There are bilingual texts in Beynon n.d. and in Brown 1992; others were published by Barbeau in English only. Swanton, as we have seen (p 189), heard many stories from a very knowledgeable Tlingit woman, Léek, in 1904, but he preserved them only in the form of English summaries. In the 1920s, T. F. McIlwraith dealt with several Nuxalk women storytellers in the same inadequate way (McIlwraith 1948). Boas did the same with the stories told to him by Heiltsuk women at Waglisla in the autumn of 1923. The authors include Q'amdemaxl (Mrs Alfred Watson, in Boas 1932: 26, 41, 54–55, 66, 71, 81–82, 91–92, 113–114, 126–129, 154–159, 166–167); Ǧagwe (Boas 1932: 73–77), and a woman identified only as Kate (Boas 1932: 27, 43–44).

16 See Birket-Smith & de Laguna 1938: 9–10, 245–246; Krauss 1982: 16–20.

17 In Oregon in 1906, Edward Sapir took extensive dictation from a speaker of Takelma, Gwìsgwashaán (Mrs Frances Johnson). These transcripts (Sapir 1907, 1909a & 1989f: vol. 8) exemplify what is missing from the Haida record. (It is interesting, for instance, that Gwìsgwashaán uses some of the technical vocabulary of basketmaking to speak of the creation of the world.) Margaret Blackman also addresses the distinction between male and female arts, and some of the conditions in which these roles could be reversed, in her biography of Daxhiigang's daughter Florence Davidson (Blackman 1982: 39–40).

18 Marianne Boelscher, Carol Eastman and Elizabeth Edwards are examples. See Boelscher 1988 and Eastman & Edwards 1991.

19 Swanton 1905a: 75.

20 The passage begins at line 1362, p 284. For the Haida text, see p 477 n 9.

21 Swanton 1905b: 149 n 59.

22 Xhaaydakuns was one of Price's names; Taan (Black Bear) was another; and as headman of the empty village of Sghan Gwaay, he was known as Nang Stins (Someone Doubled, or One Who is Two).

23 In 1903, Henry Moody formally succeeded Gidansta as headman of the empty village of Qquuna. He was then given the Tsimshian name Niiswayxs, "Grandfather," and the Haida title Nang Gayhildangaay Yuuwans, "Big One Swirling Around" (i.e., Grizzly in the Water).

24 In December 1894, Boas asked Qqiltí to repeat two of the stories he had dictated in the summer of 1891. The two versions are published side by side in Boas 1901: 50–57, 182–186.

25 David Bynum recounts, by contrast, the merciless if well-intentioned series of experiments to which Milman Parry subjected the great Montenegrin oral poet Avdo Međedović. See his introduction to Međedović 1980: x–xi. Parry's thoroughness also impressed his student Albert Lord, who repeats what Bynum has to say (Lord 1991: 98–99).

1 Swanton n.d.2: folio 43.

2 Swanton's handwritten emendation: "Capt. Kloo from here," n.d.2: folio 45; Swanton 1905b: 130.

3 Swanton n.d.2: folio 46.

4 Swanton 1905b: 133, 149 n 73.

5 The *Flyting of [William] Dunbar and [Walter] Kennedy* appears in most editions of Dunbar's poems, including James Kinsley's *The Poems of William Dunbar* (Oxford: Clarendon Press, 1979). There is a useful commentary in Kinsley and in Priscilla Bawcutt's *Dunbar the Makar* (Oxford: Clarendon Press, 1992).

6 This is the point at which Xhyuu's wife interrupted the poem, insisting that the Raven's attempt to feed the Seal by roasting his own hand should not be told as a separate episode, since it repeats the previous scene. Since she did not dictate her own version of the story, we have no way of judging whether or not she might have done a better job. Swanton says that Xhyuu accepted her objection, but in this summary of the flyting, I have let Xhyuu's three-prong parallel structure stand.

1 This is Durlach 1928, a useful book for the study of Haida literature.

2 This is Swanton n.d.3: Ms 7047, NAA, Smithsonian Institution, Washington, DC. The catalogue description has since been corrected.

3 Parry died in 1935 leaving his work far from complete. The best introduction to this work is *The Singer of Tales* (1960), by his student and colleague Albert Lord.

4 Original on folio 1 of Swanton n.d.3, continuing on folios 23–24 of Swanton n.d.2. Compare Enrico 1995: 14–21. Enrico emends the verb in line 1 to a predicate phrase, *tangaa ghagingang,* and the verb in line 7 to *xhiihlttahliyaagaas.*

5 Like many Haida nouns, *ghiinuu* has a wide and a narrow definition. It can refer to almost any intertidal holothurian, from the small (about 3 cm) black *Cucumaria vegae,* often found in mussel beds, to the big (40 or 50 cm) reddish, stippled *Parastichopus californicus.* It also often refers to the latter species alone, which is the one that is usually eaten.

Inexperienced beachcombers sometimes confuse holothurians (sea-cucumbers) with nudibranchs (sea slugs). But holothurians are echinoderms: members of the same phylum as sea urchins and starfish. Nudibranchs are molluscs: members of the phylum that includes snails, mussels, limpets and squids. As echinoderms, holothurians are animals rather than plants, but several species (notably those in the genus *Cucumaria*) are reminiscent enough of vegetables to warrant being called cucumbers of the sea. *Parastichopus californicus* – sometimes called sea-sausages – are more mobile and more obviously animal.

Living holothurians, when handled, have the disconcerting habit of transforming themselves suddenly from soft to hard or limp to stiff and back again. If handled enough, they will also ejaculate, disgorging their own viscera in apparent self-defense. This behavior is efficiently explained in a story Arthur Lewis told in Tsimshian to Gwüsḵ'aayn in the 1930s. The first holothurian, Lewis says, was the cast-off penis of the Raven (Beynon n.d.: text 95).

Though noncommittal on several important points of taxonomy (and heavily laden with typographic errors), Philip Lambert's *Sea Cucumbers* (1997) is a useful guide to *ghiinuu* found on Haida reefs and beaches.

6 At this point, Swanton inserted a very interesting passage of 18 lines dictated by Gumsiiwa. See pp 290–291.

7 The mythcreature behind the invitation is called *dang tsin·gha quunigaay,* "your grandfather the big." The qualifier *quuna*, big, has a special meaning here, as "great" does in the English phrase "great-grandfather." *Quuna* is used alone to refer to a father-in-law, who is necessarily a senior male of the *same moiety*. In the Haida kinship system, a person's own father is necessarily of the opposite moiety; so is one's mate. The father-in-law – the mate's father – is therefore always of the same side. Among grandfathers, one's mother's father is always of the opposite side, and one's father's father always of the same side. *Tsin quuna* is a male of the same moiety and the grandfather's generation, or indeed of any generation older than that. It means "male ancestor, older than a father, of the same side." The relationship between a younger male and such an ancestor is, therefore, potentially one of reincarnation.

8 Haida *yaxhudada*. Pied-bill grebes are scarce in Haida Gwaii and rarely seen on the open ocean, but *yaxhudada* was specifically identified as the pied-bill grebe by Tlaajang Quuna, an expert birder (Newcombe n.d.4). The pied-bill is also the only small grebe with a large voice. Away from the breeding grounds, horned grebes and eared grebes are virtually silent. Recent surveys (Wayne Campbell et al. 1990–99, vol 1: 166–181) have failed to recorded a single breeding site for any species of grebe in Haida Gwaii. But Ghandl, in his poems, makes some very knowledgeable references to the breeding habits of grebes. I regard this as evidence that grebes have bred in the Islands in the past. The most likely species to have done so is the pied-bill, which still breeds at many coastal sites in southwestern British Columbia. It would be nice to know if Ghandl saw breeding grebes himself before he lost his sight, or if his images preserve the observations of earlier mythtellers, perhaps made long before his time.

9 At this point in the Haida typescript, Swanton inserted an extraneous passage concerning the painting of the birds, dictated by Skaay's friend Kilxhawgins of the Qqaadasghu Qiighawaay. It did not evidently take him long to change his mind, and in his own published translation, he relocated the passage. (His

English version can be found in Swanton 1905b: 128. The Haida text is in Swanton n.d.2: folio 24.)

10 Original on folios 26–27, Swanton n.d.2. Compare Enrico 1995: 22–29.

▸ NOTES TO CHAPTER TWELVE ▸

1 Swanton n.d.2: folios 24–25. The passage is clearly out of place here, and Swanton relocated it in his translation (Swanton 1905b: 128 & 149 n 55).

2 Original on folios 31–37, Swanton n.d.2. Compare Enrico 1995: 34–46 (versos), 37–53 (rectos).

3 *Nang ttlighwaas,* "the one who lies flat," is one of Skaay's kennings for the sea. At line 1105 (p 266) is another: *nang ghagins,* "the one that is usually smooth."

4 "Someone's grave" is all Skaay says – but no one other than a shaman would be buried this way, exposed to the elements in an isolated location.

5 *Gyaan lla at gu lla taydyaasi:* "then her/him with there he/she lay," or slept, or went to bed. The euphemism usual in Haida is the same as it is in English.

6 In the world of Haida mythology and in traditional Haida life, an affair between a man and his father's sister is not a cause for scandal; the lovers, after all, are from opposite moieties. But an affair between a son and his own mother strikes at the kinship system's heart.

7 See Swanton 1905b: 284.

8 Swanton 1905b: 138–146.

9 The door implied is a hanging door or winter doorflap, hinged at the top and weighted at the bottom.

10 The mythworld is a place where speech comes true. Big Surf has just described the Raven Child as *nang ghaaxha naaghahljuu,* "a shit-assed child," and the Raven reifies his words. Skaay himself, as usual, speaks more circumspectly than his characters. All he says here is *lla qaaxuhls,* "he went outside." This is the customary euphemism in classical Haida, where a speaker of modern English might say "he went to the bathroom." The resulting Haida sentence – because it is simultaneously circumspect and absurd – is also very funny: *Gyaanhaw ttsaanuwaay sttlghaawasi jin·gi awung hlkyaa gusta lla qqaw'uwaa-was gu xhan lla qaaxuhls:* "Then beside the fire by his mother toward the door where he was sitting he 'went outside'."

11 Enrico (1995: 45) sees the dog as metaphorical and thinks that a slave in human form is meant. Such a reading is plausible, though what appears to be a real talking dog appears in the poem shortly before this, in a striking scene at the close of the second movement. In continuous performance, these episodes would be about 20 minutes apart.

12 The word *kun* can also be applied to several smaller species that visit Haida waters more sporadically. These include the pilot whale, goose-beaked whale and Stejneger's beaked whale.

13 Swanton n.d.2: 407–408 and 1905b: 286–287. The explanation is quoted – in English only – in 1905b: 287 n 3, but Swanton does not tell us who is speaking.

14 Haida *qqayskkut*. Tlaajang Quuna used this name (Newcombe n.d.4) for both the bufflehead and the hooded merganser. The hooded merganser breeds in Haida Gwaii while the bufflehead probably does not, but hooded mergansers prefer fresh water. Neither, of course, subsists on whale, but either could be drawn by other food to the vicinity of the carcass.

15 All these features tend to vanish in translation.

16 In an interesting passage (Swanton n.d.2: 765), Skaay's friend Kilxhawgins speaks of male scoters as *ghuhlghahl*. See p 327 and p 483 n 19.

17 Swanton n.d.2: folio 160 (cf. Swanton 1905b: 181):

> *Gawgiila gujaanggha xhantlinggilaay ghiista giina isdaasi*
> *gyaan kuna lla qquudlaasi.*
> *Ghuhlghahlsi.*

> *Gawgiila's daughter took something* [giina] *from the cooking box,*
> *and she bit off the tip of it.*
> *It was blue* [ghuhlghahl].

18 Swanton 1908a: 588–589.

19 Swanton 1908a: 590.

20 *Chāndogya Upaniṣad* 6.8.7, 6.9.4, 6.10.3, 6.11.3, 6.12.3, 6.13.3, 6.14.3, 6.15.3, 6.16.3. For alternate translations and commentary, see, e.g., Sarvepalli Radhakrishnan, *The Principal Upaniṣads* (London: Allen & Unwin, 1953), and Paul Deussen, *Sechzig Upanishad's des Veda* (3rd ed., Leipzig: Brockhaus, 1921). There are related passages in other classical Indian texts, e.g., *Jaiminīya Brāhmaṇa* 3.14 and *Aitareya Āraṇyaka* 2.2.4.6.

21 Boas's summary is in Swanton 1905b: 139. An analogous story was recorded in Russian from an unnamed Tlingit speaker early in the 19th century by Ivan Veniaminov. Here the Ravenchild's first kill is "a large magpielike bird, Kuzgatúli, that is, bird of heaven, with a long tail and very long, pointed shiny beak. He pulled the skin off this bird and through this obtained the power of flight. Another time he killed a large duck and gave his mother the skin, which gave her the ability to swim in the sea." See Krause 1956: ch. 10 n 7.

22 Sinjuugwaang, "Sniffing the Wind," lives in the headwaters of the Tlell River, on the east coast of Graham Island.

23 Yaahl Kingaangghu, "Calling Raven," lives near Qquuna – in the headwaters of what is now called Skedans Creek. Here Skaay uses the word *yaahl* rather than *xhuuya*. In northern Haida, *yaahl* (from Tlingit *yéil*) is the usual word for raven. Speakers of southern Haida rarely use *yaahl* except in names.

24 Qqaasta is a salmon stream southeast of Hlghagilda, shown on recent charts as the Copper River. There was formerly a village at the mouth of the creek. Skidegate people still use the area as a fishing camp at spawning time.

25 Qqaadasghu is a creek and an old village site north of Qquuna and south of Hlghagilda. It is also the site of a late-19th-century cemetery. After the small-pox epidemics emptied Ttanuu, Skaay and other survivors moved briefly to Qqaadasghu, where the deaths continued. The survivors of Qqaadasghu then moved on to Skidegate Mission.

    All four of the creeks alluded to in this passage are south of Ghahlins Kun, or Highflat Point, the home of Big Surf (Sghulghu Quuna), in whose house the feast is being held. The creeks are more or less centered on Skidegate Inlet. They are also the main salmon streams found *in between* the homes of these two spirit-beings, Sghulghu Quuna and Qinggi. The distance between these major landmarks is roughly 60 sea miles direct or 100 miles by canoe.

26 Boas n.d.2, published in Swanton 1905b: 140–141.

27 Swanton 1908a: 305.

28 Alfred Kroeber (1962: 81–82) argues that philosophy *per se* does not exist in any Native American culture. But Kroeber defines philosophy in a form that is absolutely dependant on writing. He wins his case by prearrangement, through the definition of terms, and therefore need not bother to look at the evidence.

29 Daxhiigang's story is summarized rather crudely in Boas n.d.2, published in Swanton 1905b: 320. George Dawson heard such a story at least twice in Haida Gwaii in the summer of 1878, but he too was content with a mere summary (Dawson 1993: 142, 203 n 4). These can be compared with the version that Kingagwaaw told to Swanton at Masset in the spring of 1901 (Swanton 1908a: 324). It can be measured in turn against a much more complex version written in English in 1980 by the Haida sculptor Bill Reid. Reid's version is widely pub-lished (e.g., in Reid & Bringhurst 1996: 31–37). Sculptural representations of the story, by Daxhiigang and by Reid, are also widely reproduced. See for in-stance Bringhurst & Steltzer 1992: 32–34, 40–41.

    It is crucial to Reid's version that the first human beings are all males. They are found in the shell of a phalliform mollusk (clam or cockle) and must be mated with a vulviform mollusk (chiton) to produce human beings of both sexes. In short, human beings are a byproduct of the Raven's invention of mammalian sex. This theme is missing from Daxhiigang's version as Boas recorded it, but Daxhiigang may have understood the story – and may have been trying to tell it to Boas – in these terms.

473

1 The original text is on folios 37–39 of Swanton n.d.2. Compare Enrico 1995: 46–50 (versos), 53–59 (rectos).

2 Marten and black bear live in Haida Gwaii; grizzly and mountain goat do not. There is, moreover, a proverbial relation between the former two: *Kkuuxu haw taan ghan kwaayang, wansuuga*: Marten is black bear's elder brother, they say.

3 *Nang ghagins,* "the one that is usually smooth," is a kenning for the sea, or for protected water. Skaay uses another such phrase – *nang ttlighwaas,* "the one who lies flat," – at line 667 (p 239).

4 This is the first time in the fourth movement that the Raven is actually named, and the only time in the poem that anyone calls him Voicehandler (Nang Kilstlas) instead of Voicehandler's Heir (Nang Kilstlas Hlingaay).

5 This is not where the head of the house would normally sit. Qinggi has ceded his spot in the rear of the house and come out to join the audience of villagers.

6 The common cormorant of Haida Gwaii is the pelagic cormorant, *Phalacrocorax pelagicus,* called *kkyaluu* in Haida. The cormorant mentioned here is *sghiitghun,* "red gullet." This is the double-crested cormorant, *P. auritus,* which visits the Islands in the fall.

7 A very interesting passage. Raven rattles are used by all the indigenous peoples of the northern Northwest Coast and are known by cognate names in all the northern coastal languages: *sheishóoxw* in Tlingit, *haseex* in Nishga, *sasoo* in Tsimshian, *siisaa* in Haida. They are carved in two parts: belly and back. The Raven's head, wings and tail are part of the back. So is the humanoid passenger which the rattle usually carries. The belly (Haida *qan,* meaning breast or ribcage) does not look like it could fly, and seldom has any discernibly avian elements. It is shaped like half an egg or a short canoe, and is usually engraved with the face of the Raven's marine allotrope, Ttsam'aws, the Snag. Dance etiquette and conventional wisdom on the Northwest Coast require that Raven rattles should be carried belly up most of the time, because they cannot fly away when held in that position.

8 This is the same pair, Taadlat Ghadala and Kkuxu Ginagits, or Swallow and Marten, mentioned by Sghiidagits. See p 130 and p 451 n 25.

9 Boas 1916: 565–723.

10 There are exceptions to this statement – but all are written constructs, based on Swanton's published translation of Skaay. The first such version seems to be the one compiled by William E. Myers for Edward Curtis's *The North American Indian* (vol. 11: pp 148–155; Seattle: Curtis, 1916). Myers did spend time on the Northwest Coast with Curtis in 1910–14, and he may well have heard several

stories from Henry Moody and others. There is no doubt, however, that his primary sources were printed texts – chiefly those issued by the BAE.

11 The verb in this sentence is negative but tenseless – devoid of any reference to time – and the pronoun, *dalang*, is plural.

12 Two decades later, Elsie Clew Parsons commissioned a story from almost every American anthropologist she knew, including Swanton. The anthology she produced affords considerable insight into the practice of anthropology, and the nature of the anthropologists, then at work in North America. Swanton's contribution, "Tokulki of Tulsa" (Swanton 1922), is both sensitive and substantial, but it is set in the Southeast, to which he was then devoting most of his attention. The story of his year in Haida Gwaii is one he did not write and may never really have told.

13 Swanton understood, perhaps correctly, that the Raven had ten companions in this scene, and Swanton expected all ten of them to speak. He then counted only seven insulting speeches (though there appear to me to be eight). Skaay evidently showed no interest in filling in the gaps, and Swanton came to the conclusion that "what the other three said has been forgotten" (Swanton 1905b: 125). Here it seems as if the earnest anthropologist has once again been had. Decimal and pentameral structures are basic to Haida narrative, but it is pointless to expect them to repeat with mechanical precision, just as it is pointless to expect ten syllables in every iambic pentameter, three leaves on every stalk of clover, or five fully visible fingers on every painted hand. Where a complex chain of images is central to a Haida poem – as in Ghandl's story of the Birdhunter – the arithmetic is rarely imperfect. But where ten undifferentiated objects, characters or incidents occur, as they do here, a smaller number of examples is sufficient to suggest the set.

14 Kilham 1989: 16, 31, 34, 85–86 details related behavior in crows.

15 Ravens, unlike geese, loons and many other birds, do not in fact have penises – a fact recorded and accounted for in several ways in Northwest Coast mythologies. This is probably an instance. Two less subtle explanations – both dictated to Gwüsḵ'aayn by the Tsimshian poet Arthur Lewis – are summarized on pp 144–145 and pp 469–470.

16 Swanton 1905b: 140, where the translation and orthography are Boas's: "In the village T'ano there was a chief whose name was Qîng·."

17 "The Genius of Poetry must work out its own salvation in a man: It cannot be matured by law & precept, but by sensation & watchfulness in itself — That which is creative must create itself." The passage occurs in Keats's letter to his publisher James Hessey, written 8 October 1818. See *The Letters of John Keats*, edited by Hyder Edward Rollins, 2 vols (Cambridge University Press, 1958): vol. 1: 373–374.

1 The name *xhuuya tluugha* is now used for two leguminous plants: *Lathyrus japonicus* (beach pea) and *Vicea gigantea* (giant vetch). Whether Skaay would have agreed with both these identifications or only with one is now impossible to say. The two species grow side by side in many spots along the coast. Ripe beach pea pods are often 7 or 8 cm long; vetch pods are half that length.

2 Swanton n.d.2: folios 39–42. Cf. Enrico 1995: 50–56 (versos), 59–67 (rectos).

3 *Aegolius acadicus,* the northern saw-whet owl, called *sttaw* in Haida, is the only owl that breeds in Haida Gwaii. The island birds are darker overall than their cousins on the mainland and have been classed as a distinct subspecies, *A. a. brooksi.* As owls go, they are tiny: about the size of robins. The beak is black but hardly adequate in size to replace the beak of a raven.

4 The inner bark (phloem) of the western hemlock, *Tsuga heterophylla,* is an important coastal foodstuff, like the inner bark of the pine. It is eaten fresh in springtime. In earlier days, it was also gathered in bulk during the summer, then pit-cooked, pounded and pressed into cakes or loaves. These were dried, stored and served in midwinter, with berries or fish oil, as feast food.

5 *Ghal* are blue mussels, *Mytilus edulis.* Though a delicacy elsewhere, they are basic winter food on the Northwest Coast, available at each low tide to rich and poor alike. Another reason for regarding them as workaday food and not a feast dish is that no skill is needed to prepare them. They are set beside the fire to roast; when they open, they are ready. The pussytail or pubic hair is the byssus or holdfast of the mussel, familiar to all who have cooked and eaten them.

6 Bracket fungi are as rare in Haida literature as they are in the literatures of Europe, but the Raven's choice of bracket fungus here is not fortuitous. The principal recorded use of bracket fungi by peoples of the Northwest Coast is as a medium for carving shamans' effigies and grave markers. They are known also for their insulation value and are traditionally used as protective pads for handling live coals.

The use of bracket fungus for shamanic effigies is discussed in Blanchette et al 1992 (a very important contribution to the study of Haida and Tlingit art, despite its publication in a mycological journal). For other uses, see Compton 1992: 49, 136–139, 309. The principal species involved is *Fomitopsis officinalis.*

The Haida term used here for bracket fungus is *gyaalgas naan·gha,* "sea biscuit's grandmother." This sounds, of course, like a post-contact term. If that is what it is, it would appear to be the only phrase in Skaay's entire *Raven Travelling* that does not reach back to the older tradition. But *gyaalgas* itself does not appear to be a word of recent coinage. I have a hunch that *gyaalgas naan·gha* is a precolonial idiom, and that nothing is really new here except the use of *gyaalgas* to mean sea biscuit or pilot bread.

7 I have not unravelled this name to my own satisfaction. It may be related to Nishga *siwaax* and Kwakwala *siwayu*, both meaning paddle.

8 Skaay does not say what Siiwas planted. Native tobacco is the likeliest possibility; potatoes would be next. The Haida learned about potatoes at an early date, possibly from the Tlingit, who acquired their potatoes from the Russians. Potato cultivation may already have been a part of southern Haida life when Skaay was born. It was certainly so when he was a boy.

9 This is the point at which an unnamed woman of the Stastas family supplemented Skaay's text with a sentence of her own (Swanton 1905b: 149 n 53). Swanton had some trouble understanding what she said, but it was something like what follows (cf. Swanton n.d.2: folio 42; Enrico 1995: 56):

> *Gyaanhaw ll tluu qaattlxhagaay dluu*
> *han ll suuwus,*
> *«Dii ghayat jaanggaay at dii ghayut kku'anggaay*
> *ghaatgha dii qalaa sttiiganggang.»*

This appears to mean,

> *When his canoe came into their midst*
> *he said these words:*
> *«Between my side boards and my end boards,*
> *I am altogether empty.»*

The addition fits well with the picture Skaay has painted: the Raven, dressed like a beggar but speaking in princely code, is appealing for food to hold his potlatch. But there are still some problems here that only Porpoise Woman can solve. Swanton heard the last phrase as †*dii qalaastiis*†. This sounds like nonsense, and all Swanton could find out about the verb, even in 1900, was "that Raven used it because he was hungry." Later inquiries have not absolutely resolved the problem (Swanton 1905b: 127, 149 n 53; Enrico 1995: 193 n 99).

10 The English word *potlatch* comes directly from Chinook Jargon, where it is used in two senses: (a) as noun and verb with the same meanings as in English, and (b) as a common noun and verb meaning "gift" and "to give." The root is evidently Nootka *ppaatlppiichi'atl*. This is the repetitive inceptive form of the verb *ppa*, meaning "to transfer property in the context of a public feast," thus in effect "to buy status." By the early 20th century, however, the simplified term *potlatch* had been borrowed back from the Jargon into Nootka, where it survives as the noun *pahlaach*. The original sense of *ppa* is probably "to touch" or "to reach out with the hand" – meanings that survive in Kwakwala and other northern Wakashan languages. (See Sapir & Swadesh 1939: 134, 160, 241, 261.)

11 Ghandl's Haida text is in Swanton n.d.2: folios 630–639, and Swanton's rather free translation in Swanton 1905a: 162–170. Compare Murdock 1936, especially pp 5–8. The best study of the northern potlatch is Kan 1989, but this work deals

specifically with the Tlingit memorial potlatch, _ku.éex'_. The corresponding event in the Haida world is known as _sikka_ rather than _waahlghal_. Kinga-gwaaw's description of _sikka_ potlatch procedure is in Swanton 1908a: 795–800, translated in Swanton 1905b: 176–180.

12 Original in the Dept. of Anthropology Archives, AMNH, New York. I have altered Swanton's spelling from _wāl'g.al_ to _waahlghal_.

13 Published descriptions of Haida potlatch practice differ widely from one another and err as a rule in assuming that one procedure was always and everywhere in effect. According to John Enrico, for example (Enrico & Stuart 1996: 5, 9, following George Murdock), tattoos must be applied at a housebuilding potlatch, and only to those of the hostess's moiety, while piercing must be done at the mortuary potlatch, and only to those of the moiety of the host. This is a fine and logical arrangement, but it does not agree with the detailed testimony of Ghandl and Henry Moody. The parody potlatch in Skaay's poem must in any case violate the rules to be worthy of the Raven. The violation begins with the fact that, as brother and sister, host and hostess are both of the same side.

14 Swanton n.d.2: folio 31. The reading differs from Enrico's (Enrico 1995: 34) but adopts a number of his corrections.

15 The original text is on the first leaf of Swanton n.d.3, where Swanton inserted it between lines 10 and 11 of Skaay's text. Compare Enrico 1995: 14–15.

> ▸ NOTES TO CHAPTER FIFTEEN ▸

1 The full Haida text (thicker than usual with typographic errors) is published with Swanton's translation in Swanton 1905b: 87–93.

2 On the southwest side of Qquuna Gwaay, which is shown on current charts as Louise Island.

3 A salmon stream and fish camp in the Qquuna region.

4 Waanaghan is a hereditary name normally used by the nephew and heir of the headman of the Qaagyals Qiighawaay of the Raven side, who was also, in the 19th century, usually head of the village of Qquuna. Thus, in terms of Haida social protocol, Waanaghan is the name of a suitable father for the heir to the headship of Skaay's family, the Qquuna Qiighawaay of the Eagle side.

5 It is easy to believe these two lines (22 & 23) are out of place, but I have left them where they stand. Since the place name Kkyal means Lower Leg, it is tempting even to think that they refer to Skilttakingang instead of Ttaagyaaw and belong in the following section of the poem, but it already has a place name of its own.

6 The name of a bay just south of Qquuna and of the salmon stream that feeds it.

7 In the published text (1905b: 87), this clause is missing its verb, but the intended meaning is clear. Cf. Swanton n.d.2: 678, where the speaker is Sghaagya. (Enrico 1985 discusses the grammar and concepts involved.)

8 Gwaaya and Gwiighal are small islands south and east of Qquuna. They appear on modern charts as the Low Islands (Low and South Low).

9 A bat may seem a curious creature to meet in an offshore storm accepting offerings on behalf of a killer whale – but bats routinely feed by skimming over water, and some populations live in close association with the sea. At least four species live in Haida Gwaii. The biggest of these is the silver-haired bat (*Lasionycteris noctivagans*), which is known for its long marine migrations. Another, Keen's bat (*Myotis keenii*), is endemic to the British Columbia coast. On Ghandl Kkiin Gwaayaay (Hotspring Island), near Ttanuu, Keen's bats and little brown bats (*Myotis lucifugus*) roost together in a naturally heated intertidal cave. Skaay's word for bat, by the way, is *quutgudugamhlghal*, possibly related to the Tsimshian word for bat, *ts'ogat'axtxaył*.

10 They went north and south, in other words, and they went looking far and wide. Lake Inlet (Suu Qaahli) is the head of a large bay some 50 miles south of Qquuna. (On modern charts, it is the head of Skincuttle Inlet.) Rock Point (Ttiis Kun) is a name that fits thousands of locations in Haida Gwaii and is locally applied to many. The one intended here is probably the one now charted as Gray Point, about ten miles north of Qquuna. These two locations could be said to mark the northern and southern limits of the territory claimed or overseen by the Qquuna Qiighawaay.

11 These are Cassin's auklets (*Ptychoramphus aleuticus*), *hajaa* in Haida. They spend the autumn and winter at sea, coming ashore in spring to nest in shallow burrows in the slopes above the tideline. There the eggs, the young and even the adults are easy prey for humans, gulls and other predators.

12 This is the name of the point at the east end of Gwaaya – and, of course, the hereditary name of this landform's resident killer whale.

13 Leaf barnacles (*Pollicipes polymerus*, Haida *ttlkkyaaw*) and acorn barnacles (*Balanus nubilis*, Haida *ghaawdawal*) are both important foodstuffs on the Northwest Coast, accessible at each low tide. Leaf barnacles are the smaller of the two but have much lighter armor and are easier to get.

  The name of the leaf barnacle, *ttlkkyaaw*, is made of two components which mean "thin-&-flat" and "sharp." It rhymes semantically and acoustically with *Tlghakkyaaw*, "Sharp Ground," which is the name of the barnacle harvester. This makes the story sound like literature, not history, but it may still be both. It is quite possible that Tlghakkyaaw was given this name only after his death.

14 This is standard Haida practice: the families of those who happen to be present at an accidental death pay the family of the deceased. There are of course no

moose in Haida Gwaii, and their skins could only be obtained by trading with people on the mainland.

15 Double mortuary posts were frequent in the northern Haida villages but much rarer in the south. Triple and quadruple mortuary posts were rarer still. George MacDonald records only one triple mortuary post (at Yaakkw on the northern coast) and one quadruple post (the Iidansaa mortuary, built for Gwaayang Gwanhlin's uncle, which is still in place at Kkyuusta). But there were more. George Dorsey, for example, saw a quadruple mortuary post at Qang in 1897 (Dorsey 1898: 11), which is missing from MacDonald's survey, and there is no reason to doubt Skaay's claim that a mortuary with four pillars was built for Tlghakkyaaw. Nor is there any doubt about the meaning of his words: *Ll xhaada llagha ttl hlgiistansingdaayaghan*: "His grave-post for-him they made-pillarlike-fourfold." But if this death-post really had a tree growing out of it in 1900, one might expect to find it in the early photographs – and no such structure has yet been identified.

The Iidansaa quadruple mortuary – the only current reference we have – is illustrated and mapped in MacDonald 1983: [110j], 186, 191.

16 The seaweed is *Porphyra perforata*: red laver in English, *sghyuu* in Haida.

17 Turn-of-the-Tide (Dalqqaay Hlgahlging) is one of the group of islets just outside Qquuna harbor.

18 This is the only occasion on which Skaay uses this particular closing formula, *Haw ll kunju*, "Here it [animate] forms-a-corner" or "makes-a-point." *Kun*, meaning "corner" or "point," is perfectly homophonous with *kun*, meaning "humpback whale." It is tempting to see in the classical closing formulae a suggestion that the *qqaygaang* are literary *sghaana*, while *qqayaagaang* and *gyaahlghalang* are literary *kun*. I cannot back this supposition up.

19 Swanton 1905b: 93 n 35. Incidentally, this appears to guarantee that the Gitkuna of the poem is not the Gitkuna who died in 1877 but rather some earlier bearer of the name.

20 Another name for Klemtu (Lhṁdu) is Kitasu (from Tsimshian *Kit'asgüüx*). Kilxhawgins called it by the Haida name *Gitiisda*. Swanton locates it in "Seaforth Channel, an extension of Milbank Sound [sic]" (1905b: 447). This is not quite accurate. Seaforth Channel is the easterly route out of Milbanke Sound, leading to the Heiltsuk villages of Koqui (Q'vúqvaí), Kokyet (Q'ábá) and Waglisla (Bella Bella), not to Klemtu. Finlayson Channel, the northern exit from the Sound, does lead to Klemtu. Kilxhawgins's description fits it well.

Sghaagya of the Yaakw Gitinaay, who had more combat experience than any other Haida Swanton met, recounted another raid on the same place, with a similar outcome (Swanton n.d.2: folios 664–665; 1905b: 371–372). I have not read or heard any account of these attacks that is told from the defenders' point of view, but there are plenty of other accounts by mainlanders of raids by – and raids against – the Haida. Boas 1928: 136–147, for example, includes several such accounts in Heiltsuk, evidently dictated by Willie Gladstone.

21 The full Haida text appears in Swanton n.d.2: folios 809–813. There is a full English translation in Swanton 1905b: 444–448.

22 That is, on *siigaay*, Hecate Strait, between Haida Gwaii and the mainland.

23 This appears to be the Haida form of the Tsimshian *Kitgya'ts*, "[Country of the] People to the South," which is the Southern Tsimshian coast.

24 The taking of heads and scalps is rarely mentioned in the myths, but both Kilxhawgins and Sghaagya refer to it often (Swanton 1905b: 373, 377, 386, 393, 412, 415, 416, 418, 419, 420, 423, 434, 435, 438, 439). In most of these passages, Kilxhawgins seems to speak as an historian. Here he speaks from his personal experience. Sghaagya is almost always recounting exploits of his own.

25 Gyaagujang was head of the Qqaadasghu Qiighawaay, Kilxhawgins's lineage.

26 The war canoe belonging to Gitkuna, headman of the Qquuna Qiighawaay and headman of Ttanuu.

27 Swanton 1905b: 448 n 20.

28 John Work gave the population of Qquuna as 439 around 1840, and the population of Ttanuu as 545 (Dawson 1993: 165). The later figures for Ttanuu and Qqaadasghu come from Duff n.d.: file 111.

▸ NOTES TO CHAPTER SIXTEEN ▸

1 According to Swanton, Kilxhawgins and Xhyuu were the only Haida initiates of the Ulalala society still alive in 1900 (Swanton to Boas, 30 Sept 1900, AMNH; Swanton 1905a: 156–157).

2 Charles Newcombe recorded the Haida names of Kilxhawgins and his wife (Newcombe n.d.1: v 35 f 1). The baptismal record is in Crosby et al. n.d.

3 Swanton n.d.2: 367–368, 391, 407–408, 411–412, 415–416, 470–471, 474–476, 480–483, 597–598, 627–629, 729–730, 733–736, 741–745, 751–752, 755–757, 760–766, 774–776, 780–783, 809–813, and 1905b: 33–35. Swanton's translations of these texts are in 1905b: 32–34, 269–270, 281, 286–291, 305–315, 354–355, 401–448 and 1905a: 157–158. (In the latter case, Kilxhawgins is the unnamed "old man just referred to," identified in n.d.2: 627.)

4 Swanton n.d.2, folio 760. For another translation, see Swanton 1905b: 418.

5 The word used here is *kunaan*, which nowadays usually means the medicinal roots of *Urtica dioica*, stinging nettle. But the procedure described – steaming, then peeling, coupled with expressions of delight – suggests that the women are actually preparing the sweet roots of *Lupinus littoralis*, the beach lupine.

Lupine roots are known now in Haida by the nickname *taaghan skkyaaw,* "black bear's tail," but it looks to me as though Kilxhawgins called them *kunaan.* For better or for worse, I have followed this hunch in the translation.

6 Guuhlgha was a village site just south of Hlghagilda. It is also where Swanton lived during the fall of 1900. On modern charts, it is Skidegate Landing.

7 Daghas means "Owner." The name was used by the headman of one of the Inlet families, the Hlghaayu Llaanas, who owned the town of Gawjaaws (Drum), on Lina Island, in Skidegate Inlet.

8 The full text is in Swanton n.d.2: 760–766. For another translation, see Swanton 1905b: 418–424.

9 A ranking member of the Qquuna Qiighawaay.

10 The woman belonged, in other words, to a family from the Ttanuu and Hlqiinul area, and was married to a man from the region of Sghan Gwaay, at the southern tip of the archipelago.

11 Ttaahldi is a salmon stream and inlet at the head of what is now called Klunkwoi Bay, traditionally owned by the headman of Ttanuu. The area was ravaged by miners during the early 20th century and was for a time the site of a cannery. It has been healing since the 1940s.

   One of Kilxhawgins's stories about shamans opens with the following words (Swanton n.d.2: 474; cf. 1905b: 308):

> *Hlinagit sghaay haw lla ghii saawaghan.*
> *Ll sghaaga qawdihaw*
> *ghaatxhan Ttaahldi gha ttl skansulandyaay dluu*
> *tsiina suugha qqulaay giitgha lla ghii saawaghan.*
> *Gaydluuhaw gamhaw aasi gwaayaay gut tsiinaggangghangang wansuugang.*
> *Gaydluu tajaw sqaagistlguns gangaang tsinaay isttlxhaayang wansuugang.*

> *A Tlingit spirit-being spoke through him.*
> *After he had acted as a shaman for a time,*
> *when they were all camped at Ttaahldi,*
> *the son of the leader of the salmon spoke through him.*
> *They say there were no salmon in these islands then.*
> *And then, they say, the salmon blew in like a gale.*

12 At the time of these events, Ginaaskilas of the Qquuna Qiighawaay was headman of Ttanuu. A later bearer of this name (active circa 1870) was also a noted carver and one of the best of the early Haida silversmiths.

13 Redcedar dugouts are normally rough-hewn outside and inside, then finished to shape on the outside and adzed from the inside to uniform thickness. Then they are steamed. One false move with the adze in the intermediate stage leaves a thin spot in the hull. A few false strokes in a row, and the hull is lost.

Cracks (which soon develop even in the best boats) are easily repaired with twisted cedar limbs for caulking. But outright punctures – especially in a raw hull, not yet steamed – are cause for despair.

14 Alder and The Grandson (Qals and Ttakkinaay) were two of the roughly two dozen house chiefs of the village of Ttanuu in the second half of the 19th century. Both belonged to the Jigwahl Llaanas of the Eagle side and both were, in the loose sense, uncles of Ginaaskilas, the headman of the town. Both, that is, belonged to the same moiety as he, though not to the same lineage. Ginaaskilas and Alder in particular are favorite characters in Kilxhawgins's history. They appear again in Swanton n.d.2: 741–745 & 774–776, translated in Swanton 1905b: 408–412, 425–427.

15 Seal Beach in Haida is Xhuut Tsiixwas, "Harbor-Seal Ebb-Tide." It was one of several villages that ringed Tlgakun Gwaay ("Earthpoint Island," now called Lyell Island). At the time of this narrative, it seems that all the Tlgakun Gwaay villages, including the main village of Hlkkyaa, had already been abandoned.

16 West Coast Cloud (Dawyanaay of the Jigwahl Llaanas of the Eagle side) was Alder's sister. Out of courtesy, Kilxhawgins does not name the other woman – whose lineage is his own.

17 Ganxhwat was headman of Hlghagilda – thus the bearer of the title Sghiidagits – in the early years of the 19th century. MacDonald (1983: 40) has estimated that he died around 1832. When Swanton was at Skidegate in 1900, Ghanxhwat's mortuary house had already been disturbed and his bones buried on instructions from the missionary, but "the remnants of his grave box and the Chilkat blanket that was wound around his body were still to be seen" (Swanton 1905b: 417 n 3).

18 This is the Flower Pot Island of current charts.

19 Three species of scoter breed in North America. All can be found in Haida Gwaii. The males of these species (*Melanitta nigra, M. perspicillata* and *M. fusca*) have the most decorative bills of any North American ducks. Kilxhawgins calls them *ghuhlghahl sghil*: blue (or blueblack) scoters, a description that would fit the males of all three species.

20 The word used here for muskrat is *nikkigha,* from Tsimshian *nak'eeda.* Muskrats were not found in Haida Gwaii until humans introduced them, probably late in the 19th century, but the fur trade had made them into a form of local currency before that. It is in trade with the Tsimshian and the Nishga that Kilxhawgins (or his predecessors) would have established the rate of exchange between scoter bills and muskrat skins.

21 The Hlghagilda people have chased their attackers straight across Skidegate Inlet. Kun·ghaay, "The Point," is the Onward Point of modern charts (known locally as Welcome Point), on the south shore of the mouth of the inlet.

22 The taking of heads, like the classification of languages and the definition of poetry, has provoked large quantities of nonsense mildly disguised as scientific prose. Kilxhawgins and Sghaagya give us some of the most lucid, unpretentious information on the subject to be found in any language. But the taking of heads on the Northwest Coast of North America has not been studied with the care that has been lavished on the same deep-seated cultural phenomenon in Asia and Oceania. (The more readable studies include McKinley 1976, Rosaldo 1980, Hoskins 1989 & 1996.) Nor have headtaking practices around the Pacific Rim as yet been studied, as they evidently should, in comparison with each other. It seems clear that the practice was less overtly ritualized in Haida Gwaii than in Sumba, Sulawesi or Luzon. It is also clear that a detailed etiquette and logic was nonetheless at work, and that this logic might be fruitfully explored.

23 Gwiisukuunas, like Alder, was one of Ginaaskilas's uncles. The housepole of a later bearer of this name is visible in the photos on pp 108–109.

24 Swanton n.d.2: 710. For the context, see Swanton 1905b: 392.

> ▶ NOTES TO CHAPTER SEVENTEEN ◀

1 Kroeber 1951: 72. The following quotations are from the same source.

2 Kroeber 1951: 71.

3 Kroeber 1948: 37. The phenomenon of dream songs and dream poems is not, of course, limited to the Mojave – nor is it limited to the human species. See Marcia Barinaga, "Birds May Refine Their Songs While Sleeping," New York: *Science* 282 (18 Dec 1998): 2163–2165, and the further references therein.

4 Kroeber thought anthropology a wonderful adventure, but even the wisest Native Americans he met seemed to him "unspeakably ignorant" and their cultural traditions "puny." (These assessments are quoted in Heizer & Kroeber 1979: 123, and there are many such remarks in Kroeber's writings.)

5 Wissler & Duvall 1909: 5.

> ▶ NOTES TO CHAPTER EIGHTEEN ◀

1 At least two of these family heads were master politicians. One was Wiiha, the headman of Ghaw, who was baptized as Chief Stephen in 1882. Another was Daxhiigang's uncle Gwaayang Gwanhlin, baptized as Albert Edward Edenshaw in 1883 after moving his people to Ghaw from Kkyuusta. There is no doubt that Gwaayang Gwanhlin chose his Christian names with care. However little he knew of British history, he was aware of current events and knew that Albert Edward was the name of the ranking British male – the widowed Queen Victoria's eldest son and heir apparent to the British throne.

2 Fort Victoria was founded in 1843 as the Hudson's Bay Co. regional headquar-

ters. In 1849 it was named the capital of the British colony of Vancouver Island, and in 1868, capital of the colony of British Columbia.

3 Swanton 1905a: 16.

4 There are persistent scholarly rumors of a third Haida dialect, spoken in the Ghangxhiit region – that is, at Sqaay, Sghan Gwaay and other towns around the southern tip of Haida Gwaii. But there are no surviving speakers and no texts in this dialect. Swanton transcribed one substantial story from the sculptor Xhaaydakuns (Tom Price) of the Saahgi Qiighawaay (Swanton n.d.2: 202–205; cf. Swanton 1905b: 203–206 and Enrico 1995: 146–158). Xhaaydakuns was one of few survivors from Sghan Gwaay still alive in 1900 and was the headman of the empty village. He ought to have been a speaker of the Ghangxhiit dialect if anyone was, but his Haida, in transcription, seems dialectally no different from that of other people at Skidegate.

Ghandl mentions *Ghangxhiit Xhaaydaghaay kihlgha*, "the speech of the Ghangxhiit people," and I think he would have mimicked this speech at the same time (Swanton n.d.2: 53; cf. Swanton 1905b: 138). But again there is no sign of *dialectal* distinction. It seems most likely that the Ghangxhiit people had a perceptibly southern *accent*, not in the linguistic sense a dialect of their own.

5 Swanton 1908a: 273.

6 The Haida text and Swanton's translation are in Swanton 1905b: 36–43.

7 Big Inlet, otherwise known as Masset Inlet, is the largest sea loch in Haida Gwaii, some 40 miles long and up to eight miles broad.

8 The text says *Skyamskun Xhiila*, "Pierced by a Blue Falcon." Swanton did not, it seems, ask Ghandl if he might have meant to say *Dattsi Xhiila*, Pierced by a Wren. A few lines later we will meet another spirit named *Skyamskun Ttawjugins*, "Floating Falcon Feather."

9 Again, Ghandl says *Skyamskun Xhiila*, "Pierced by a Blue Falcon," and I have emended his text to read *Dattsi Xhiila*, "Pierced by a Wren."

10 There is nothing in the text to indicate who is the subject in this stanza (lines 186–190). Swanton understood a change of subject, from Tl·laajaat (Fairweather Woman) to Stan Gwaay (the resident spirit of Charcoal Island). I presume his reading is based on clarification from Ghandl, so I follow Swanton's lead.

11 The Haida text and Swanton's translation are in Swanton 1908a: 370–376.

12 The Tallgrass River is Qqanan Ghandlaay, near the old village of Ttii, which is mentioned later in the poem. These are sites 90 & 91 on the map, pp 24–25.

13 The Haida word is *sghaana* (or in Haayas's dialect, *s'aan*), which is the same word normally applied to killer whales. Herakleitos of Ephesos explains the sense in which *theos* or *theoi* in Greek and *god* or *gods* in English are appropri-

ate translations in this context. Fragment 62 (DK 22B62): Ἀθάνατοι θνητοί, θνητοὶ ἀθάνατοι, ζῶντες τὸν ἐκείνων θάνατον, τὸν Δε ἐκείνων βίον τεθνεῶτες: "The deathless are mortal, mortals are deathless, each living the death of the other, each dying the life of the other."

14 This is normal. Haida dugouts are beached stern first, ready for departure.

15 *Jaatahl Qqaygaanga,* Story Woman or Myth Woman, is the name that Daxhiigang gave his youngest daughter, born in 1896. Her uncle Kihlguulins gave her her English name, Florence. Her biography (Blackman 1982) alludes to some of the pain and consternation that a prized name such as Myth Woman could cause for someone who lived in a missionized culture.

   Swanton, incidentally, is mistaken in remarking (1908a: 375 n 1) that Haayas omits this name from his list the first time through. The name is there in the manuscript (Swanton n.d.4: 129) and also in the printed Haida text. It is missing only from Swanton's translation.

16 The text reads †*Nang sghwan han nang sghwan*† *Jaat Ghulaang Quunwas hin kyaasang.* A phrase has been mistakenly repeated or a phrase has been left out. I have assumed the former.

17 The Haida text here is corrupt, and in Swanton's translation there are phrases with no Haida counterpart (Swanton n.d.4: 129; cf. 1908a: 375). I think that Swanton dropped a line of Haida when he copied the text from his notebook but kept the corresponding line when typing his translation. The sense of the passage does not seem to be in doubt.

▸ NOTES TO CHAPTER NINETEEN ▸

1 Enrico & Stuart 1996 at last joins the study of music and text and discusses the differences between the language of song and that of ordinary speech.

2 Swanton recorded the name of only one individual singer – a man, who sang him two songs – and of only one composer – again a man, to whom one song is credited. The singer's name is Skilqwiitlas; the composer's is Qajiquukw. Both belonged to the Sttlinga Llaanas, a northern lineage of the Raven side. Whether Skilqwiitlas composed the songs he sang for Swanton is not clear. (See Swanton 1912: 58–59, songs 94, 95 & 97.)

3 Swanton 1912: 51.

4 Swanton 1912: 59.

5 Swanton 1912: 62.

6 Kroeber 1962: 81–86 lays out the jaundiced case for the absence of both philosophy and poetry in aboriginal American cultures.

7 Letter to Frank Speck, 2 October 1914. Speck collection, APSL, Philadelphia.

8 Sidney 1595: folios c3r, f3v.

9 This preface has been included, I believe, in all editions of Eliot's translation of *Anabase*. It is also reprinted in Saint-John Perse 1971: 675–678.

10 Calvert Watkins's *How to Kill a Dragon* (1995) is, among other things, a study of the associations of verse and poetry in Indo-European culture.

11 Evidence to this effect – from North and South America, North Asia and Oceania – has been abundantly available for a century or more, but it has not impeded Eurocentric scholarship. G.S. Kirk, for instance, tells us that "musical accompaniment is an almost essential and invariable part of oral poetry" and that "the vast majority of oral traditions, and all rich and prolific ones, have depended on musical accompaniment" (*The Songs of Homer* [Cambridge University Press, 1962]: 313). That statement is inaccurate even for Europe, Asia and Africa. For Oceania and the Americas, it is without the slightest foundation.

12 Northrop Frye, "Verse and Prose," in *Princeton Encyclopedia of Poetry and Poetics,* edited by Alex Preminger (Princeton University Press, 1965): 885–890. The view is restated in Frye 1988: 111–114. But Frye was scarcely dead before this article acknowledging a third kind of literary language was bumped from the standard work of reference for which it was written and replaced by an entry skillfully reasserting the old binary division. (The replacement article is T.V.F. Brogan, "Verse and Prose," in *The New Princeton Encyclopedia of Poetry and Poetics,* edited by Preminger & Brogan [Princeton, 1993]: 1346–1351.)

Albert Lord's article "Oral Poetry," in both the 1965 and 1993 editions of the same encyclopedia, rests on the same conflation of verse and poetry. Lord insists here that "the two main types of oral traditional narrative poetry are epic and ballad," the former stichic, the latter stanzaic. The corpus of Native American oral narrative poetry is vast, but it includes very little that fits either of these classes.

13 Hopkins 1959: 267. These notes, admittedly, were not available to Boas when he needed them most. They were published first in 1937. Pound's essay "How to Read," however, was serialized in the New York *Herald Tribune* in January 1929, when Boas was at Columbia. There Pound identifies "three 'kinds' of poetry":

MELOPOEIA, *wherein the words are charged, over and above their plain meaning, with some musical property....*
PHANOPOEIA, *which is a casting of images upon the visual imagination.*
LOGOPOEIA, *'the dance of the intellect among words'....*

This list hardly seems exhaustive. But only in the first of these is the organization primarily acoustic. [See Pound 1929: part 2 = 1954: 25. The definitions are restated and enlarged in Pound 1934: chapters 4 & 8.]

If Boas knew nothing about the work of Pound and his colleagues, it is also true that Pound, though he was born in Shoshone country and advocated study of all the world's poetry, knew nothing about the work on which Boas, Bunzel, Sapir, Swanton and their colleagues were engaged. Only Sapir, it seems – and in his own way Roman Jakobson – formed a conscious link between these worlds.

14 Dell Hymes has very convincingly demonstrated both microscopic and macroscopic patterns in the oral literatures of the southern Northwest Coast. Judith Berman has done likewise for the oral literatures of the central Northwest Coast. In the oral literatures of the northern coast (Tlingit and Haida), the microscopic patterns have not yet, to my knowledge, been reliably described. See Hymes 1981 and Berman 1991, along with Hymes's translations of the Kathlamet mythteller Qqiltí [Charles Cultee], the Kalapuya mythteller William Hartless and the Kiksht [Clackamas] mythteller Victoria Howard, and Berman's translation of the Mamaliliqula (Kwakwala-speaking) mythteller T'łabid (all in Swann 1994: 273–310, 250–272). For the northern coast, see Dauenhauer & Dauenhauer 1987 and 1990, and Nyman & Leer 1993.

15 Hymes uses the terms *stanzas* and *verses* to name both the conceptual and the syntactic units he has found in oral narrative. (Hymes 1981: 318 explains the terminology.) He is borrowing the terms of acoustic prosody to address noetic prosody. I resist the transfer of terms but applaud his analyses. Some works germane to the subject: Sapir 1921a, Jacobs 1959, Finnegan 1977, Jakobson 1979 & 1981, Chafe 1981, Tedlock 1983, Swann 1983, Swann & Krupat 1987.

16 Liú Xié, *Wén xīn diāo lóng*: 文心雕龍 [*The Literary Mind and the Carving of Dragons*] §1.1: *Rì yuè ... shān chuān ... cǐ gài dào zhī wén yě*: 日月 ⋯ 山川 ⋯ 此蓋道之文也.

17 Shláwtxan spoke no English but received two English names: Joe Hunt and Joe Hollingsworth. His biography is summarized in Jacobs 1929: 242–243.

18 Jacobs 1929: 181–182. Bruce Rigsby kindly respelled the text at my request. The orthography is explained in appendix 3. Noel Rude later supplied me with a second retranscription and a morpheme-by-morpheme gloss. In line 21, the first person singular nominative pronoun, *ínk*, appears to me extraneous. An alternate reading, *inmí tíin*, "my people," is also plausible, and that is how Jacobs evidently understood the phrase, though not how he wrote it.

▶ NOTES TO CHAPTER TWENTY ◀

1 I owe my knowledge of this form to John Enrico.

2 "Die Erde ist schmal und scharf wie ein Messer" – Boas 1895: 319. The story is repeated, evidently from an independent Tlingit source, in Rev. Livingston F. Jones's otherwise unrewarding *Study of the Thlingets of Alaska* (New York: Revell, 1914), pp 181–182, and Boas also discusses it briefly in an earlier publication, Boas 1889: 238. A thousand kilometers to the south, in 1913, one of Sapir's Nuuchahnulth teachers – probably Saayaacchapis – expressed the prin-

ciple in a similar image, saying, "A man walks ahead as though on a straight line as slender as a hair. If he misses a step, he drops down and dies." The Nootka original for this phrase should be in Sapir's manuscripts, but I have not found it. For the English, see Sapir & Swadesh 1939: 108–109 & 223 n 184.

3 Kihlguulins (Henry Edenshaw) told this story to Swanton at Ghaw in the spring of 1901, not long before the end of Swanton's stay in Haida Gwaii. It is published in Swanton 1905a: 37. The original fieldnote entry survives in Swanton n.d.1, vol. 2: 372–373.

4 Swanton heard this phrase from Richard of the Daw Gitinaay and others at Ghaw, and from Tlaajang Quuna at Hlghagilda (Swanton n.d.2: 497; 1908a: 411). It remains in use.

5 Newcombe recorded the funeral in his diary (Newcombe n.d.1: v 33 f 8).

6 Swanton n.d.2: 278–279; 1905b: 235–237. There are also, of course, the portions of *Raven Travelling* told by Xhyuu, discussed in chapter 8.

7 Swanton n.d.2: folios 371–373.

8 Haida *stan sghaana*. The geoduck – *stan* in Haida, *Panopea generosa* in Latin – is the largest clam on the Northwest Coast.

> NOTES TO CHAPTER TWENTY-ONE >

1 Sheldon 1912: 151–152. (See also the photo of Glower and his wife, facing p 150.)

2 Albert Lord's *The Singer of Tales* (1960) and Milman Parry's belatedly published *The Making of Homeric Verse* (1971) remain the major contributions to this field. But Parry and Lord focussed exclusively on the neolithic tradition, in which poetry is cast as oral-formulaic metered verse. Dell Hymes's *"In Vain I Tried to Tell You"* (1981) remains the most perceptive work to date on compositional techniques in mesolithic oral poetry. An important recent work on the metaphysics of oral literature, both paleolithic and neolithic, is Sean Kane's *Wisdom of the Mythtellers* (2nd ed., 1998).

3 The reference is to Antti Aarne, *The Types of the Folktale*, translated and enlarged by Stith Thompson, 1st revision (Helsinki: Suomalainen Tiedeakatemia, 1928). The work has since been updated by a 2nd revision (i.e., 3rd edition) published in 1961.

4 Delargy 1945: 183–186. Ó Conaill died in 1931, but a substantial collection of his stories, with a biographical sketch and brief autobiography, is published as Ó Duilearga 1977 & 1981. For a parallel account of the Lushootseed storyteller Gʷəqʷulčəʔ (Gwuqwults'u' or Susie Sampson Peter), see Peter 1995: xiii–xv.

5 The early demographic studies of John Work are reported in Dawson 1880: 173 = 1993: 165. His figures are substantiated by an archaeological survey con-

ducted in 1969–70, which identified the sites of 15 houses (MacDonald 1983: 116–120). To Work, Qaysun and Ttsaa'ahl are Kish-a-win and Kow-welth; to Dawson they are Kai-shun and Cha-atl, and to MacDonald, Kaisun and Chaatl.

6 Newcombe n.d.2: 12.

7 Swanton 1905a: 287–289; MacDonald 1983: 60–65.

8 *Contributions to the Ethnology of the Haida* (1905a).

9 Swanton n.d.1, vol. 2: 402ff.

10 Ekunélyel's stories are in Petitot 1888: 507–509, 525–547. Kanyátaííyo' is published in Hewitt 1928 and in Gibson 1992. Casa Maria is in Goddard 1911. Isidor Solovyov is in Bergsland & Dirks 1990: 60–247. Saayaacchapis is in Sapir & Swadesh 1939: 138–177. Kâ-kîsikâw-pîhtokêw and Nâh-namiskwêkâpaw are in Bloomfield 1930 & 1934.

11 Bill Ray is in Goddard 1908. Hánc'ibyjim (Tom Young) is in Dixon 1912, with new translations by William Shipley in Hánc'ibyjim 1991. Qqiltí is in Boas 1896 & 1901, with some new translations by Hymes in Swann 1994. François Mandeville is in Li & Scollon 1976. Weyiiletpuu (Wayílatpu) is in Phinney 1934. Kâ-kîsikâw-pîhtokêw, to repeat, is in Bloomfield 1930 & 1934. Chiishch'ilíts'ósí is in Sapir 1942 and Haile 1943. Kootye is in Boas 1925–28.

> NOTES TO CHAPTER TWENTY-TWO >

1 The Haida text is on folios 381–385, Swanton n.d.2.

2 Spruce bark for roofing (rather than hemlock or pine bark for food or cedar bark for clothing) is apparently what Ghandl has in mind.

3 *Sghunskaxhawa* means "all alone." This is the Haida name for the largest size of California mussel, *Mytilus californianus*. The meat makes good eating and the shells make good adze-blades and knives.

4 The three lines in angle brackets are my interpolations.

5 *Skyaal* is the common cockle of the Pacific Coast, *Clinocardium nuttallii*, typically about 15 cm in diameter.

6 Where Xhyuu said *stan sghaana*, a geoduck spirit-being, Ghandl says *sqaaw sghaana*, a horseclam spirit-being. Geoduck (*Panopea generosa*) and horseclam (*Tresus nuttallii*) are much the largest, strongest bivalves found in Haida waters. Geoducks are, on average, slightly larger and their burrows somewhat deeper, but horseclams range a little farther out to sea. Each of the two mythtellers chooses the species that best fits the story as he tells it.

7 This detail confirms what we should now suspect about the uncle. A big topknot (*kyuuyuu jiwaagas*) is the conventional hairstyle for a Haida shaman.

8 Among the many interesting analogues is a story told by Nick Tumaka to Ruth Bunzel at Zuni in 1926, published in Bunzel 1933: 199–209. Closer to home, there is a well-made version of the story told by Mark Luther in Tsimshian around 1938 and recorded by Gwüsḵ'aayn (Beynon n.d.: text 78).

9 Eagles, αἰετοί, appear nine times in the *Iliad,* always as omens of Zeus, which is their usual role in the Greek mythworld. They appear in the *Odyssey* seven times (2.146; 15.161; 19.538, 543, 548; 20.243; 24.538), but there they are never omens of Zeus; they are always outright personifications of Odysseus or omens of his return and restoration.

10 Daxhiigang's version of the story (recorded in English only) is in Boas n.d.2 and Swanton 1905b: 273–276. Kingagwaaw's is in Swanton 1908a: 513–517.

11 Wolfram Prinz, "Die Darstellung Christi im Tempel und die Bildnisse des Andrea Mantegna," *Berliner Museen* 12 (1962). Mantegna and Nicolosia were evidently married late in 1453 or early in 1454. Dates as late as 1466 have been suggested for the painting.

12 Bellini's painting, insecurely dated to the 1460s, is in the Pinacoteca Querini Stampalia in Venice. The central figures in the two works are patently the same, though they are rendered by different hands. The background characters are different – and in Bellini's work no reference to the painter or his sister or other relatives has been spotted.

> ▸   NOTES TO THE APPENDICES   ▸

1 Each of these systems has developed over time and varied from publication to publication, depending evidently on the writer's whim, the audience intended and, of course, on the typographic resources available.

2 One area treated very differently by different scholars is vowel length. Swanton understood the importance of vowel length but did not learn how to write it with consistency. Levine chose not to recognize it at all. Enrico has established the first consistent and rational system, though applying this system to the classical texts remains problematic, because it differs so extensively from Swanton's more impressionistic record.

3 Enrico 1995.

4 Swanton 1905a and Swanton to Boas, 19 October 1903. Original in the APSL, Philadelphia.

5 Newcombe n.d.2 is the report of a physical survey made in 1901, but it covers only the southern part of the archipelago. This document names and locates 70 village sites and close to 30 camps. About 30 of these villages, including some of the largest, are missing from Swanton's list.

Select Bibliography

T HESE ABBREVIATIONS appear here and in the notes:
AES = American Ethnological Society (New York)
AMNH = American Museum of Natural History (New York)
APSL = American Philosophical Society Library (Philadelphia)
BAE = Bureau of American Ethnology (Washington, DC)
IJAL = *International Journal of American Linguistics* (Chicago)
NAA = National Anthropological Archives (Washington, DC)

Abbott, Donald N., ed.
 1981 *The World Is as Sharp as a Knife: An Anthology in Honour of Wilson Duff.* Victoria, BC: British Columbia Provincial Museum.
Banfield, A.W.F.
 1974 *The Mammals of Canada.* Toronto: University of Toronto Press.
Basso, Keith H.
 1996 *Wisdom Sits in Places: Landscape and Language among the Western Apache.* Albuquerque: University of New Mexico Press.
Benedict, Ruth
 1935 *Zuni Mythology.* 2 vols. Columbia University Contributions to Anthropology 21. New York: Columbia University Press.
Bennett, Sam, & Don Gasin
 1992 *Na Maalsga Walps Nisłgümiik: The Story of the House of Nisłgümiik.* Suwilaay'msga Na Ga'niiyatgm 7. [Prince Rupert, BC: Tsimshian Tribal Council.]
Bergsland, Knut, & Moses Dirks, ed.
 1990 *Unangam Ungiikangin kayux Tunusangin: Unangam Uniikangis ama Tunuzangis: Aleut Tales and Narratives, collected 1909–1910 by Waldemar Jochelson.* Fairbanks: Alaska Native Language Center.
Berman, Judith
 1991 The Seal's Sleeping Cave: The Interpretation of Boas' Kwakw'ala Texts. Ph.D. dissertation, University of Pennsylvania.
 1996 "'The Culture as It Appears to the Indian Himself': Boas, George Hunt, and the Methods of Ethnography." In Stocking 1996: 215–256.

Beynon, William [= Gwüsḵ'aayn]
n.d.   "The Beynon Manuscript." Columbia University Library, New
        York. [Individually paginated holograph texts numbered from 5 to
        253, with a few omissions. In Tsimshian with Gwüsḵ'aayn's
        interlinear English translation.]

Birket-Smith, Kaj, & Frederica de Laguna
1938   *The Eyak Indians of the Copper River Delta, Alaska.* Copenhagen:
        Levin & Munksgaard.

Blackman, Margaret B.
1972   "Nei:wons, the 'Monster' House of Chief Wi:ha: An Exercise in
        Ethnohistorical, Archaeological, and Ethnological Reasoning."
        Victoria, BC: *Syesis* 5: 211–225.
1982   *During My Time: Florence Edenshaw Davidson, a Haida Woman.*
        Seattle: University of Washington Press.

Blanchette, Robert A., et al.
1992   "Nineteenth Century Shaman Grave Guardians Are Carved
        Fomitopsis officinalis Sporophores." New York: *Mycologia* 84.1:
        119–124.

Bloomfield, Leonard
n.d.   Cree Texts, series 2. Ms Boas Coll. A1a.1 = Freeman 785. APSL,
        Philadelphia.
1930   *Sacred Stories of the Sweet Grass Cree.* National Museum of Canada
        Bulletin 60. Ottawa: Department of Mines.
1934   *Plains Cree Texts.* New York: Publications of the AES 16.

Blyth, Gladys Young
1991   *Salmon Canneries: British Columbia North Coast.* Lantzville, BC:
        Oolichan Books.

Boas, Franz
n.d.1   Haida word lists, grammatical notes and phrases. Holograph.
        Ms 4117-B, NAA, Smithsonian Institution, Washington, DC.
n.d.2   Myths and interpretations of artworks obtained from Daxhiigang.
        Typescript. Dept. of Anthropology Archives, AMNH, New York.
1888   "Die Tsimschian." Berlin: *Zeitschrift für Ethnologie* 20: 231–247.
1889   "Preliminary Notes on the Indians of British Columbia." London:
        *58th Report of the British Association for the Advancement of
        Science*: 236–242.
1894   *Chinook Texts.* [BAE Bulletin 20]. Washington, DC: BAE.
1895   *Indianische Sagen von der Nord-Pacifischen Küste Amerikas.* Berlin:
        Asher.
1898a   *Facial Paintings of the Indians of Northern British Columbia.* Jesup
        North Pacific Expedition 1.1. New York: AMNH.
1898b   *The Mythology of the Bella Coola Indians.* Jesup North Pacific
        Expedition 1.2. New York: AMNH.
1901   *Kathlamet Texts.* Washington, DC: BAE Bulletin 26.

494

1902   *Tsimshian Texts*. Washington, DC: BAE Bulletin 27.

1908   "Eine Sonnensage der Tsimschian." *Zeitschrift für Ethnologie*. Berlin: Behrend: 776–797.

1910   *Kwakiutl Tales*. Columbia University Contributions to Anthropology 2. New York: Columbia University Press.

1911   *Handbook of American Indian Languages*, vol. 1. Washington, DC: BAE Bulletin 40.

1916   *Tsimshian Mythology*. Washington, DC: BAE Annual Report 31.

1923   "A Keresan Text." IJAL 2: 171–180.

1925   *Contributions to the Ethnology of the Kwakiutl*. Columbia University Contributions to Anthropology 3. New York: Columbia University Press.

1925–28 *Keresan Texts*. 2 vols. New York: Publications of the AES 8.

1927   *Primitive Art*. Oslo: Aschehoug. [Reissued, Harvard University Press, 1928.]

1928   *Bella Bella Texts*. Columbia University Contributions to Anthropology 5. New York: Columbia University Press.

1930   *The Religion of the Kwakiutl Indians*. 2 vols. Columbia University Contributions to Anthropology 10. New York: Columbia University Press.

1932   *Bella Bella Tales*. New York: Memoirs of the American Folk-Lore Society 25.

1935–43 *Kwakiutl Tales (New Series)*. 2 vols. Columbia University Contributions to Anthropology 26. New York: Columbia University Press.

1940   *Race, Language, and Culture*. New York: Macmillan.

Boas, Franz, & George Hunt [= Q'iẋitasu']

1902–5   *Kwakiutl Texts*. 3 vols. Jesup North Pacific Expedition 3.1–3. New York: AMNH.

1906   *Kwakiutl Texts: Second Series*. Jesup North Pacific Expedition 10.1. New York: AMNH.

Boas, Franz, et al.

1938   *General Anthropology*. Boston: D.C. Heath.

Boelscher, Marianne

1988   *The Curtain Within: Haida Social and Mythical Discourse*. Vancouver: UBC Press.

Bogoras, Waldemar [= Vladimir Germanovich Bogoraz]

1900   Материалы по изучению чукотскаго языка и фольклора. St Petersburg: Akademia Nauk.

1902   "The Folklore of Northeastern Asia as Compared with That of Northwestern America." Lancaster, Penn.: *American Anthropologist* n.s. 4: 577–683.

1910   *Chukchee Mythology*. Jesup North Pacific Expedition 8.1. New York: AMNH.

1917   *Koryak Texts.* Publications of the AES 5. Leiden: E.J. Brill.
1918   *Tales of Yukaghir, Lamut, and Russianized Natives of Eastern Siberia.* New York: AMNH Anthropological Papers 20.1.

Boit, John
1794–6 "The Journal of a Voyage Round the Globe." Log and Remarks of the Sloop *Union,* 29 August 1794 – 8 July 1796. Bound holograph. [The original, formerly held by the Massachusetts Historical Society, has been listed as missing since the 1960s. Photographic replicas are on deposit at the MHS and other institutions.]

Boyd, Robert
1990   "Demographic History, 1774–1874." In *Handbook of North American Indians,* vol. 7: Northwest Coast: 135–148.
1994   "Smallpox in the Pacific Northwest." Vancouver: *BC Studies* 101: 5–40.

Bright, William
1984   *American Indian Linguistics and Literature.* Berlin: Mouton.

Bringhurst, Robert
1994   "A Story as Sharp as a Knife, Part 3: The Polyhistorical Mind." Peterborough, Ontario: *Journal of Canadian Studies* 29.2: 165–175.
1995a   "Raven Travelling: Page One." Vancouver: *Canadian Literature* 144: 98–111.
1995b   "Everywhere Being Is Dancing, Knowing Is Known." In *Poetry and Knowing,* edited by Tim Lilburn. Kingston, Ontario: Quarry Press: 52–64.
1998   *Native American Oral Literatures and the Unity of the Humanities.* The 1998 Garnett Sedgewick Memorial Lecture. Vancouver: University of British Columbia.

Bringhurst, Robert, & Ulli Steltzer
1992   *The Black Canoe: Bill Reid and the Spirit of Haida Gwaii.* 2nd ed. Vancouver/Toronto: Douglas & McIntyre.

Brown, Dorothy
1992   *Saaban: The Tsimshian and Europeans Meet.* Suwilaay'msga Na Ga'niiyatgm 3. [Prince Rupert, BC: Tsimshian Tribal Council.]

Bunzel, Ruth L.
1929   *The Pueblo Potter: A Study of Creative Imagination in Primitive Art.* Columbia University Contributions to Anthropology 8. New York: Columbia University Press.
1932   *Introduction to Zuni Ceremonialism; Zuni Origin Myths; Zuni Ritual Poetry* and *Zuni Katcinas: An Analytical Study.* Washington, DC: BAE Annual Report 47.
1933   *Zuni Texts.* New York: Publications of the AES 15.

Butler, Gregory
1983   "Ordering Problems in J.S. Bach's *Art of Fugue* Resolved." New York: *The Musical Quarterly* 49: 44–61.

Calder, James A., & Roy L. Taylor
1968   *Flora of the Queen Charlotte Islands.* 2 vols. Ottawa: Department of
        Agriculture.
Campbell, Lyle
1997   *American Indian Languages: The Historical Linguistics of Native
        America.* New York: Oxford University Press.
Campbell, Lyle, & Marianne Mithun, ed.
1979   *The Languages of Native America.* Austin: University of Texas Press.
Campbell, R. Wayne, et al.
1990–99 *The Birds of British Columbia.* 4 vols. Vancouver: UBC Press.
Canada. Department of Fisheries & Oceans
1991   *Sailing Directions: British Columbia Coast,* vol. 2 (North Portion).
        12th ed. Ottawa: Canadian Hydrographic Service.
Canizzo, Jeanne
1983   "George Hunt and the Invention of Kwakiutl Culture." Toronto:
        Canadian Review of Sociology and Anthropology 20: 44–58.
Cannon, Aubrey
1991   *The Economic Prehistory of Namu.* Simon Fraser University
        Archaeology pub. 19. Burnaby, BC: Archaeology Press.
Carlson, Barry F., ed.
1977   *Northwest Coast Texts.* IJAL Native American Texts Series 2.3.
        University of Chicago Press.
Carlson, Roy L., ed.
[1983] *Indian Art Traditions of the Northwest Coast.* Burnaby, BC:
        Archaeology Press.
Carlson, Roy L., & Luke Dalla Bona, ed.
1996   *Early Human Occupation in British Columbia.* Vancouver: UBC
        Press.
Chafe, Wallace
1981   "Differences between Colloquial and Ritual Seneca, or How Oral
        Literature Is Literary." In *Survey Reports, 1981.* [Berkeley]: Survey
        of California and Other Indian Languages, Report 1: 131–145.
Chafe, Wallace, & Johanna Nichols, ed.
1986   *Evidentiality: The Linguistic Coding of Epistemology.* Norwood, NJ:
        Ablex.
Chittenden, Newton
1884   *Official Report of the Exploration of the Queen Charlotte Islands.*
        Victoria, BC: Government of British Columbia.
Chowning, Ann
1962   "Raven Myths in Northwestern North America and Northeastern
        Asia." Madison, Wisconsin: *Arctic Anthropology* 1.1: 1–5.
Cole, Douglas
1995   *Captured Heritage: The Scramble for Northwest Coast Artifacts.* 2nd
        ed. [but labelled "reprint"]. Vancouver: UBC Press.

Cole, Douglas, & Ira Chaikin
  1990   *An Iron Hand upon the People: The Law against the Potlatch on the
            Northwest Coast.* Vancouver/Toronto: Douglas & McIntyre.
Compton, Brian
  1993   Upper North Wakashan and Southern Tsimshian Ethnobotany.
            Ph.D. dissertation, University of British Columbia, Vancouver.
Cook, Eung-Do, & Donna B. Gerdts, ed.
  1984   *The Syntax of Native American Languages.* Orlando: Academic
            Press.
Cornell, George L.
  1987   "The Imposition of Western Definitions of Literature on Indian
            Oral Traditions." In *The Native in Literature,* edited by Thomas
            King, Cheryl Calver & Helen Hoy. Toronto: ECW: 174–187.
Coupland, Gary
  1988   "Prehistoric Economic and Social Change in the Tsimshian Area." In
            Prehistoric Economies of the Pacific Northwest Coast, edited by Barry
            L. Isaac. Greenwich, Connecticut: JAI Press: 211–243.
Crosby, Thomas, et al.
  n.d.   Church ledger for Skidegate, Gold Harbour and Clue, vol. 1
            [1884–1916]. Unnumbered ms., United Church of Canada, British
            Columbia Conference Archives, Vancouver. [Bound holograph in
            many hands, 96 pp including intermittent blanks.]
Darnell, Regna
  1990   *Edward Sapir: Linguist, Anthropologist, Humanist.* Berkeley:
            University of California Press.
Dauenhauer, Nora Marks, & Richard Dauenhauer
  1987   *Haa Shuká, Our Ancestors: Tlingit Oral Narratives.* Seattle:
            University of Washington Press.
  1990   *Haa Tuwunáagu Yís, For Healing Our Spirit: Tlingit Oratory.* Seattle:
            University of Washington Press.
Davis, Philip W., & Ross Saunders, ed.
  1980   *Bella Coola Texts.* Victoria, BC: British Columbia Provincial
            Museum.
Dawson, George M.
  1880   *On the Haida of the Queen Charlotte Islands.* Montreal: Geological
            Survey of Canada. [Reprinted in Dawson 1993: 97–166.]
  1993   *To the Charlottes,* edited by Douglas Cole & Bradley Lockner.
            Vancouver: UBC Press.
Delargy, James H. [= Séamus Ó Duilearga]
  1945   "The Gaelic Story-Teller." London: *Proceedings of the British
            Academy* 31: 177-221.
Deloria, Ella Cara
  n.d.1   Dakota Song Texts. Ms Freeman 840. APSL, Philadelphia.
  n.d.2   Teton Myths. Ms Freeman 852. APSL, Philadelphia.

1932   *Dakota Texts.* New York: Publications of the AES 14.
Denevan, William M.
1992   *The Native Population of the Americas in 1492.* 2nd ed. Madison: University of Wisconsin Press.
Denny, J. Peter
1986   "Cultural Ecology of Mathematics: Ojibway and Inuit Hunters." In *Native American Mathematics,* edited by Michael P. Closs. Austin: University of Texas Press: 129–180.
Dixon, Roland B.
1912   *Maidu Texts.* Publications of the AES 4. Leiden: E.J. Brill.
1916   "The Swan-Maiden Theme in the Oceanic Area." In *Holmes Anniversary Volume,* edited by Frederick Webb Hodge. Washington, DC: J.W. Bryan: 80–87.
Dorsey, George A.
1898   *A Cruise among Haida and Tlingit Villages about Dixon's Entrance.* New York: Appleton.
Douglas, George W., Gerald B. Stanley & Del Meidinger, ed.
1989–94 *The Vascular Plants of British Columbia.* Victoria, BC: Ministry of Forests. 4 vols.
Duff, Wilson
n.d.   Wilson Duff papers. Ms GR-2809, British Columbia Archives, Victoria.
1964   *The Indian History of British Columbia,* vol. 1: *The Impact of the White Man.* Victoria, BC: British Columbia Provincial Museum.
1975   *Images Stone B.C.* Saanichton, BC: Hancock.
1983   "The World Is as Sharp as a Knife: Meaning in Northern Northwest Coast Art." In Roy Carlson [1983]: 47–66.
Duff, Wilson, et al.
1967   *Arts of the Raven.* Vancouver: Vancouver Art Gallery.
Durlach, Theresa Mayer
1928   *The Relationship Systems of the Tlingit, Haida and Tsimshian.* New York: Publications of the AES 11.
Eastman, Carol, & Elizabeth Edwards
1991   *Gyaehlingaay: Traditions, Tales and Images of the Kaigani Haida.* Seattle: Burke Museum.
Edmonson, Munro S.
1971   *The Book of Counsel: The Popol Vuh of the Quiche Maya of Guatemala.* New Orleans: Middle American Research Institute, Tulane University.
1985   (ed.) *Supplement to the Handbook of Middle American Indians,* vol. 3: *Literatures.* Austin: University of Texas Press.
Egesdal, Steven M.
1992   *Stylized Characters' Speech in Thompson Salish Narrative.* Missoula: University of Montana Occasional Papers in Linguistics 9.

Ellis, C. Douglas, ed.

1995   *Âtalôhkâna nêsta tipâcimôwina: Cree Legends and Narratives from the West Coast of James Bay.* Winnipeg: University of Manitoba Press.

Ellis, David W., & Solomon Wilson

1981   *The Knowledge and Usage of Marine Invertebrates by the Skidegate Haida People of the Queen Charlotte Islands.* [Skidegate, BC]: Queen Charlotte Islands Museum Society.

Enrico, John

1983   "Tense in the Haida Relative Clause." IJAL 49: 134–166.

1985   "The Fire as Conduit to the Other World: A Note on Haida Deixis and Haida Belief." IJAL 51: 400–402.

1986   "Word Order, Focus and Topic in Haida." IJAL 52: 91–123.

1989   "The Haida Language." In Scudder & Gessler: 123–147.

1995   *Skidegate Haida Myths and Histories.* Skidegate, BC: Queen Charlotte Islands Museum Press.

Enrico, John, & Wendy Bross Stuart

1996   *Northern Haida Songs.* Lincoln: University of Nebraska Press.

Farrand, Livingston

1900   *Traditions of the Chilcotin Indians.* Jesup North Pacific Expedition 2.1. New York: AMNH.

1902   *Traditions of the Quinault Indians.* Jesup North Pacific Expedition 2.3. New York: AMNH.

Fenton, William N.

1959   "John Reed Swanton, 1873–1958." Menasha, Wisconsin: *American Anthropologist* 61.4: 663–668.

Finnegan, Ruth

1977   *Oral Poetry: Its Nature, Significance and Social Context.* Cambridge University Press.

1988   *Literacy and Orality: Studies in the Technology of Communication.* Oxford: Blackwell.

Fitzhugh, William W., & Aron Crowell, ed.

1988   *Crossroads of Continents: Cultures of Siberia and Alaska.* Washington, DC: Smithsonian Institution.

Fladmark, Knut

1986   *British Columbia Prehistory.* Ottawa: National Museum of Man.

1989   "The Native Culture History of the Queen Charlotte Islands." In Scudder & Gessler: 199–221.

Foster, J. Bristol

1964   "Evolution of Mammals on Islands." London: *Nature* 202: 234–235.

Fowler, Catherine S., & Don D. Fowler

1986   "Edward Sapir, Tony Tillohash and Southern Paiute Studies." In *New Perspectives in Language, Culture, and Personality,* edited by William Cowan et al. Amsterdam: John Benjamins: 41–65.

Frachtenberg, Leo J.

1917   "Myths of the Alsea Indians of Northwestern Oregon." IJAL 1:
        64–75.

1920   Alsea Texts and Myths. Washington, DC: BAE Bulletin 67.

Freeman, John F.

1966   *A Guide to Manuscripts Relating to the American Indian in the
        Library of the American Philosophical Society.* Philadelphia:
        American Philosophical Society. [Supplemented by Kendall 1982.]

Frye, Northrop

1988   *On Education.* Markham, Ontario: Fitzhenry & Whiteside.

1990   *Myth and Metaphor: Selected Essays 1974–1978.* Charlottesville:
        University Press of Virginia.

1993   *The Eternal Act of Creation: Essays 1979–1990.* Bloomington:
        Indiana University Press.

Galois, Robert

1994   *Kwakwaka'wakw Settlements, 1775–1920: A Geographical Analysis
        and Gazetteer.* Vancouver: UBC Press.

1996   "Measles, 1847–1850." Vancouver: *BC Studies* 109: 31–43.

Garibay Kintana, Angel María

1964–68 *Poesía náhuatl.* 3 vols. México, DF: Universidad Nacional
        Autónoma de México.

1971   *Historia de la literatura náhuatl.* 2 vols. 2ª ed. México, DF: Porrua.

Gatschet, Albert S.

1890   *The Klamath Indians of Southwestern Oregon.* 2 vols. Contributions
        to North American Ethnology 2. Washington, DC: Dept. of the
        Interior.

Gibson, John A. [– Kanyátaííyo']

1992   *Concerning the League: The Iroquois Tradition as Dictated in
        Onondaga by John Arthur Gibson,* edited & translated by Hanni
        Woodbury et al. Winnipeg: Algonquian & Iroquoian Linguistics.

Goddard, Pliny Earle

1908   *Kato Texts.* Berkeley: University of California Publications in
        American Archaeology & Ethnology 5.3.

1911   *Jicarilla Apache Texts.* New York: AMNH Anthropological Papers 8.

1914   *Chilula Texts.* Berkeley: University of California Publications in
        American Archaeology & Ethnology 10.7.

Goldman, Irving

1975   *The Mouth of Heaven: An Introduction to Kwakiutl Religious
        Thought.* New York: Wiley.

Goldschmidt, Walter, ed.

1959   *The Anthropology of Franz Boas.* Menasha, Wisconsin: American
        Anthropological Association Memoir 89 = *American Anthropologist*
        n.s. 61.5, pt 2.

Golla, Victor, ed.

  1984   *The Sapir-Kroeber Correspondence.* Berkeley: University of
            California Press.

Golla, Victor, & Shirley Silver, ed.

  1977   *Northern California Texts.* IJAL Native American Texts Series 2.2.
            University of Chicago Press.

Gottesfeld, Leslie Johnson

  1992   "The Importance of Bark Products in the Aboriginal Economies of
            Northwestern British Columbia." New York: *Economic Botany* 46.2:
            145–157.

Greenberg, Joseph H.

  1987   *Language in the Americas.* Stanford University Press.

  1996   "In Defense of Amerind." IJAL 62: 131–194.

Haas, Mary R.

  1969   *The Prehistory of Languages.* Janua Linguarum Series Minor 57. The
            Hague: Mouton.

Haile, Berard

  1943   *Origin Legend of the Navajo Flintway.* University of Chicago Press.

Haldane, Victor

  1986   "Shag and the Raven" and "Story of the Double Fin Killer Whale,"
            translated from the Haida by Erma Lawrence. Anchorage: *Alaska
            Quarterly Review* 4.3–4: 32–33.

Hamilton, George

  1986   "Haida Hunters and Legend of the Two Fin Killer Whale,"
            translated from the Haida by Erma Lawrence. Anchorage: *Alaska
            Quarterly Review* 4.3–4: 34–35.

Hánc'ibyjim

  1991   *The Maidu Indian Myths and Stories of Hánc'ibyjim,* edited &
            translated by William Shipley. Berkeley: Heyday.

Handbook of North American Indians

  1978–   20 vols. Washington, DC: Smithsonian Institution.

Harrington, John Peabody

  1930   "Karuk Texts." IJAL 6: 121–161.

Heizer, Robert F., & Theodora Kroeber, ed.

  1979   *Ishi, the Last Yahi: A Documentary History.* Berkeley: University of
            California Press.

Herskovits, Melville J.

  1953   *Franz Boas: The Science of Man in the Making.* New York: Scribners.

Hewitt, J.N.B.

  1903   *Iroquoian Cosmology, First Part.* Washington, DC: BAE Annual
            Report 21: 127–339.

  1928   *Iroquoian Cosmology, Second Part.* Washington, DC: BAE Annual
            Report 43: 449–819.

Holm, Bill

1965   *Northwest Coast Indian Art: An Analysis of Form.* Seattle:
University of Washington Press.

1981   "Will the Real Charles Edensaw Please Stand Up? The Problem of
Attribution in Northwest Coast Indian Art." In Abbott: 175–200.

1990   "Art." In *Handbook of North American Indians,* vol. 7: Northwest
Coast: 602–632.

Holm, Bill, & Bill Reid

1975   *Form and Freedom: A Dialogue on Northwest Coast Indian Art.*
Houston: Institute for the Arts, Rice University. [Reissued as
*Indian Art of the Northwest Coast: A Dialogue on Craftsmanship and
Aesthetics.* Vancouver/Toronto: Douglas & McIntyre, 1978.]

Hopkins, Gerard Manley

1959   *The Journals and Papers of Gerard Manley Hopkins,* edited by
Humphry House & Graham Storey. Oxford University Press.

Hoskins, Janet

1989   "On Losing and Getting a Head: Warfare, Exchange and Alliance in
a Changing Sumba, 1888–1988." Arlington, Virginia: *American
Ethnologist* 16: 419–440.

1996   (ed.) *Headhunting and the Social Imagination in Southeast Asia.*
Stanford University Press.

Hyatt, Marshall

1990   *Franz Boas: Social Activist.* Westport, Connecticut: Greenwood.

Hymes, Dell

1971   "Masset Mourning Songs." New York: *Alcheringa* 2: 53–63.

1975   "Folklore's Nature and the Sun's Myth." Austin, Texas: *Journal of
American Folklore* 88: 345–369.

1980   "Tonkawa Poetics: John Rush Buffalo's 'Coyote and Eagle's
Daughter'." In *On Linguistic Anthropology: Essays in Honor of
Harry Hoijer,* edited by Jacques Maquet. Malibu, California:
Undena: 33–88.

1981   *"In Vain I Tried to Tell You": Essays in Native American Ethnopoetics.*
Philadelphia: University of Pennsylvania Press.

1990   "Mythology." In *Handbook of North American Indians,* vol. 7:
Northwest Coast: 593–601.

1995   "Na-Dene Ethnopoetics, A Preliminary Report: Haida and Tlingit."
In *Language and Culture in Native North America,* edited by
Michael Dürr, Egon Renner & Wolfgang Oleschinski. München:
Lincom: 265–311.

Hymes, Dell, & Henry Zenk

1987   "Narrative Structure in Chinook Jargon." In *Pidgin and Creole
Languages: Essays in Honor of John E. Reinecke,* edited by Glenn G.
Gilbert. Honolulu: University of Hawaii Press: 445–465.

Jacknis, Ira
    1985   "Franz Boas and Exhibits: On the Limitations of the Museum
               Method in Anthropology." In *Objects and Others: Essays on
               Museums and Material Culture,* edited by George W. Stocking.
               Madison: University of Wisconsin Press: 75–111.

Jacobs, Melville
    1929   *Northwest Sahaptin Texts,* 1. Seattle: University of Washington
               Publications in Anthropology 2.6.
    1939   *Coos Narrative and Ethnologic Texts.* Seattle: University of
               Washington Publications in Anthropology 8.1.
    1940   *Coos Myth Texts.* Seattle: University of Washington Publications in
               Anthropology 8.2.
    1957   "Titles in an Oral Literature." New York: *Journal of American
               Folklore* 70: 157–172.
    1958–9   *Clackamas Chinook Texts.* 2 vols. Bloomington: Indiana University
               Research Center in Anthropology, Folklore & Linguistics,
               Publications 8 & 11 = IJAL 24.1, part 2, & 25.2, part 2.
    1959   *The Content and Style of an Oral Literature.* University of Chicago
               Press.
    1960   *The People Are Coming Soon: Analyses of Clackamas Chinook Myths
               and Tales.* Seattle: University of Washington Press.
    1962   "The Fate of Indian Oral Literatures in Oregon." Eugene, Oregon:
               Northwest Review 5: 90–99.
    1966   "A Look Ahead in Oral Literature Research." New York: *Journal of
               American Folklore* 79: 413–427.

Jakobson, Roman
    1973   *Question de poétique.* Paris: Seuil.
    1979   *Selected Writings,* vol. 5: *On Verse, Its Masters and Explorers.* The
               Hague: Mouton.
    1981   *Selected Writings,* vol. 3: *Poetry of Grammar and Grammar of Poetry,*
               edited by Stephen Rudy. The Hague: Mouton.

Jochelson, Waldemar [= Vladimir Il'ich Iokhel'son]
    1900   Материалы по изучению юкагирскаго языка и фольклора.
               St Petersburg: Akademia Nauk.
    1905   "Essay on the Grammar of the Yukaghir Language." Lancaster,
               Pennsylvania: *American Anthropologist* n.s. 7.2: 369–424.
    1908   *The Koryak.* Jesup North Pacific Expedition 6. New York: AMNH.
    1926   *The Yukaghir and the Yukaghirized Tungus.* Jesup North Pacific
               Expedition 9.2. New York: AMNH.

Jonaitis, Aldona
    1988   *From the Land of the Totem Poles: The Northwest Coast Indian Art
               Collection at the American Museum of Natural History.* New York:
               AMNH.

Jones, William
  1917–19 *Ojibwa Texts,* edited by Truman Michaelson. 2 vols. Publications of
           the AES 7. Leiden: E.J. Brill.

Judd, Neil M.
  1967   *The Bureau of American Ethnology: A Partial History.* Norman:
           University of Oklahoma Press.

Kaiser, Rudolf
  1987   "Chief Seattle's Speech(es): American Origin and European
           Reception." In Swann & Krupat: 497-536.

Kan, Sergei
  1989   *Symbolic Immortality: The Tlingit Potlatch of the Nineteenth
           Century.* Washington, DC: Smithsonian Institution.

Kane, Sean
  1998   *Wisdom of the Mythtellers.* 2nd ed. Peterborough, Ontario:
           Broadview.

Kendall, Daythal
  1982   *Supplement to "A Guide to Manuscripts Relating to the American
           Indian in the Library of the American Philosophical Society."*
           Philadelphia: American Philosophical Society. [Supplement to
           Freeman 1966.]

Kilham, Lawrence
  1989   *The American Crow and the Common Raven.* College Station, Texas:
           Texas A&M University Press.

Kleivan, Inge
  1962   *The Swan Maiden Myth among the Eskimo.* Acta Arctica 13.
           Copenhagen: Munksgaard.

Krause, Aurel
  1885   *Die Tlinkit-Indianer: Ergebnisse einer Reise nach der Nordwestkuste
           von Amerika und der Beringstraße.* Jena: Costenoble.
  1956   *The Tlingit Indians.* Translated by Erna Gunther. Seattle: University
           of Washington Press. [Translation of Krause 1885.]

Krauss, Michael E.
  1982   *In Honor of Eyak: The Art of Anna Nelson Harry.* Fairbanks: Alaska
           Native Language Center.
  1986   "Edward Sapir and Athabaskan Linguistics." In *New Perspectives in
           Language, Culture, and Personality,* edited by William Cowan et al.
           Amsterdam: John Benjamins: 147–190.

Kroeber, Alfred L.
  1917   "The Superorganic." Lancaster, Penn.: *American Anthropologist* 19:
           163–213.
  1940   "The Work of John R. Swanton." In *Essays in Historical
           Anthropology of North America.* Washington, DC: Smithsonian
           Miscellaneous Collections 100: 1–9.

1948   *Seven Mohave Myths.* Anthropological Records 11.1 Berkeley: University of California Press.

1951   *A Mohave Historical Epic.* Anthropological Records 11.2. Berkeley: University of California Press.

1962   *A Roster of Civilizations and Cultures.* Viking Fund Publications in Anthropology 33. New York: Wenner-Gren Foundation.

1972   *More Mohave Myths.* Anthropological Records 27. Berkeley: University of California Press.

Kroeber, Alfred L., & Clyde Kluckhohn

1952   *Culture: A Review of Concepts and Definitions.* Cambridge, Mass.: Papers of the Peabody Museum 47.1.

Kroeber, Alfred L., et al.

1943   *Franz Boas.* Menasha, Wisconsin: American Anthropological Association Memoir 61 = *American Anthropologist* n.s. 45.3, pt 2.

Kuhnlein, Harriet V., & Nancy J. Turner

1991   *Traditional Plant Foods of Canadian Indigenous Peoples.* New York: Gordon & Breach.

Lambert, Philip

1997   *Sea Cucumbers of British Columbia, Southeast Alaska and Puget Sound.* Vancouver: UBC Press.

Lawrence, Erma, et al.

1977   *Haida Dictionary.* Fairbanks: Alaska Native Language Center.

Lee, Dorothy Demetracopoulou

1938   "Conceptual Implications of an Indian Language." Baltimore: *Philosophy of Science* 5.1: 89–102.

Leer, Jeff

1991   "Evidence for a Northern Northwest Coast Language Area: Promiscuous Number Marking and Periphrastic Possessive Constructions in Haida, Eyak and Aleut." IJAL 57: 158–193.

Léon-Portilla, Miguel

1967   *Trece poetas del mundo azteca.* México, DF: Universidad Nacional Autónoma.

1992   *Fifteen poets of the Aztec World.* Norman: University of Oklahoma Press. [Revision of Léon-Portilla 1967. Issued in Spanish as *Quince poetas del mundo azteca.* México, DF: Diana, 1994.]

Leman, Wayne

1987   *Náévåhóo'ȯhtséme / We Are Going Back Home: Cheyenne History and Stories Told by James Shoulderblade and Others.* Winnipeg: Algonquian & Iroquoian Linguistics Memoir 4.

Levine, Robert D.

1977   The Skidegate Dialect of Haida. Ph.D. dissertation, Columbia University, New York.

1979   "Haida and Na-Dene: A New Look at the Evidence." IJAL 45: 157–170.

Lévi-Strauss, Claude

1964–71 *Mythologiques*. 4 vols (*Le Cru et le cuit; Du Miel aux cendres; L'Origine des manières de table; L'Homme nu*). Paris: Plon.

1969–81 *Introduction to a Science of Mythology*. 4 vols (*The Raw and the Cooked; From Honey to Ashes; The Origin of Table Manners; The Naked Man*). New York: Harper & Row. [Translation of Lévi-Strauss 1964–71.]

1979 *La Voie des masques*. 2ᵉ éd. Paris: Plon.

1982 *The Way of the Masks*. Vancouver/Toronto: Douglas & McIntyre. [Translation of Lévi-Strauss 1979.]

1989 *Des Symboles et leurs doubles*. Paris: Plon.

Li, Fang-kuei, & Ronald Scollon

1976 *Chipewyan Texts*. Nankang, Taipei: Institute of History and Philology, Academica Sinica.

Lillard, Charles, ed.

1984 *Warriors of the North Pacific: Missionary Accounts of the Northwest Coast, the Skeena and Stikine Rivers and the Klondike, 1829–1900*. Victoria, BC: Sono Nis.

1989 *The Ghostland People: A Documentary History of the Queen Charlotte Islands, 1859–1906*. Victoria, BC: Sono Nis.

López-Rey, José

1963 *Velázquez: A Catalogue Raisonné of His Oeuvre*. London: Faber & Faber.

Lord, Albert B.

1960 *The Singer of Tales*. Cambridge, Mass.: Harvard University Press.

1991 *Epic Singers and Oral Tradition*. Ithaca, NY: Cornell University Press.

1995 *The Singer Resumes the Tale*, edited by Mary Louise Lord. Ithaca, NY: Cornell University Press.

Low, Jean

1982 "Dr Charles Frederick Newcombe." Winnipeg: *The Beaver* 312.4: 32–39.

Lowie, Robert H.

1960 *Crow Texts*. Berkeley: University of California Press.

MacArthur, Robert H., & Edward O. Wilson

1967 *The Theory of Island Biogeography*. Princeton University Press.

MacDonald, George F.

1983 *Haida Monumental Art*. Vancouver: UBC Press.

McIlwraith, T. F.

1948 *The Bella Coola Indians*. 2 vols. University of Toronto Press. [Reissued 1992 with a new preface by John Barker.]

McKinley, Robert

1976 "Human and Proud of It! A Structural Treatment of Headhunting Rites and the Social Definition of Enemies." In *Studies in Borneo*

Societies: Social Process and Anthropological Explanation, edited by
G.N. Appell. [DeKalb, Illinois]: Center for Southeast Asian Studies,
Northern Illinois University: 92–126.

McNeley, James K.

1981   *Holy Wind in Navajo Philosophy.* Tucson: University of Arizona
Press.

Malotki, Ekkehart, [& Herschel Talashoma]

1978   *Hopitutuwutsi.* Flagstaff: Museum of Northern Arizona Press.

Manaster Ramer, Alexis

1996   "Sapir's Classifications: Haida and the Other Na-Dene Languages."
Bloomington, Indiana: *Anthropological Linguistics* 38.2: 179–215.

Marsden, Susan, ed.

1992   *Na Amwaaltga Ts'msiyeen: The Tsimshian, Trade, and the Northwest
Coast Economy.* Suwilaay'msga Na Ga'niiyatgm 1. [Prince Rupert,
BC: Tsimshian Tribal Council.]

Matson, R.G., & Gary Coupland

1995   *The Prehistory of the Northwest Coast.* San Diego: Academic Press.

Maud, Ralph

1982   *A Guide to B.C. Indian Myth and Legend.* Vancouver: Talonbooks.

1989   "The Henry Tate–Franz Boas Collaboration on Tsimshian
Mythology." Arlington, Virginia: *American Ethnologist* 16: 158–162.

Međedović, Avdo

1974   *The Wedding of Smailagić Meho.* Translated with introduction, notes
& commentary by Albert B. Lord. Serbo-Croatian Heroic Songs 3.
Cambridge, Mass.: Milman Parry Collection, Harvard University.

1980   *Ženidba Vlahinjić Alije, Osmanbeg Delibegović i Pavičević Luka,*
edited with prolegomena & notes by David E. Bynum. Serbo-
Croatian Heroic Songs 6. Cambridge, Mass.: Milman Parry
Collection, Harvard University.

Mishler, Craig

1981   "'He Said, They Say': The Uses of Reporting Speech in Native
American Folk Narrative." *Fabula* 22. Berlin: Mouton de Gruyter:
239–249.

Murdock, George Peter

1936   *Rank and Potlatch Among the Haida.* New Haven: Yale University
Publications in Anthropology 13.

Murko, Mathias [= Matija Murko]

1929   *La Poésie populaire épique en Yougoslavie au début du xxᵉ siècle.*
Paris: Honoré Champion.

Muskett, Henry Joseph

1902   Diary for the summer and fall of 1902. Add. Ms 2232, British
Columbia Archives, Victoria.

Nagorsen, David W., et al.

1993–   *The Mammals of British Columbia.* 6 vols. Vancouver: UBC Press.

Needham, Joseph, & Lu Gwei-Djen
 1985   *Trans-Pacific Echoes and Resonances: Listening Once Again.*
         Singapore: World Scientific.
Newcombe, Charles F.
 n.d.1   Newcombe papers. Add. Ms 1077, British Columbia Archives,
         Victoria.
 n.d.2   "Notes of a Journey Round the Southern Islands of the Queen
         Charlotte Group, British Columbia, in the year 1901." Dept. of
         Anthropology Archives, AMNH, New York. [Newcombe's
         holograph (1901 or 1902) and Museum's 41-page typed transcript
         (1936?). Page references are to the sometimes inaccurate
         typescript, checked against the holograph.]
 n.d.3   "List of plants collected by Dr John R. Swanton." Latin and Haida.
         Ms 4117-A(2), NAA, Smithsonian Institution, Washington, DC
         [where it is catalogued as Swanton's].
 n.d.4   Annotated checklist of British Columbia birds, with Haida names
         supplied by Tlaajang Quuna [Tom Stevens]. Ms 4117-A(3), NAA,
         Smithsonian Institution, Washington, DC [where it is catalogued
         as Swanton's].
 n.d.5   "List of mollusca [and fishes, crustacea, etc.] collected in the Queen
         Charlotte Islands." Ms 4117-A(4), NAA, Smithsonian Institution,
         Washington, DC [where it is catalogued as Swanton's].
 n.d.6   Botanical specimen labels. Latin, English and Haida. Dept. of
         Anthropology Archives, AMNH, New York.
 1906   "The Haida Indians." Québec: *Congrès internationale des
         americanistes*, XVe session, vol. 1: 135–149.
 1909   *Guide to Anthropological Collections in the Provincial Museum.*
         Victoria, BC: King's Printer.
Niblack, Albert P.
 1890   *The Coast Indians of Southern Alaska and Northern British
         Columbia.* Washington, DC: US National Museum Annual Report
         for 1888.
Nichols, Frances S.
 1940   "Bibliography of Anthropological Papers by John R. Swanton." In
         Essays in Historical Anthropology of North America. Washington,
         DC: Smithsonian Miscellaneous Collections 100: 593–600.
Nyman, Elizabeth, & Jeff Leer
 1993   *Gágiwdul.àt: Brought Forth to Reconfirm: The Legacy of a Taku River
         Tlingit Clan*, with an introduction by Robert Bringhurst. Fairbanks:
         Alaska Native Language Center.
Ó Duilearga, Séamus [= James Delargy], ed.
 1977   *Leabhar Sheáin Í Chonaill: Sgéalta agus Seanchas ó Íbh Ráthach.*
         Baile Átha Cliath (Dublin): Comhairle Bhéaloideas Éireann.

1981   *Sean Ó Conaill's Book: Stories and Traditions from Iveragh,* translated
        by Máire MacNeill. Baile Átha Cliath: Comhairle Bhéaloideas
        Éireann. [Translation of Ó Duilearga 1977.]

Ọlatunji, Ọlatunde O.

1984   *Features of Yorùbá Oral Poetry.* Ibadan: University Press.

Ortega y Gasset, José

1957–83 *Obras completas,* 12 vols. Madrid: Revista de Occidente & Alianza.

Parezo, Nancy J.

1992   Introduction to *Zuni Ceremonialism* by Ruth Bunzel. Albuquerque:
        University of New Mexico Press: vii–xxxix.

Parks, Douglas R.

1991   *Traditional Narratives of the Arikara Indians.* 4 vols. Lincoln:
        University of Nebraska Press.

Parry, Milman

1971   *The Making of Homeric Verse: The Collected Papers of Milman Parry,*
        edited by Adam Parry. Oxford: Clarendon Press.

Peter, Susie Sampson [= Gʷəqʷulćəʔ = Gwuqwults'u']

1995   *X̌ačusadəʔ ʔə gʷəqʷulćəʔ,* edited by Vi Taqʷšəblu Hilbert & Jay
        Miller. Seattle: Lushootseed Research.

Petitot, Émile.

1888   *Traditions indiennes du Canada nord-ouest: textes originaux et
        traduction littérale.* Alençon: Renaut de Broise.

Philippi, Donald L.

1979   *Songs of Gods, Songs of Humans: The Epic Tradition of the Ainu.*
        Princeton University Press.

Phinney, Archie

1934   *Nez Percé Texts.* Columbia University Contributions to
        Anthropology 25. New York: Columbia University Press.

Pinnow, Heinz-Jürgen

1985   "Sprachhistorische Untersuchung zur Stellung des Haida." Berlin:
        Indiana 10: 25–76.

1985–6 *Das Haida als Na-Dene-Sprache: Materialien zu den Wortfeldern und
        zur Komparation des Verbs.* 4 vols. Nortorf, Schleswig-Holstein:
        Völkerkundliche Arbeitsgemeinschaft.

Pound, Ezra

1929   "How to Read." 3 parts. New York *Herald Tribune Books,* 13, 20 & 27
        January 1929. [Reprinted in Pound 1954: 15–40.]

1934   *ABC of Reading.* New Haven: Yale University Press.

1954   *Literary Essays,* edited by T.S. Eliot. New York: New Directions.

Radin, Paul

1915   *Literary Aspects of North American Mythology.* Museum Bulletin
        16. Ottawa: Department of Mines, Geological Survey of Canada.

1926   "Literary Aspects of Winnebago Mythology." New York: *Journal of
        American Folk-Lore* 39: 18–52.

1948   *Winnebago Hero Cycles: A Study in Aboriginal Literature.* IJAL Memoir 1. Baltimore: Waverly Press; Bloomington: Indiana University.

1949   *The Culture of the Winnebago as Described by Themselves.* Bollingen Foundation Special Publication 1 = IJAL Memoir 2. Bloomington: Indiana University.

1950   *The Origin Myth of the Medicine Rite: Three Versions.* Bollingen Foundation Special Publication 2 = IJAL Memoir 3. Baltimore: Waverly Press; Bloomington: Indiana University.

Rankin, Robert L.

1992   Review of Joseph Greenberg, *Language in America* (1987). IJAL 58: 324–351.

Reeves, Henry

1992   *Adawga G̱ant Wilaaytga Gyetga Suwildook: Rituals of Respect and the Sea Otter Hunt.* Suwilaay'msga Na G̱a'niiyatgm 2. [Prince Rupert, BC: Tsimshian Tribal Council.]

Reid, Bill, & Robert Bringhurst

1996   *The Raven Steals the Light.* 2nd ed, with a preface by Claude Lévi-Strauss. Vancouver/Toronto: Douglas & McIntyre.

Rivet, Paul

1943   "Franz Boas." New York: *Renaissance* 1.2: 313–314.

Robertson, Gordon, et al.

1990   *Bax^walanusiwa.* Supplément 3, *Amerindia* 14. Paris: Association d'Ethnolinguistique Amérindienne.

Robins, Robert H., & Eugenius M. Uhlenbeck, ed.

1991   *Endangered Languages.* Oxford: Berg.

Rohner, Ronald P., ed.

1969   *The Ethnography of Franz Boas.* University of Chicago Press.

Rosaldo, Renato

1980   *Ilongot Headhunting, 1883–1974.* Stanford University Press.

Ruhlen, Merritt

1987   *A Guide to the World's Languages,* vol. 1: Classification. Stanford University Press.

1994   *On the Origin of Languages.* Stanford University Press.

Saint-John Perse

1971   *Collected Poems.* [French text with English translations by various hands.] Bollingen Series 87. Princeton University Press.

Samuel, Cheryl

1982   *The Chilkat Dancing Blanket.* Seattle: Pacific Search Press.

1987   *The Raven's Tail.* Vancouver: UBC Press.

Sapir, Edward

n.d.1   Comparative Na-Dene Dictionary. 4 vols. Holograph. Ms Boas Coll. NA20A.3 = Kendall 4552. APSL, Philadelphia.

n.d.2   Hupa Texts. 11 vols. Holograph. Ms Freeman 4369, APSL,
        Philadelphia. [Forthcoming in *Collected Works.*]
n.d.3   Nootka Texts & Linguistic Materials. 24 vols + approx. 1600 pp.
        Holograph & typescript. Ms Kendall 4586. APSL, Philadelphia.
1907   "Religious Ideas of the Takelma Indians of Southwestern Oregon."
        Boston: *Journal of American Folk-Lore* 20.76: 33–49.
1909a   *Takelma Texts.* University of Pennsylvania Anthropological
        Publications 2.1. Philadelphia: University Museum. [Reprinted in
        Collected Works, vol 8.]
1909b   *Wishram Texts.* Publications of the AES 2. Leiden: E.J. Brill.
        [Reprinted in *Collected Works,* vol 7.]
1921a   "The Musical Foundations of Verse." Urbana, Illinois: *Journal of
        English and Germanic Philology* 20.2: 213–228.
1921b   *Language: An Introduction to the Study of Speech.* New York:
        Harcourt, Brace & World.
1925   "Sound Patterns in Language." Baltimore: *Language* 1.1: 37–51.
1942   *Navaho Texts,* edited by Harry Hoijer. Iowa City, Iowa: Linguistic
        Society of America.
1949   *Selected Writings,* edited by David G. Mandelbaum, Berkeley:
        University of California Press.
1989–   *Collected Works.* 16 vols. Berlin: Mouton de Gruyter.
Sapir, Edward, & Morris Swadesh
1939   *Nootka Texts: Tales and Ethnological Narratives, with Grammatical
        Notes and Lexical Materials.* Philadelphia: Linguistic Society of
        America.
1955   *Native Accounts of Nootka Ethnography.* Bloomington: Indiana
        University Research Center in Anthropology, Folklore, and
        Linguistics.
Schlichter, Alice [= Alice Shepherd]
1981   "Notes on the Wintu Shamanistic Jargon." In *Survey Reports, 1981.*
        [Berkeley]: Survey of California and Other Indian Languages,
        Report 1: 95–130.
Schulenburg, Albrecht C. von
1894   *Die Sprache der Zimshian-Indianer in Nordwest-America.*
        Braunschweig: Richard Sattler.
Scudder, Geoffrey G.E., & Nicholas Gessler
1989   *The Outer Shores.* Skidegate, BC: Queen Charlotte Islands
        Museum.
Seiler, Hansjakob
1970   *Cahuilla Texts.* Bloomington: Indiana University Research Center
        for Language Sciences.
Sheldon, Charles
1912   *Wilderness of the North Pacific Coast Islands.* New York: Charles
        Scribner's Sons.

Shepherd, Alice [= Alice Schlichter]

1989   *Wintu Texts.* Berkeley: University of California Publications in
        Linguistics 117.

1997   *In My Own Words: The Stories, Songs, and Memories of Grace
        McKibben.* Berkeley: Heyday.

Shimkin, Demitri Boris

1947   "Wind River Shoshone Literary Forms: An Introduction." Menasha,
        Wisconsin: *Journal of the Washington Academy of Sciences* 37.10:
        329–352.

1949   "Shoshone I: Linguistic Sketch and Text." IJAL 15: 175–188.

Sidney, Philip

1595   *The Defence of Poesie.* London: William Ponsonby.

Silver, Shirley, & Wick R. Miller

1998   *American Indian Languages: Cultural and Social Contexts.* Tucson:
        University of Arizona Press.

Skutch, Alexander F.

1996   *The Minds of Birds.* College Station: Texas A&M University Press.

Snyder, Gary

1979   *He Who Hunted Birds in His Father's Village: The Dimensions of a
        Haida Myth.* Bolinas, California: Grey Fox.

Steward, Julian H.

1960   "John Reed Swanton, February 19, 1873 – May 2, 1958."
        Washington, DC: *National Academy of Sciences Biographical
        Memoirs* 34: 329–349.

Stocking, George W., ed.

1974   *The Shaping of American Anthropology, 1883–1911: A Franz Boas
        Reader.* New York: Basic Books.

1996   *Volksgeist as Method and Ethic: Essays on Boasian Ethnography and
        the German Anthropological Tradition.* Madison: University of
        Wisconsin Press.

Suas, Jean-Baptiste

1911–12 "Mythes et légendes des indigènes des Nouvelles-Hébrides
        (Océanie)." 4 parts in 2. Vienna: *Anthropos* 6: 901–910, 7: 33–66.

Swan, James G.

1883a   Daybook for summer 1883. Diary 32, Swan Papers, Manuscript
        Division, University of Washington Library, Seattle.

1883b   "Journal of a Trip to Queen Charlotte's Islands, B.C. for the
        Smithsonian Institution...." Diary 33, Swan Papers, Manuscript
        Division, University of Washington Library, Seattle.

Swann, Brian, ed.

1983   *Smoothing the Ground: Essays on Native American Oral Literature.*
        Berkeley: University of California Press.

1992   *On the Translation of Native American Literatures.* Washington, DC:
        Smithsonian Institution.

1994 *Coming to Light: Contemporary Translations of the Native Literatures of North America.* New York: Random House.

Swann, Brian, & Arnold Krupat, ed.

1987 *Recovering the Word: Essays on Native American Literature.* Berkeley: University of California Press.

Swanton, John R.

n.d.1 Haida notebooks. 2 vols [216 + 432 pp]. Holograph. Ms 4162, NAA, Smithsonian Institution, Washington, DC.

n.d.2 Skidegate Haida texts. Typescript with holograph corrections. Ms Boas Coll. N1.5 = Freeman 1543. APSL, Philadelphia. [Formerly 819 leaves; now 350 leaves, numbered 23 to 813 with many gaps. First 32 leaves also numbered 2–33; other secondary numberings throughout.]

n.d.3 Skidegate Haida texts. Ms 7047, NAA, Smithsonian Institution, Washington, DC. [394 leaves: uncorrected carbon of an earlier state of Swanton n.d.2.]

n.d.4 Masset Haida texts. Typescript with holograph corrections. Ms Boas Coll. N1.4 = Freeman 1544. APSL, Philadelphia. [333 folios numbered 4--786, with many gaps.]

n.d.5 Koasati Texts, 1st series. Holograph. BAE ms 4154, NAA, Smithsonian Institution, Washington, DC.

n.d.6 Koasati Texts, 2nd series. Hologra BAE ms 1818, NAA, Smithsonian Institution, Washington, DC.

n.d.7 "Notes Regarding My Adventures in Anthropology and with Anthropologists." Typescript. Ms 4651, NAA, Smithsonian Institution, Washington, DC.

1900 "Morphology of the Chinook Verb." Lancaster, Penn.: *American Anthropologist* n.s. 2: 199–237.

1903 "The Haida Calendar." Lancaster, Penn.: *American Anthropologist* n.s. 5: 331–335.

1905a *Contributions to the Ethnology of the Haida.* Jesup North Pacific Expedition 5.1. New York: AMNH.

1905b *Haida Texts and Myths: Skidegate Dialect.* Washington, DC: BAE Bulletin 29.

1907 "A Concordance of American Myths." Boston: *Journal of American Folk-Lore* 20.78: 220–222.

1908a *Haida Texts: Masset Dialect.* Jesup North Pacific Expedition 10.2. New York: AMNH.

1908b "Social Conditions, Beliefs and Linguistic Relationships of the Tlingit Indians." Washington, DC: BAE Annual Report 26: 391–486.

1909 *Tlingit Myths and Texts.* Washington, DC: BAE Bulletin 39.

1910 *Haida: An Illustrative Sketch.* Washington, DC: Government Printing Office. [Reissued in Boas 1911: 205–282.]

1912   *Haida Songs.* In one volume with Franz Boas, *Tsimshian Texts* (*New
        Series*). Publications of the AES 3. Leiden: E.J. Brill.

1922   "Tokulki of Tulsa." In *American Indian Life,* edited by Elsie Clews
        Parsons. New York: Huebsch: 127–145.

1928   *Emanuel Swedenborg: Prophet of the Higher Evolution.* New York:
        New Church Press.

1929   *Myths and Tales of the Southeastern Indians.* Washington, DC: BAE
        Bulletin 88.

1952   *The Indian Tribes of North America.* Washington, DC: BAE Bulletin
        145.

Tate, Henry

1993   *The Porcupine Hunter and Other Stories,* edited by Ralph Maud.
        Vancouver: Talonbooks.

Tedlock, Dennis

1983   *The Spoken Word and the Work of Interpretation.* Philadelphia:
        University of Pennsylvania Press.

1985   *Popol Vuh: The Mayan Book of the Dawn of Life.* New York: Simon &
        Schuster.

Thornton, Russell

1987   *American Indian Holocaust and Survival: A Population History since
        1492.* Norman: University of Oklahoma Press.

Turner, Nancy Jean

1974   *Plant Taxonomic Systems and Ethnobotany of Three Contemporary
        Indian Groups of the Pacific Northwest.* Victoria, BC: *Syesis* 7,
        Supplement 1.

1979   *Plants in British Columbia Indian Technology.* Victoria, BC: British
        Columbia Provincial Museum.

1995   *Food Plants of Coastal First Peoples.* 2nd ed. Vancouver: UBC Press.

Turner, Nancy J., & Roy L. Taylor

1972   "A Review of the Northwest Coast Tobacco Mystery." Victoria, BC:
        Syesis 5: 249–257.

Uhlenbeck, Christianus Cornelius

1911   *Original Blackfoot Texts.* Verhandelingen der Koninklijke Akademie
        van Wetenschappen, Afdeeling Letterkunde, nieuwe reeks 12.1.
        Amsterdam: Müller.

1912   *A New Series of Blackfoot Texts.* Verhandelingen der Koninklijke
        Akademie van Wetenschappen, Afdeeling Letterkunde, nieuwe
        reeks 13.1. Amsterdam: Müller.

Veniaminov, Ivan (St Innokentii)

1840   Записки объ островахъ уналашкинскаго отдѣла. 3 vols.
        St Petersburg: Rossiisko-Amerikanskaia Kompanii.

1984   *Notes on the Islands of the Unalashka District.* Translated by Lydia
        Black & R.H. Geoghegan; edited by Richard A. Pierce. Kingston,
        Ontario: Limestone Press. [Translated from Veniaminov 1840.]

Verano, John W., & Douglas H. Ubelaker, ed.

    1992   *Disease and Demography in the Americas.* Washington, DC: Smithsonian Institution.

Voegelin, Charles Frederick, & Florence Marie Voegelin

    1977   *Classification and Index of the World's Languages.* New York: Elsevir.

Walkus, Simon

    1982   *Oowekeeno Oral Traditions as Told by the Late Chief Simon Walkus Sr.,* edited by Susanne Storie & John C. Rath. Mercury Series 84. Ottawa: National Museums of Canada.

Wardwell, Allen

    1978   *Objects of Bright Pride: Northwest Coast Indian Art from the American Museum of Natural History.* New York: Center for Inter-American Relations.

Watkins, Calvert

    1995   *How to Kill a Dragon: Aspects of Indo-European Poetics.* New York: Oxford University Press.

Weltfish, Gene

    1937   *Caddoan Texts: Pawnee, South Band Dialect.* Publications of the AES 17. New York: Stechert.

    1958   "The Linguistic Study of Material Culture." IJAL 24: 301–311.

Wissler, Clark, & David C. Duvall

    1909   *Mythology of the Blackfoot Indians.* New York: AMNH Anthropological Papers 2.1.

Yeats, William Butler

    1920   "Swedenborg, Mediums, and the Desolate Places." In *Visions and Beliefs in the West of Ireland,* by Isabella Augusta Gregory. New York: Putnam: vol. 2: 295–339.

Index

Haida authors are in **boldface**.
Authors in other Native American
languages are in SMALL CAPS. The
names of Native American languages
and literatures are in *sanserif italic*.

Aeschylus 295, 336
AHYŌ'IINI (*c.* 1834–1899) 193
Ainu 156, 456
Aleut 100, 156, 390
Alsea 455
American Museum of Natural
    History 58, 153, 182, 336
anonymity
  of mythtellers 16, 136
  of women 204–208, 306–308, 319
Arikara 423, 447, 467
Arnold, Matthew (1822–1888) 366
Aristotle 363
Athapaskan languages 159
Athens 385
autobiography 165f, 203f, 466

Bach, Johann Sebastian (1685–1750)
  15, 335
  Die Kunst der Fuge 197
BARNABY (*fl. c.* 1914) 464
bats 300, 479
Baudelaire, Charles (1821–1867) 363,
  365
BEAULIEU, FRANÇOIS (1774–1875)
  460

Beethoven, Ludwig van (1770–1827)
  132
  Opus 18 quartets 196f
Bellini, Giovanni (*c.* 1430–1516) 413
Bellini, Nicolosia (*c.* 1435–*c.* 1500)
  413
Benedict, Ruth (1887–1948) 136f
Bentley, Richard (1662–1742) 460
Beowulf 67, 121, 335
Beynon, William, *see* Gwüsḵ'aayn
Big Surf (Sghulghu Quuna) 241,
  243f, 257f, 277, 289, 471
Birket-Smith, Kaj 206
Black Death 70
Blackfoot 115, 335–338, 423
Blake, William (1757–1827) 150
blindness, in mythtellers 390f
Bloomfield, Leonard (1887–1949)
  390, 466, 490
Boas, Franz (1858–1942) 58, 66, 135f,
  151–154, 191–195, 205f, 336, 362,
  368f, 372, 418, 487, 488
  appraisal of Swanton 191f
  comparative studies 135f, 269
  correspondence with Swanton 69,
    75, 157, 173–179, 181–186, 189,
    195, 285f
  editing of Swanton 185f
  importance as a critic 453, 464
  instructions to Swanton 153f
  on oral literature 191, 211, 463
  on verse & prose 363–365

525

Two principal text types are used in this book. The serifed
type is Aldus, designed for Mergenthaler Linotype in
Frankfurt by Hermann Zapf. The unserifed type is Scala Sans,
designed for the Vredenburg concert hall in Utrecht by
Martin Majoor. Supplementary types include Vadim
Lazurski's Lazurski Cyrillic, Victor Scholderer's New Hellenic,
Sumner Stone & John Renner's Stone Phonetic, Carol
Twombly's Trajan and Hermann Zapf's Palatino bold.

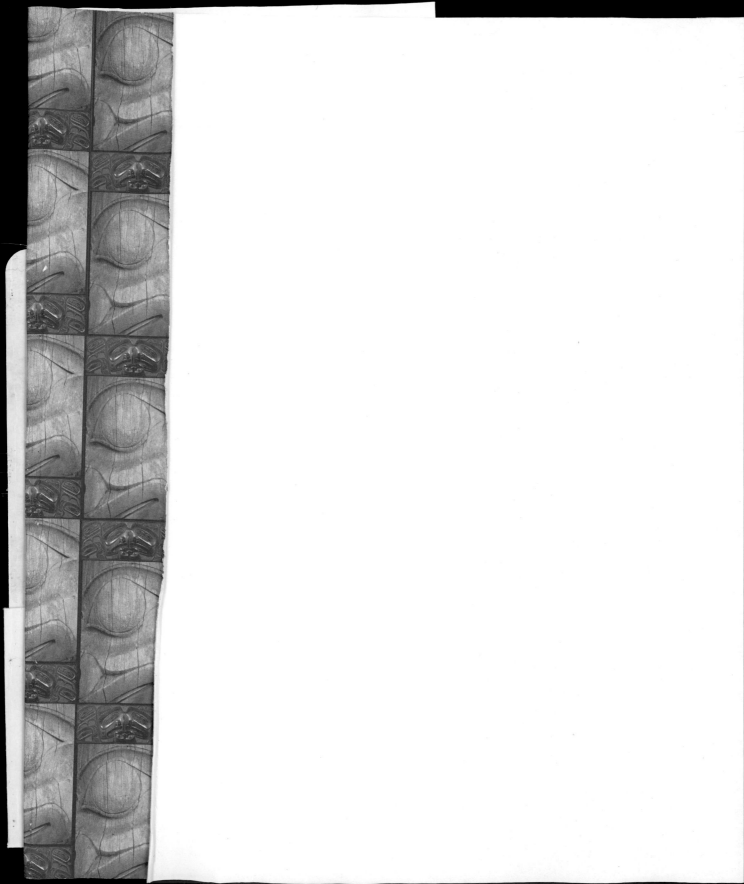

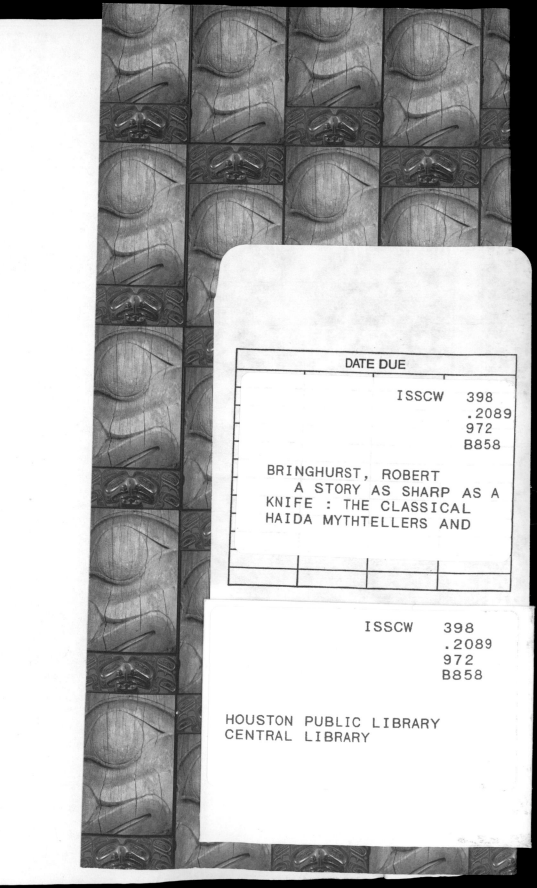